FRENCH
RENAISSANCE
STUDIES

1540–70

♦

FOR FRANCE, MY WIFE

FRENCH RENAISSANCE STUDIES

1540–70

Humanism and the Encyclopedia

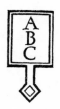

EDITOR
PETER SHARRATT

AT THE UNIVERSITY PRESS
EDINBURGH
1976

© Edinburgh University Press 1976
22 George Square, Edinburgh
ISBN 0 85224 276 X
Printed in Great Britain by
Western Printing Services Ltd
Bristol

CONTENTS

Preface vii

v

Contents

PREFACE

THE PAPERS PUBLISHED IN this volume were all delivered at a conference held in the University of Edinburgh, from the 1st to the 5th of April, 1974.

Some of them appear almost exactly as they were given, and others have been altered in the light of the discussions which took place; many of them have been enriched with copious notes. The reader will be struck by the variety of scholarly approaches and attitudes.

The Edinburgh colloquium was designed to carry on the good work begun in 1969 at a conference organized by the School of French Studies in the University of Warwick, and a second one that took place in Turin and Venice in 1971, under the aegis of the Accademia delle Scienze di Torino, in collaboration with the Fondazione Giorgio Cini of Venice, and organized by the Istituto di Lingua e Letteratura Francese of Turin. The *Acta* of both these previous conferences have been published: *Humanism in France at the end of the Middle Ages and in the early Renaissance,* edited by A. H. T. Levi, Manchester University Press, 1970, and *Culture et politique en France à l'époque de l'humanisme et de la renaissance,* edited by Franco Simone, Accademia delle Scienze, Turin, 1974.

The subject proposed to the speakers who had been invited to Edinburgh was a study of French Renaissance education, and in particular of the trivium and quadrivium, together with any other areas of the university curriculum that were usually associated with the seven liberal arts. It was also suggested that we would pay attention to the importance of such a study for a true understanding of the literature of the period. Of the fifteen papers read to the conference, some attempted an overall view of a particular discipline, some concentrated on themes or topics, and the rest were more strictly literary. It will be seen that there was no attempt to treat the encyclopedia exhaustively or methodically, but rather to give the flavour of university teaching and suggest further lines of enquiry.

One of the papers is, unfortunately, missing from this volume. James P. Thorne spoke on 'The Humanist attack upon scholastic theories of language', showing how the scholastics' concern with the truth condition of sentences in natural languages was not shared by the humanists. Since, however, this brilliant scholarly tirade had not previously been committed to paper, it could not be reproduced here.

Our volume opens with the inaugural address by Alan J. Steele, which set the tone of 'docta amicitia' that was characteristic of the conference. My own paper, 'Peter Ramus and the Reform of the University: the Divorce of Philosophy and Eloquence?' aims to show what were some of the preoccupations of Parisian academics at the time, and links Ramus's reforms with his divergent attitude to literature and its uses. The rest of this first day was entirely devoted to the trivium. Christopher Armstrong, in 'The Dialectical Road to Truth: the Dialogue' deals with rhetoric and logic and their interdependence and relation to literature. Terence Cave, in 'Copia and Cornucopia' is more specifically concerned with rhetoric, and with imaginative literature. Brian Barron's paper, 'Poet and Orator in Le Caron's *Dialogue de la poësie*' examines in detail Le Caron's contribution to poetic theory. On the second day the quadrivium was introduced by W.P.D.Wightman in 'Cosmological and Technological Trends in the French Renaissance'. The author shows the achievement and the limitations of the scientific movement in France in the sixteenth century, and accounts for the late acceptance of Copernicus's theories. Guy Demerson ('Météorologie et poésie française de la Renaissance') and Dudley Wilson ('The Quadrivium in the Scientific Poetry of Guy Lefèvre de la Boderie') both deal with scientific poetry, a genre which is now attracting renewed attention; Demerson stresses the wonder and curiosity of the poet and philosopher which is different from the attitude of the scientist, and Wilson presents the scientific poet as a Magus. J.-C.Margolin, in 'L'Enseignement des mathématiques en France (1540-70): Charles de Bovelles, Fine, Peletier, Ramus', demonstrates how the study of mathematics is at the centre of the humanist movement, and is of cultural rather than scientific importance. Kathleen Hall's paper on 'Pontus de Tyard' reappraises Pontus's platonism, his account of the furies, and his attitude to the encyclopedia. Ian McFarlane unites a paper on the quadrivium with something of Scottish interest. In 'The History of George Buchanan's *Sphæra*' he sketches in the humanist background to the story of the publication of this 'scientific' text.

From the seven liberal arts we turn to medicine, ethics and law. M.A.Screech's paper on 'Medicine and Literature: Aspects of Rabelais and Montaigne' appeals for close attention to the difficult but rewarding texts which were familiar to the men of the sixteenth century and now often increasingly more inaccessible. A.H.T.Levi ('Ethics and the Encyclopedia in the Sixteenth Century') attempts to get to grips with the elusive ideal of the encyclopedia, and notes a progression from an 'educational' to an ethical aim. In the next paper

('Un Thème majeur du second humanisme français (1540–70): l'orateur et le citoyen. De l'humanisme à la réalité vécue'), André Stegmann links together many of the topics already discussed, and describes the 'finality' of much of the writing on education, with its political and religious implications, and relates this to the troubled history of the time. Finally, Franco Simone ('La Notion d'Encyclopédie: Elément caractéristique de la Renaissance française') provides an overall historical account of the encyclopedia and its moral and cultural importance, tracing it from classical times, and showing its development in the Christian writers of the Middle Ages, and through the Renaissance. The author attempts to define what Rabelais meant by 'le vrays puys et abisme de encyclopédie'.

The papers offered to the conference received visual support in the splendid exhibition of books that had been mounted in the University Library, with the help of Miss M. Robertson. It drew on the library's own substantial Renaissance holdings, those of the National Library of Scotland, Glasgow University Library, The Edinburgh Royal College of Physicians, and the Edinburgh Royal Observatory.

We are grateful to Professor W. Beattie, Director of the Institute for Advanced Studies in the Humanities, for his support of the conference, to the British Academy, to M. Philippe North of the Institut français d'Ecosse, and the French *Ministère des Affaires culturelles*, for further financial help, and to the University of Edinburgh for its hospitality. We appreciate too the help given in committee by Professor Denys Hay, Vice-Principal of the University, and Professor John MacQueen, of the School of Scottish Studies. We are grateful also to the Edinburgh University Press for agreeing to publish these papers, and to Miss P. Duncan for editorial assistance. Finally, we wish to thank the speakers, and the listeners, and urge that another conference be arranged somewhere else when the time is opportune.

Peter Sharratt
Edinburgh 1975

ALAN J. STEELE

Opening Address

ORES QUE JE VOUS voy ci assemblez, non moins chers amis que doctes indagateurs, venuz de tant diverses et esloingnees parties du monde, il m'agree vous saluer tous et de grand cœur bienveingner en nostre froidureuse Escosse, mesmement en ceste bonne ville et alme université d'Edimbourg, vous merciant d'avoir baillé responce favorable à nostre invitation, et vous souhaictant trouver copie de bonne et plaisante doctrine au banquet que pour vous avons dressé.

Combien que soyons nombreux, si sommes nous privés (et en demeurons marris) de la societé et commerce d'aulcuns, lesquelz encontre leur vouloir n'ont pu venir en nostre pays, qui pour la longueur et incommodité du voyage, qui pour n'estre à ceste heure en assez bon poinct, qui pour aultres empesches. Telz sont Raymond Lebegue parisien, Gaultier Ong d'Amerique, Henry Weber occitanien, Frances Yates docte autant que vertueuse demoiselle londonienne, et aultres.

D'avanture demandera on, à quelle fin avons voulu rassembler quasi soubz le pole artique une si grand et honneste compaignie? A ce respondray je, que selon nostre conception aultre chose ne faisons icy, que suivre les glorieux vestiges des majeurs, translatans ores en Escosse ces nobles estudes, lesquelles ayans pris naissance en Angleterre par la non jamais assez louee emprise de ces bons Warvicquois, furent puis en honneur en Italie, soubz la guide et conduicte de Franc Simon turinois, et meshuy seront non du tout indignement celebrees icy, advenant que Phoebus benignement nous œillade. Comme aulcunesfois de nuict on void les prompts ardens blubluetter de place en place, menans à l'entour leurs esbats et carolles, ainsi nos brandons espars esclattent briefvement leurs vifs rayons, tantost deça, tantost dela. Tandis, aux rives de la Loire ard une flamme perpetuelle.

Nous doncques, deliberans à nostre tour ordonner quelque feste apollinique, avions premier eslu pour matiere et subject d'icelle les artz qu'ordinairement on denomme liberaux; voulans par telle diffinition desseigner le cerne d'une belle lice, en laquelle nos genereux pensers, ardens vouloirs, et curieux desirs, voulentiers borneroient, ce cuidions nous, leurs courses et galopades. Las, si parfaicte liaison, enchainure, et harmonieuse circuition, n'avons nous pu accomplir. Et de ce ne se faut esmerveiller. N'a dict Platon la figure ronde estre la forme sans plus de la divine perfection, de quoy ça bas ne pouvons veoir sinon tant seulement quelque imaige inconstant et umbratile? Possible avez vous remerqué ès desers armoriques ces grand pierres, lesquelles nos peres gaulois, ce dist on, esleverent en rond pour à leurs dieux faire homage et honneur. Et combien que plusieurs en aient eté ruees jus, ou soient du tout disparues, si pouvons nous aulcunement concevoir le grand cerne du temple. Non aultrement meshuy, faillans quelques maillons de nostre chaine, ou qui diroit mieux, fleurons de ceste belle couronne encyclopedique, toutesfois pourra on recoignoistre l'idee de ceste cy, à l'avanture par inspiration et fureur divine. Parquoy ne nous doibt on reprendre d'avoir œuvré, non selon telle perfection, ainçois selon nostre suffisance pure humaine.

Davantage, veu que pour neant voudroit on arrester la Fortune, et pour telle raison voyons en nos tableaux ceste lubrique Deesse juchee sus un siege non carré, ains spherique, la mesme Encyclopedie ne peut estre dicte du tout exempte de la vicissitude et branle des choses mondaines, je ne dy en son essence celeste, oui bien en son terrestre imaige. Ores la revere on, ores on la met en doubte et oubliance. Pour ce avons deliberé ficher nos yeux aux utiles-doulx ouvrages que nos François ont mis en lumiere, s'escoulans les annees marquees sus nostre rollet, c'est à sçavoir, de l'an mil quinze cens et quarante, jusques en l'an mil quinze cens et septante. Car au commencement ne pouvoit on aulcunement croire le siecle d'or debvoir quelque jour renaistre, et les Muses estre remises en honneur et gloire? Las, mais incontinent apres, tel doulx songe s'est mué en dubitative incertitude, voire en cauchemar angoisseux. Tracer le decours d'une si grand mutation, et esplucher les causes d'icelle tant soient secretes, est chose tres-digne sans contredict de curieuse estude.

Espoinçonné doncques de tel haut desir, nostre bon ami Peter Sharratt novocastrien nous fist propos de tenir ces assises academiques. A quoy tres-voulentiers nous consentimes, d'autant que luy d'abord se chargea du grand labeur et soin à ce duysant, non toutesfois sans l'ayde de ce sien jeune disciple Brian Barron orinessien, à peine hors de page. Dont je les veulx grandement louer et remercier. Graces soient rendues pareillement aux aultres regens, docteurs, et officiers de nostre université qui gaillardement nous ont faict espaule, et quant et quant à messieurs les libraires de la Librairie d'Escosse, lesquelz avecques monsieur Hermann Bruck astronome de sa royale

Majesté, nous ont presté de tant beaux et rares volumes pour vous en faire monstre. Ni je ne veulx oublier celle illustrissime compaignie qui a nom *The British Academy*: d'elle avons nous receu en pur don deux cens livres bien sonnantes et trebuchantes, dont Dieu la benisse. Joinct que messire Philippe North principal de l'Institut François d'Escosse nous a semblablement porté ayde, secours, et reconfort. Finablement, de peculiere gratitude debvons nous remercier ces bons et bien disans orateurs dont les noms sont en nostre rollet, lesquelz vont verser dans nos memoires l'ambroisie de bon et honneste sçavoir.

Que diray je plus, amis? Il me prend fantasie de parangonner nostre trouppe à ces magnanimes nautonniers ahannans de rames et de voiles en la navire Argon pour conquerir au loin un riche tresor. Dont se pourroient tirer belles narrations à plenté et copieuses descriptions esloingnees du vulgaire, qui y mettroit peine et estude. Mais de ce n'ayez peur. Jà trop plus long tems que raison je vous ai arrestez au reciter de ces miennes langagieres bourdes et circonbilivaginations. Pour ouyr si faictes billevesees n'estes vous pas venuz. Or sus doncques, gentilz esprits, clers engins, compains et mignons des Muses! Ne soyez ocieux, ains intentifs aux doulx sonnans accors du portelyre faictes moy bondir nostre nef isnellement sus les flotz blanchissans, jusques à tant que surgissans enfin au port de Sapience et Vertu, en rapportions hardiment celle tant glorieuse Toison d'or!

PETER SHARRATT

Peter Ramus and the Reform of the University: the Divorce of Philosophy and Eloquence?

'NEQUE UNQUAM AUT MEDICO turpe habitum est, nescire leges; aut iurisperito vel medicinam, vel astrorum scientiam non tenere. Nos uni sumus, quibus omnis illa liberalium artium varietas non pertractanda quidem, ac pernoscenda penitus; sed degustanda tamen, et delibanda necessario est', ut dixit Muretus noster in oratione de studiis literarum Venetiis habita.[1]

The official languages of this conference—apart from sixteenth-century French—are Latin, French, Italian, Scots and English. A Scottish teacher who worked in Poitiers in the sixteenth century, Thomas Bicarton from St Andrews, recounts in his *Miscellanea* how when he was in France he met a foreigner and attempted to converse with him in Latin, but neither could understand the other. His acquaintance, he found out later, was an Englishman. I think therefore that it will be better if I speak to you in English.[2]

In the course of last year there was an exhibition, held in the chapel of the Sorbonne, devoted to the history of the University of Paris. One of the exhibits consisted of four photographs of large groups of people chatting idly in the courtyard. Some people felt that these pictures did not entirely do justice to certain events of five years previously. There was another omission, equally surprising, and much less easy to account for, the sixteenth century. Yet the sixteenth century, and especially the middle years, say from about 1540 to 1570, witnessed the highest point, and perhaps the lowest point in the history of the University of Paris, if not of French education.

This was one of the richest and most creative moments in the history of French literature; it was during these years that French classical scholarship came into its own with the teaching and editorial work of Marc-Antoine Muret, Adrien Turnèbe, Denis Lambin and the inspiring, self-effacing ubiquitous Jean Dorat; during these years that the Collège Royal, later the Collège de France, knew its first and second generation of lecturers, when French academic printing could boast of the Estiennes, Wechel, Vascosan, Turnèbe himself and a host of lesser names; during these years that Calvin

4

published the different versions of the *Institutes*, and ensured the meteoric rise and establishment of French protestantism; that Ignatius, a student in Paris, made reforms of a different kind; when the movement for scientific and technical writing in the vernacular made an irreversible step forward; when finally a spirit of French nationalism became linked with a democratic rejection of authority.

This was the world of Peter Ramus, one of the most controversial figures in that polemical age; he mirrors now the uneasy ill-fitting humanism of the last scholastics, now the measured, harmonious, if complacent aspirations of the new classical commentators, and sometimes even anticipates the methodical probing outlook of the scientific revolution. His active life spans the entire period. During the thirties he studied at the Collège de Navarre (in 1533 he saw Ronsard come and go), and taught in some of the small colleges; he was to stay in Paris, teaching at the Collège de Presles, and from 1551 also at the Collège Royal, with two relatively short periods of salutary absence, until his death in 1572.[3]

Of his early life and studies we know little. We can leave aside the tradition that in 1536 he defended an MA thesis on the subject 'Everything Aristotle said was false', since this was not attested in his lifetime, and as Walter Ong has proved 'commentitia', in the apparently simple alleged title, means something else.[4] But the title can express for us, with our hindsight, his reforming spirit during these years. In an age familiar with Erasmus, Melanchthon, Sturm, Vives, Linacre, Rabelais, Calvin and later Montaigne, it was evident to all that reforms in education were long overdue, that the university was suffering from a serious *malaise* if not from a chronic and almost incurable disease. Ramus's own adhesion to the movement of reform —I mean of the university, for his protestantism develops less surely —results partly from the climate of the time, and partly from his own restless, fractious, contesting temperament.

In 1543 he published his first works, two small books about logic, the *Dialecticae partitiones* and the *Aristotelicae animadversiones*, rubbing shoulders, by a curious quirk of chronology, if at a distance, with Copernicus and Vesalius. If he had found himself classed in the company of these immortals, especially an astronomer and a doctor, the self-trumpetting Ramus would have revelled in the association. It is an association one wants to reject, but it would be wrong to do so. It is true that histories of logic have little to say about Ramus, but then general histories of any art or science have little enough to say about the sixteenth century, sandwiched as it is between the passionate, and colourful, but so hopelessly erroneous, thought of the middle ages, and the objective truth, scientific certainty and modernity of the seventeenth century. But the impact of Ramus on the thought of his time, and that of the following generations was considerable.

These two works of logic, hopefully addressed to the most illustrious Academy of Paris, caused a furore in university circles. The tendentious coat-trailing remarks against Aristotle aroused bitter controversy because they contained an implicit attack on the establishment and the authority of the university. Ramus was condemned first by the faculty of theology, at the instigation of Pierre Galland, rector of the faculty of arts, then by the Parlement, at the instigation of the Portuguese jurist Antoine de Gouveia; the matter was finally referred to François Ier himself and a public debate between Ramus and Gouveia was organized, in the presence of senior representatives of all the faculties. He was accordingly prohibited from teaching or writing philosophy. The authority of Aristotle was shown to be still unshaken, the supremacy of the theological faculty over the faculty of arts acknowledged. Not that at this stage he had any clear thoughts of the reform of the university. Yet he was proposing changes in the teaching of logic, perhaps the most important subject in the curriculum, and through the years his reform of the university was to be inextricably bound up with his logical reform of the content of each discipline.

Almost immediately Ramus turned his attention to teaching the strange combination of mathematics and rhetoric. As a shrewd opportunist he interpreted his condemnation in the strictest possible sense, in other words, according to its letter rather than its spirit. In 1544 he was content to say that philosophy was synonymous with logic, and that was all he was not allowed to teach. If we are to make any sense at all of the writings on education at the time we must always bear in mind that philosophy had a variety of meanings, with an ambiguous or at least undefined relationship to the encyclopedia of the liberal arts and the university curriculum, sometimes synonymous with logic, sometimes with ethics, sometimes these together with physics, sometimes even the whole of the seven liberal arts. In the *Dialecticae partitiones* Ramus uses it in a very general sense with strong Platonic overtones. In the following year in his *Oratio de studiis mathematicis* he equates it with logic, and removes mathematics from its control. In 1546 in his commentary on Cicero's *Somnium Scipionis* he makes his first statement about the union of philosophy and eloquence — this was, of course, a commonplace of Renaissance writing, a commonplace, and therefore understood in a different sense by everybody. In its simplest terms, for Ramus, it meant teaching philosophy by illustrating it from literary texts. The circumstances in which he published the work might alert us to the fact that he was giving it a new twist. In the same year this topic was the subject of his first lecture of the year at the Collège de Presles of which he was now head, *Oratio de studiis philosophiae et eloquentiae coniungendis*. Already he has seen the problem of the classification of the sciences and the relation of the arts and sciences to one another. He insists that each art, each subject of the curriculum has a clearly defined scope, absolutely distinct from that of any other. Yet the method for explaining each art is identical and they have a common purpose in the presentation of knowledge. His colleague Talon would teach philosophy, that is logic, in the morning, and he would teach rhetoric in the afternoon. The planned relationship between the parallel series of classes is made clear. He also brought out a new edition of his logic, under Talon's name, in which he gave the first real account of method, the central point of his later writing.

After the accession of Henri II in 1547 and because of the new-found power and prestige of his old school-fellow Charles de Guise, later Cardinal de Lorraine, the prohibition on teaching and writing was removed, and Ramus went from strength to strength. Ong has of course unravelled the story of Ramus's incessant, laborious remodelling of the work on logic through many editions, and established the bibliography of the sixty-odd other publications.[5] My aim is to concentrate on works concerned with the reform of the university. The first of these is *Pro philosophica Parisiensis Academiae disciplina oratio* (1551) in which Ramus aims to justify his teaching-methods and practice. His critics claim that the much-vaunted union of philosophy and eloquence is not acceptable in a teacher, and in his case this is made worse by the fact that he refuses to teach the books laid down by the university statutes. In reply Ramus sets out and defends the timetable in his own college: the pupils were taught five hours in the morning and five in the afternoon, in each case made up of one hour's lecture on classical literature, two of 'edis-cendi', that is studying or memorizing, and two more of debate and practice (pp. 26–7). Behind this procedure lies his theory of analysis and genesis leading to original composition (pp. 28–43). The course lasts seven and a half years (from the age of seven to fifteen): in the first three years there is a graded study of grammar and syntax, in the fourth year rhetoric, and then begins the 'tempus philosophicum' starting with logic in the fifth year, ethics in the sixth (the first four books of Aristotle) and mathematics, that is arithmetic and geom-etry, music and optics. The final year is devoted to physics (the first eight books of Aristotle), including meteorology and some astron-omy—'Physicam veram, mathematicis rationibus fundatam' he calls

PETER SHARRATT

it, though his own *Scholae physicae* (1556) fall far short of this. As in all the other subjects, physics would be studied through literature, in this case Virgil's *Georgics*, Ovid's *Metamorphoses*, and some Lucretius, Seneca and Pliny (pp. 44–5), a union if you like of science and poetry, but poetic science rather than scientific poetry. At the end the student graduates master of arts, 'not just in name but in truth' says Ramus, already, at the ripe age of fifteen years prepared to teach other people, or to study law, medicine or theology and ultimately play a useful part in society (p. 49).

The system Ramus describes represents an attempt to shorten the course (a glance at Egasse Du Boulay's *Historia Universitatis Parisiensis*, 1673, shows that this was a recurrent topic in faculty and university business), and, significantly, to restore or even inaugurate the quadrivium. It is easy to be misled by our knowledge of early encyclopedias such as Martianus Capella's *De nuptiis Philologiae et Mercurii* and Gregorius Reisch's *Margarita philosophica* into thinking that they mirror university teaching throughout the sixteenth century. It is doubtful whether the quadrivium was ever taught extensively anywhere and it is highly unlikely that it was taught at all in Paris during our period. Ramus also points to the progressive cumulative value of his teaching: the precepts of each art are taught separately, each in its own place and subject, but they have a common aim. In an extended metaphor he compares the process of education to the different branches of farming, where fruits of all sorts are gathered in and taken back to the farmyard for a common or similar purpose. So it is in 'animorum cultura' where the ultimate fruits ('animi perfectio') are to be found in public life, implemented 'in forum, in Senatum, in concionem populi, in omnem hominum conventum' (pp. 50–1).[6]

Ramus's statement about his teaching elicited a vigorous reply from Galland in *Pro schola Parisiensi contra novam academiam Petri Rami oratio*.[7] For seven years now Ramus has been seditiously disturbing 'tranquillity and the repose of letters', by the rejection of the established authors in his new academy. The attempted linking of philosophy and eloquence is 'umbratilis', 'vaga' and 'volatica', and, Galland claims, Ramus teaches neither Aristotle nor philosophy but mere poetry. He misquotes the laws of Estouteville (1452) and is unoriginal—have not Agricola, Vives, Melanchthon and Agrippa said it all before?—and repetitive, serving up to us this offensive dish of warmed-up cabbage ('nobis iam toties veluti crambem recoctam moleste apponis'—the proverb perhaps comes to him from Juvenal) and most readers will derive no benefit from him but will 'read him as they would the vernacular books of the ridiculous Pantagruel, for fun and pleasure'.[8]

8

For Galland, the relation between philosophy and the preliminary arts is like that between Penelope and her attendants. The suitors of Penelope were distracted from their purpose by her beautiful hand-maidens, dissipated their efforts on them, and never reached Penelope. The pursuit of philosophy is an equally serious business which calls for intimate and exclusive attention if you are to profit from it and enjoy it. Now the handmaidens of philosophy are grammar, rhetoric, poetry and history, already taught in all the Paris colleges as an obligatory introduction to philosophy.

Galland does not entirely disapprove of the union, but says that each subject should be taught 'discretis professionibus', which sounds remarkably like Ramus's own view. The simple difference is that Ramus wants every art to be taught separately, except that literature, which is not an art, can be used to explain and illustrate any other. Galland is clearly afraid that the higher faculties (theology, medicine and the two laws) will suffer from the contemporary vogue in favour of literature and especially poetry. There is a danger, he says, that 'people will be tainted by the allurements of the poets, captivated by the facility of the other less important arts, and will devote themselves to the study of them.'[9] Is this an indirect reference to the practice of Dorat at Coqueret and Muret at Boncourt, where literature is being taught almost as an autonomous discipline and not as a repository of grammatical oddities, rhetorical tropes or moral aphorisms? Galland even notes that university privileges do not extend to poetry and teachers of poetry. He warns of the dangers inherent in the teaching of literature. Remember what became of the companions of Ulysses, once they had tasted the fruit of the Lotus, they wanted to stay among the lotus-eaters, transformed by Circe's potions into swine. This will happen to those who practise your in-famous union, led astray by this humanist food. They will be attrac-ted by the siren to the rocks of poetry and oratory, and will spurn the healing medicine of philosophy after the first bitter mouthful as though it were absinth. Philosophy is the methodical examination of divine and human things, which has received its most perfect expres-sion in Aristotle. Poets and orators give you merely the nail-parings and hair-clippings and external skin of philosophy, but nothing solid, no blood, nerves, marrow, bone. Galland concludes by asking if it is really possible that there are people who think that logic can be taught better from Virgil than from Aristotle and make this practice part of the programme of rebuilding the Academy of Paris.[10] If I have dwelt on this topic, it is because it is the only time Ramus is ever accused of being on the side of poetry.

No wonder that Rabelais and Du Bellay entered this dispute,

though the new preface to the fourth book which recommends the petrifaction of these two Peters does not suggest that Rabelais had read either of the texts.[11]

Ramus's reinstatement was greatly strengthened during this same year 1551 when he was given a post at the Collège Royal with the unprecedented and never to be repeated title of Professor of Philosophy and Eloquence. During the early years of his professorship he was busy publishing his classical commentaries, mainly of Cicero and Virgil, his Arithmetic and the French translation of the *Dialectica*. By way of digression I wish to make three brief points about the *Dialectique* of 1555. Firstly, it is a pity that most people now approach Ramus through this relatively unimportant edition. This beautiful Wechel production does contain some translations by Ronsard, Du Bellay and others, and it is the best example of Ramus's practical linking of philosophy and eloquence. He himself, however, attached little importance to it. Secondly, his relationship with the poets has been exaggerated into a close friendship when all the evidence suggests that it was nothing of the kind.[12] Thirdly, the *Dialectique* long established as the first original work of philosophy to be written in French must now give pride of place to a curious little work which I have recently turned up, *Dialectique en françois pour les Barbiers et Chirurgiens composée par Maistre Adrien l'Alemant, docteur en medecine à Paris*, published in 1553 by the same Thomas Richard who brought out Ramus's *Euclid* in 1549 and 1558 and the *Somnium Scipionis* in 1557.[13] This earlier French logic (dare I say first French logic?) modifies our ideas about Ramus's French philosophical neologisms. Like Ramus's book, it was not a university text-book; if it is in French it is precisely because it is directed to the non-academic public, in this case barbers and surgeons, because, he says wrily, they are more given to argument.

I wish now to draw attention to a work which is more directly related to the reform of the university and which demonstrates a less well-known side of Ramus's character and activities. In 1557 he published a pamphlet entitled *Oratio de legatione*, which was translated by one of his friends as *Harangue de Pierre de la Ramée, touchant ce qu'ont fait les deputez de l'Université de Paris envers le Roy*. Here is Ramus, the university administrator, a diplomat, a friend of the students and sympathizer with their cause, and someone with antimonastic leanings. The point at issue was the much-disputed Pré-aux-clercs, an expanse of open land between the monastery of St Germain-des-Prés and the river, which theoretically belonged to the university for the use of the students. This right was intermittently threatened by the monks who made inroads into it for their own use, and by the university itself which illegally sold parts of it for housing and other purposes. The students manifested against these abuses and had been severely treated by a Royal Edict and a decree of the Parlement. Ramus (with Turnèbe and others) was on a commission (post factum) which was to report to the king. He objects to the closure of the college gates at six in the afternoon, and the cancellation of public lectures in order to keep the students inside the colleges. Ramus claims that this would transform 'un college d'exercice' into an 'obscure et salle prison, non pas une escole de letres' (p. 6). He rejects also the idea that students should be made to surrender their arms to the Hôtel de Ville, for 'Qu'est ce autre chose que condamner les escoliers, c'est à dire les nourrisons de repos et de paix, comme s'ils estoient ennemis?' (ibid.) and throw them on the mercy of their cut-throat neighbours in the Quartier latin. He is adamant that peace will not come from repression. This is particularly so in the case of foreign students expelled from the country by the edict. They are not enemies of the crown, 'Et ne fault pas estimer que l'Université de Paris soit particuliere aux Françoys seulement, mais que c'est aussi la commune escole de toutes nations.' (p. 15) The suppression of non-resident students too, is unreasonable because if they disappear the university will become deserted. Ramus is always on the side of the 'pauvres escoliers' who cannot afford to live in a college. His practical proposals for resolving the conflict are (i) to leave standing those fine old houses already built on the Petit Pré, though the revenue from them should go to finance public lectures, and to demolish the ugly modern houses on the Grand Pré: (ii) the university should procure even more green open spaces, outside the Porte St Jacques and the Porte St Victor, to cater for the increased number of colleges, by appropriating lands belonging to the monks. The usurpation of the Pré-aux-clercs, and the destruction of the playing-fields has already resulted in immorality such as excessive use of the *jeux de paume, cabaretz* and *bordeaux*. Ramus also has a fascinating scheme for making water flow once more through the Roman *Termae* near the Hôtel de Cluny for the refreshment of the university. But he is aware that the physical well-being of the university is less urgent than good relations between the university and the King (pp. 14–15). In a phrase with an uncannily modern ring he says 'si par la follie de quelques uns il s'est faict quelque esmeute, il ne s'ensuit pas qu'elle ayt esté faicte du conseil, vouloir, authorité, ny du Recteur, ny des quatre facultés, ny des colleges, ny des principaux, ny des procureurs de chasque nation: ny (pour dire en un mot) de l'Université.' (p. 8) The university itself should not be blamed as seditious or rebellious, nor should the student body be globally condemned. The deputation ended successfully since the edict and the 'arrest' were rescinded. The speech ends on an optimistic if un-prophetic note—'Je concluray priant Dieu le tresbon et tres grand, que ceste tempeste soit l'expiation pour jamais de toutes les mal-heurtés qui pourroient menacer l'Université de Paris.' (p. 32)[14]

At the end of the fifties and the beginning of the sixties Ramus published his grammars, French, Latin and Greek. At the same time he was preparing a key work on the reform of the university, pub-lished anonymously in 1562 as *Prœmium reformandae Parisiensis Academiae* and simultaneously in a French version. Since 1557 he had in fact served on a commission which had been studying this ques-tion. Addressing himself to Charles ix he reminds us that reform was initially proposed by the Three Estates meeting at Orléans (they had asked in particular that certain regents should be chosen and paid for by the state); the Privy Council had agreed and the king had ordered that the university should be reformed 'au naif patron d'une forme et maniere legitime'. From the time of François Ier onwards reforms had been taking place, especially in the schools of grammar and rhetoric, because of the king's reawakening of 'l'estude de l'humanité'. Disputatious methods have already disappeared from the classroom along with the *Doctrinale* of Alexander de Villa Dei, the *Graecismus* of Eberhard of Béthune and the Theodoletus, and in their place we now find poets, historians and orators, used to train young boys to read and write Latin and Greek. Ramus contends that the reforms have not extended beyond grammar and rhetoric, and all the indications that we have (apart from the new rhetorical orientation of logic since Agricola and Sturm) are that he is right. For the most part, in spite of a new spirit in scientific publications, the higher faculties and the philosophy course of the faculty of arts have not yet been reformed according to any humanist principles. The university has evolved a cumbersome system of co-opting new teaching members which has resulted in an infinite number of newly graduated regents, and yet the number of students has remained the same. In our terms, the staff-student ratio was unacceptable because there were far too many staff. The regents were paid entirely out of the fees which the students provided and these had risen inevitably to keep pace with the ever-increasing number of new staff. In colour-ful satirical terms Ramus shows that the actual fees and expenses demanded of the students are at least four times what the laws allow. Apart from the fees charged by the regents, which were variable, there were many fixed honoraria and legal-type administrative charges which supplemented the income of the regents and other officials. An expensive recurrent annual item appears to be the

Regents' Banquet, the origin presumably of the picnic at Arcueil given by Ronsard and his fellow-students to Dorat. Out of this social abuse, if it was one, grew the poetry of *Les Bacchanales* and *Ad Fontem Arculei*.

Ramus writes: 'Et quel argument suffisant ont les gantz, les bonnetz, les banquetz, pour prouver la diligence et suffisance du disciple, et combien il a prouffité en Philosophie?' (p. 12), and goes on to show that there is a further abuse in the fact that part of these extra fees is distributed among honorary regents who do nothing, and priests who say mass—'Bref, l'argent et la recepte du degré de Philosophie est administré de façon, que ceux qui portent moins de proufit à ceux qui estudient en Philosophie, sont ceux mesmes qui en pillent la meilleure part.' (p. 13) The burden of his argument (the result of personal experience) is that learning should not depend on wealth: 'Car c'est chose fort indigne que le chemin pour venir à la cognoissance de la Philosophie, soit clos et deffendu à la pouvreté, encores qu'elle feust docte et bien apprise.' (p. 14) In order to provide the money necessary to pay a small number of chosen regents, it would be sufficient for the king to order certain monasteries and colleges of canons to supply the funds, which they would gladly do. Ramus has by this date irrevocably joined the ranks of the reformers. He concludes on this point of student expenses: 'Que la seule et legitime depence que face l'escolier soit, d'auoir vescu, de s'estre entretenu d'accoustrements, d'auoir acheté liures, d'auoir trauaillé, veillé, et passé la meilleure part de sa vie aux lettres.' (pp. 14–15) It is true that in 1534 the faculty of law had undertaken some serious reforms in the matter of expenses, though Ramus felt that even the remaining fees should be abolished. It had been intended that similar reforms should be made in medicine and theology, but the theologians, the worst offenders, accused the proposer of heresy and there the matter rested (pp. 16–17).

A second criticism which he makes is that so much teaching, especially that of philosophy now takes place privately in the colleges, instead of publicly in the rue du Fouarre as the statutes both of university and college decreed. Each college had four teachers of philosophy (le Sommeliste, le Logicien, le Physicien and l'Intrant) say a hundred for all Paris, whereas if all lectures were public, then a few specialists would be enough. Grammar, rhetoric and logic should still be taught privately in the colleges, but the rest, mathematics, physics and ethics must be public, in the university and not just at the Collège Royal (pp. 38–50).

A third criticism concerns also the faculty of theology which has retained the ancient form of teaching by 'questionnaires' (instanced as Principes, Tentatives, Grande et Petite Ordinaire, and Vesperie) which it has substituted for the teaching of the Bible (pp. 72–100 and esp. p. 83).

In medicine, as in every other art, Ramus calls for more practical work, in words which remind us at once of Vesalius and Rabelais: 'que le docteur regent en une saison de l'année menast ses escoliers philosopher sur les herbes, plantes et toutes especes de simples, par les prez, jardins et boys: en une autre, qu'il les exerçast à la section des corps: en l'autre, et qui est la principale, qu'il leurs communicast en la cure des malades les consultations, les medicamentz, et tout l'ordre qu'il y tiendroit . . .' (pp. 73–4).[15]

Throughout the sixties Ramus continued the revision of his earlier works, such as the *Dialectica*. Within the university most of his energies were engaged in a stormy controversy about the teaching of mathematics and philosophy with Jacques Charpentier, newly appointed, in scandalous circumstances, to the chair of mathematics. I mention this incident to remind you of the close relation between proposals for university reform, such as those concerning the scope of philosophy and mathematics, and personal disagreements.[16]

From August 1568 until summer 1570, because of the political climate, Ramus was on leave from the university, travelling in Germany and Switzerland, inspecting the curricula of other universities. When he returned to Paris he found that there had been various measures against protestants which deprived him of his teaching, though luckily he was left with his title and his salary. The final version of the *Dialectica* came out in 1572 just before his death; in it he equates the method of logic with that of geometry, extending it to all the arts of the encyclopedia. Ten days before his death he wrote to Johann Freige, sending him books on the first three liberal arts, and promising to send books on the other four at a later date. His murder in late August cut short this plan for a final systematic presentation of the encyclopedia, though Freige in his *Paedagogus* and in his *Professio Regia in septem artes liberales* went some way to accomplishing it, and in 1587 Christofle de Savigny in a summary though visually exciting form presented an amplified Ramist encyclopedia.

In this account of the reform of the university I have emphasized Ramus's practical suggestions about the length and structure of the course, his sensitivity to relations between teachers and students, and between the university and the authorities. I have noted also his attempt to introduce a strict logical method into teaching, a method which would be the same in each science, and yet ensure the separation of one science from another. His treatise *Quod sit unica doctrinae*

14

instituendae methodus (1557) a reworking of one edition of the *Aristotelicae animadversiones* is a summary of this. This one method is sometimes divided into the method of teaching and the method of prudence, which is another way of expressing the idea of philosophy and eloquence. I propose therefore to look again at this topic, and to see how Ramus stands in the debates, central to educational problems, and indeed to the reform of the university, and to the question of literary theories and attitudes.

Adrien Turnèbe, in his *Animadversiones in Rullianos Petri Rami commentarios* (1553), one of the items in a lengthy exchange of pamphlets on Cicero's idea of fate, accuses Ramus of fraudulently arrogating to himself this title of Professor of Philosophy and Eloquence (though of course it was real and official) because he does not fulfil its promise—we are tempted to say, because his idea of philosophy does not coincide with that of Turnèbe. Ramus, he says, is 'illiteratus', 'ignarus litterarum' (p. 81) (this is the opposite of what Galland had said about him), believing that all philosophy and eloquence is contained in his insipid artifices which amount to no more than a new technical jargon. What solid philosophy there is in Ramus could be learned in three days by a very busy man (p. 73). The abridged simplicity, of which Ramus, incidentally, was so proud, is valueless, for what is the good of a philosophy or eloquence which can be circumscribed 'in these tiny little precepts, in such a small compass'. For Turnèbe, there is 'nothing here which helps us to understand nature or other writers or for the enrichment of speech' (ibid.). In a striking phrase he says to him 'personatus prodis orator et philosophus' (p. 81), a phrase redolent of Descartes's 'larvatus prodeo'; Turnèbe adds that Ramus's mask is that of the incompetent actor.[17]

Logic, moreover, he says elsewhere, is a mere part of philosophy, not the whole. For Turnèbe, after Cicero, philosophy is 'rerum divinarum et humanarum cognitio, et causarum quibus quaequae res gerantur notitia'; it studies the 'penetralia mundi' as well as the stars, is admitted to the councils of the gods as well as describing human behaviour and duties, and includes all the other arts in its scope (p. 41). Their rights are derivative, 'precaria', which means 'uncertain because depending on the will of' philosophy, literally lent by philosophy, borrowed money which she may call in some day. Now since for Ramus philosophy was synonymous with teaching the implications are obvious. As so often, this is a matter of principle underlying a demarcation dispute between teachers who have no clear brief or contract about what they are supposed to teach. Like Ramus Turnèbe repeats the Ciceronian equation of philosophy with the cultivation of the mind, 'animi culturam, tanquam agri'. The other arts do no more than prepare the ground to receive the seed of philosophy; we must go beyond philosophical fore-play to the study of wisdom, leaving aside the 'progymnasmata' as Turnèbe calls the other arts (p. 44). Aristotle himself joined eloquence with philosophy and he can only gain by being interpreted by men of our profession, teachers of good Greek and Latin literature. Turnèbe is not, in fact, quarrelling with Ramus's aim, but with the way he sets about achieving it. Like Ramus he claims that philosophy includes everything. What he is taking exception to is rather Ramus's brand of eloquence, his illiterate way of expressing his philosophy.[18]

Muret, too, treated this subject on several occasions. In 1555 in *De studiis literarum* he discusses the relation between literature and philosophy, seeing them as closer together than some would allow. Teachers of literature are not just 'masters of words, interpreters of fables, architects of trifles' (p. 21). Literature, synonymous here with eloquence, does not merely result in some empty delight, for under cover of the fables there is to be found 'all elegant doctrine, all knowledge worthy of a noble man, all wisdom' (p. 22). We are reminded of Dorat's teaching as Ronsard describes it to us in the *Hymne de l'Automne* (1563):

Disciple de d'Aurat, qui long temps fut mon maistre,
M'aprist la Poësie, et me montra comment
On doit feindre et cacher les fables proprement,
Et à bien deguiser la vérité des choses
D'un fabuleux manteau dont elles sont encloses.[19]

For Muret teachers of literature have to be learned in many fields, to be able to explain the material from all other arts and sciences which authors have introduced into their works. He claims, though this was contested, that practitioners of other arts, such as logic or physics, medicine or law, can be totally ignorant of all the others. It is not thought disgraceful for a doctor to be ignorant of the law or of astronomy. 'We alone', he writes, and I return to my initial quotation, 'the teachers of literature, although we do not have to study and become thoroughly acquainted with all the liberal arts, we must still appreciate and acquire a real taste for them.' He goes on to ask, if you are unfamiliar with astronomy and geography, can you really say that you are a satisfactory critic and interpreter of poetry (pp. 26–7)?[20] Muret's own practice was to implement the union of philosophy and eloquence, as we learn from his speech on this subject in Venice in 1557, by teaching an oration of Cicero one year and a work of philosophy the next. Muret suggests several reasons why anyone should oppose the union of the two: blindness, jealousy, incompetence, snobbery, or a desire to separate the scope of different subjects, again a teachers' demarcation dispute (p. 33). His definition of philosophy, too, is the Ciceronian one, and he sets out clearly the two sides of the question, that you cannot be eloquent, you cannot excel in speaking or in public affairs unless you have first been schooled in the workshop of the philosophers, since 'all liberal doctrine, all history, the variety of all the arts comes from the philosophers' (p. 38) (in what way precisely he does not make clear); on the other hand, elegance of language is necessary, since beauty and dignity of dress is better than mere protection from the elements, and nature usually joins beauty with usefulness; Muret is particularly hard on those who intentionally cultivate barbarity of speech, who think that philosophy must use jargon. They are like that community of people in antiquity who lived in squalid filth, dressed in rags, were always unwashed, unshaven, uncombed and claimed that therefore they were philosophers (p. 44).[21]

Denis Lambin, for his part, in his *De philosophia cum arte dicendi coniungenda oratio* (1568) is even more eloquent, saying that the union is like the commerce between Venus and the muses, or graces. If he were to draw a child's crayon-sketch of philosophy he would give her a face with virginal modesty and innocence and yet matronly dignity, her hair neither wantonly shoulder length nor unduly crisped and curled, somewhere between sumptuous luxuriousness and illiberal negligence. Philosophy has a natural beauty of her own and despises adventitious aids. She does not need to make her eyebrows blacker than they are naturally, nor her cheeks redder or whiter. Nor does she seek out the public. Rhetoric on the other hand displays herself to the people, decked out in gold and purple, with fetching curls and seductive make-up. Lambin seems to forget that he is supposed to be praising the union of philosophy and eloquence and ends by roundly abusing rhetoric who is so unbridled and excitable that she rushes headlong into disordered garrulity and blind furious madness. For Lambin, the marriage, or rather affair, between philosophy and eloquence is decidedly morganatic.[22]

To return to Ramus: few humanists have been as enthusiastic as he was about this marriage of philosophy and eloquence. As it was initially proposed, the union was a humanist reaction against scholastic jargon after the rediscovery of the Greek and Latin classics, with a concomitant claim that the new university philosophy (which is mainly Cicero with a certain amount of Plato) is itself naturally eloquent. It is usually also an emphasis on rhetoric and moral and political philosophy at the expense of both logic and science. The question is further complicated by the new idea of literature and especially poetry which was emerging, put forward by French poets writing in the vernacular and supported by some teachers of Greek and Latin literature. Superficially, though for him logic is more important than ethics, Ramus shares these aims. The fact that he was rejected by poets, philosophers, humanists and men of science should surely make us wonder why they saw him as so different from themselves. His temperament is one thing, but it does not explain all the animosity. Nor even does the fact that he was a logician, and therefore offered, to use Montaigne's phrase, 'cette image triste, querelleuse, despite, menaceuse, mineuse' of philosophy.[23] Equally, if not more, important is his attitude to literature. He had in fact small Latin and less Greek, never giving the impression of being well-versed in Roman, and having no familiarity at all with Greek literature. His reputation for being one of France's greatest orators may be merited, but this rarely appears from his printed page. Perhaps Scaliger was right when he said that he was a good orator but wrote badly.[24] There is abundant evidence in Nancel's *Petri Rami vita* of his lack of poetic sensibility.[25] What I want to suggest is that his calling on poets and orators to illustrate philosophy and his hunting for syllogisms and tropes in literature was totally discordant with the new literary sensibility. It was a devaluation of literature, and led to the divorce of philosophy and eloquence which is evident in all the Ramist encyclopedias, such as Freige's, where the scheme of university teaching has been radically reformed, systematized, dichotomized, bracketed, emasculated out of existence, and poetry squeezed in as an afterthought. Muret, Turnèbe and Lambin, for all their cloying Ciceronianism, are steeped in Greek and Latin and are poets themselves.

From his first brush with the authorities in 1543 to his detailed project of 1562, and including his representation of the students' cause in the incident of the Pré-aux-clercs we see his dedicated concern to establish a new order and adopt a new approach to the running of his university of Paris, which he once called, in a delightful phrase, 'la plus belle boutique du monde'. Underlying all his ideas there is the belief that there is one method for all teaching, all philosophy. His reorganization should be more scientific, because more methodical, and at the same time more humanistic, because linked with literature. But he is protesting too much and in vain. Practising poets in France were not interested in his teaching and the teachers of literature were already doing what he suggested, much better and with much less fuss. His encyclopedia effectively restricts the scope both of philosophy and of eloquence or literature. The preparation of an encyclopedia by one person (one of his critics ironically labelled him 'omniscium') indicates a belief in the perfection rather than the perfectibility of knowledge, and shows that the old humanist ideal is disintegrating. We have the impression that we are watching at the bedside during the last illness of *uomo universale*.

The theorists of poetry in the sixteenth century in France set a high ideal for the education of the poet: Du Bellay said that he should be 'instruict de tous bons arts et sciences' and Peletier that he should be familiar with 'toute la Philosophie'.[26] Muret, in the Latin quotation with which I began, says that the *teacher* of poetry must have a taste for knowledge of all sorts. As we now start this conference which aims to study the state of learning in the sixteenth century in relation to French literature, may I, with Muret, wish you 'bonne dégustation', and, reminding you of another Renaissance commonplace on the two fruits of learning, hope that the conference will lead to *utilitas* if not *voluptas*.

NOTES

1 M.-A. Muret, 'Aduersus quosdam litterarum humaniorum uituperatores, oratio, habita Venetiis postridie Non. Oct. Anno MDLV', in *Orationes XXIII* (Venice, Aldus, 1576), 26.

2 Thomas Bicarton, *Miscellanea* (Poitiers, Bochets, 1588).

3 The literature on Ramus and Ramism is vast. My own greatest debts are to Walter Ong, especially in his *Ramus, Method and the Decay of Dialogue* and his *Ramus and Talon Inventory*, both published in 1958 in Cambridge, Mass., to J. J. Verdonk in *Petrus Ramus en de wiskunde* (Assen 1966), and to Cesare Vasoli, *La Dialettica e la retorica dell'umanesimo* (Milan 1968). A fuller bibliographical account will be found in my 'Present State of Studies on Ramus' *Studi Francesi*, n. 47-8 (1972) 201–13.

4 Even Verdonk has been misled into accepting the traditional, but erroneous, view about Ramus's thesis.

5 Ong, *Ramus and Talon Inventory, passim.*

6 Ramus, *Pro philosophica Parisiensis disciplina oratio* (Paris, M. David, 1551). All references are to this edition.

7 This work, and its place in the present controversy, has been recently studied by Charles Schmitt, in *Cicero Scepticus* (The Hague 1972) esp. 92–102.

8 Galland, *Pro schola Parisiensi*, 1551, f. 9 v: 'Melior pars eorum qui hasce tuas nugas lectitant Rame (ne hinc tibi nimium placeas) non ad fructum aliquem ex iis capiendum, sed ueluti uernaculos ridiculi Pantagruelis libros ad lusum et animi oblectationem lectitant.'

9 f. 30 v: 'Quid ita? quoniam multos non defuturos arbitrati sunt qui poetarum illecebris deliniti, caeterarumque leuiorum artium facilitate capti, in iis studiose uersarentur.'

10 f. 63 v.
11 It seems to me that M. Guy Demerson, in his excellent edition of Rabelais's *Œuvres complètes* (Paris 1973) 573 mixes up Galland and Ramus.
12 M. Dassonville in 'La collaboration de la Pléiade à la *Dialectique* de Pierre de la Ramée (1555)' *BHR*, 25 (1963) 337–48, and edition of *La Dialectique* (1555) (Geneva 1966). Most scholars now repeat Dassonville's statements without examination.
13 Copies are to be found in the BN, 8° T 18 I, and in the Bibl. Sainte Geneviève, T 8° 143 inv. 1368 (Rés).
14 *Harangue touchant ce qu'ont faict les deputez de l'Université de Paris envers le Roy* (Paris, A. Wechel, 1557).
15 All references here are to the French version *Advertissements sur la Reformation de l'Université de Paris,* 1562.
16 The fullest account of the controversy with Charpentier will be found in Vasoli, op. cit.
17 References are to *Opera* (1600) t. 1.
18 *Adriani Turnebi oratio habita cum philosophiam profiteri coepit,* also contained in *Opera* (1600) t. 111 to which reference is made.
19 Ronsard, ed. Laumonier, XII, 50.
20 M.-A. Muret, ed. cit., see note 1.
21 M.-A. Muret, *De philosophiae et eloquentiae coniunctione oratio, habita Venetiis mense Octobri Anno* MDLVII, in *Orationes XXIII* (Venice, Aldus, 1576) 28–49: 'a philosophis omnis doctrina liberalis, a philosophis omnis historia, a philosophis omnis artium uarietas sumi potest' (p. 38); 'qui dedita opera barbariem in loquendo diligunt, et non aliter se philosophos uisum iri putant, quam si dictione inquinatissima utantur, et, ut sues in luto ac cœno, sic ipsi in orationis sordibus uolutentur. Antiquis temporibus quoddam stultorum genus fuisse proditum est, qui pedore ac squalore horridi, pannis obsiti, semper illoti, semper intonsi, semper impexi, illo ipso incultu ac neglectu corporis philosophorum nomen in uulgus assequebantur. Non ualde dissimilis est eorum amentia, qui orationem nullo studio excultam, nulla diligentia expolitam, nullo artificio elaboratam, philosophiae professoribus conuenire aiunt' (p. 44).
22 Lambin, *De philosophia cum arte dicendi coniugenda, Oratio, habita in gymnasio Samarobrinensi a.d. VII. Idus Ianuarias, anno M.D.LXVIII...* (Paris 1568) Apud Ioannem Benenatum, 3–4.
23 Montaigne, *Essais,* 1, 26.
24 'Bonus orator, qui facultatem dicendi sibi comparaverat...', and 'Ramus male scribebat', *Prima Scaligerana* and *Secunda Scaligerana,* s.v. *Ramus* (Amsterdam 1740). It is of course possible that Scaliger was here referring to his handwriting and not to his style—see Nancel, *Petri Rami vita,* 61.
25 Op. cit., 22, 32, 33, 81–2.
26 Du Bellay, *La Deffence et illustration de la langue françoyse,* 11, ch. 5; Peletier, *L'Art poëtique,* ed. A. Boulanger, 216–17.

BRIAN BARRON

Poet and Orator in Louis le Caron's Dialogue de la poësie *(1556)*

IN THE INTRODUCTION TO his *Dialogues*, Louis le Caron states that although his previous works have not been very well received by the public, he has decided to overcome his personal disappointment and carry on publishing his philosophy for the sake of posterity.[1] Posterity, it must be admitted, has not shown very much gratitude, and has dealt almost as unkindly with the *Dialogues de Loys le Caron Parisien* as it has with his *Poësie* and his *Philosophie*.[2] The fourth of the series of dialogues, entitled *Ronsard, ou de la poësie* is the only exception, and has attracted the attention of critics of French sixteenth-century poetic theory. However, these critics have used the dialogue mainly as a means of documenting or substantiating points of theory which it is supposed were held in common by sixteenth-century poets and critics, and as a consequence, their use of Le Caron's dialogue is highly selective. Marcel Raymond does not see much of originality in the dialogue; for him it is mainly a proof of the rapid spread of the neo-platonic view of poetry in France.[3] Henri Weber has since pointed out the interest of the section Le Caron devotes to the function of myth in poetry,[4] and more recently still Grahame Castor has indicated how Le Caron already has some grasp of Aristotle's theory of the *vraisemblable* as early as 1556.[5]

What I want to do here is to look at Le Caron's dialogue as a whole—that is as a total statement on poetry—and also to place it within the context of the series of dialogues it belongs to. It seems to me that this exercise will be worthwhile for two reasons. First, Louis le Caron is not a major literary figure, but has something of the status of an educated amateur, and therefore his views may legitimately be taken to reflect something of the expectations and attitudes of the thoughtful sixteenth-century reader. Secondly, and perhaps paradoxically, Le Caron is a *very* well educated amateur, widely read in Greek literature and philosophy, and an overall examination of the dialogue will show whether his erudition has enabled him to make any original contribution to criticism in France. The dialogue form itself is obviously of importance here: it is true that in the few examples we have in this volume Le Caron's use of the dialogue is not always very subtle, but just the same, in the case of the *Dialogue de la poësie*, he does seem to be juxtaposing several strands of poetic theory and several attitudes to poetry in order to extract from the resulting discussion some kind of stable and coherent criteria for its assessment.[6]

But before getting down to an analysis of the dialogue itself I want to have a more general look at the whole series in order to get an idea of what Le Caron was aiming at. The one volume that appeared in 1556 is in fact only the first part of a projected three-volume work that never got any further—or at least volumes two and three never got into print. However, Le Caron gives the titles of all his intended dialogues at the beginning of volume one, and even a brief glance at them shows just how ambitious his project was. He seems to have been aiming for some kind of encyclopedic work, based mainly on Plato, but with contributions from other authors of antiquity, notably Cicero. It is worthwhile pointing out though that Le Caron does claim some degree of independence from his sources in his *avant-propos*:[7]

> Maintenant je te presente trois livres de Dialogues, desquelz tu rapporteras et ce que les anciens ont congneu, et ce qu'ilz ont ignoré. Car je ne suis ne trop serf admirateur, ne trop ignorant despriseur de l'antiquité.

His intention then would seem to be to take the best of ancient philosophy, build on it and complement it. The list of dialogues is as follows:

Book 1. Le Courtisan premier, ou que le prince doit philosopher.
  Le Courtisan second, ou, de la vraie sagesse, et des louanges de la philosophie.
  Valton, de la tranquilité de l'Esprit, ou du souverain bien.
  Ronsard, ou de la poësie.
  Claire, ou de la beauté iiii dialo. desquelz le premier est comme l'argument, ou epitome des autres. (Only the first of these was published, the others being deferred to the second volume.)
Book 2. Le Chaldean, ou des divinations ii dia.
  Pasquier, ou l'Orateur ii dia.
  Le Solitaire, ou la description du monde iiii dia.
  Le Sophiste, ou de la science.
  Faulchet, ou de l'utilité, qu'apporte la congnoissance des choses naturelles ii dia.
Book 3. Le nouveau Narcisse, ou de la nature de l'homme ii dia.

Le nouveau Heraclite, ou des secrets de la philosophie non
encores congneus ne revelez iii dia.
Le nouveau Parmenide, ou de l'Estant, et des Idées.
Le nouveau Pytagore, ou des nombres et de l'harmonie vi
dia.
Le Senateur, ou de la Chose publique x dia.

In this list of titles it is I think possible to discern Le Caron's general
aim, in that there is a gradual broadening of philosophical scope and
a gradual move towards greater abstraction as we progress through
the volumes. The first dialogue—*Que le prince doit philosopher*—is an
introduction to the main body of the work, a praise of philosophy
which develops into a treatise on the education of princes and the
need for them to attain *sagesse* through the study of philosophy.[8] Le
Caron then sets out to explore the various aspects of human experience and knowledge, which he would no doubt have eventually
synthesized and applied in the creation of his own ideal Republic in
the last ten dialogues.

The *avant-propos* does in fact warn the reader that he should be
aware of the deliberate structuring of the work, although Le Caron
does not comment on the structure himself, being content to tell us
that there is more to his dialogues than meets the eye:

> Quant a l'ordre, que j'ay suivi, trop long seroit de t'en rendre
> raison: toutefois asseure toi, que je n'ai rien disposé sans grande
> prudence: et ne m'est besoing de censeur, comme aux nouveaux
> apprentis, qui font leur coup d'essai.

This may of course be bluff, but apart from the elements of structure
already mentioned, each book does seem to have some kind of unifying theme or element. The second, for example, deals largely with
natural philosophy, while the third starts with a discussion of the
nature of man—including no doubt his capacity for abstract thought
—and moves on to metaphysics. From our point of view, it is
interesting to note that the dialogues devoted to the orator—and
there were to be two of them as opposed to only one on poetry—are
placed later in the series than the *Dialogue de la poësie*, after the discussion of the poetic, erotic and vatic furies, and before the dialogues
dealing with natural philosophy. This may suggest that in Le
Caron's view the orator and his art are more closely involved with
the communication and acquisition of knowledge than are the poet
and his. The evidence is slight, but this idea is given some credence
by Le Caron's mildly hostile attitude to poetry in those parts of the
dialogues not expressly concerned with it—this in spite of his own
attempts at poetry, or perhaps precisely because of their failure. The

first dialogue, for example, does not see the popularity of poetry as an unqualified blessing. Le Caron and his companion Philarete deplore the state of the country and attribute it to the scornful attitude of the French to philosophy; Le Caron (here speaking in his own name) declares that he will not rest until he has made the French as keen on philosophy as they are on poetry:

> . . . nous tombâmes en la plainte des ennuis, que l'injurieuse malice du temps fait injustement souffrir a plusieurs: tellement que je disois tel desordre et perturbation du repos des hommes ne venir d'allieurs, que de l'ignorance et mepris de la philosophie (en laquelle chacun devroit mettre le meilleur de ses ans) et quant a moy, ma deliberation estre de ne jamais reposer, tant que je la voie un jour autant fleurissante entre les Francois, que la poësie.

So we have here a clear distinction between poetry and the knowledge and wisdom which make up *philosophie*. This is not necessarily to deprecate poetry, but Le Caron makes the direction his thought is taking clear in his next speech where he describes what *does* appeal to the frivolous French:

> rien ne leur est agreable, que ce qui est elegant et fardé des plaisantes mignardises de bien dire, desquelles je confesse mon oraison n'estre exquisement decorée: car je ne recognoi rien en moi, qu'une pure et franche affection envers la Chose-publique.

The implication is that the betterment of the public ought to be the aim of any writer, and that plain speaking is the way to achieve this; stylistic effects are appreciated for their own sake and thus divert attention away from the acquisition of knowledge and the public good.

This separation of form and content ties up with the general unifying theme of the first book, which seems to be the dichotomy between sense and spirit. The last dialogue, concerning beauty, asks whether the appreciation of beauty necessarily involves the senses, or whether a wholly intellectual perception of beauty is possible. More important still is the fact that in his third dialogue, *Valton, de la tranquilité de l'esprit, ou du souverain bien,* Le Caron expounds his theory of knowledge, describing the sensitive faculty and its connections with memory, imagination and the faculty called *entendement*.[9] He also discusses here whether human behaviour is regulated by *vertu* or by *volupté*. Indeed he puts into the mouth of no less a spokesman than Rabelais some interesting arguments on the connections between these, the desire for virtue and knowledge being seen as inspired by the pleasure which accompany them. The 'delectation du corps' and that of the spirit join together to produce 'la vraie volupté de tout l'homme'. And Rabelais concludes as follows:

On ne peut vivre joieusement, si non aussi sagement, honneste-
ment et justement: ne par mesme raison sagement, honneste-
ment et justement, si non joieusement. Et le fruit et guerdon de
la vertu est icelle-meme volupté.[10]

Valton is given the last word however, and he sees contentment in
rather more exclusively spiritual terms: 'la tranquillité de l'esprit' is
eventually identified with the intellectual rapture of the philosopher:

Quelle plus grande joie peut avoir l'homme, que de jouir de
soi-même, c'est a dire du repos et contentement lequel il se
donne par les pensées, conceptions et discours, qu'il fait en lui-
mesme des choses excellentes et louables. (f. 126r)

This then is the background to the *Dialogue de la poësie*. Le Caron can
now go on to examine how poetry operates within the epistemo-
logical scheme outlined in the third dialogue. Being a student of
Plato, he will be particularly interested in establishing whether
poetry is capable of acting as a bridge between the world of appear-
ances and the transcendental reality. He will also wish to examine
poetry's appeal to *volupté* and to *vertu*.

The participants in the dialogue are two poets, Ronsard and
Jodelle, and two 'orateurs', Pasquier and Fauchet. It is not known
whether Le Caron ever met either of the poets, but the 'orateurs'
were both young lawyers at the same time as he was and he would
certainly have professional connections with them, and in the case of
Pasquier at least, there was real friendship.[11] This may explain why
Pasquier's role in the dialogue is such an important one, as I hope to
show. The nature of the participants obviously adds another issue
to those outlined above—the relationship between poetry and
rhetoric and the social function of the poet and the orator respectively. In fact the two 'orators' very quickly concentrate the discussion on the moral justification of poetry, and its contribution to the
public good.

In this connection, we should perhaps note here that Le Caron's
dialogue stands apart from other French literary criticism of the
time, which has a definite practical bias and is not much concerned
with the metaphysical and moral justification of the arts.[12] Le
Caron's standpoint leads him to an approach rather more common
among Italian critics of the time, and to a kind of objectivity
which is of course helped by the clash of ideas the dialogue form
permits.

Ronsard is the first to speak, and he sets out to prove the excellence of poetry. His argument makes three major points: it estab-
lishes the primacy of poetry over philosophy, it declares that poetry
is capable of penetrating the ideal world, and it states that poetry is

'useful' in the sense that it has a positive effect on public morality. Ronsard's justification, that is, like nearly all poetic theory of the time, combines the neo-platonic inspiration theory with the combination of 'doux' and 'utile' derived from Cicero and Horace.

The primacy of poetry is proved by a long series of examples showing how many of Plato's ideas are already to be found in Pindar and other early poets, whom Plato himself designated as 'les peres et Capitaines de sagesse'. It is implied that this temporal primacy automatically means that poetry is a superior form of philosophy since it is closer to the divine origins of mankind. (f. 129v) The relationship of poetry with the world of Ideas is made clear in an interesting analogy between poetry and painting—all the more interesting because although these comparisons are commonplace in Italian criticism they are rather less frequent in French critics, and also because it will come up again later in Le Caron's dialogue in a rather different form. Here, the analogy shows how the artist combines the sensual and the spiritual:

> ... [la poësie] n'est grandement diverse de la peinture de Polygnote ou Zeusis non moins doctes es autres arts, qu'excellents en leur profession: Lesquelz se proposoient deux choses, l'une de leur art, et l'autre qui dependoit de la vertu et cognoissance des autres choses. C'etait bien de leur art de representer au vif l'image du corps, qu'ilz designoient de peindre, mais il venait de leur vertu et plus haulte science d'exprimer la perfection d'une beauté en toutes ses graces et bienseances. (f. 130v)

Any artist of genius is therefore also necessarily a philosopher, and only such genius is capable of producing the perfect work of art where particular and ideal, or form and content, unite. Ronsard, however, seems to be pulled in two contrary directions by his own analogy. On the one hand, the ultimate aim of the neo-platonic artist must be abstraction, the suppression of the particular:

> Phidias se proposant de faire l'image de Jupiter ou de Minerve n'addressoit son projet a aucun, pour en tirer de lui la semblance: ains une Idée de la souveraine beauté estoit engravée en son esprit, a l'imitation de laquelle il dressoit l'art et la main. (f. 131r)

But on the other hand, 'art' cannot be wholly dispensed with; abstract statement is repugnant and must be accompanied by appropriate decoration if it is to make any impression:

> tant soit la beauté belle, si elle n'est parée de riches ornements, de nul sera cogneue et estimée: aussi tant soit la sentence excellente, si elle n'est enrichie d'inventions bien agensées et appropriées au sujet, qui lui donnent grâce, couleur et autorité, ne

faut esperer qu'elle soit recueillie de telle faveur, que paraventure elle merite. (f. 133r)

The notion of appropriateness is however crucial, and if this criterion is respected, the fusion of form and content is assured, producing what Ronsard proceeds to define as 'une exquise imitation de la nature des choses':

> Je rejette avec Pindare les fables bigarrés de variables mensonges, d'inutiles et vaines moqueries: celles me plaisent seulement qui ont une exquise imitation de la nature des choses, et avec la delectation l'utilité conjointe. (ibid.)

The criteria outlined here—appropriateness, consistency, depth of meaning—indicate the middle path that poetry must follow between unattractive abstraction and overindulgent decoration. This middle path also assures the conjunction of pleasure and profit demanded by Horace, and this leads us to the third section of Ronsard's argument.

All that we have said so far concerns only the relationship between the artist and his work. As soon as the idea of the usefulness of poetry is introduced, things start to get complicated, and the delicate balance between form and content is upset by the obligation to consider the needs and potential of the audience. The 'profit' side of poetry, according to Ronsard, goes back to its origins with the civilizing of primitive man by the songs of Amphion and Orpheus. And it is important to note that this civilizing effect was achieved, in the first instance at least, by the sensual power of poetry and the pleasure it gave.

> Il falloit reveiller ces premiers esprits endormis en une horreur de vie par l'attraiante volupté de ce qui est plus agreable aux oreilles. Qui est l'homme si mal né et si grossier et lourd d'entendement, qui ne sent en soi toutes ses parties plus nobles se ravir au chant d'une gracieuse chanson, et i prendre quelquefois si grand plaisir, qu'il semble estre transporté de tout autre pensement? (f. 129v)

Primitive man, that is, was tricked or charmed into becoming civilized through the pleasurable attractions of poetry. We may refer back here to the sentiments expressed by Rabelais in the previous dialogue. There are in fact two ways of looking at a poem, depending on the quality of the reader, who may either be one of those whom Le Caron calls 'bien né', or belong to the 'vulgaire'. Ronsard uses two rather different images to express the function of style in poetry corresponding to these different types of reader. First of all, the poet's use of *fable* is seen as an *amorce*, with its double meaning of a bait or temptation and also a starting point, in a thoroughly neoplatonic view of poetry:

> Quel grand plaisir se donne l'esprit, quand ravi et abstrait des
>   pensements terrestres il cherche et recherche franchement, in-
>   vente, concoit, entend, traitte et designe infinis discours, pour
>   trouver la verité, de laquelle la subtile fable lui donne quelque
>   amorce. (f. 133r)

We are obviously very close here to the neo-platonic ideas of Pontus
de Tyard's *Solitaire premier*, published four years earlier in 1552.
There too poetry is seen as only the first step in the 'aliénation d'entendement' which leads the soul to God. Now if it is to fulfil this
purpose, it must be obscure, and its imagery must above all be *subtle*
since its only function is to stimulate the intellectual curiosity of the
reader and set in motion a kind of internal dialectic that is pleasurable in itself but that goes beyond language, and therefore has only
very tenuous connections with the poem. Indeed the poem must be
self-effacing, prepared to give way to the free-ranging speculations
of the reader. The intellectual pleasure experienced by the 'bien né'
when he reads poetry corresponds to Valton's definition of contentment in the previous dialogue as opposed to Rabelais's. The image
of the *amorce* is also manifestly similar to that of the *veil* used by the
real Ronsard in his own works, and Le Caron does in fact introduce
the notion of the poet *concealing* the truth elsewhere in this speech.
Here then, the poet is concerned only with an intellectual elite; the
vulgaire are scorned, and obscurity is the order of the day.

Secondly, *fable* is also seen to make the poet's work useful in its
effect on the *vulgaire*, by civilizing them in the same way as Orpheus
did the primitives. A number of related images is used to designate
this effect of poetry; fable is seen as the sugar-coating on the bitter
pill, as a cosmetic or disguise:

> Nous voions les medecins quand ils veulent presenter au malade
> facheus et difficile un bruvage de saveur amere, avoir de cous-
> tume de le deguiser par quelque douce liqueur. En mesme
> maniere l'ancienne philosophie a gaigné son premier honneur
> par le voile et couverture des fables, des carmes et des chants
> desquelz elle fardoit la gravité de ses sentences. (f. 133v)

This image involves a total reversal of the values contained in the
other one; no longer a free exploration of the mysteries by an
elevated understanding, but a kind of propaganda or brainwashing,
involving the imposition of one man's opinion on another. What the
vulgaire get out of it is a spontaneous but rather unspecific pleasure,
which can only be qualified as mindless: the kind of automatic
response one gives when one is *tickled*.

> J'admire non sans cause les poëtes, lesquels se proposoient de
> contenter et les plus excellents et le commun. Car si les secretz

cachez et enveloppez de leurs rares inventions ne pouvoient
estre de chacun entendus: au moins le plaisir du discours
chatouilloit et les uns et les autres, se rendant digne d'estre
embrassé de touts. (f. 133r)

So, from another point of view, the perfect fusion of form and content described earlier can be seen as a compromise made inevitable
by the nature of the audience.

So far so good. In this speech by Ronsard, Le Caron has given us
a clear statement of the kind of ideas about poetry that were in the
air in the 1550s and were often used by poets talking about their
work. One might even say that it is one of the best such statements,
and Le Caron has been complimented for expressing Ronsard's
views on poetry better and earlier than Ronsard himself. This explains why critics of French sixteenth-century poetic theory find
themselves drawn to this section of the dialogue. But as far as Le
Caron is concerned, this is only the first stage of the examination of
poetry; Ronsard's pronouncement does not give the answers, it is
no more or less than the basis for the subsequent discussion.

The next to speak is Jodelle, whose function seems to be to fill in
the neo-platonic background to what Ronsard has said. He explains
the doctrine of poetic fury and the intimate connection that exists
between poetry, philosophy and music. The idea of harmony—
divine, social, and psychological—is introduced. Jodelle's neoplatonism is rather vehement, and it is he who really drives home the
idea that the artist should scorn what he calls 'la sotte multitude'.
Interestingly, Jodelle the neo-platonist states explicitly that he cannot accept one of the things that Plato says about inspiration—what
Socrates says in the *Io* about it often being the worst poets who are
inspired. By bringing this point up at all, it seems to me that Le
Caron is letting us know that he is aware that Plato himself treats the
idea of inspiration with a certain irony, and that he, unlike most of
his contemporaries, has chosen not to ignore this irony. He is pointing out, in fact, that Jodelle is tampering with Plato to suit his own
ends.

The arguments of the two poets are now taken up and answered
by the two orators. Their tactic is to turn the points made in the
defence of poetry against the poets in such a way as to destroy their
justification of the art. In particular, they pick on the 'moral utility'
argument of Ronsard which is, as we have seen, rather a weak one
since it involves compromising so as to make poetry accessible to
the *vulgaire*. It is also natural that they should be most interested in
the moral question, given their status as 'orators' and men of law.
Poetic theory stole the idea of 'usefulness' and 'teaching' from

rhetoric; here two professional public speakers set out to show that poetry is not a fit medium for teaching.

Pasquier begins by adopting Ronsard's earlier tactic of comparing poetry and philosophy. He expresses his admiration for Homer, and in a series of examples proves to his own satisfaction at least that the poet's works express symbolically or allegorically the philosophy of Plato. Thus Homer ought to be the ideal poet described by Ronsard in his speech, and indeed, says Pasquier, echoing the reference made by Ronsard, Plato himself calls Homer divine, and 'le vrai Capitaine des sages'. (f. 140v) If then Homer possesses this quality, his poetic version of Plato ought to make the truth more accessible and palatable to the people, yet Plato bans all poets including Homer from his Republic. The reason for this is that the historical primacy used by Ronsard as a way of glorifying poetry does not mean that poetry is a superior kind of philosophy, rather quite the opposite. The philosopher's understanding has matured to a point where he no longer needs the stimulus of poetry to reach the world of Ideas, and at this point of abstraction poetry becomes unacceptable for the very reasons Ronsard had brought up in its favour—the metaphysical and moral arguments start to work against it. Plato's aim is to do away with the 'desordre des pensées et actions humaines' (ff. 142v–143r) by providing mankind with certain stable, immutable principles of thought. The poet inevitably depicts the diversity of the world, and his attachment to the individual and the particular as perceived by the senses militates against him in Plato's eyes. To illustrate this, Pasquier gives us a different version of the poetry-painting analogy—that of the composite ideal, which Italian critics often use in their justifications of poetry, but which serves here both to belittle it and to undermine Ronsard's earlier use of the analogy:

> [Platon] n'a point imité les vulgaires imagiers, lesquelz de toutes parts recueillent les fleurs et traits de beauté, et ingenieusement les enrichissent de diverses couleurs: afin que de plusieurs pourtraits ilz tirent une beauté entiere et accomplie. (f. 143r)

There is also a resemblance between this view of painting and the real Ronsard's description of his own creative processes in the opening lines of the *Ode à Michel de l'Hôpital*. Even the best of poets, then, are concerned to some extent with the particular, since as Ronsard himself said in his speech, abstraction is repugnant to the reader. And not only does this make poetry metaphysically inferior to philosophy, but it also condemns it for moral reasons. Attachment to the individual makes the poet fall away from the unity of truth into the diversity of opinion which is the hallmark of the human condition, and his work can thus be seen as nothing more than an attempt to persuade his readers that his opinion *is* the truth:

> Aucuns [poëtes] se rendent trop populaires et semblent estre serfs des afections humaines, les autres et ceux plus graves et excellents (comme Homere) imitent les mœurs des hommes, qui ont esté ou vertueux ou vicieux, et plus souvent se bigarrent selon les diverses opinions du vulgaire. Davantage Platon, qui n'a rien traitté, que tres-exquisement et en telle majesté que sa grandeur meritoit, s'est tousjours proposé de suivre une vraie et certaine raison, reputant indigne de *chatouiller* ses citoiens de je ne scai quelles blandices et *amorces* des fables, desquelles la jeunesse ne peut rapporter aucune utilité. (ff. 143r–v, my italics).

However, Pasquier is a lover of poetry and admires Homer, so his condemnation is not as total as Plato's. The fact that the poet was banned from the ideal republic does not mean that society should reject him, but only that they should be careful in their dealings. Since poetry could be a powerful immoral force, it should only be available to those of sound judgement. (Hence the reference to 'la jeunesse' who presumably are not.) Poetry, he concludes is 'non a touts et n'en touts lieux convenable'. (ibid.)

Pasquier's speech is followed by Fauchet's, which serves the same purpose as did Jodelle's in that it backs up and expresses rather more vehemently the arguments of the previous speaker. He explains for example how artistic imitation is for Plato at two removes from reality. But he is mainly interested in the moral argument. For him, youth, whose judgment is not yet formed, should be exposed only to literature of an edifying character. The arguments that the pleasure side of poetry stimulates the understanding, and that the fables hide an allegorical meaning are both rejected, the first because 'ne faut estimer la volupté tant chere, qu'elle soit preferée a la vertu', the second because 'on ne les scauroit tant farder et deguiser d'allegories, qu'elles doivent estre apprises par les enfants, qui ne les peuvent discerner'. (f. 144v) This completely reverses Ronsard's earlier use of the image—the allegorical explanation is seen only as an excuse for putting in the pleasurable fable. The argument is turned on its head; poetry is no longer a spur to virtue, but a positive barrier. The crucial point in Fauchet's argument is the freedom the poet claims: freedom to write about whatever subject he likes. If poetry is to be justified as a *moral* art, censorship must be applied for the sake of the public:

> Si toutes choses meritoient d'estre honnorées, on pourroit reputer l'imitation d'elles indifférente . . . le bon poëte qui rapporte son estude au bien public, ne se doit accommoder a autres

descriptions, que celles, qui sont les vraies images de l'hon-nesteté. (f. 145r)

If the poet, that is, wishes to assume the 'teaching' function that Cicero attributes to the orator, he must subject himself and his imagination to the same discipline as orators do for the sake of the 'bien public'. In reality, poets do quite the opposite:

Mais les poëtes ne trouvent rien, qui ne soit convenable a leur imitation, et ne donnent moins aux choses vituperables leur grace et bienseance, qu'aux louables et vertueuses. (f. 146r)

Fauchet also expands Pasquier's point about the force of poetry and its power over the reader. This section is not only a rejection of what is implied in the image of 'fard' or 'deguisement', it also comes across as a reply to Du Bellay's definition of the perfect poet in the *Deffence et illustration*:

Mais si telle est la force de la poësie, que si vivement elle exprime les mœurs et affections des hommes, que nul tant soit il grave et seure, ne pourroit flechir allieurs sa pensée, qu'en cete part, a laquelle la vehemence poëtique l'auroit emeu et attiré: il me semble que par elle la raison est grandement offensé. (f. 145v)[13]

So as long as the poet insists on his imaginative power and the freedom his imagination must have, he cannot justify his art by alleging that it is 'useful' to society.

Pasquier now speaks again, partly agreeing with Fauchet's demand for censorship, but also pointing out that the poet's subject matters less than the way he treats it—he can describe bad conduct in such a way as to make it seem unworthy. This leads on to a new, more important point: that although some poems *may* be praise-worthy on purely moral grounds, the real criterion for judging poetry is an aesthetic one:

On doit considerer en la poësie ou les excellentes et admirables sentences desquelles elle est toute pleine, ou l'agensement et convenance des personnes et des choses accommodées a l'argument proposé. (f. 147r)

We now move away from Plato and start following Aristotle's definition of imitation at the beginning of the *Poetics*, including his analysis of the pleasure such imitations can give us. Beauty is no longer the issue, as aesthetic pleasure seems to be a matter of life-likeness. This pleasure makes it possible for us to contemplate things we would find unbearable in life 'non que telles choses apparoissent belles: mais par ce que naïvement depeintes et represen-tées de leurs vraies et non feintes couleurs elles semblent avoir quelque vie . . .' (ibid.) The work of art, then, is not to be judged with reference to the transcendental reality, which it is necessarily incapable of expressing, but only with reference to itself and the life it contains, and to the 'appearance' that it represents. The analogy with painting comes up again here, but in Aristotle's version and with rather a different emphasis:

> Telle est l'imitation de la poësie, laquelle nous appelons la vive ou parlante peinture, et cette-ci la muëtte poësie. Quand donc les poëtes descrivent quelques choses horribles, quelques faits tristes et miserables, quelques mœurs et afections vehementes, il ne faut tant regarder au sujet, qu'a la bienseance de l'art qui l'a diligemment exprimé. (ibid.)[14]

Pasquier is here reasserting the rights of *art* which is so often deprecated in sixteenth-century theory, and not least in the statement Le Caron has just put into Ronsard's mouth. But ultimately, he says, poetry must be appreciated and judged on artistic merit alone, irrespective of the 'truth' it claims to portray. If truth and utility are to be accepted as criteria, it has to be recognized that Plato, 'le divin Platon', is the only true poet. The emptiness of the neo-platonic theory of inspiration is shown up by Jodelle when he replies—rather petulantly—to Fauchet's condemnation by telling us that poetry has never achieved perfection. The ancients, he tells us, made many mistakes 'mesmement en la poësie, laquelle je ne puis dire n'avoir encores esté traittée ne par les Grecs, ne par les Romains, beaucoup moins par les Italiens et aultres estrangers en telle dignité qu'elle merite'. One can therefore assume that Jodelle's hope—that 'un jour la France verra la poësie au plus hault lustre de sa perfection' is a pious if patriotic one.

Ronsard sums up with an attempt to return to the inspiration theory, distinguishing between 'les inventions inspirées de Dieu' and 'celles lesquelles l'imagination humaine feint et concoit a son plaisir'. Such truly inspired poetry cannot but be moral and needs no further justification. But all this argument does is to take us back to the beginning of the dialogue.

In conclusion then, I think it is justified to say that the dialogue as a whole aims at undermining the neo-platonic inspirational view of poetry, which Le Caron is unable to swallow because he himself is too well versed in Plato. Participation in the divine mysteries and expression of the transcendental reality is a laudable aim, but an unattainable one for poetry, since such a criterion would reveal Plato as the only real poet, and those readers who are able to keep up with his 'divin entendement' are few and far between. Poetry then can only be justified in the long run by the *pleasure* it gives, and although such pleasure may be entirely intellectual, like that given

BRIAN BARRON

by the dialectic sparked off in the mind of the 'bien né' by the poetic allegory, such readers are rare, and the pleasure is in any case only marginally imputable to poetry. More common is the pleasure afforded by imitation in the sense Le Caron derives from the *Poetics*. All such pleasure is legitimate, but it is always essential that the reader should be aware of the nature of poetry, of its metaphysical status and its relationship with truth before he embarks on his reading. Le Caron then, has attempted to replace the inspirational, but more particularly the utilitarian justification of poetry by a more properly aesthetic one, based on a more honest appraisal of the relationship between poem and reader, and that quite a long time before such ideas became generalized in France. His introduction of Aristotle's *Poetics*, even imperfectly understood, also seems to be the first systematic use of this treatise in French criticism.[15] Ultimately then, the dialogue must be seen as an appeal for honesty in literary criticism, for a justification of poetry which is based on the reality of the reader's response rather than on the supposed 'divinity' of the art. As such, it embodies an attitude which, emerging as it does from the clash of ideas that the form permits and encourages, belongs to Le Caron himself rather than to any of his debaters. It is for this reason surely that the author specifically points to the fictitious nature of the participants here, although he does so nowhere else in the volume.[16] Le Caron believes he is being controversial, and, as he himself says, in a neat piece of self-congratulation voiced by his fictitious Ronsard, they have gone a long way further than might have been expected:

> Notre dispute a trouvé plus ample discours, que ne pensois au commencement: telle est la suite des propos, quand une fois ilz tombent es meilleurs esprits, comme sont les vostres. (f. 149r)

NOTES

1 *Les Dialogues de Loys le Caron Parisien* (Paris 1556) f. 2r.
2 *La Poësie de Loys le Caron Parisien* (Paris 1554); *La Philosophie de Loys le Caron Parisien* (Paris 1555).
3 Marcel Raymond, *L'influence de Ronsard sur la poésie française (1550–1585)* (Geneva 1965) second ed., vol. 1, 314–6.
4 Henri Weber, *La Création poétique au XVIe siècle en France* (Paris 1956) 127; 133–4.
5 Grahame Castor, *Pléiade Poetics. A Study in Sixteenth Century Thought and Terminology* (Cambridge 1964) 61–2 and 170 n. 3.
6 On Louis le Caron see A. Pinvert, *Clermontois et Beauvaisis* (Paris 1901) which includes a section on Le Caron by Lucien Pinvert, also published in *Revue de la Renaissance*, 2 (1902); cf. also, Ferdinand Gohin,

De Lud. Charondae vita et versibus (Paris 1902). On Le Caron and the dialogue form, cf. Eva Kushner, 'Réflexions sur le dialogue en France au xvıᵉ siècle' *Revue des Sciences Humaines* (1972) 493.

7 *Dialogues*, f. 2r. According to Pasquier in his *Recherches de la France* Le Caron invented the word 'avant-propos' as a French equivalent to the Greek 'prologue'. Le Caron was interested in the advancement of the French language and the 'vulgarisation' of knowledge. It is to this end that he published his *Philosophie*, wishing to 'communiquer aux Francois ce que les excellens esprits de la Grece avoient exquisement escrit de la philosophie'.

8 This first dialogue repeats and expands points made in a previous dialogue, published in *La Philosophie* and entitled 'Le Philosophe, ou que la philosophie est toute roïale'.

9 cf. Castor, op. cit., ch. 14.

10 f. 115 r. cf. A. Lefranc 'Un entretien philosophique de Rabelais rapporté par Charondas, 1556', *Revue des Etudes Rabelaisiennes*, 1 (1903) 193–201.

11 Ronsard and Jodelle are chosen because they are 'à bon droit reputez les premiers poëtes de nostre tems'; the 'orateurs' are Pasquier and Fauchet 'lesquelz l'excellence de leur esprit pour la bonne esperance d'eux m'a fait toujours aimer'.

Pasquier's friendship for Le Caron stretched far enough to merit the inclusion of the latter in the chapter of the *Recherches de la France* on 'la grande flotte de Poëtes que produisit le règne du Roy Henry deuxiesme'.

12 cf. J. E. Spingarn, *A History of Literary Criticism in the Renaissance* (New York 1925) 171–2.

13 cf. *La Deffence et illustration de la langue françoyse*, ed. Chamard, STFM (1966) 179.

14 The general concern with morality in the dialogue, the mention of youth and the reference to Simonides's aphorism, also suggests a familiarity with Plutarch's *De audiendis poetis*.

15 cf. note 5 above.

16 'Mais si aucun d'eux s'estonne que je le fai parler de ce que paraventure il n'a jamais ne dit ne pensé, ou est entierement contraire à son opinion, je croi que se resouvenant de la coustume des dialogues il ne trouvera estrange que j'aie emprunté son nom et sa personne' (ff. 128 r–v).

C. J. R. ARMSTRONG

The Dialectical Road to Truth:
the Dialogue

THE RESTORED LOGIC OR dialectic of the Renaissance, with its roots in the humanists' revival of classical letters in Italy, and with Rudolf Agricola as its prophet in northern Europe from the turn of the fifteenth century, has not had a good press. William and Martha Kneale and Walter Ong are among the historians of logic writing in English who, as far as their discipline is concerned, see the period from Valla to Ramus largely as a doldrums. That is, a period when the relatively stern demands of rigour, which were associated with Aristotle and the high scholastics, and the promising nascent formalism of certain nominalist logicians, were forced to make way for a *rhetorical*, if not—in Ong's words—a *pedagogical* 'juggernaut'. This juggernaut was powered mainly by the fusion of rhetorical and dialectical *topoi* that were found broadcast in ancient authorities, and by a simplistic reduction of argumentation to the arts of literary composition.[1] Historians of the revival of letters, on the other hand, have generally felt such matters to be beyond their ken. Several distinguished literary scholars have evidently felt sufficient fellow-feeling with, for example, Ramus, to take him under their wing, even to defend him on the ground of his logic—for he wrote not a word of 'literature'; but, in general, in spite of the example of, for instance, Quirinus Breen on Calvin's argumentative style[2] or, more recently, Brian Vickers on Francis Bacon's,[3] there has been relatively little attempt to relate the labours of these 'woolly' dialecticians to the literature of their age, Latin or vernacular, and this notwithstanding their own and others' oft repeated assertions that letters and logic, rhetoric and philosophy (in the Ciceronian formula), should always and everywhere be intimately connected.[4]

I cannot, in the time available, demonstrate conclusively that such a *rapprochement* is overdue. I *do* venture to assert my own conviction —and I will also try to illustrate the utility of such a thesis—that *both* sides of the equation, that is, both the literary logicians and the contemporary literary genres, especially those of an even vaguely 'philosophical' flavour, such as the dialogue, should be studied together if the fullest possible insight is to be obtained. If this has not already been done, the reason is, I suggest, at least in part, that we too readily impose our own twentieth-century procedural and critical categories on the far more fluid nature of the works we study, supposing in this case that ostensibly logical books and treatises should be left to historians of logic or philosophy and literary works to literary men. The topic I have chosen is really only an instance of this general theme; by which I mean that I have yet to see any serious attempt to correlate Renaissance dialogue with the specific literary and philosophical ethos of Agricola and his followers. Hirzel, historian of the dialogue, makes not the slightest gesture in this direction;[5] Charles Herford, who has possibly some of the best pages in English on the subject of the dialogue, offers no allusion to dialectic,[6] nor do Howell and others, who have approached sixteenth-century dialectic, if they have considered it at all, purely as rhetoric.[7] I need scarcely add that there is no sign of dialogue in such standard histories of logic as those of Prantl or Risse, of the Kneales and (for our period) of Fr Ong.[8]

I find this unwillingness to bring together dialogue and dialectic surprising. Some critics, such as Pierre Villey, have come close to forging a link between literature and the dialectical cast of mind of the age but, to my mind, even in Villey the bulk of the story is missing.[9] For, on the face of it, everything urges us to relate the fifteenth- and sixteenth-centuries' endemic tendency to write and publish dialogues with those centuries' evident interest in and avid absorption (at least in youth) of their own special brand of logic which, for good reason, they called 'dialectic'. We will even find the two notions connected among the definitions given *sub verbo* 'dialectique' in our *Petit Robert*.[10]

What is common knowledge to lexicographers of the twentieth century was, as we should expect, still more widely known in the sixteenth century. From the side of those writing *ex professo* on the dialogue—a select band, it is true—the message is unanimous. Thus, early in Sigonio's *De dialogo* (1562) comes the following:

> Because the disputation is a rational investigation conducted among learned men by means of question and answer (a procedure the Greeks termed *dialégesthai*), the ancients maintained that dialogues should be composed of questions and answers and thus come under the competence of dialectic, which is charged with finding the arguments whereby we confirm or refute anything.[11]

A little later, Sigonio lists dialectic at the head of the three *artes* indispensable to the would-be composer of dialogues. The others are the art of the poet, who deals with the aspect of *mimesis* or *imitatio*, with the *decorum* of the *mise-en-scène*, and the suiting of words to speakers; and the art of the orator, who sees to the suitable embellishment of the language. But in order of interest and importance dialectic clearly leads in Sigonio's mind. He devotes a good deal of attention to *decorum*, but is decidedly jejune on eloquence—naturally, because, as he says, it is so fully dealt with elsewhere.[12]

Speroni, also, in his *Apologia dei dialoghi* closely links dialogue and dialectic, bringing out more strongly than Sigonio the probabilistic nature of dialectical discussion in dialogues, a point to which I will return.[13] Torquato Tasso, likewise, affirms that the dialogue is peculiarly the province of the dialectician: I am indebted to Tasso for the best short categorical statement of the matter, though all three of these Italians are at one here: 'Il dialogo,' says Tasso, 'farà imitazione d'una disputa dialettica.'[14] Perhaps M. Robert had been reading in Tasso! Perhaps, but his own words suggest that he was aware of the utterances and practice of Plato and of other evidence for the universal association of the two in ancient letters such as Quintilian *Institutions* v, 14, 27–28.

The treatise on the dialogue occurs late in the history of the Renaissance dialogue. In view of the statements I have just quoted, it would be surprising indeed if dialogue were wholly absent from the *dialectical* works of the age. On the whole it has to be admitted that its presence is more implicit than otherwise, but we do have, even as early as Agricola's important and influential *De inventione dialectica* (so brilliantly thrown into relief by Ong) a fully explicit if slight treatment of dialogue, introduced under the heading: *Quomodo oblectandus oratione auditor*.[15] Lest one should think, however, that this is the only treatment of dialogue in the pages of Agricola besides the small number of incidental references,[16] it is well to remember that for him, as for most 'Ciceronian' dialecticians, *all oratio* is in some sense divided into *oratio concisa* on the one hand, and *oratio continens* or *perpetua* on the other, and that the former includes within its scope 'disputationes et alternantia scholasticorum certamina', that is to say: dialogues.[17] In other words, dialectic here reigns over the whole field of serious discourse (*oratio*) whether it be arranged as a single continuous piece (e.g., an oration or treatise) or as alternating fragments of the spoken word (i.e., a 'dispute' in the narrow sense, or dialogue, between two or more interlocutors). Most writers on dialectic abstract for most of the time from this distinction of 'genera dicendi', as Cicero calls them,[18] even when they mention it. Agricola for most of his book is a case in point.

One who decided that the dialogue deserved a study on its own within the dialectical context is that most distinguished of Agricola's successors, the teacher of Ramus at Paris, Ioannes Sturmius or Sturm. In his *Partitionum dialecticarum libri*, which began to be published in 1539 but was complete in four books, I think—*pace* Ong—in 1548–9,[19] we find no less than 23 chapters in Book III devoted to the dialogue as such, and to the tricks of the dialectical trade which may enhance its composition. In the course of this rather rambling disquisition, Sturm makes considerable play with Greek terminology of very learned if not baffling appearance. Some of these terms are undoubtedly Aristotelian for, like other exponents of this subject, Sturm is highly preoccupied with Book VIII of Aristotle's *Topics*, and the *Rhetoric* also plays a part in one section.[20] Much of this terminology remains at present, so far as I am concerned, of uncertain provenance, despite Sturm's appeal to ancient precedent and my own recourse to expert advice in the matter.

The importance of such treatments of the art of dialogue-writing could easily be exaggerated. On the other hand, it would have been surprising, to me at least, to find that *no* dialectical manual paid attention to the dialogue, given the normal insistence of such books that *their* brand of dialectic as compared, for example, with that of Peter of Spain, Lull, Heytesbury, Ockham, Buridan and other pedlars of 'sophistica cavillatio' and / or 'garrulitas' in the preceding age, is supremely useful and applicable[21]: *useful* for the real business of comparing, defending and recommending positions; *applicable*, also of course, to the writing of books in which such activity is permanently captured for the general good, or one's own or one's country's or one's church's glory. When Strebaeus (Jacques d'Estrebay), for example, in a work published in Paris in 1540, says that 'dialectic is much more important as an aid to writing books or composing discourses, than for priming quarrelsome shouting-matches which render the throat hoarse and the mind confused',[22] we catch a glimpse of this practical emphasis which led the humanists, or some of them, to think, not only that every serious composition had its 'logical' or 'dialectical' aspect or dimension, but that knowledge of, and skill in, logical techniques could contribute to the lucidity and forcefulness of discourse in general and the art of composing dialogues (by definition *not* 'shouting-matches') in particular.

Is this association of dialectic and dialogue too banal to have deserved reference or further comment?[23] While there are reasons for suggesting this, there are, also, I think, still weightier ones for pursuing the matter. These, for the purposes of this paper, I will resume under three headings: first, that at least an influential section of sixteenth-century authorities considered ancient dialogue to be in a rather special sense dialectically constructed. The evidence for this is largely in commentaries but can also be found elsewhere: 'What', says Melanchthon, 'are Cicero's philosophical dialogues but dialectic with the added embellishment of *elocutio* ?' In the *De officiis*, for example, 'et in aliis multis disputationibus precepta dialectica sequitur in docendo et addit elocutionem ex rhetorica.'[24] I have also a vivid picture in my mind of poor Sturm in one of his prefaces having to admit that his efforts to fit the quart of a Socratic dialogue into the pint-pot of his dialectic have been a total failure. Wily old Socrates, Sturm confesses, has covered his tracks too well![25]

My second reason for suggesting that the relations of dialectic and dialogue might profitably be pursued, is that there are, as a matter of fact, in a number of Latin, French, Italian and Spanish dialogues (to cite but them) fairly numerous implicit or explicit references to the powers of reasoning and persuasion there employed, which echo closely similar remarks in the books treating immediately or indirectly of dialectic. This point would be difficult to develop in a convincing way in a paragraph and I trust that those who are familiar with a cross-section of dialogues between, say, Valla and Guy de Bruès inclusively, will be able to recall the sort of thing to which I am referring. Some points of contact will emerge in the course of what follows.

Thirdly, and I shall stay with this point for the rest of the paper, there is, it seems to me, a marked convergence of views, one might almost call it an attitude of connivance, between the writers on dialectic and the composers of dialogues concerning the whole business of truth-seeking and argumentation, which I find it very hard to dismiss as insignificant or coincidental given the other reasons for, as I have put it, at least 'associating' the art and the literary activity concerned.[26]

For the truth, whatever one understands by the term, *is* central. The first thing the tyro dialectician learns at the professorial knee is that truth or, possibly, *the* truth, is the subject of his discipline. Similarly, in the dialogues, one or other of the interlocutors is almost bound sooner or later to say something like: 'Of course I'm not saying this because I really think it but in order that truth may be brought out more clearly.'[27] *Alii aliter*, of course: thus Pontus de Tyard, writing *in propria persona* and with a suitably glittering display of relevant quotations, opens his *Univers* (a dialogue) with copious expatiation on the twin themes: 'homo naturaliter vult scire' and 'vera scientia est per causas' which lead naturally *via* the topic of scientific certitude in general to that of mathematics and astronomy in particular, where the dialogue remains focussed.[28]

But what *does* happen to truth in Renaissance dialectic and in a certain type of Renaissance dialogue? If there is one thing many Renaissance *dialogues* are characteristically short of (and I am not here concerned with propagandist or polemical dialogues—evidently) it is *truth*: not that they tend to deliver *falsehood*—they just don't say anything at all. This observation is not original. Let us hear, for example, Etienne Pasquier whose opinion is generally worth consideration:

> Ie ne veux pas vous ramentevoir, he writes to a certain M. Bigot, l'aage de nos peres; nous vismes en nostre enfance uns Longueil, Contarein, Bembe, Sadolet, Pole, Bonamie, et plusieurs tels autres qui s'acquirent le bruit de sçavans parmy le peuple pour dicter biens unes lettres en langue latine et toutefois lettres dans lesquelles il n'y a qu'un amas de paroles bien choisies de Cicéron et proprement rapportées à leur ouvrage, en forme de marqueterie.[29]

Pasquier's central judgment here, that the early sixteenth-century writers (in *Latin*—but may not the scope be extended to include e.g. Pontus de Tyard, Guy de Bruès, Louis Le Caron, Louis Le Roy?) produced an exiguous amount of solid matter from a plethora of words, is equally that of, among others, Samuel Johnson and Francis Bacon. This trio of disparate and highly independent judges pass, broadly speaking, the same sentence: the men of the early sixteenth century were infatuated with words but had nothing to say: they were intent on *copie*, says Bacon, rather than *weight*; so blinded by the light of the new learning, says Johnson, that they were unable to digest their reading sufficiently and come to any conclusions.[30]

The humanists may indeed have been infatuated by words. If they themselves constantly harp on the importance of *res* over *verba* this is no doubt because of their incurable habit of quoting Cicero, who said it first.[31] However, my point is that I do not think this is the whole or only explanation for the existence of so much sixteenth-century writing which labours gigantically to produce the tiny mouse it has to communicate. I suspect that behind and sustaining this apparently too wordy façade is a certain attitude to what I have called the whole business of truth-seeking and argumentation, an attitude which can be seen in sharper relief if we read the dialogues of the time in particular alongside their rational philosophical counterparts: the manuals of dialectic. This type of attitude I would describe as fundamentally *Ciceronian,* endowing this term (i.e., 'Ciceronian') with dimensions and values which it commonly lacks in current critical usage. This Ciceronian attitude, then, sees in dialectic not what Socrates, or, rather, his disciple, Plato, saw in it: a royal road to the citadel of the Ideas, of Truth, at which he who is faithful to his godlike reason will infallibly arrive.[32] No, this attitude, in so far as we can recapture it in the words of such as Agricola and Vives, Valla, Bembo, Ramus and others—Erasmus, I think, among them (I shall return to Cicero himself in a moment), suggests that the rules of reason do not of themselves deliver the answers we sometimes impiously expect from them.[33] While demonstration is in principle possible, given a subject sufficiently perspicuous (mathematics is the example universally appealed to), the general obscurity of all natural knowledge not only rules out its use in arguing about the supernaturally revealed 'mirabilia super nos' but also in normal discussion of a large number of sub-lunary philosophical topics. In *these* discussions also the man who insists on the logical knock-out by means of *soi-disant* epideictic syllogisms or close argumentation simply betrays an absurd presumption of certitude where everybody who knows anything knows that he knows nothing.[34] Given that nothing in practice is exempt from the shadow of doubt, each must construct the case he has as plausibly as possible and preferably without appearing too obviously to do so. Let there be reasoning but let it be latent. The cut and thrust of technical disputation is on Agricola's view, and he is not alone, 'puerile', to be confined within the walls of the 'schools'.[35] Since, on his view, dialectic is responsible not only for informing the auditor (*docere*, i.e., 'rem ex ignota facere notiorem') but also for moving him (*movere*, i.e., 'pacatam tranquillamque mentem affectibus perturbare') it follows that arguments should be presented *in the right way* to such an end, which is certainly not, in Agricola's *milieu*, that of overt syllogistic reasoning which involves generalization and is devoid of appeal.[36] In the last analysis, what is true is what *seems* true to whomsoever the dialectician aims to convince, in a word whatever is, or has been so constructed dialectically as to appear to be, *probabile*. The rules of the game are fundamentally the same whether one is taking sides on the vexed question of the priority of hens and eggs, defending an innocent man on trial for his life or arguing an abstruse point in philosophy.[37]

Small wonder then, that a humanist such as Vives, breathing the same relaxed atmosphere and evoking its antecedents in the golden Platonic and Ciceronian era before the barbarous logomachies of the scholastics, should write that 'there used to be among adults and older folk a certain mutual comparing of opinions and reasonings, which was not aimed at anyone's winning but at eliciting the truth'.[38] This dialectic, concerned as its name implies, with greater and less probability, was decidedly not conceived as delivering 'answers' in the way that a well-conducted piece of algebraic reasoning delivers the values of x, y, and z. It is no longer a closed system, the yardstick of true and false, but subordinate, relative. 'Dialectic', writes Agricola again, 'does not arrogate to itself the role of judging, does not by its own resources clinch this or that dubious matter; it simply furnishes the wherewithal for such a judgment to be made by someone conversant with the subject-matter.'[39] In a later day Jacques Charpentier specifies that the tools for judgment are provided in the art of epideictic demonstration which alone can *decide* the issues debated with probability by dialectic. But such precision is not for Agricola.[40]

Agricola's dialectical viewpoint should be compared with that of Cicero. In Cicero's philosophical dialogues, for example, *all* the speakers are clearly using dialectic, but every man's dialectic has equal rights with every other man's. None is represented as 'victorious'; none is privileged *eo ipso* like the dialectic of Socrates in *Phaedrus*.[41] Likewise, each interlocutor remains at the end, as at the beginning, in secure possession of his original opinion, again so unlike the young men reduced to a state of *aporía* by Socrates. The decision in the matter under discussion (I am not speaking of the *Tusculans* or the *De officiis* here, though these are certainly relevant to Cicero's method in general) is left to someone outside the discussion itself: to you and me, the readers, to Brutus to whom the dialogue has been sent as to a judge ('iudex') who will adjudicate ('diiudicaberis') in the debate.[42] In one sense the atmosphere of such dialogue is caught quite well by Montaigne who thinks, in the passage I shall quote, that he is describing Plato but, like Vives and others, reads Plato as though he were Cicero:

> Platon me semble avoir aymé cette forme de philosopher par dialogues à escient pour loger plus decemment en diverses bouches la diversité et variation de ses propres fantaisies.[43]

This comparison of dialectically orchestrated positions is, for Cicero, what philosophy, *doing* philosophy, *is*: 'Quum philosophia', as he puts it, 'ex rationum collatione constet'—since philosophy consists of a conferring together of reasoned positions.[44]

Whatever justification he seeks in the teaching and practice of Aristotle, who allegedly encouraged copious dialectical debates *in utramque partem*,[45] such theory and practice admirably suited Cicero's own philosophical probabilism, his rhetor's preoccupation with *copia* and his barrister's approach to handling problems. Such ideas or habits in combination have their dangers. Let us add another voice to those we have already heard pronouncing on what is essentially one and the same method:

The conflict [about the true doctrine of the Academics] endured, says Augustine, to the time of our own Tullius, when with its last gasp it finally inflated Latin letters. For what could be more inflated than to have bestowed such copiousness, so much rhetorical ornament on philosophical positions in which he himself did not believe.[46]

And yet Augustine, too, in spite of this apparent hostility to the Ciceronian method, had not when he wrote this dialogue *Contra academicos* entirely shaken himself free of the master's influence. He lived to regret the little movement of self-deprecation and joking acceptance of merely dialectical or probabilist values, which rounds off the discussion. 'I refuted his arguments with most cogent reasoning' says the later, indignant Augustine in his *Retractationes*, now by so much closer to Calvin than to Cicero.[47]

But we may if we wish view the phenomena which chiefly interest us here, these sixteenth-century 'attitudes', through the eyes of *contemporaries* whom they did not please. For Agricola, Vives, Sturm, Ramus and their ilk, with their emphasis on a merely probabilist dialectic, did not go unnoticed in their time. By the middle years of the century, if not before, some yearned for the good old days when an argument was an argument and no mere *regula lesbia*, unfit even to whack a pupil's palm.[48] Melanchthon early in his, in other respects, highly nominalist Dialectic of 1531 embraced the cause of 'stiffening up' dialectic, adopting an idea to be found also, curiously enough, in Vives and not entirely absent from Cicero himself, namely the Stoic and Euclidean notion of the *dignitates insculptae in anima* or *koinoi ennoiai*, the so-called 'common notions'.[49] Yet Melanchthon too, despite his battles against academics and sceptics, is capable in his turn of demonstrating the figures of logical argumentation in the merely persuasive context of Greek and Latin orations or contemporary religious, or even political, polemic concerning the *adiáphora*, thereby undoubtedly undermining the force of his insistence on the possibility and necessity of strict demonstration in philosophy and natural theology by such means.[50]

It is precisely this endemic tendency of our literary logicians to reduce argumentation, even when fortified with syllogistic, to the level and criteria of *vraisemblance* demanded by persuasive oratory or literary composition, which lends weight to Galland's accusation of Academic scepticism levelled against Ramus in 1551, a Ramus found guilty among other things of admiring Cicero's philosophical works above his books on rhetoric (an admiration emulated by his lieutenant, Omer Talon), a mis-demeanour classed as a crime of *lèse-Aristote* verging on impiety by his accuser.[51] But most explicit of such commentators is, perhaps, the expatriot medical writer, keen Galenist and tepid Aristotelian, Bartolomeo Viotti, who, from his vantage post in Bordeaux, a few years later (1560), casts a retrospective glance over the scene and reveals the whole sordid intrigue mounted by the sappers of logical morale. Viotti names as ringleaders: Agricola, Valla, Trapezuntius, Titelmanus, Caesarius, Melanchthon himself, and 'similar writers of dialectics', who are all, because of their dialectical probabilism and insistence on argumentation *in utramque partem à la* Cicero, little better than Academic sceptics who, like the Harpies, contaminate all they touch.[52]

Is it possible that Galland and Viotti were anticipated by another learned man of science, François Rabelais? Chapters 35 and 36 of the *Tiers Livre*, coming so soon after Ramus's early and scandalous denunciation of Aristotle in the name of the truly Platonic and Academic philosophy, could just possibly, perhaps, reflect the sensation caused and the reaction to the whole affair in all its dimensions among a certain 'old guard', represented by the father of Pantagruel. Such a reference might seem oblique in the extreme yet it would have been a fine, an artistic stroke, to have represented the consequences of rhetorical dialectic and inconclusive copiousness in the curt, dim and monosyllabic mumblings of that dull dog, Trouillogan. In a much later day and age, a similar reluctance was pilloried by Samuel Butler *via* his professors of hypothetics among the Erewhonians, afflicted, they in their turn, by that classic 'Academic' disease called 'sitting on the fence'.[53]

The accusation of scepticism was levelled at our dialecticians by their enemies; it is not infrequently levelled today at the writers of dialogues by their critics and commentators, though of course *today* the 'accusation' is intended as a compliment. In the one case, that of the dialecticians, some, such as Melanchthon, Vives, Ramus, deliberately measure their distance from thoroughgoing Academic scepticism; of others the least that can be said is that they do cater for epideictic demonstration somewhere along the route. In the case of the dialogue-writers, I do not think the case for anything resembling what a modern would call scepticism can be sustained with reference to their method and intentions, though the evidence for a certain inconclusiveness is indisputable. What I personally have found interesting in this connection is not the existence of a sceptical or indeed any other particular philosophical '-ismus' in the early sixteenth century but the evidence I feel sure exists for a dialectical, probabilist, in a word, *humane* approach to the business of philosophical discussion and argumentation. For me there are those who make this attitude their own—and there are those who don't. I will illustrate with a final example and conclude.

A world separates the logical method of the so-called humanist, Calvin, and that of his fellow-humanist, Castellio. In the one, as we may study him in his writings, taking a hint from Breen's article already mentioned, the logical instrument is implicitly apprehended as imperious, conclusive, welding the parts of the continuous discourse together in one, and one only, acceptable, true, statement of the nature of things. Such 'dialectic'—but here indeed we must speak of 'logic'—if it becomes political ideology, is not questioned without a price being paid.[54] Castellio, on the other hand, as we see from his two treatises, the *De haereticis* of 1554 and the long unpublished *De arte dubitandi*, composed shortly after, had a very different idea of the nature of truth, and the way to it, and the way to safeguard it once found. At one point, in the second of these books, having stated that there is a God, a truth, Castellio says, which is beyond dispute since it is of faith, he raises the problem of the Trinity and what it means, 'a hard question,' Castellio continues, 'and one on which it would be rash to pronounce with certainty. For this reason I shall refrain from asserting anything as fact and offer to the reflections of my readers a short discussion in the form of a dialogue. . . .'[55]

If one is sceptically inclined oneself, or has read a lot of books about sixteenth-century philosophy, or for any of a number of more or less good reasons, one may favour the view that this attitude of Castellio smacks of 'scepticism'. I believe that his approach, whatever one calls it—and I should like to reinstate some such term as 'Ciceronian' or 'humane', but 'dialectical' will do—is shared by many of his generation and background, and by some of their teachers. Certainly I do not think it rash to assert that we ourselves tend to view Castellio's rather than Calvin's method as 'enlightened'. But then we are academics. Possibly we, too, tend to hesitate and doubt, to talk *round* subjects rather a lot, yes, in a phrase, 'to sit on the fence'. The only danger is that our fences should become too comfortable. Humpty Dumpty, we are told, sat on a *wall*—and we all know what happened to *him*. But Humpty Dumpty, if we believe Lewis Carroll, was not only as loquacious and inconclusive as Trouillogan was curt and inconclusive, he was opinionated and egotistical as well.[56] Probabilist dialectic and Ciceronian dialogue both signify a certain open-ness. It was with some such awareness, implicit or explicit in their minds, as I believe, that many sixteenth-century writers apprehended them.

46

NOTES

1 Walter J. Ong, *Ramus, Method and the Decay of Dialogue* (Cambridge Mass. 1958); especially chapters v and vii. William and Martha Kneale, *The Development of Logic* (Oxford 1962); chapters iv and v, especially 300 ff. Ong's heavy emphasis on the teaching orientation of Renaissance logicians is occasionally nuanced by such statements as: 'The weakness of Agricola's *Dialectical Invention* as a formal philosophical treatise (which it hardly pretends to be), is compensated for by the relevance of the work to the unstated and complex psychological needs, pedagogical, linguistic and literary, created by the maturing humanist outlook' (op. cit., 123).

2 Quirinus Breen, 'John Calvin and the Rhetorical Tradition', *Church History*, 26 (March 1957) 3–21.

3 Brian Vickers, *Francis Bacon and Renaissance Prose* (Cambridge 1968).

4 René Radouant, 'L'union de l'éloquence et de la rhétorique au temps de Ramus', *Revue d'histoire littéraire de la France*, 31 (1924) 161–92. If the fact that the formula *is* Ciceronian (so far as the Renaissance is concerned) were more widely emphasized it would perhaps be seen that it has implications beyond the mere improvement of the style of learned discourse (cf. *De oratore*, i, 42, 188; iii, 31, 123; *Orator*, 32, 113). That Cicero's espousal of dialectic (one of the three branches of 'philosophy') was serious and thorough is put beyond doubt by Alain Michel, *Rhétorique et philosophie chez Cicéron* (Paris 1960).

5 Rudolf Hirzel, *Der Dialog, Ein literar-historischer Versuch* (Leipzig 1898).

6 Charles H. Herford, *Studies in the Literary Relations of England and Germany in the Sixteenth Century* (Cambridge 1886) ch. 11. Herford is chiefly concerned with polemical and satirical dialogues. He does less than justice to Ciceronian dialogue, describing it at one point as 'merely a device to facilitate monologue' (p. 32). But he is writing of dialogue in *England*.

7 Wilbur Samuel Howell, *Logic and Rhetoric in England, 1500–1700* (Princeton 1956).

8 Carl von Prantl, *Geschichte der Logik in Abendlande, Leipzig* 1855–70, 4 vols.; Wilhelm Risse, *Die Logik der Neuzeit*, vol. 1, *1500 bis 1640*. (Stuttgart 1964).

9 Pierre Villey, *Les sources et évolution des Essais de Montaigne* (Paris 1908) 2 vols. See, e.g., vol. 2, p. 34f. on collections of antique lore organized by the method of contrary instances. Yet Villey barely mentions the dialectical habit of thought of the age.

10 *Petit Robert* (Paris 1967) s.v. *dialectique*, 1, 2: 'Philo. Dans Platon, Art de discuter par demandes et réponses. v. Dialogue, maïeutique' (p. 476). Cf. Liddell and Scott, *Greek–English Lexicon* (1940), s.v. *dialégo*, 11, B, 2: 'In philosophy, practise dialectic, elicit conclusions by discussion.'

11 Carolus Sigonius, *De dialogo* (Venice 1562), ff. 12r–v: 'Itaque quoniam disputatio, quaedam est disquisitio rationis, quae inter eruditos homines percontando, et respondendo versatur, quod graece διαλέγεσθαι dicitur, ea de re dialogum antiqui tradiderunt ex interrogatione, et responsione compositum, dialecticae nimirum ipsius spectantes potestatem, quam constat inveniendorum esse facult-

atem argumentorum, quibus confirmemus, vel refellamus quid,
adversario ita interrogationibus impellendo, ut ei optionem relin-
quamus, utrum velit repugnantium partem accipiendi.' See also f. 14v.

12 Ibid., ff. 8r–v, 17r.

13 Sperone Speroni, *Apologia dei dialoghi*, in *Opere* (Venice 1740) vol. 1,
266–85. Here pp. 280 ff. Speroni's emphatic probabilism appears on
p. 283.

14 Torquato Tasso, *Dell'arte del dialogo discorso*, in *Opere* (Venice 1737)
vol. 7, 16–23. Here p. 19.

15 Rudolfus Agricola, *De inventione dialectica*, ed. I. M. Phrissemius (Paris
1534). Bk. 2, pp. 424 ff.

16 Ibid., Bk. 2, pp. 278, 492, 495.

17 Ibid., Bk. 2, p. 283.

18 M. T. Cicero, *De officiis*, I, i, 3.

19 Cf. Ong, op. cit., 233 and 361 n. 25. I base this assertion on the
Cambridge University Library copy: *Joannis Sturmii Partitionum
Dialecticarum Libri Quatuor* Emendati et Aucti, Strasbourg (per
Wendelium Rihelium), Anno MDXLIX. Cf. Charles Schmidt, *La Vie
et les travaux de Jean Sturm* (Strasbourg 1855), 315. Ong misquotes
Schmidt in his note (loc. cit.). Schmidt gives the following history of
these *Partitiones dialecticae*: first two books (Paris 1539); liber III—De
demonstratione liber unus (Strasbourg 1543); libri IV, Strasbourg
1548—for which *four-book* edition he cites Strobel as authority. Then a
'second edition' 1554 at Strasbourg and a 'third' also at Strasbourg
1560. The 1554 edition in the Mazarin library, Paris, printed at Lyons,
has all four books. Ong himself quotes from an edition of 1572.

20 Sturm, *Partitiones dialecticae* (1549) 94r and ff. These chapters deserve
and, it is hoped, will receive, separate treatment elsewhere. For
Aristotle's *Topics*, see Martin Grabmann, *Geschichte der scholastischen
Methode* (Freiburg-im-Breisgau 1909) 450–1; Ong, op. cit., 106, 113.
The primordial text for the Renaissance would seem to be Cicero,
De oratore II, 36, 132 where Catullus urges appropriation of Aristotle's
topics 'from philosophy' (cf. Quintilian, *Institutiones oratoriae*, XII, 2, 6–
10; Teubner edit. (1965) 381–2). In fact, although Cicero's book on
Topics professes to be derived from the philosopher the relationship is
far from close (Kneale & Kneale, op. cit., 178f.).

21 The point is heavily stressed, for example, by Phrissemius, comparing
Peter of Spain and Rudolf Agricola at the opening of his commentary
on the *De inventione dialectica*. But the theme is entirely commonplace,
see, also: Rabelais, *Gargantua*, ch. 13–14, 20–1. Academic logic has,
indeed, only recently ceased to be 'useful'.

22 *M. Tullii Ciceronis ad M. Brutum Orator Iacobi Strebaei commentariis . . .
illustratus* (Paris 1540) f. 15r: 'Usus enim dialecticae prestantior est aut
in constituendis libris aut in perpetuitate disserendi, quam in conten-
tiosa vociferatione quę raucim gutturi, confusionem animo parit.'
Agricola, too, had already hinted at dialectic's utility for writing
books: *De inventione dialectica*, Bk. III, 487.

23 Ramus's custom of reducing discourse to dialectic, even to syllogistic,
may incite to ridicule (Ong, op. cit., 191, 250, 263–5) yet Michel's
analysis of the dialectical structure of Ciceronian *oratio* is wholly after
Ramus's heart and would seem largely to justify him. This type of
analysis (Ong calls it 'shrinking') may be seen applied to the *Pro*

Milone in Michel, *Rhétorique et philosophie*, 177 ff. Cf. Agricola, *De inventione dialectica*, Bk 11, 194–5, where Agricola also looks at this oration 'dialectically'.

24 Melanchthon, *De elementis rhetoricis* (1542), in *Opera*, vol. XIII, col. 420 (*Corpus Reformatorum*, ed. C. G. Bretschneider et al., Halle 1934).

25 *Platonis Gorgias . . . Ioannis Sturmii Praefatio de Ratione interrogandi atque collocandi dialectica ad Iacobum Bonerum* (Strasbourg 1541) f. a2r–v. According to Sturm, the *Gorgias* is a golden example of 'Aristotelica praecepta' in action (a4r).

26 The full title of Ong's *Ramus, Method* announces the 'decay of dialogue' (viz. in the Renaissance). Others have felt that 'dialogue' in its various manifestations had as tight a grip on Ramus's contemporaries and immediate predecessors as had 'dialectic'. Cf. Lucien Febvre, *Origène et Des Périers* (Paris 1942) 26–7.

27 Thus Antonio in L. Valla's *De libero arbitrio*: 'An existimas me aliquid affirmare, ac non disputandi gratia quaerere?' to which Valla replies: 'Quasi ego victoriae causa pugnem potius quam veritatis' ed. Mario Anfossi (Florence 1934) 25. See also *The Dialogues of Guy de Bruès*, A Critical Edition . . . by Panos Paul Morphos (Baltimore 1953) 182, the statement of Nicot: 'Les plus opiniastres disputes sont les plus asseurées espies de la vérité' etc.; cp. p. 281, similar words of Aubert.

28 *The Universe of Pontus de Tyard*, with Introduction and Notes by John Lapp (Ithaca 1950) [p. 3].

29 Etienne Pasquier, *Œuvres* (Amsterdam 1727) vol. 2, livre 11, lettre 11, cols. 27 ff.

30 Francis Bacon, *Advancement of Learning*, in *The Philosophical Works of Francis Bacon*, Reprinted from Ellis and Spedding (London 1905) 54; Samuel Johnson in *Johnson's Journey to the Western Islands of Scotland* etc., edit. R. W. Chapman (Oxford 1970) 13.

31 Cicero, *Orator*, 23, 77; cf. *Tusculanae disputationes*, V, II, 32.

32 Cf. the analysis of Michel, *Rhétorique et philosophie*, 93 ff.

33 All this raises the large question of the 'Academic scepticism' of the period. It may in the end prove more accurate to speak of a return to some such concept as Ciceronian probabilism, largely discussed, e.g., by Vives, in *De disputatione, De ratione dicendi, De causis corruptarum artium, De instrumento probabilitatis*, etc. Erasmus both wrote dialectical dialogue (the *Antibarbari*, with its interesting sequel in Fisher's misunderstanding after reading only the half he had been sent, see P. S. Allen, *Desiderii Erasmi Opus Epistolarum* (Oxford 1906) IV, p. 279, ll. 25–32), and pleaded for 'dialogue' with Luther in which discussion of probability might replace the bare assertion and demonstration of certainties, see *De libero arbitrio*, especially the lengthy opening sections, in *Opera* (Leyden 1703–6) IX, cols 1215 ff.

34 The prevalent tendency to belittle the powers of reasoning with certitude may be studied in Vives: *De causis corruptarum artium* (doubting, for example, the utility of Aristotle's norms for apodeictic demonstration, described as a 'lesbia norma' given human fallibility) should be compared with Agricola's vigorous projection of 'dialectices' which opens *De inventione dialectica*. Bk 2 (edit. cit. 184f). The sweeping competence claimed for dialectic here accurately reflects his

statement opening Bk I: 'Exigua enim portio eorum quae discimus certa et immota est . . .' (ibid., 3).

35 Agricola, op. cit., Bk. III, 486–7.

36 This notion that rational arguments 'move' those to whom they are addressed illustrates both the rhetorical view of the 'force of reason' and its essential pragmatism. Agricola, op. cit., Bk II, 198 ff.; the same point is made much of by Strebaeus in *M. Tul. Ciceronis De Partitione Oratoria Dialogus Iacobi Strebaei ac Georgii Vallae commentariis illustratus* (Lyons 1538) 19.

37 Agricola, op. cit., Bk II, 184–7.

38 Vives, *De causis corrupt. art.*, in *Opera*, vol. VI, 49: 'Inter viros, aut natu grandiores fuit quaedam opinionum ac rationum collatio, non ad victoriam intenta, sed ad enucleandum verum.' Cp. Cicero, note 44 below.

39 Agricola, op. cit., Bk II, 210: 'Dialectices disserendi probabiliter rationem tradit, hoc est, instrumentum tantum veri falsique discernendi, cuius usu ministerioque expeditius cuncti artifices, quid veri aut falsi sit in rebus sibi propositis explorent. Quod si tamen volumus istud accipere ita ut sit discernendo vero et falso destinata: non abnuerim id quidem, non ut ipsa discernat, hoc est iudicet (hoc enim singularium est artium) sed ut instrumentum praebeat, sine quo nullo pacto ista discerni possint.'

40 Jacques Charpentier (Carpentarius), *Compendium in universam dialecticam* (Paris 1551) II.v: 'Ex probabilibus pronunciatis dialectica ratiocinatio, opinioni potius quam scientiae gignendae accomodata, componitur. In qua argumentorum turba magis aestimantur quam exacta iudicandi regula. Quo fit ut in ipsis locis, ex quibus talia eruuntur, posita sit ratio inveniendi: totius artis disserendi pars natura prior ad ad communem usum potior: praesertim cum ea facultate instructi, quam adfert locorum cognitio, de omni quaestione proposita in utramque partem ex probabilibus disserere possimus: aut ipsi, si quid in disputatione defendamus, diligenter cavere ne quid dicamus repugnans: in eoque longo usu exercitati, tandem quid in quaque re verum sit, quid falsum, adhibita demonstrationis certissima regula, diiudicare.'

41 Cicero describes this as writing 'Aristoteleo more' (*Epist. ad diversos*, I, 9) i.e., disputing 'in contrarias partes' (*Tusculanae disputationes* II, 3, 9); this is for Cicero both Socratic and according to the model of Carneades (*De finibus* IV, 10). In *Orator* 32, 114–17, it is said that the orator may use both the 'praecepta disserendi' of Aristotle and the 'spinier' logic of Chrysippus. Examples of Stoic and Epicurean, as well as 'Aristotelian' logic or dialectic occur in the *philosophica* of Cicero.

42 Cicero, *De finibus* III, 2, 6; cf. *De nat. deorum* I, 7, 17; *De legibus* I, 20, 53. See Michel, *Rhétorique et philosophie*, 93 for *De officiis* II, 14, 19. The espousal of Cicero's *iudex* by Renaissance dialogue is a subject in itself. It always remains an open possibility that a writer of dialectical dialogue in a Ciceronian sense is offering it to *himself* as judge; so Antoine de Mouchy (Antonius de Mocharis) *In octo libros Topicorum Aristotelis . . . Hypomena* (Paris 1535); f. 14r: 'Dialecticus enim et quisquis hac methodo iuste fuerit instructus, utramque contradictionis partem rei propositae argumentis probabilibus ancipitem reddere

potest: et is facile in re quavis, et quid verum et quid falsum sit perspiciet, et quid sequandum intelliget, quemadmodum iudex auditis utriusque rationibus, quid iustum et quid iniustum, veri lumine intuetur.'

43 Michel de Montaigne, *Essais* 11, 12, in *Œuvres complètes*, ed. Thibaudet et Rat (Paris 1962) 489f.

44 Cicero, *Tusculanae disputationes* 1V, 38, 84; cf. *De divinatione* 11, 72, 150: 'conferre causas'; *Tusculanae disputationes* 111, 39, 95; V, 29, 83. The method of *De officiis* is expressly distanced from this procedure of 'nostra Academia' in *De officiis* 111, 4, 20.

45 Cicero, *Orator* 14, 46 and parallels.

46 Augustine, *Contra academicos* 111, 18, 41 in *Opera omnia* (Paris 1836) vol. 1 col. 486. My own translation.

47 Augustine, *Contra academicos* 111, 20, 45; *Retractationes* 1, 1, 4. In edit. cit., vol. 1, col. 489 and cols. 26–7.

48 The phrase is used of Ramus's logic by Pierre Galland, *Adversus Petri Rami novam academiam* (Paris 1551) f. 62v.

49 Melanchthon, *De dialectica libri quatuor* (Witemberg 1531) f. Gviiivᵒ; Vives, *De disputatione* in *Opera*, vol. 3, p. 69. Cicero refers to the *pronunciatum* or ἀξίομα as an element in dialectics in *Tusculanae disputationes* 1, 6, 14. Cf. Michel, *Rhétorique et philosophie*, 170. See also G. de Bruès, *Dialogues*, edit. cit., 162, for 'les notices et divines informations desquelles Cicéron parle en tant de lieux'.

50 This is especially marked in Bk 111 of the 1531 *Dialectica*. In Bk 11 it is noticeable that Melanchthon, too, believes in 'shrinking' orations. Melanchthon's anti-Academic stance is most pronounced (as well it might be) in his *Initia doctrinae physicae* (1549), in *Opera (Corpus Reformatorum)*, vol. x111, cols. 179 ff.

51 Galland, *Adversus Petri Rami novam academiam*, ff. 4r, 5v, 23r, 53r, 62v. Ramus tackles head-on the issue of probabilist and demonstrative logics in his 1555 *Dialectique*, ed. Dassonville (Geneva 1964, 64) but Galland seems not to have had impact here. Ramus does however express disapproval of Cicero's dialectical method with special reference to *De fato* (1550). There is a discrepancy between the attitudes expressed in this preface and those of Talon in his to Cicero's *Academica* [sic]; see Petrus Ramus, Audomarus Talaeus, *Collectaneae Praefationes, Epistolae, Orationes*, With an introduction by Walter J. Ong (Hildesheim 1969) 77 ff. (Talon), 109 ff. (Ramus).

52 Bartolomeo Viotti, *De demonstratione libri V* (Paris 1560) ff. eiiiv and ff.

53 Samuel Butler, *Erewhon*, chaps. xx1–xx11: *The Colleges of Unreason*.

54 Thus also Sperone Speroni in his *Dialogo della rhetorica*: 'Ragione è bene che le nostre reppubliche, non da scienze dimostrative vere e certe per ogni tempo, ma con retoriche opinioni variabili e tramutabili-quali son l'opere e le leggi nostre-prudentemente sian governate.' Quoted by Eugenio Garin, *L'umanesimo italiano* (Bari 1952) 202. Several of Speroni's dialogues illustrate his interest in these questions.

55 Sébastien Castellio, *De l'art de douter et de croire, d'ignorer et de savoir*, trans. by Charles Badouin (Geneva 1953) 127.

56 Lewis Carroll, *Through the Looking Glass*, chap. v1: *Humpty Dumpty*.

TERENCE CAVE

Copia and Cornucopia

It is now widely recognized that Erasmus's handbook *De copia* made a considerable impact on the teaching of rhetoric in the sixteenth century. Melanchthon was able to omit from his *Elementa rhetorices* more than the briefest reference to *copia* on the grounds that 'omnibus in manu sunt Erasmi libelli' (I quote from the edition published in Paris in 1532);[1] between 1530 and 1540, a dozen editions appeared in Paris alone; the same period saw the publication of an epitome of the manual as well as Veltkirchius's commentary on it; while the 1525 *Enchiridion* of Thierry Morel, which provides variations on a large number of 'useful formulas' in a pale imitation of the Erasmian manner, was to be successful for a quarter of a century.[2]

There has also been much sympathy for Bolgar's claim that Erasmus's outline of a method of collecting and redeploying the materials of classical literature provides a key to the aesthetic of both Rabelais and the Pléiade.[3] The virtuoso use of sources and the pre-occupation with linguistic or poetic abundance are certainly common to the major vernacular writers of the mid-sixteenth century, and it is tempting to postulate a cause and effect relationship between humanist teaching and literary practice; Laumonier long ago inferred (without reference to the *De copia*) that the mode of imitation recommended by Dorat to his pupils at Coqueret was based on a principle of systematic compilation.[4] However, a more detailed and nuanced account must be given of how the notion of *copia* might have enriched and facilitated the rise of vernacular literature in France. Problems occur at two levels. The first is provided by the sudden halt in the publication of the *De copia* in Paris after 1540 (only one edition, dated 1547, has been identified). It is true that editions continued to appear in Lyon, that Paris publishers were no doubt reluctant to handle works by Erasmus in a period of greatly increased censorship, and that many copies of the earlier editions must have remained in circulation throughout this period. However, the new handbooks on rhetoric seem to have absorbed little of Erasmus's method; as Ong has pointed out, the Ramist rhetorics scarcely ever refer to *copia* as a principle of stylistic elaboration and of imitation.[5] Likewise, it is interesting to note that, in his study on *Ronsard et la rhétorique*, Gordon says nothing about *copia* and, in order to illustrate Ronsard's practice, exploits the rhetoric of Antoine Fouquelin (or Foclin), which is wholly Ramist and un-Erasmian.[6]

A second set of problems arises from the fact that there is an apparent difference of register between a methodology designed to produce eloquence in Latin prose and the composition of imaginative literature in the vernacular. In particular, Erasmus's cast of mind, his wit, his intellectual style, seem at first sight far removed from the aesthetic preoccupations of the Pléiade. Furthermore, the famous 'notebook' method of compilation, although clearly important to Erasmus, is contained in a single section of the second book of the *De copia*; it nourishes the notion of *copia*, but by no means defines it.

In order to tackle these problems, it will be necessary first to look at some of the implications of the word *copia* as it is used by Erasmus. This will be followed by a review of certain areas of humanist concern in which a stress on copiousness appears to be central; and as this concern is often of an imaginative as well as a conceptual order, I have found it instructive to use an image, that of the horn of plenty, as a means of isolating and comparing different texts. This approach will I hope have the advantage of replacing over-simplified assumptions about 'influence' with a sense of the context within which the popularity of the *De copia* may be better understood, both as a symptom and as a contributory cause of major developments in sixteenth-century humanism and literature. Finally, I will return to the question of the relative disappearance of *copia* method from sixteenth-century rhetoric in France.

The notion of copiousness in both thought and language is of course a recurrent one in the rhetorical theory of Cicero and Quintilian, though it is scarcely ever treated by them as a specific device or topic in its own right. Erasmus would certainly have seen it in this context; but he might also have observed its appearance in the work of fifteenth-century Italian humanists.[7] It is possible, too, that he was acquainted with Agricola's treatment of the topic in the *De dialectica* before he wrote his own handbook. This last point is doubtful, since the first version of the *De copia* was certainly written before the publication of the *De dialectica* in 1515.[8] However, it is known that Erasmus was enthusiastic about Agricola's work, and it will be relevant to comment briefly on the *De dialectica* before moving on to the *De copia*.

For Agricola, copiousness of thought arises in the first place from an exact knowledge of how to unfold the concepts of the mind, how to move appropriately through the 'places' of logic. In this sense, *copia* is a function of one specific discipline. But in the last analysis, this discipline enables us, as Cicero recommended in the *De oratore*, to speak about any matter at all: dialectic is the key to the encyclopedia of knowledge and its deployment in language. In the concluding section of his treatise, Agricola introduces a further principle, that of *imitatio* as the best means of *exercitatio*: since the encyclopedia is mirrored in the corpus of classical literature and thought, the potential riches of this corpus must be reactivated by the individual after a process of absorption and reflection:

> Usum duabus his in rebus fore accipio: scriptis authorum cuiusque generis expendendis, et nostris deinde ad illorum exemplum quantum datur effingendis. Quorum illud est ad artis perceptionem commodius, istud ad efficiendi facultatem efficacius. Sunt autem revolvendi authores, non in hoc solum, ut inventionis acumen, dispositionis decorem, in omni rerum orationisque genere noscamus; sed communis rerum humanarum sensus peritiaque accipitur, et copia quaedam orationis ad omnem usum paratur. Unde semper velut ex thesauro, vel proferamus ea quae disposuimus, vel eorum similia effingamus . . . Legendum est ergo authorum omne genus . . .[9]

But Agricola, in this treatise at least, remains a topical logician; he is not much interested in the production of imaginative literature. Indeed, when he speaks of metaphor (*translatio*), he scathingly ascribes its use to the requirements of the *hebetes*,[10] and others (Melanchthon, for example) will take a similar view. For Erasmus, on the other hand, *figura* in general and *translatio* in particular are fundamental to the literary exploitation of *copia*.

These varying attitudes imply important differences of emphasis within that notoriously shifting territory where dialectic and rhetoric overlap. It is not the purpose of this paper to show exactly what kind of relationship between the two disciplines is established by any given theorist. It is necessary however to allude to the fact that the relationship was considered throughout this period to be a crucial one, and that the problems to which it gave rise were solved in different ways; but that even where *inventio* is absorbed wholly into dialectic at the expense of rhetoric, as in Ramist method, the primary aim of the major theorists is to establish the need for total congruence between speech and thought. The notion of speech as a mirror-image of the mind (echoed in the play on *ratio* and *oratio*) is a recurrent and fruitful one in the work of Erasmus and his contemporaries.

In the opening chapters of the *De copia*, a similar concern is implied in Erasmus's treatment of the relationship between *copia* and *brevitas*. Although extension and compression of language had not always been treated as antithetical and mutually exclusive techniques in rhetorical theory, Erasmus's insistence that they are complementary is of particular interest. A writer who has a talent for one is likely to have a talent for the other, he says, and Quintilian cites Homer as a supreme master of both.[11] This observation is related to Erasmus's keen awareness of the dangers of empty loquacity, on which he was to write his essay *Lingua* and for which antecedents may be found in classical rhetorical theory, in Plutarch, and in Petrarch; the first chapter of the *De copia*, indeed, is entitled 'Periculosam esse Copiae affectationem'. The importance of the balance between *copia* and *brevitas* is that it enables Erasmus to suggest that true plenitude of language is to be found not in simple extension, but in inventive and imaginative richness.

This use of an apparent antithesis to point to a principle which transcends formal categorization is characteristic of the whole work, and not least of its division into two books, the first on *copia verborum*, the second on *copia rerum*. Although Erasmus sketches out categories and definitions in both sections, pedagogical method in this sense is subordinate, in the economy of the treatise, to the lively exploration of how the act of writing works. He is not concerned to isolate a particular set of techniques so much as to communicate to the reader a sense of the potentialities of language: *copia* and its implications constitute a thematic core which cannot be reduced to mechanical procedures.[12] One of the most striking examples of this approach is provided by the celebrated double set of variations which (in the earlier editions) conclude Book I, the virtuosity of which has provoked comparisons with Queneau's *Exercices de style*. Unlike Morel's drab lists of alternative phrasings, or the strings of synonymous epithets produced by Holofernes in *Love's Labour's Lost*, Erasmus's variations are dynamic and imaginative. The first in particular becomes more and more exuberant as it proceeds, each version of the sentence being richer than the one before; and the sense of *crescendo* includes also a development by association. Towards the end of the sequence, the sense of pleasure contained in the formula of thanks is explored through a series of metaphors involving drinking and feasting, so that a kind of 'symposium' atmosphere is conjured up out of what began as a banal phrase:

> Nullum ego nectar tuis scriptis anteposuerim. An ego ullum mel Atticum cum tuis amantissimis literis contulerim? Saccarum non est saccarum, si cum literis tuis componatur. Nulli

mortalium tam sapit lotus, quam mihi literae tuae sapiunt. Quod sitienti vinum, hoc mihi tuae sunt literae . . . Ubi recœpissem tantopere expectatas tuas literas, dixisses Erasmum plane gaudiis ebrium. Ut redditae sunt abs te literae, statim vidisses nos nimia quadam laetitia quasi temulentos . . . Non tam pallato blandiuntur ullae cupediae, quam animum meum tuae literae deliniunt. Nullae lautitiae suavius titillant palatum, quam tua scripta mentem titillant . . .[13]

The sequence closes with a strong stress on imagery of abundance: 'your letters are a wagon full of pleasures', 'a well of pleasures', 'a sea of joys'; and Erasmus's verbal excitement is further indicated, perhaps, by his use of Greek words and phrases to denote these images.[14] No doubt these developments are in one sense gratuitous and accidental; but this is precisely why the example is important. Erasmus has abandoned *doctrina* for *exercitatio* (or *experientia*, as he calls it here), and has created a sequence which celebrates abundance of language as a form of positive intoxication, as a feast of the mind. Plenitude is here intuitively felt, whether in the compressed richness of each variation or in the dynamic expansion of the sequence as a whole; it is not a function of any schematic conjunction of *verba* and *res*. Furthermore, *copia* is envisaged not as a quantitative, linear process (as, once again, in Morel's lists) but as the deployment of a creative impulse, releasing and bringing to life, as in poetry, the potential *nuances* of a single bare statement. Indeed, as if Erasmus has become aware retrospectively of the poetic implications of the sequence he has just composed, he immediately adds the following adjustment:

> In his porro si qua videbuntur eiusmodi, ut in oratione soluta vix toleranda putentur, meminerit hanc exercitationem ad carminis quoque compositionem accommodari.[15]

The notion of a creative force operative in literary composition appears as early as chapter viii in Book i, where Erasmus is distinguishing between dull repetition and true *copia* which depends on *varietas*:

> Tantam ubique vim habet varietas, ut nihil omnino tam nitidum sit, quod non squalere videatur, citra huius commendationem. Gaudet ipsa natura vel in primis varietate, quae in tam immensa rerum turba nihil usquam reliquit, quod non admirabili quodam varietatis artificio depinxerit.[16]

The profusion of the natural world thus becomes the model for *copia* in discourse; while a sentence or two later, the image of Protean transformation is introduced to clarify the principle involved:

> Hoc igitur tantum malum [i.e. repetition without variation]

facile vitabit, cui promptum erit sententiam eandem in plureis formas vertere, quam Proteus ipse se transformasse dicitur.[17] The same image occurs at the beginning of chapter xxxiii to illustrate the principle underlying the ensuing set of variations. The notion of transformation which it embodies may recall those passages in contemporary rhetorical and poetic theory which deal with the moving of the passions: the listener (and sometimes the speaker or writer as well) undergoes a process of metamorphosis in which he is identified wholly with the passion evoked. Comparable imagery will be found, for example, in Du Bellay's *Deffence et illustration*, and again in La Taille's preface on the art of tragedy, while Daniel d'Auge (in his *Deux dialogues de l'invention poétique* of 1560, largely translated from the dialogues of Alessandro Lionardi) refers twice to the Protean activities of the poet.[18] Erasmus's use of the image is slightly different, but in connection with the variation exercise of chapter xxxiii it conveys forcefully the sense of a writer wholly engaged in writing as a living and infinitely variable experience.[19]

Before leaving Erasmus, we may cite one further example of *copia* as an imaginative principle. The second book of the *De copia* gives particular prominence to *enargeia* (or *evidentia*, or *demonstratio*, or *hypotyposis*, as it is variously known), that is to say the bringing alive of a scene or an object. This figure was to be important to the poets of the Pléiade: Ronsard cultivated it, as did Belleau, and the posthumous preface to the *Franciade* dwells on it at length. The importance of the procedure is that—unlike the medieval *descriptio*—it again suggests a creative approach to composition rather than prescribing a set of techniques. Erasmus alludes to theatrical representation, to epic description, to descriptions of banquets or of armour, to the transcription of paintings, sculptures, tapestry, the shields of Achilles and Aeneas, as well as to 'fabulous' descriptions, which include mythological figures and personifications. *Copia* is here represented primarily in terms of abundance of surface decoration, of colours and textures; or more generally, as an aesthetic which gathers together the materials of the visual world and reactivates them through language.[20]

Erasmus's handbook thus sketches out some of the implications of the word *copia*, which comes to denote both a loose set of procedures and, more importantly, a living process of composition. Like Agricola's *De dialectica*, though with a very different emphasis, it includes the need for a thorough assimilation of the whole body of materials supplied by antiquity (primarily classical, but also Biblical). This is to be achieved by the 'notebook' method, and, as Bolgar points out, any such method of compilation would produce in practice a result similar to the compendia of various kinds which were popular throughout the sixteenth century. Erasmus's *Adages* constitute one of the earliest and most influential examples; but Crinitus, Ravisius Textor, Raphael Regius, the *Dictionarium poeticum* of 1556, the mythological handbooks of Conti and Giraldi, also supplied ample sources of *res*, while De La Porte, Morel and dictionaries such as Robert Estienne's provided a basis for copiousness of words. The preface of the *Dictionarium poeticum* speaks of weaving a garland of flowers derived from the fertile gardens of Hesiod, Homer, Quintus Calabrius, Ovid, Diodorus, Hyginus, Phornutus and Palephatus; one is tempted to recall in this connection the image of poetic creation in the first stanza of Ronsard's *Ode à Michel de l'Hospital*, but the dictionary itself is of course still only a catalogue of materials and not an imaginative composition. Similarly, the section of Ravisius Textor's *Theatrum poeticum* entitled *Cornucopia* is simply a list of places in which certain things are found in abundance. Such works are important for their sheer proliferation and for the variety which they offered to the potential writer; concepts and images denoting abundance occur frequently in their titles or prefatory material. But for a qualitative rather than a quantitative view of the gardens of Homer, Hesiod and the rest one must turn to the current editions of the authors themselves. Such editions often include detailed cross-reference to and quotation from other authors, forming a set of concordances clustered around the original text; they thus provide a starting-point for the kind of critical reflection which Scaliger was to develop more explicitly in the closing books of his *Poetices*. Furthermore, the major authors—in particular Hesiod, Homer, Virgil and Ovid—were explicitly seen as encyclopedic treasure-houses of knowledge and of rhetorical or poetic ornament, each containing a quintessence of the whole range of classical literary insights and styles. Already in the *De copia* Erasmus speaks of Homer and Virgil as models of variety, followed closely by Ovid in spite of a reservation about his suspect prolixity; Melanchthon presents Homer and Hesiod as paradigms among those authors 'qui simul et rerum scientiam alerent, et ad parandam sermonis copiam plurimum conducerent', as masters of ethics, physics and rhetoric.[21] Similarly, Salel's translation of Homer, echoing a classical commonplace transmitted by Politian among others, emphasizes his universality, while Habert and Aneau claim the same advantage for Ovid in the prefaces to their translations of the *Metamorphoses*.

Thus a long-standing reverence for Virgil as a source of *loci*, or for the *Metamorphoses* as a *Bible des poëtes*, is reconstituted in terms of a much enlarged frame of reference and a new stress on significant abundance. There emerges from these various editions and translations an image of an ideally rich work of literature, a living and inexhaustible paradigm of the humanist encyclopedia. The size or length of a work is not of cardinal importance here; one episode of the Iliad, the making of Achilles's shield, embodies the notion of a complete microcosm expressed in terms of ornamentation; in the *Metamorphoses*, what counts is not only the bulk of myths it contains but also the principle of change itself, which operates on a level more profound than that of narrative content:

> Or est il vray que entre toutes les Poësies Latines n'en y a point de si ample, ne de tant riche, si diverse, et tant universelle que la Metamorphose d'Ovide qui contient en quinze livres composez en beaux vers Heroiques toutes les fabulations, (ou à peu pres) des Poëtes, et scripteurs anciens tellement liées l'une à l'autre, et si bien enchainées par continuelle poursuyte, et par artificielles transitions: que l'une semble naistre, et dependre de l'autre successivement, et non abruptement: combien qu'elles soient merveilleusement dissemblables de diverses personnes, matieres, temps, et lieux. Par toutes lesquelles fables il ne veult autre chose faire entendre sinon qu'en la nature des choses les formes se muent continuellement, la matiere non perissante: comme luy mesme le demonstre au quinsiesme et dernier livre soubz la personne et en l'opinion de Pythagoras.[22]

Again, the preface by Laurentius Humfridus to the 1558 edition of the Eustathius commentary on Homer, celebrating Homer in traditional manner as a master of *copia* and *brevitas*, as a source of tropes, figures and adages, and as a fount of wisdom, uses images from the *Odyssey* itself to render imaginatively the qualities of the whole work:

> Hic Nectar Deorum, hic domus Alcinoi pulcherrima Vulcani arte extructa, hic horti Alcinoi in quo pirus piro succedit, pomaque pomis, deaeque virent, quarum fructus numquam perit, nec hyeme deficit nec aestate. Hic Moly flore lacteo, radice nigra, Hic Nepenthe, malorum levamentum et vitiorum expultrix.[23]

Such statements, in which themes or episodes of the works become emblems of their own moral and aesthetic character, suggest a profound attempt to grasp the creative centre from which a great masterpiece arises, and thence the source of creativity itself. In virtually every instance, the underlying notion is one of abundance, fertility and fruitfulness, a notion which is crystallized in the image of the cornucopia, used as a title both for the compendium already referred to and for the Basle edition of Homer with Eustathius's commentaries. It is true that there are classical precedents for this: Aulus Gellius twice refers to ἀμαλθείας κέρας or *copiae cornu* as an appropriate title for a miscellany;[24] Melanchthon calls the works of Pliny a cornucopia of *paideia*.[25] Nevertheless, it is not I think insignificant that in the mid-sixteenth century the greatest of all classical literary works was known by a title which denotes not its narrative content but its quintessential literary character.[26]

Hence, if one looks at the compendia and the editions as a set of materials to be exploited by the writer, one finds no doubt at one end of the scale a principle of enumeration; but at the other end may be discerned an attempt to render—in the form of images rather than precepts—the fundamental character of literary expression as an art of *copia*, as the endless unfolding of beautiful and significant materials.

The various insights suggested by the identity of *copia* and *brevitas*, by Erasmus's exuberant set of variations, and by the image of cornucopia imply the notion of potentiality and its release rather than simply of extension and multiplicity. In the psychological domain, *copia* may thus be traced back (like dialectic in Agricola's treatise) to its source in the mind, the point at which language emerges and unlocks the treasure-house of mental concepts. Talon refers thus in his *Institutiones oratoriae* of 1545 to the origin of thought and language:

> Deus enim celeres ingeniorum motus ingeneravit nobis, qui sunt ad omnem cogitationem mentis, prudentiamque rationis explicandam, et ornandam uberes, et copiosi: quos, cum doctrine cognitio, et assiduus meditationis labor confirmavit, praeclarum, atque eximium eloquentiae munus existit.[27]

The context here is that of a traditional distinction between *natura*, *doctrina* and *exercitatio*; the essential basis for rhetorical fluency is seen as *natura*, identified explicitly with God's creative action in generating copious movements in the mind which comprise both its cognitive and its expressive powers. The terminology appears to be derived from Cicero's *De oratore*, which refers to the rapid movements of the mind ('animi . . . celeres . . . motus') arising from *natura*, and describes them as 'uberes';[28] Talon adds the word 'copiosi', perhaps simply as a reflex action ('uberes et copiosi' is a commonplace Ciceronian doublet); more importantly, he attributes the *motus* to a specifically divine source, a shift which deepens the implications of the passage considerably, drawing attention to the supernatural *generation* of natural abundance in the domain of eloquence. He omitted this analysis of mental and linguistic activity from his later discussions of rhetoric, so that no such fertile image of inspired abundance filters through, say, to Fouquelin's rather dry and schematic rhetoric. Nevertheless, as a very precise definition of the role of nature in rhetoric it provides a useful point of reference and shows how a positively valued abundance of language may be seen to originate from and thus be guaranteed by the creative power of God.

This means of excluding *a priori* the negative aspects of copious discourse is analogous to (though not identical with) that provided by the Platonist divine fury, which of course was becoming a major focus of attention in France in the 1540s and provided a structure within which imaginative abundance might be linked to and vindicated by an act of supernatural generation. Within the limits of the present paper, it is impossible to probe the analogy more deeply; but one may recall in passing that the analysis of the furies in the *Symposium* and the *Io*, and in the Ficinian commentaries thereon, focuses on the theme of potential and actual abundance in the mental and linguistic spheres; and also that the notion of encyclopedic knowledge, embodied in the arts (one thinks, for example, of Love as master of the arts), or allegorized in the Muses, is fully incorporated into the dynamics of divine inspiration.[29]

Talon, then, isolates the source of mental and linguistic abundance, ensuring that identity of *philosophia* and eloquence (or, in a slightly different register, of dialectic and rhetoric) which is a central preoccupation of Ramist no less than Erasmian thought. Although he is not here making a moral point, one would expect such a fusion ideally to carry with it as a corollary the ethical fulfilment which is an essential component of *humanitas*. In this moral domain, too, imagery of abundance is frequently used by contemporary writers to denote an enriching insight. Thus Melanchthon, in the context of the Homeric encyclopedia:

> Non distendit crumenam auro et argento Homerus, non ventrem pinguedine, non cingit digitos gemmatis annulis: At certe mentem, quae praestantior, quae immortalis pars nostri est, ingentibus, ac longe nobilioribus, aeternisque divitiis cumulat, ornat, ditatque.[30]

This distinction between worldly and spiritual riches may be compared with Budé's interpretation of the cornucopia image in the *De contemptu rerum fortuitarum* (1520) and the *De transitu hellenismi* (1534). In the earlier text, he concedes that pagan moral philosophy may be fruitful, but denies to it the power of overcoming all worldly afflictions:

Ne philosophia quidem moralis tam uberem penum habet, unde promere cito fomenta lenimentaque possit ad aegritudinem animi angentem et enecantem. Multa quidem ipsa visenda, iucunda, fructuosaque docet, sed quae imparia sint saepe dolori, si cum eo committantur in re praesenti.[31]

Once *doctrina*, *ratio* and *natura* have been defeated by adversity, 'unica salutis spes est sacrosancta oracula librosque hierographos adeuntibus, in fidemque et opem divinam venientibus'. This strongly evangelical emphasis determines the sense of the subsequent reference to the 'cornu Amaltheae' itself:

Itaque auferat sane quidvis Fortuna, cornu tantum illud Amaltheae, id est, animi aequitatem, dono det mihi providentia, id ego instar esse ducam protinus copiae exuberantis, ut enim multa desiderem, pauca tamen exposcam.[32]

In the *De transitu*, the contemplation of Christ crucified similarly provides the essential foundation for true tranquillity of mind, and is translated again into an image of cornucopia:

Postremo hoc habet philosophia tanquam divinae cornu copiae, unde non alimenta modo theoriae, sed etiam delicias suppeditet contemplationi editae et reconditae: unde divitias summas animi studiosi promat, fidem, spem, charitatem: unde in rebus acerbissimis, aequum animum, in secundis, vitae contemptum.[33]

It is of course important not to blur the fundamental difference of context between Budé's Christian cornucopia on the one hand, which transcends and supersedes the wealth of pagan ethics, and the claims made for the Homeric encyclopedia on the other; Melanchthon's enthusiasm, for example, is made possible by an optimistic application of the *duplex regimen*, while Budé is deliberately tilting the balance in the opposite direction. Nevertheless, the notion of supreme moral enrichment is explored in each case through imagery of abundance; furthermore, this imagery implies a vision of moral fulfilment which is dependent not so much on formal precepts as on the fruition of inward potentialities. Once again, the cornucopia expresses what might be called the dynamics of intuition.

The sense of delight which is attached to the notion of the horn of plenty is explicit in the text from the *De transitu*, while aesthetic pleasure is a necessary part of the appreciation of Homeric *humanitas*. One might evoke in this context a long series of variations on the *locus amoenus* as an allegory of moral fruitfulness, not the least of which is the garden situated on the rock of Virtue: we are here touching on the crucial question of the relationship between *virtus* and *voluptas*. This enormous field of enquiry may however be restricted for present purposes to a further examination of the gloss on cornucopia as an image of moral goods. Two ethical applications of the image are indicated by Erasmus in Adage 1.vi.2 (*Copiae cornu*). In the first, it simply denotes an abundance of virtues: Philostratus Dionem sophistam appellat ἀμαλθείας κέρας, velut omni genere virtutum expolitum.

The second invokes Plutarch's phrase 'At qui Stoicam acceperit Amaltheam',

irridens paradoxa Stoicorum, qui suo sapienti tribuunt universa, divitias, libertatem, sanitatem, regnum.[34]

The Stoic paradox referred to here is the claim that the truly wise man will enjoy not only all 'internal' goods, but also all 'external' ones; Plutarch on several occasions (including a passage in the *De tranquillitate animi*)[35] rejects the literal sense of the paradox in favour of the more orthodox Stoic aspiration to an exclusively moral enrichment. A similarly ironic presentation of this 'paradox' occurs in Horace's *Satires* 1,3, while Cicero, in the *De natura deorum*, gives a positive version, attributing it to Socrates:

Magnis autem viris prosperae semper omnes res, siquidem satis a nostris et a principe philosophiae Socrate dictum est de ubertatibus virtutis et copiis.[36]

Although Erasmus does not provide all these allusions, it is clear that we are here dealing with a central area of classical ethical concern, familiar to sixteenth-century humanists, in which various forms of moral fulfilment are associated with copiousness.

A more richly imaginative example is provided by the triumph of Vertumnus and Pomona in the *Hypnerotomachia*. Pomona carries a cornucopia, and the inscription for the procession is as follows (I give the French version of Jean Martin):

Je donne et presente a ceulx la qui me servent, perfecte santé de corps, ferme et stable vigueur de leurs personnes, pures et chastes delices en banquetz, avec bienheureuse tranquillité d'esprit.[37]

The triumph is an allegory of the seasons; but it is also an allegory of ethical fulfilment based on mental and physical harmony and vindicating a purified hedonism. *Tranquillitas animi* (or *securitas animi*, as the Latin version of the motto has it) does not arise from a rigorously Stoic apathy, nor, at the other end of the scale, from physical power and riches, but rather from a right ordering of natural appetite. The Rabelais of Louis Le Caron's Dialogue *Valton, de la tranquillité d'esprit, Ou du souverain bien*, or indeed the Rabelais of the *Quart Livre*, would have concurred with this ideal equilibrium of *virtus* and *voluptas*; it tallies rather less directly, perhaps, with the presentation of the child Gargantua's *braguette* as a kind of sexual cornucopia.[38]

Ripa's *Iconologia* retrospectively suggests some rather more straightforward moral associations for the cornucopia: it is a metaphor for natural and mental fertility (*Fecondità*), it symbolizes the consequences of Good Fortune (*Fortuna*), and more specifically the fruits of labour:

> Il cornucopia accenna il frutto conseguito delle fatiche, senza le quali è impossibile arrivare alla felicità, che per mezzo d'esse si conosce, e desidera. (*Felicità publica*)

'Felicità' is further defined in the same emblem as 'un riposo dell' animo in un bene sommamente conosciuto, e desiderato, e desiderabile'. It is perhaps relevant to add that the emblem *Tranquillità*, in which a ship is depicted together with a cornucopia and other motifs, glosses the cornucopia as showing that the tranquillity of sky and sea produces abundance, a 'physical' interpretation which could easily be shifted to the moral sphere.[39]

This group of samples, although fragmentary, clarifies the range of possible contacts between cornucopia and tranquillity, a conjunction which may well seem somewhat strange at first sight. In each case, the sense of fulfilment is presented not as a static conclusion but as an ultimate opening up of enriching possibilities; equilibrium is reached at the ideal point where satiety and potentiality become identified. The horn of plenty thus denotes, once again, not sheer quantity of goods but a principle of inexhaustibility. For Budé, it points towards a silent inward contemplation; for the editors of the Homeric canon, it suggests an expressive unfolding of language and of the universal insight contained therein. Broadly speaking, this is the range of options investigated in different ways by Rabelais and Ronsard.

The concept of *copia* and the image of cornucopia might well be used to measure the precise differences of rhetorical and ethical standpoint suggested by the varied contexts in which they appear. Conversely, their convergence can be seen to indicate certain fundamental preoccupations which form a part of the specific character of the Renaissance in France and of its literature. There is little doubt, I think, that the emergence of the word *copia* as a focal point of rhetorical theory is symptomatic of the way in which interest begins to shift in the earlier sixteenth century in northern Europe towards imaginative literature as an alternative to, even a superior substitute for, formal modes of thought (whether scholastic logic or topical logic). For Cicero and Quintilian, it had indicated both a characteristic of elevated style and the storehouse of devices which an orator must have at his disposal. Erasmus's treatise raised it to the level of a stylistic and imaginative ideal which subsumes a broadly based technique of imitation as well as a set of devices designed to produce linguistic exuberance. Prepared by the rehabilitation of rhetoric and by the notion of the union of philosophy and eloquence, this use has the advantage of cutting across commonplace distinctions to suggest a central principle of mental creativity comprising both *res* and *verba*, *inventio* and *elocutio*, *natura*, *doctrina* and *exercitatio*. Its value is precisely that it does not create categories and distinctions, but provides a context in which to explore both the source of mental and linguistic activity and the ideal end-product of that activity.

These characteristics are underlined if we compare the concept of *copia* with the rhetorical term *amplificatio*. For the classical rhetoricians, *amplificatio* had been a device used in judicial and demonstrative rhetoric to give weight and substance to an argument or to praise a person or an act: it is the cause which is amplified, rather than the style itself. Medieval rhetoric shifted it eventually to a specifically stylistic context: it became a general label for the various ways of saying more about a topic, of extending or spinning out a discourse. Used in this sense, it was indeed one of the central principles of medieval rhetoric. The humanist rhetoricians of the Renaissance restored the term to its classical sense, so that it is regularly treated under the rubric of *inventio* rather than that of *elocutio*; and, as Ong has pointed out, *copia* takes the place of the medieval *amplificatio*.[40] Melanchthon and others sometimes continue to use *amplificatio* as a synonym for *copia*; but the shift from medieval *amplificatio* to Renaissance *copia* is nevertheless a major one. A term used to denote a formal set of procedures which can be learnt and deployed systematically by any writer is replaced by a concept which, while including many of the same procedures, may also lead in sophisticated contexts to an intuitive insight into literary aesthetics.

The richness of the notion of *copia* is in direct proportion to its value as an image. Frequently coupled with its synonym *ubertas* (or, in the adjectival form, *copiosus/uberis*), it evokes associations of plenitude and fertility which in their turn invite comparisons with other domains of activity: those of the natural world, of moral experience, or of supernatural intuition. The recurrence of the cornucopia image is one particularly striking instance of an imaginative preoccupation with fruitfulness in these central areas of experience; many others could be adduced—the symposium, the Golden Age, Penia and Porus, imagery of sexual and seasonal generation and so on. Hence the conceptual patterns of humanist thought are enriched by a metaphorical apparatus which is in no sense merely ornamental: it may shift the whole emphasis of a discussion, or even illustrate the origin and nature of the shift itself. At key points, *copia* and cornucopia become emblems of release from the categories of formal thought, signalling the movement into an intuitive domain of overwhelming potentiality.

This awareness of a fertile mode of perception and expression does not of course undercut the humanist encyclopedia: on the contrary, it allows—ideally—the full flowering of *humanitas* and the liberal arts. But in mid-sixteenth-century France, imaginative excitement is generated not so much within the realms of rhetoric or ethics proper as in that of literary creation. While absorbing into itself many of the preoccupations and ideals of *humanitas*, the literary work follows an uncompromisingly intuitive path, with the result that the encyclopedic vision becomes centrifugal and eventually fragmented. The substitution of intuitive perception for externally structured knowledge opened up the enclosed space of the encyclopedia and made it subject to a principle of unresolved expansion: in consequence, the world-view of mid-sixteenth-century French literature is one which asserts and explores the necessity of change, of an inquiry which must remain open-ended. In theory, then, the cornucopia may symbolize a harmonious balance of potentiality and realization; in practice, the dynamics of intuition purchase fruitfulness at the expense of stability.

In the light of this analysis, we may in conclusion attempt to explain the relative lack of *copia* in rhetorical theory after 1540. In the first place, it seems clear that the kind of orientation which Erasmus gives to *copia* in his handbook, while relevant to many forms of writing, is ultimately of greatest concern to imaginative literature. As Margaret Mann Phillips has put it in a recent article:

Il [the *De copia*] contenait en somme toute la théorie d'une nouvelle littérature basée sur le modèle antique: en latin, certes, mais en présupposant un style très individualiste, libéré du pédantisme, et qui faisait place aux préférences personnelles, à la création même. On se demande en lisant le *De copia* si le plus clair de son importance n'est pas précisément de ce côté-là, puisque ses préceptes transposés étaient valables pour toute tentative littéraire . . .[41]

This message was certainly absorbed by Rabelais; meanwhile, poetic theory was soon to begin to establish itself as the appropriate domain in which to explore such questions. It could be demonstrated, I think, that the French vernacular poetics of the mid-century are much closer to the *De copia* in their doctrine and, above all, in their implied assumptions than they are to rhetorical treatises like Fouquelin's. An imitation theory anchored to the criterion of intuitive identity between the poet and his model; an eclectic and richly allusive use of source-material from every available area; a stylistic emphasis on colourful texture and on mimetic procedures like *enargeia*; the attempt to understand the principles by which emotive impetus can be achieved and communicated: in all these respects, Pléiade theory and practice echo Erasmus without once referring to his example. The notion of *copia* has by now become thoroughly naturalized in the vernacular; its implications are being worked out in poetry—often in terms of cornucopian imagery—while rhetoric follows paths of its own.[42]

NOTES

1 P. Melanchthon, *Elementorum rhetorices libri duo* (Paris, Simon de Colines, 1532) f. 45 v.
2 See H. Rix, 'The Editions of Erasmus' *De copia*', *Studies in Philology* (University of North Carolina), XLIII (1946) 595–605. An indication of the popularity of the term *copia* and its vernacular derivatives is provided by Guillaume Télin's *Bref sommaire des sept vertus/sept ars liberaulx/ sept ars de Poesie* . . ., Paris, Nicolas Cousteau for Galliot du Pré, 1533 o.s., in which 'copieux' and 'copieusement' are used repeatedly o. to describe the style of various Latin authors. The point is reinforced by the fact that this is hardly an avant-garde text, if only in that it was printed in Gothic type.
3 R. R. Bolgar, *The Classical Heritage and its Beneficiaries* (New York 1964) 272–5, 297–8, 320 ff.
4 P. Laumonier, *Ronsard, poète lyrique* (Paris 1909) 379 ff.
5 W. J. Ong, *Ramus, Method, and the Decay of Dialogue* (Cambridge, Mass., 1958) 212.
6 A. Gordon, *Ronsard et la rhétorique* (Geneva 1970) (*Travaux d'humanisme et renaissance* CXI).
7 See G. Vallese, 'Erasme et le *De duplici copia verborum ac rerum*', in *Colloquia Erasmiana Turonensia* (Douzième stage international d'études humanistes, Tours 1969), vol. I (Paris 1972) 235–6.
8 See Margaret Mann Phillips, 'Erasmus and the Art of Writing', in *Scrinium Erasmianum*, vol. I (Leiden 1969) 348–9. This article is as a whole particularly relevant to the present paper.
9 R. Agricola, *De inventione dialectica libri tres* (Paris, Simon de Colines, 1538) 440–1.
10 Ibid., 119.
11 Erasmus, *Omnia opera* (Basle, Froben, 1540) vol. I, 2 (Book I, ch. iii): 'Homerus, teste Fabio, utracque iuxta re mirabilis est, tum copia, tum brevitate.' Cf. p. 3 (I, v): 'non alius artifex melius ad brevitatem arctabit orationem, quam qui calleat eandem quam maxime varia supellectile locupletare'.
12 In Book I, chapter vii, Erasmus stresses that he has only distinguished

between *res* and *verba* for teaching purposes: they are separate in theory rather than in practice. J. K. Sowards, in his 'Erasmus and the Apologetic Textbook', *Studies in Philology* (University of North Carolina), LV (1958), 122–35, points out Erasmus's characteristic device of choosing examples which have an intrinsic moral or religious message to offer, thus injecting *philosophia* into what is ostensibly a study of stylistic technique.

13 *Omnia opera*, vol. I, p. 20 (Book I, chapter xxxiii). Banquet imagery is also to be found in I, x (p. 6).

14 The final variation ('Mihi plane tuae literae fuerunt quod Persis διὸς ἐγκέφαλος, quemadmodum aiunt Graeci') is explained by Adage I.vi.lx (*Iovis et regis cerebrum*): De cibo vehementer opiparo ac suavi. Aut de molliter delicateque viventibus. Clearchus apud Zenodotum scribit, oppiparas epulas apud Persas, Iovis ac regis cerebrum appellari . . . (*Omnia opera*, vol. II, 215). One might cautiously read this image of supreme gastronomic delight as also implying a sense of superior wisdom, bearing in mind the myth of the birth of Minerva from the brain of Jupiter.

15 Ed. cit., p. 21 (I, xxxiii). In I, viii (p. 4), Erasmus claims that *copia* is useful, *inter alia*, for the composition of verse.

16 Ibid., p. 4 (I, viii).

17 Loc. cit. This image is further connected with the cultivation of extempore fluency, thus stressing the notion of an intuitive and spontaneous mode of discourse which can adapt itself to the needs of the moment.

18 J. Du Bellay, *La Deffence et illustration de la langue françoyse*, ed. H. Chamard (Paris 1948) 37, 42, 46; Jean de La Taille, *Dramatic Works*, ed. Kathleen M. Hall and C. N. Smith (London 1972) 20; D. d'Auge (Augentius), *Deux dialogues de l'invention poétique, de la vraye cognoissance de l'histoire, de l'art Oratoire, et de la fiction de la fable* (Paris, R. Breton, 1560) f. 58v, 77r.

19 See also the extraordinary inventory of transformation *exempla* in Book II, the section *Ratio colligendi exempla* (89–90).

20 Book II, *Quinta ratio* (66 ff.). This preoccupation with *enargeia* and related figures must, I think, be carefully distinguished from the Ramist notion of the visual representation of concepts, which tends to be formal and schematic. Ramist rhetorics do not dwell much on the rendering of sense-impressions.

21 P. Melanchthon, *Praefatio in Hesiodum*, in *Liber selectarum declamationum . . . Adiectae sunt eiusdem Praefationes in aliquot illustres Autores* (Argentorati, ex officina Cratonis Mylii, 1541) 613. Cf. also the *Praefatio in Homerum* in the same collection, 385–406. The principal classical source for the view of Homer as universal author is the pseudo-Plutarchan *De vita et poesi Homeri*.

22 B. Aneau, *Trois premiers livres de la Metamorphose d'Ovide, Traduictz en vers François. Le premier et second, par Cl. Marot. Le tiers par B. Aneau* (Lyon, Guillaume Rouille, 1556) f. b5 r–v.

23 Eustathius, *Copiae cornu, sive oceanus enarrationum Homericarum* (Basle, Froben, 1558) 2.

24 Aulus Gellius, *Noctes Atticae*, Praef. 6; I, viii, 1.

25 P. Melanchthon, *De corrigendis adolescentiae studiis* (*Declamatio* of 29 August 1518, at Wittenberg), in *Corpus Reformatorum* XI, col. 22.

26 Cf. Rabelais's reference to his book, in the prologue of the *Tiers Livre*, as 'un vray Cornucopie'.
27 O. Talon (A. Talaeus), *Institutiones oratoriae, ad celeberrimam et illustrissimam Lutetiae Parisiorum Academiam* (Paris, J. Bogard, 1545) 6.
28 Cicero, *De oratore* i, 25 (113).
29 The *Symposium* myth of Porus and Penia and its interpretation by Ficino and Ebreo provide a striking example of this theme in the neoplatonist context.
30 P. Melanchthon, *Praefatio in Homerum*, in *Liber selectarum declamationum*, 405.
31 G. Budé, *De contemptu rerum fortuitarum*, in *Omnia opera* (Basle, apud Nicolaum Episcopium Iuniorem, 1557) vol. i, 128.
32 Ibid., 129.
33 G. Budé, *De transitu hellenismi ad christianismum*, in *Omnia opera*, vol. i, 166.
34 Erasmus, *Omnia opera*, vol. ii, 193.
35 Plutarch, *De tranquillitate animi*, 472; cf. *Stoicos absurdiora poetis dicere*, (5). For an early source, see von Arnim, *Stoic. Vet. Frag.*, iii, p. 164, Frag. 655.
36 Cicero, *De natura deorum* ii, lxvi.
37 *Discours du songe de Poliphile . . .* (Paris, J. Kerver, 1546) f. 67 v.
38 F. Rabelais, *Gargantua*, chapter vii. In the *Songe de Poliphile*, the cornucopia recurs as an attribute of both Ceres (summer) and Bacchus (autumn) in the decoration of the altar at which the followers of Vertumnus and Pomona worship (f. 68 r); these seasonal allegories are followed by an explicitly phallic triumph of Priapus which, Poliphile says, 'me donna plus d'admiration que de plaisir, et ne me sembla point si divin que les precedens' (f. 68 v). Thus a difference of register is indicated in what is nevertheless a closely interrelated group of symbolic themes.
39 C. Ripa, *Iconologia* (Padua, Pietro Paolo Tozzi, 1611) 160, 183, 167, 521 respectively. Cf. G. de Tervarent, *Attributs et symboles dans l'art profane, 1450–1600*, 2 vols. (Geneva 1958–9) (*Travaux d'humanisme et renaissance* xxix), where the cornucopia is shown to be an attribute (always favourable) of a wide range of notions and deities, including Felicity, Prudence, Hope, Charity, Venus, Eros, Tellus, Religion, Equity. The cornucopia represents Fortune in Alciati's emblem 'Virtuti fortuna comes', while the political message of 'Ex pace ubertas' is conveyed by a depiction of Halcyon on a nest of wheat-ears and vines (almost, but not quite, a cornucopia).
40 W. J. Ong, op. cit., 211, 213.
41 Margaret Mann Phillips, 'Erasme et Montaigne ii: *De duplici copia verborum ac rerum* et *Essais*', in *Colloquia Erasmiana Turonensia*, vol. i, 491. Cf. the concluding page (489) of the first part of the same article, on the substitution of instinctive for logical order in Erasmus and Montaigne.
42 This paper owes much to Professor Guy Demerson, who first indicated to me Budé's interpretation of the horn of Amaltheia. I am also indebted to Mr George Kerferd and Mr Philip O'Prey, whose detailed research (as yet unpublished) on early sixteenth-century humanists has greatly nourished my own reflections on these topics.

WILLIAM P.D.WIGHTMAN

Cosmological and Technological Trends in the French Renaissance

IN A PUBLIC LECTURE it may generally be assumed that at least the lecturer knows what he is talking about, even if the audience doesn't. But in this case I must frankly admit that I have no clear and distinct ideas of what science, French or Renaissance mean. 'Renaissance' I shall dodge, since it would take a whole lecture to state and support my provisional interpretation. The word 'science' according to the OED was first used in the modern English sense of 'natural science' by James Hutton of this city and by Richard Kirwan of Dublin about the same time. Cosmology being conveniently vague will however do to cover both astronomy and what was then called 'physics' roughly corresponding to Aristotle's τὰ φυσικά, 'natural things'. Aristotle chose to deal in separate books with what he called History of Animals—the word 'animal' being equivalent to those beings that were 'ensouled', and this of course included plants about which Aristotle probably wrote, but our knowledge of Greek botanical studies rests on the two small but admirable works of his successor at the Lyceum, Theophrastos. The *princeps* of each of these was issued as part of the Aldine Aristotle in 1498. Apart from the elder Scaliger these works, though displaying an admirably scientific temper, were relatively neglected during the sixteenth century. By that time the study of plants was dominated by the need of the medical schools established on the basis of the *De materia medica* of the Greek Dioskurides on which an undoubted Frenchman, Jean Ruel, composed one of the earliest scholarly commentaries in 1515. Why do I say 'undoubted'? Well this brings me to my third ill-defined term, 'French'. It is particularly significant for the study of plants, since some of the greatest masters of the so-called Low Country herbalists, who succeeded the German pioneers, found it convenient, though born in France, to follow their countryman, Christophe Plantin, to Antwerp, where nearly all their works were published.[1] Even the most passionate claimants for 'La Gloire' would hesitate before including Antwerp within the realm of France, but the case of Louvain is not so easily dismissed; and there it was in the *Collegium trium linguarum* that the most talented and progressive workers on the frontiers between astronomy and technology were already at work before 1548. I shall return to Louvain; but why 1548? Because it was in that year that a remarkable claim for the opening of a new world-epoch was published. To many of you it may be already familiar, but it is so fundamental to my assessment that I must consider it in some detail: 'To speak candidly about this our age, the disciplines and arts that had been buried nearly twelve hundred years ago and had really fallen into a state of complete extinction have now completely revived and regained, I might even say surpassed, their former splendour, so that this age need envy that former time in hardly any respect.' Men of very varied attainments, the writer went on to point out, had created 'many magnificent works that yield nothing to those more ancient ones whose fame is on everyone's lips'. And not only was this true, he emphasized, in respect of the fine arts and letters but also of military engines, fire bombs, printing, and the discovery of new lands. This remarkable document was written only a little less than a century after the invention of printing from movable type—the only triumph of human ingenuity, other than fire bombs, the author chose to mention. Many of its phrases suggest that it was based on a similar claim made by Leon Battista Alberti a few years *before* the introduction of printing. Yet the author was no hack writer, but Jean Fernel, the most influential physician in France if not in Europe during the second half of the sixteenth century; and it was he who had also made the first western measurement of an arc of meridian. Allowance must be made for the fact that he was addressing the French king Henry 11 in the dedication of his book, *On the secret causes of things* and Henry was not likely to be a very enlightened critic. But it was a very learned (if dated) book in which Fernel would surely have taken some care to avoid appearing so sadly behind the times as the tenor of the dedication suggests that he was. The truth seems to be that French cultural development *was* behind the times; fifty years previously the same sort of nonsense as that with which the passage opens might have passed muster in Italy but hardly in 1547—four years we may remind ourselves, after the publication of those truly epoch-making books of Copernicus and Vesalius. We must not however 'draw up an indictment against a whole nation' on the evidence of a single document.

First let us recall the names of a few of those who had been prominent in the 'arts and sciences' during the hundred years separating the manifestos of Alberti and Fernel—Toscanelli, Nicholas of Cues, Regiomontanus, Dürer, Giovanni Manardi, Paracelsus. None of these, it must be admitted, stands out prominently in a history of *science* as commonly understood; but in an age of the 'transvaluation of all values' they, and many more could be named, saw further and with surer vision than their contemporaries into what was to become natural science. In France we should look in vain for anyone (with the possible exception of Nicolas Chuquet, whose *original* ideas were unknown until the nineteenth century) of whom the same could be said. To avoid any suspicion of national bias I must candidly admit that if France was the most backward cultural scene in western Europe England was a close second! The only thing to be said for my native land is that the light of science dawned there a little earlier than it did in France, as we shall see. But to return to Fernel.

Sir Charles Sherrington (who as it were introduced me to Fernel in his Gifford Lectures about fifty years ago) regarded him as a typical 'Renaissance Man'. Insofar as this abstraction really exists I think Fernel would exemplify him as well as any. His later works reveal a humane, scholarly, systematic, and wise physician; his failure to recognize the three chief growing points of positive knowledge of the sixteenth century, namely, algebra, natural history of plants and animals, and anatomy suggests however that he was out of touch with the times. Perhaps he was; but tied to the court and dedicated to his craft and his writing he must have had to rely largely on the reports of others. And within 100 miles of Paris there do not appear to have been any others who could have enlightened him. In fact one is tempted to say that the further you went from Paris—eastward to Louvain and Antwerp; southward to Lyon and Montpellier—the greater chance you had of meeting progressive spirits. The temptation must however be resisted before a rather more searching look has been made at the circle of Jacques Dubois (Sylvius).[2] Until comparatively lately Sylvius has had a bad press; a junior assistant who has caught the professor out in more than one howler is not the most reliable witness as to the latter's competence. Vesalius was not the first nor, alas, the last to fail to correct the professor's errors in a manner discreet enough to earn his gratitude rather than to raise his wrath. And on the other hand Sylvius was foolish enough to publish an unbridled attack on Vesalius after the latter had produced the greatest work on anatomy since Galen's *De anatomicis administrationibus* (which incidentally had been translated into Latin by another of Sylvius's assistants, Guinther of Andernach, and beautifully printed by Simon de Colines in 1531). So to form a completely just estimate of Vesalius' debt to Sylvius is now probably impossible. But for our purpose it is sufficient to know that, as Vesalius admitted, Sylvius was a skilled anatomist of *animals* and that he gave his students, who also included Miguel Servet, ample opportunities for dissection and demonstration. The tragedy was that Sylvius regarded himself as the self-appointed and dedicated defender of Galen down to the last bone and fibre—a species of idolatry for which I fancy Galen wouldn't have thanked him. Needless to say Sylvius was never admitted to the *Faculté*; for them he seems to have been *too* progressive.

There is an even more startling omission from Fernel's list of 'triumphs'—the publication four years earlier of Copernicus's blueprint for a cosmic reassessment. Three years before the appearance of this blue-print there had been printed at Dantzig a letter previously written by Copernicus's devoted assistant, Ioachimus Rheticus, to Io. Schöner, and since known as the *Narratio prima* of the Copernican system. In fact the outline of this system had been circulated in manuscript by Copernicus himself many years earlier and this so-called *Commentariolus* was shown to Clement VII in 1536 with a strong recommendation that the author should be urged to revise it for the press. Copernicus himself, probably recognizing more clearly than the Holy See that the theory on which the calculations were based was a time bomb, took a lot of persuading. However Rheticus, having joined Copernicus at Frauenburg and having assisted him to arrange and complete the intricate calculations and diagrams based on fresh observations, at last obtained a still rather reluctant permission to prepare the text for publication. The happy issue of the long struggle to persuade Copernicus was announced to the world in the *Narratio prima*. The epoch-making *De revolutionibus orbium coelestium* appeared in 1543 from the press of Io. Petreius of Nuremberg.

According to Professor René Taton three Frenchmen looked favourably—but no more—on the new system: the algebraist Jacques Peletier, Jean Péna and the polymath Pontus de Tyard. Taton does not however mention the *démarche* of Pierre de la Ramée which, though it happened nearly twenty years after the event raised an issue that from the time of Aristotle and especially in thirteenth- and fourteenth-century Paris had been regarded as of fundamental importance.[3] In 1563 La Ramée wrote a letter to Rheticus in which he congratulated him on having proved that the hypotheses based on epicycles and excentrics (which of course Copernicus had been compelled to use as the geometrical basis of his demonstration of the heliostatic system) were in La Ramée's words 'absurd and false'. La Ramée had seen this alleged demonstration in the *Foreword* to Copernicus's *De revolutionibus* and had understandably assumed (*ni fallor*, as he was careful to add) that the *Foreword* was the work of Rheticus. The fact that, as was revealed only decades later, it was written by another Lutheran, Andreas Osiander, who undertook the final preparation of Copernicus's manuscript, is for our purpose of no particular consequence; what is of special interest is the actual form of the argument on which the verdict of 'falsity' was made to rest: this was the distinction recognized by Aristotle, but categorically enunciated by the sixth-century neoplatonist, Simplikios, in a passage that became and has remained the *locus classicus*; the distinction was between the 'astronomer' and the 'physicist'. While both had to assume hypotheses from which consequences could be validly drawn and thereafter tested by reference to the phenomena, those of the astronomer need not in themselves be 'true' in any sense; it was the business of the 'physicist', or as he came to be called the 'philosopher', to decide whether they were consistent with the accepted cosmology—'how things actually are and could not be otherwise' as Aristotle puts it in the *Posterior Analytics*.

What La Ramée was demanding of Rheticus was what he misleadingly called 'an astronomy free from hypotheses'—a 'scientific' system embodying nothing but what Auguste Comte was to call 'positive' knowledge. Such had been the basis of the Occamite controversy in fourteenth-century Paris, admirably documented by Pierre Duhem in his masterly Σώζειν τὰ φαινόμενα; in a modified form six centuries later it was to be the basis of the unresolved conflict of views between the solitary Albert Einstein on the one hand and Max Born and Werner Heisenberg on the other.

Of course history has shown the ultimate sterility of the exclusive form in which La Ramée expressed his demand: the only astronomy that has ever come near to fulfilling the condition of being devoid of hypotheses is that embodying the Babylonian Venus Tables expressed in the so-called z-functions—of great historical interest but in themselves a dead-end. Nevertheless it is in the light of this demand that we must judge those sixteenth-century men who openly expressed their views on the new heliostatic cosmology.

I must first remind you that Osiander's cautionary 'positivism' was totally at variance with Copernicus's own belief. In his dedication to Paul III Copernicus claimed that 'the heavens themselves become so bound together that nothing in any part thereof could be moved from its place without producing confusion of all the other parts of the Universe as a whole'. Though I suppose it could be rather unconvincingly argued that this is no more than a rhetorical reference to purely mathematical 'movement' and 'confusion', the matter is put beyond all reasonable doubt by the characteristic role attributed to the Sun in another rhetorical outburst to which I shall make later reference. But since, before the book could be widely read, Copernicus had already passed to a realm where philosophical

niceties presumably play no dominant role he took no part in the
ensuing apologetics.

The earliest and most pragmatic effect of the new system was the
publication by Erasmus Reinhold of the Prutenic Tables marking a
significant if not very considerable advance on the centuries old
Alphonsine Tables and which at last made possible the long awaited
reform of the calendar towards which so much astronomical activity
had been motivated at least since the efforts of Pierre d'Ailly. It was
formerly accepted that Reinhold was the first to embrace the
Copernican cosmology; recent scholarship has however cast serious
doubts on whether his acceptance ran to anything more than that of
an 'astronomer' concerned solely with the calculation of tables
while at the same time rejecting the 'truth' of the hypotheses on
which the model was based. It has so far never been established that
any *astronomer* of note ever went any further than this until Kepler,
who mentions that at Tübingen towards the end of the century he
had heard Michael Maestlin make frequent serious references to the
Copernican system. To Tycho Brahe, by far the greatest of the
sixteenth-century astronomers, the heliostatic hypothesis seemed
'physically absurd' and he died in 1602 consoled in the faith that his
unsurpassed observations would be used to establish his own geocentric version. The absence in France of any forthright questioning
—the case of La Ramée seems to be not free from some ambiguity—
of the Aristotelian world-system can not therefore be regarded as a
mark of rabid conservatism. What however is significant is that
among the perhaps half dozen men who before 1600 accepted the
Copernican world view as a fundamental 'revolution' three were
English, one Italian, one Frisian. A fourth Englishman, William
Gilbert, supported it for somewhat anomalous reasons in his *De
magnete* of 1600. None of these men could be strictly described as
'astronomers': four were primarily concerned with technological
problems, the Italian was of course that aberrant genius Giordano
Bruno. Finally the Frisian, Reinerus Gemma, was closely associated
with the vigorous school of applied mathematics at Louvain. The
quality of this school is attested by the fact that among its associates
was Gerhard de Kremer (better known as 'Mercator') early employed by Charles v as leading instrument maker, and who later
learnt enough mathematics from Gemma to construct (1569) the
*Nova et aucta orbis terrae descriptio ad usum navigantium emendate accom-
modata* containing the projective system known to every schoolboy.
Also had François Rabelais written a little later than he did he would
surely have had Gargantua recommend Gemma's *Arithmeticae
practicae methodus facilis* instead of Cuthbert Tunstall's ponderous *Ars*

supputandi which, though ostensibly written for money changers and others, ran to only one edition, while one rapidly loses count of Gemma's reprints and translations. Before 1548 Gemma had announced the method of triangulation that remains to this day the basis of terrestrial (as against aerial) survey and cartography.

It remains to add that apart from Bruno, whose speculations went far beyond what Copernicus or anyone else could have demonstrated, the only unambiguous acceptances of the Copernican system were by the English physician, mathematical teacher, and administrator, Robert Recorde, and by Thomas Digges, who in an Appendix to his father's *Prognostication Everlasting*, shattered the concept of a cosmos enclosed by a changeless sphere of fixed stars. It was the latter rather than Copernicus, who was responsible for Donne's lament of 'all coherence gone . . .'

You will have noticed that Digge's epoch-making claim was spread abroad through the medium of an astrological almanac, as indeed had been Gemma's welcome of the Copernican system. The widespread concern with astrology in the sixteenth-century at all levels of credulity needs no emphasis—almost every ruler, great or small (Catherine de Medici being one of the most addicted) maintained a domestic astronomer (or 'mathematician' as he was often called) whose pay was rarely for the advancement of knowledge, but for discovering the most propitious times for political action, whether for war or for the foundation of a university. On the value of timing medical therapy by the stars opinions were sharply divided. I am able to cite three documents of French provenance.

Claude Dariot's *Ad astrorum iudicia facilis introductio . . . Quibus accessit fragmentum de morbis & diebus criticis ex astrorum motu cognoscendis* was printed at Lyon 1557 and partly translated into French (Lyon) in 1588. It was Englished with additions by one Fabian Wither five years earlier. Its original appearance in Latin shows that it was no popular almanac but intended for the learned, mainly medical. Despite its two translations (after a longish interval) the author is only very briefly noticed in the standard biographies; better known and near contemporary was Ogier Ferrier, one of whose works was dedicated to Catherine and another to Cardinal Castillion on his designation as Archbishop of Toulouse; Ferrier dealt with both nativities and 'critical days'.

Reference to my third document will enable us to form a fairly representative judgment of the attitude to astrology of both a seat of learning and the Church. It is a lecture given to the fairly recently founded University of Douai by a sixteenth-century alumnus of the University of Aberdeen at King's College where I was able to make a study of all his works in the original editions. His *curriculum vitae* is of one of the most interesting of the minor 'scientific' figures of the French Renaissance—that is if I may be permitted to stretch this period to 1576.

James Cheyne was born of an Aberdeenshire-Norman family in about 1545 and claimed to have graduated in 'philosophy' at King's College in 1566.[4] In 1572 he became lecturer in 'philosophy and mathematics' at Douai. His books show that this profession covered astronomy, geography, and 'physics'. Although composed in the form of text-books they were of a most enlightened kind: dogmatic assertion was not enough; frequently there was appeal to the 'fabric of nature', as William Harvey was later to call it, and exercises with the instruments, grants for which called forth his gratitude to the municipality. He was a 'Renaissance Man' in that while clearly basing his teaching and books on the admirable thirteenth-century didactic masterpiece, Ioannes de Sacrobosco's *Tractatus de sphaera*, he paid tribute only to the 'ancients' and 'moderns' (including Reinerus Gemma) and ignored the medievals. It is true that he fails even to mention Ptolemy on the one hand and Copernicus on the other: but probably he thought that for teaching at the equivalent of the grammar school level they were too difficult. Perhaps they would have appeared in a final part of his *Astronomy* in course of composition but never published. Above all he was willing to accept, on the good faith of the observers, the existence of new stars (the Southern Cross) and a total repudiation of the alleged uninhabitability of the tropics and antipodes—and this in an institution founded mainly for the training of secular priests who would act as the advance guard of the Counter-Reformation. I have asked you to take rather a wide-ranging look at this undistinguished man before stating his contribution to the problem of astrology. I could add many other documented details of his wide experience, European-mindedness, and of the high esteem in which he was held by one of the outstanding personalities of the age—Thomas Dempster. The university lecture to which primarily I wish to direct your attention was delivered at Douai in 1576 and printed there in the following year; its title *De praedictionibus astrologorum*. Though he had used his astronomical skill to calculate the nativity of James VI of Scotland there is no evidence that he used the associated data of 'ascendants' and 'houses' to forecast the fate of the subject. His attitude to the limits of astrological forecast is clearly indicated by the lines at the close of the *schola*:

> Those general divinations derived either from the stars or from
> natural causes, in which category are those which are accepted

as aids in navigation, agriculture, and medicine, seem to me the least objectionable (*vanas*): as to the rest, those to which is ascribed any kind of power (*iuris*), whether over matters of chance or of human actions, I regard, as would anyone of noble and liberal education, especially if he be a Christian, as utterly unworthy.

Granted the acceptance of the geocentric Aristotelian cosmos with the associated concentric spheres apparently demanded by astronomers and theologians it is difficult to see anything unscientific about astrology expressed in his terms. If, as a very little later men came to do, you deny the premises, then of course it is possible, but without logical fallacy not necessary, to deny the consequences. Arnoldus Massius, Doctor in Theology, presumably expressed the current attitude of the Church when he added that the *schola* was 'docta[e] et catholica[e] nec quicquam continet quodpias aures offendat'. Which was just as well, since Cheyne ended his days as canon and 'magnus poenitentiarius' of the cathedral of Tournai.

It was perhaps too late to mend the rent fabric of Christendom; yet if there had been others like Cheyne perhaps nearly a century of horror in France and later in Germany, comparable to Vietnam, might have been avoided. But in the city of David Hume it ill behoves one to confuse 'is' and 'ought'!

Only recently has it become respectable to consider the influence of magic on science. In France Marcelin Berthelot, one of the greatest chemists of all times, laid the basis of the new approach. But it was, I think, Alexandre Koyré who in his work on Paracelsus extended the study of this topic into the Renaissance. Of the influence of the *Corpus Hermeticum* on literature you are far better informed than I could be; but of a complementary aspect of this question it may be worth while to say a few words.

First I will remind you of a revealing *cri du cœur* that I have already hinted at. Though Copernicus's treatise is one of the most austerely mathematical of the great classics of science it contains a single famous passage, in which he claims support for the heliostatic system from the most unexpected sources, which here are not the Pythagoreans or Aristarchos of Samos but the *Electra* of Sophocles and Hermes Trismegistos. Where, he asks, could the Sun be more appropriately placed than at the centre where 'upon a royal throne he may rule his children the planets that circle round him?' This 'rule' was effected not by 'gravity', which Copernicus regarded in Aristotelian style as of the Earth earthy, but by the almost celestial radiation of power well known to Grosseteste and adapted by Paracelsus to his *Lichtmetaphysik* theory of stellar pathology. That this hermetic element in Copernicus's macrocosm took strange forms and metamorphoses for nearly a century, or more, of poetic imagery I shall illustrate by citing some famous lines that in this place and time will have a threefold function.

The first of these, which I hope you will not regard as ignoble, is the purely personal one of trusting to persuade you that, though illiterate in French and outstandingly so in respect of the French Renaissance, I am not insensitive to the beauty. Here are the lines:

Je la sens distiller goutte à goutte à mon cœur,
Pure, saincte, parfaite, angelique liqueur,
Qui m'eschaufe le sang d'une chaleur extreme.
Mon ame la reçoit avec un tel plaisir,
Que tout esvanouy, je n'ay pas le loisir
Ny de goutter mon bien, ny penser à moymesme.

The second function of this citation is to remind you of a similar but not identical 'picture' presented by that less sentimental writer, René Descartes. Although he spoke more than once in terms of high praise for William Harvey's demonstration of the purely mechanical action of the heart in relation to the circulation of the blood he pictured 'le sang' as falling 'goutte à goutte' into the left ventricle where 'elle s'enfle promptement et se dilate' owing to the innate heat of the heart, showing that he had but half understood what Harvey had demonstrated.[5] Harvey for his part was even more 'hermetic'—and in a sense nearer to Ronsard. The living blood is endowed with an innate power—'perfervid' he calls it—which it yields up to the tissues, thereafter by a purely mechanical process being returned to the heart there to be recharged with a 'saincte, parfaite angelique liqueur'. Well, not quite in so many words, but with 'balsam'—a purely hermetic term used by his early contemporaries such as Joseph Du Chesne (Quercetanus), the Paracelsian.

The third derivative of Ronsard's lovely lines is that for the history of science there is a lesson recognized—how clearly we can not tell—by Aristotle: that διότι (*propter quid*) must be drawn from the intuitional common stock, τί ὅτι from 'what we see'. And they must never be confused. In relation to the fundamental science of vertebrate physiology Harvey, as he made plain in a letter to the younger Jean Riolan, understood this; Descartes, whatever he may have achieved in the abstract science of motion, never did. That is why I maintain that the astonishing development of mathematics started by François Viète and his contemporaries, by itself and without the *genuine* Aristotelian insight of Harvey and others, would never have brought about what is rather regrettably called the 'Scientific Revolution' of the seventeenth century.[6]

NOTES

1 E.g., Charles de l'Ecluse (Clusius) and Mathias de l'Obel (Lobelius). See A. Arber, *Herbals—Their origin and evolution*, 2nd ed. (Cambridge 1953).
2 Cf. C. E. Kellett, 'Vesalius in Paris' in *Commemoration . . . de la mort de Vésale*, *Académie royale de médecine de Belgique* (1964) 91–119.
3 Cf. Edward Rosen, 'The Ramus-Rheticus Correspondance', *JHI* 1 (1940) 363–8.
4 For a fuller account see my original article, 'James Cheyne of Arnage', *Aberdeen University Review*, 30 (1954) 369–83, or a somewhat abridged version in *Mélanges Alexandre Koyré* (Paris 1964).
5 Cf. E. Gilson, *Etudes sur le rôle de la pensée médiévale dans la formation du système cartésien* (Paris 1930) 73f., and Descartes, *Discours de la méthode*, 5ième partie.
6 Cf. W. P. D. Wightman, 'Essay on myth and method in seventeenth-century biological thought', *J. Hist. Biol.* 2, 321–36.

GUY DEMERSON

Météorologie et Poésie Française de la Renaissance

EN 1539, AMERBACH EDITE à Strasbourg les *Météores* du Napolitain Pontano; à la même date, Johannes Velcurio fait paraître à Leipzig un manuel de physique dont la section météorologique semble bien avoir servi d'aide-mémoire à J.-A. de Baïf quand il composa ses *Météores* de 1567, réédités en 1573, puis démarqués par du Bartas et Isaac Habert; Pierre du Val, J. Peletier du Mans, Pontus de Tyard, Ronsard et bien d'autres poètes se sont inspirés de la science météorologique.[1] L'aspect *descriptif* de ces œuvres a été analysé avec pertinence par D. B. Wilson,[2] mais leur côté proprement *scientifique*, cette 'médiocrité savante' définie par Albert-Marie Schmidt,[3] semble leur dénier non seulement tout mérite poétique, mais aussi toute valeur cognitive sérieuse; un historien de Baïf exécute en ces termes les *Météores*: 'l'ignorance de Baïf en ces matières n'est point douteuse; celle de Pontano, son modèle, était aggravée de superstition';[4] on nous renvoie donc aux spécialistes du néo-latin pour expliquer l'inexplicable engouement des poètes et du public pour la météorologie.

Cette science avait sa spécificité;[5] section importante de la physique aristotélicienne, elle étudie les *météores* ou 'mixtes imparfaits', phénomènes dont le lieu de production est, selon l'étymologie, une région *élevée* de l'atmosphère, échappant à une observation proche:[6] météores humides et réels, comme les nuages, les pluies, la neige; phénomènes lumineux 'apparents' comme le halo, l'arc-en-ciel; météores ignés, comme l'étoile filante, l'éclair, la comète, la voie lactée, les feux follets; phénomènes aériens comme les vents et leurs effets, etc. D'après les *Tableaux* (1587) de Christophle de Savigny, la météorologie est du domaine des arts libéraux 'qui se peuvent attribuer à la philosophie'; spécialisée dans les *qualités* des corps composés et inanimés, elle est donc sœur de la métallographie et cousine à la fois de l'astronomie—qui traite des corps simples célestes—et de la biologie—qui étudie les corps composés animés.[7] Ce chapitre considérable des manuels de Philosophie Naturelle et de toutes les compilations encyclopédiques constituait un élément fort apprécié du programme de physique dans les facultés des arts et de philosophie; à Padoue, à Venise, à Paris, dans toute l'Europe, les professeurs publiaient volontiers leurs cours sous forme de commentaires sur les *Météorologiques* d'Aristote, que venaient parfois illustrer des leçons sur *l'Histoire Naturelle* de Pline ou de Sénèque; ainsi les travaux de Jacques Charpentier, professeur au Collège de France depuis 1561, ont pu inspirer à Baïf un sujet et une méthode au moment où il promettait au jeune Charles IX un poème scientifique.[8]

L'étude des causes de phénomènes lointains et anomaux, irréguliers, était privée à la fois d'instruments d'observation et d'un modèle mathématique comparable à celui de l'astronomie; sa méthode, spéculative, consistait donc à enchaîner des suites de raisonnements formels pour parvenir à une supputation des séries de causes. Pour Ronsard, *la cognoissance des méthéores* était le type même du divertissement philosophique, détourné de l'action.[9] Mais dans le grand public et à la cour, l'intérêt pour les météores n'avait pas ce caractère abstrait: 'les médecins experts, les sages laboureurs, les rusez pilotes, les prudents guerriers' savaient que la vie de provinces entières dépendait des grêles, des frimas ou des orages, tandis que les météores 'extraordinaires', étoiles barbues ou tombantes, 'sont ceux desquelz Dieu se sert pour resveiller la stupidité du monde' selon les termes de Simon Goulart.[10] Imprévisible, inquiétant, le météore est un *monstre*; les singularités des 'impressions' lumineuses, des pluies prodigieuses, étaient consignées en de multiples feuilles volantes. Dans l'entourage de la Florentine Catherine de Médicis, à qui Baïf dédie ses *Météores*, on était sensible au retentissement dans l'opinion publique des *flammes apparaissantes* qui accompagnaient avec prédilection les déplacements ou la mort des princes: étoiles mobiles, colonnes ardentes, feux aériens qui clignotaient jusque sur les vêtements du souverain[11]...

De nos jours, on reconnaît volontiers le caractère 'poétique' de ces sentiments naïfs d'*admiration*, source de surprises fécondes en évocations émues, voire d'élans d'une religiosité méditative, où nous discernons encore le plus haut lyrisme;[12] on s'accorde par contre à estimer que la déduction syllogistique, la réflexion rationnelle sur les causes, la classification formelle, qui caractérisent justement l'ancienne science météorologique, ne peuvent qu'être fatales à l'œuvre versifiée où elles ont pu venir s'insérer; pour l'esprit moderne, la démarche scientifique, qui est découverte méthodique et impersonnelle des lois naturelles, ne saurait, sans profanation réciproque, s'allier à l'allure poétique, exploration fantaisiste ou fantastique de domaines que jamais l'on ne verra deux fois. Le problème qui se pose[13] est de savoir si cette séparation méthodologique, par laquelle nous confinons l'irrationnel en des sortes de réserves, de zones pour pensée sauvage, ne nous gêne pas pour interpréter correctement l'effort spirituel de la poésie scientifique à la Renaissance. C'est la poésie météorologique, qui, de par la nature même de son objet lointain mais étonnant, se trouve présenter *conjointement* les deux aspects les plus nets et, apparemment, les plus contradictoires[14] de la poésie scientifique:

1. la recherche des causes expliquant, en une théorie *unique*, ces apparences émouvantes;

2. l'évocation (visionnaire ou simplement descriptive) des faits de la nature, infiniment *variée*;

> Deux langages différents: celui du poète est nécessairement ambigu, plurivoque, surdéterminé . . . parce que l'homme tout entier, avec tous ses pouvoirs et en premier lieu par le moyen de ses sensations, essaye d'épouser le plein des choses—tandis que le langage du savant tend à l'univocité et à la saisie d'une vérité qui sera susceptible de démonstration logique ou mathématique[15].

Cette distinction est un héritage de Descartes, qui a donné pour tâche, précisément à ses *Météores* (1637) d''exorciser l'esprit humain' du sentiment le plus pernicieux qui soit: 'l'étonnement, toujours mauvais et nuisible à la science en (...) ce qu'il *immobilise* l'esprit en un ébahissement stupide devant un fait réputé merveilleux';[16] tandis que la première page du traité affirme qu''il est possible de trouver des causes de tout ce qu'il y a de plus admirable sur la terre', la dernière page proclame: 'on ne verra rien dans les nues à l'avenir qui donne sujet d'*admiration*'. La découverte des causes a la vertu salubre de stériliser l'admiration; la littérature scientifique serait-elle incompatible avec ce sentiment qui est essentiel au lyrisme?

Précisément, ceux de nos écrivains qui font des météores le sujet principal d'un poème, exposent systématiquement le mécanisme de leur formation en vue d''*asseurer* les humains, les guarissant du mal d'Ignorance', selon l'expression de Ronsard: pour lui, la poésie météorologique collabore avec la Philosophie, qui sait 'comme se faict la gresle, comme se faict la neige & la nièle, les tourbillons', les vents, les séismes,

> Et d'où se font en l'air ces longs images
> Qui nous troubloient d'époventementz vains.[17]

Soixante-dix ans avant Descartes, Baïf faisait de ses *Météores* un agent civilisateur destiné à débarrasser de ses étonnements stupides une mentalité que nous qualifierions de primitive:

> Si quelque chose advient, tant petite soit-elle,
> Outre l'acoustumé, pource qu'elle est nouvelle,
> Des homes estonez sotement curieux,

Elle vient empescher les pensers & les yeux (. . .)
Mais le sage & sçavant, qui ne se paist de bourdes,
Qui au caquet du peuple a les oreilles sourdes,
Ces foles peurs ne sent. Heureux l'home qui sçait
Les segrets de Nature, & coment tout se fait! (. . .)
Il ne s'étone pas de voir luire un Comète
Dedans le Ciel, sçachant que toute chose est fète
Par un ordre certain, & cherchant la raison
Trouvera que ce n'est rien qu'une exalaison (v. 625-680)[18]

Mais, ce que Baïf condamne ici, n'est que la *sotte* curiosité: pour
l'esprit humain, l'apparition des météores a un avantage sur le retour
régulier des astres; cette irrégularité même en effet réveille la faculté
d'admiration émoussée par l'habitude: 'L'acoustumance éteint des
choses la grandeur' (v. 624). Jacques Peletier développait une telle
idée, toute opposée à la position qui sera celle de Descartes, dans le
Premiere Proème de son *Algèbre* (1554): 'La variété des objets met en
mouvement les vertus de l'âme de degré en degré jusqu'à l'ébahissement'.[19]

Dans cette perspective, l'exposé théorique, rationnel, du système
aristotélicien apparaît comme une propédeutique à une connaissance
supérieure de l'univers; certes les poètes météorologiques apprécient
unanimement, et explicitement, le génie, divinatoire selon Giordano
Bruno,[20] des théories d'Aristote, qui fournissent, par l'induction,
ἐπαγωγή, une explication unique à des données multiformes[21]; mais
l'essentiel de leur projet littéraire n'est pas de donner un résumé
versifié de l'hypothèse des deux exhalaisons ou de celle des qualités
essentielles des quatre éléments: c'est ainsi que les exposés didac-
tiques énoncés par du Bartas dans le *Second Iour* de la *I. Sepmaine*
(1578) et par Joseph du Chesne dans le *Grand Miroir du Monde*
requerront tous deux un commentaire de Simon Goulart, consti-
tuant un cours plus complet et plus clair de météorologie. Pour un
poète, l'*explication* intellectuelle ne se suffit pas, elle ne porte pas sa
fin en soi car elle se réfère à un *sens* qui l'ordonne;[22] on comprend
ainsi que la conception scientifique d'un système explicatif des
phénomènes atmosphériques manifeste l'originalité de la pensée et
de la spiritualité de chaque poète; c'est à propos de la météorologie
que l'on discerne combien relative était la soumission des esprits à
la tradition ancienne: sans aller jusqu'à l'originalité du sieur de La
Violette, qui fera intervenir dans la formation des météores non plus
la mixture des quatre éléments, mais la transmutation des trois
principes élémentaires: soufre, sel et mercure,[23] beaucoup d'écrivains
se refusent, pour des raisons de logique ou de dogme religieux, à

ranger, comme Aristote, les comètes et la voie lactée parmi les météores, objets sublunaires.[24] Le poète qui accueille la tradition scientifique ne la considère pas comme une révélation immuable; l'effort créateur de sa pensée est concurrent et comme contemporain de l'effort investigateur du savant.[25] Comme l'écrit G. Lanson, 'chaque science appartient à la littérature précisément par ce qui reste d'incertain et d'inconnu . . . La poésie de la science doit être cherchée . . . dans l'agitation de l'âme consolée ou blessée par la connaissance'.[26] La contemplation des enchaînements de causalité procure donc des joies spirituelles dont la littérature révèle le caractère poétique, même dans la démarche scientifique.[27]

Certes, ce n'est plus par leurs exposés déductifs, mais par leurs descriptions brillantes, voire hallucinantes, que les poètes météorologiques nous enchantent aujourd'hui; déjà ils aimaient guider et encourager l'attention du lecteur en plaçant, au premier plan de leurs évocations du ciel nuageux ou obscur, des observateurs semblables à ces silhouettes dont les cartographes ornaient leurs plans perspectifs: berger revenant de la verte prairie, soldat en faction, voyageur égaré, amoureux insomniaque.[28] Comme l'a montré D. B. Wilson, la description des météores a donné matière, par exemple chez Peletier, à d'intéressantes recherches rythmiques et phoniques destinées à reproduire par le moyen du langage[29] l'étrangeté fascinante ou obsédante de ces jeux de l'eau avec la terre, de l'air avec le feu et surtout des métamorphoses perpétuelles des quatre éléments.[30] Mais l'*évocation* des phénomènes n'est pas seulement inventaire et description; la présentation la plus pittoresque dénote déjà une volonté d'explication: ainsi les comparaisons ne sont pas des ornements plus ou moins brillants, risquant de détourner l'attention de l'observateur sur un 'signifiant' étranger au météore 'signifié'; comme l'écrit Peletier, 'le dû à la comparaison est . . . d'*éclaircir*, exprimer et représenter les choses comme si on les santoit';[31] l'image a déjà une fonction cognitive: faire comprendre un processus de formation non seulement par une analogie pédagogique, mais par une analogie de structure; sa pertinence repose sur la conviction que des correspondances réelles se retrouvent dans le mécanisme de formation et dans le déroulement des phénomènes en diverses parties de la nature; on pense même que le corps humain a ses météores, aqueux, ignés, venteux.[32] Quand Baïf, suivi par du Bartas, Habert, du Monin, du Chesne, compare le brasillement des étoiles bondissantes au pétillement des flammes éparses parmi les pailles d'un chaume,[33] il révèle clairement que, dans les deux cas, la nature du combustible conditionne l'apparence prise par la flamme: ici, l'exhalaison ignée,

'Sèche, épanduë & rare, & qui n'est continuë' determine la forme du météore. Cette méthode du schéma analogique, qui explique la cause inaccessible par le processus familier, remonte à Aristote: chez Baïf (*Météores*, v. 444), la comparaison du jaillissement de la foudre avec l'expulsion d'un noyau de cerise pressé entre les doigts paraît du dernier ridicule à certains critiques,[34] ou d'un réalisme original à A.-M. Schmidt,[35] alors qu'elle est prise dans Aristote,[36] ou plus exactement au *Commentaire* de saint Thomas, à qui Baïf doit la précision: *nux cerasii* (*Comment. in Meteorolog. I*, VI); ici, l'analogie descriptive est une méthode d'analyse du mouvement oblique d'un projectile soumis à une composition de forces. La doctrine de Jacques Toussain, le professeur de Baïf, pour qui les comparaisons des poètes antiques éclairent la compréhension savante du monde physique,[37] laisse présager l'expression de Claudel: 'la beauté elle-même n'est qu'un moyen de recherche.'[38] L'anthropomorphisme des images supposait, déjà chez Aristote,[39] l'identité des phénomènes soumis à la finalité avec un acte raisonnable: l'image suggère qu'une *cause finale* simple a ordonné la marche de la nature.

Cette notion de l'unité organique de la nature qui sous-tend les images a une valeur explicative, et non décorative; c'est pourquoi tous les poèmes météorologiques français comportent un rejet explicite de recours aux fables mythologiques: à l'époque de la plus grande vogue des légendes classiques, la poésie météorologique, à la différence de l'inspiration astronomique,[40] se défie du style ornemental; Guy Amerbach, le commentateur des *Météores* latins de Pontano, en recommandait encore la facture mythologique;[41] par ailleurs, on répète traditionnellement que Baïf est tributaire de Pontano sous prétexte qu'il résume le fameux mythe de la Giganto-machie par lequel le Napolitain donnait une explication fabuleuse de la voie lactée; or il suffit de prendre la peine de lire Baïf pour se rendre compte que le but de l'auteur français est bel et bien de con-damner ce genre d'explication fabuleuse, en le rangeant parmi les *vieils contes*, les théories hâtives du *vieil tems*, les raisons mal fondées du *vieil age* (*Météores*, v. 845, 925, 953). A la suite d'Aristote, de saint Thomas (*De Anima* I, VIII), Baïf, qui se proclame pourtant érudit en légendes antiques (*Météores*, v. 876), se méfie d'un style plus orne-mental qu'analytique lorsqu'il s'agit de la Philosophie, qui

Ayme trop mieux estre bien démonstrée
Qu'estre sans plus d'un beau langage aornée.

Les *Dialogues* de Guy de Bruès (1557) lui prêtent cette sentence.[42] La poésie météorologique poursuit l'effort de la philosophie grecque, qui tendait à arracher le concept du monde à la sphère de la pensée mythique;[43] le poète, fidèle à la règle d'or de la physique aristotélicienne, doit 'sauver les phénomènes', c'est-à-dire qu'il revient sans cesse à l'image même des météores, mais à une image enrichie, épurée, sublimée par l'aspect intellectuel que l'explication confère sans cesse à la vision.

Mais, au-delà de la suggestion sensible donnée par les descriptions, l'évocation du monde des météores vise à un type de perception plus ambitieux: la vision directe des causes, non pas intuition surréelle, mais, au contraire, plongée au cœur de la réalité; volontiers le poète, quand son esprit s'est échauffé par la prière et l'étude, entreprend un voyage cosmique où, derrière le pittoresque des apparences, il perçoit les sources de l'être et du déploiement des causes: si Jacques Peletier est monté 'par voées inconnues (. . .) dessus la région des Nues', s'il traverse 'le milieu froédureus', par delà 'pluyes & tourbilhons', c'est d'abord pour s'apercevoir qu'il apprend, en une révélation proprement poétique,

commant sont causées
Les tandres & basses Rosées,
Puis les Brouées & Frimaz,
La Pluye, la Nège, la Grêle
E l'Etoèle aus crins portanteus
E Foudres eyans davant eus
L'Ecler qui les Nues démêle.[44]

Cette ambition d'une perception plus directe, parce que plus pure, des causes est une tendance typique de la science ancienne, impatiente des longueurs d'une théorie discursive,[45] διάνοια θεωρητική, qui, selon, les aristotéliciens, est la condition du progrès. Pour la météorologie, vouée à une approche spéculative, *per speculum*, des causes physiques, l'esprit poétique pouvait apparaître comme un instrument, un *speculum* précieux grâce à la finesse, à la sensibilité de ses intuitions,[46] surtout si l'on voit dans les lois naturelles l'expression d'une intelligence ordonnatrice, à la façon des platoniciens qui se refusaient à considérer l'ordre du monde comme un compromis fortuit, empiriquement établi entre des forces aveugles.[47] Il est significatif que les poèmes consacrés aux météores commencent presque tous par énoncer le mythe du Chaos débrouillé par l'Esprit: la production des météores est une conséquence de l'harmonie imposée aux éléments;[48] la hantise de la poésie météorologique est celle de l'ordre, ordre caché derrière les bizarreries et les anomalies de la nature, mais aussi ordre de l'esprit dominant la matière: dans le *Microcosme* (1562), Scève évoque la fragilité du premier couple humain chassé de l'Eden et affronté aux météores dangereux et incompréhensibles, exhalaisons mêlant l'humide et le froid, épouvantables fulgurations, pluies monstrueuses; mais

l'humanité humiliée se redresse après l'épreuve due au courroux
du Juge céleste et à ses Esprits souffleurs; le génie inventif de
l'homme trouvera des protections contre les dangers météorologiques.[49]

Ainsi, avant Descartes, on n'opposait pas la connaissance des causes
à l'admiration, bien au contraire; chez du Bartas, comme chez
Habert, comme chez Baïf, l'exposé même des causes est plus impres-
sionnant que ne serait la *peinture* du gouffre de feu ou du serpent
d'étoiles; la mention des vapeurs qui se roulent et s'embrassent dans
les espaces infinis, se cherchent ou se combattent, fait participer
l'intelligence à d'immenses mutations au sein de l'atmosphère;
vision et compréhension se complètent pour délivrer l'esprit de ses
craintes:
> [Quand] tu *verras* là-haut une flamme courante (...)
> Ecoute les *raisons* pour ne t'en estoner,
écrit Baïf, montrant le passage d'une admiration sensible à une
compréhension intellectuelle pleine de sérénité (*Météores*, v.469–
472). S'il n'y a pas d'antinomie entre poésie descriptive et poésie
explicative, c'est que l'étude de l'univers mouvant des météores
trouvait obligatoirement son aboutissement dans une vision de
l'harmonie cosmique enfin décelée. L'*ébahissement* de la sensibilité
devant des spectacles extraordinaires conduit à l'*émerveillement* de
l'âme devant l'œuvre du Créateur, en passant par la *curiosité* devant
les causes secrètes des transmutations atmosphériques. En 1557,
Couillard du Pavillon écrit que l'intelligence de l'ordre primordial
institué par l'Esprit entre les quatre éléments et la 'spéculation du
ciel' retrouvent la trace de la splendeur créatrice dans la vision des
météores, qui 'font frémir les créatures raisonnables et hurler les
irraisonnables',[50] et Peletier écrira:
> Sciance adrece l'homme à connoêtre les fez
> De la Divinité, par causes e efez (*Louanges*, 1581, f. 52)
Les poèmes météorologiques introduisent à la glorification de l'ordre
providentiel: J. du Bellay résume en un sonnet la portée de l'œuvre
de Pierre du Val, évêque de Sées, *De la grandeur de Dieu, et de la
Cognoissance qu'on peut avoir de luy par ses Œuvres* (1553):
> le Feu, l'Air & la Terre, & l'Onde
> Liez ensemble en accords discordans (...)
> De toutes parts racontent aux humains
> Du grand Ouvrier les œuvres nompareilles.[51]
Du Val avait montré que les pluies, les exhalaisons, font percevoir
> Du Seigneur Dieu la haute providence
et permettent de remonter à la Cause initiale, 'de tous les moteurs

l'extrême et le dernier'.[52] Les traités de météorologie ajoutent volontiers aux causes matérielles et formelles des phénomènes une étude
sur leurs causes finales; selon la *Meteorologia* de Wolfgang Meurer
(1513–85), la production des météores a quatre causes finales,
toutes tournées vers le bien de l'homme: purifier l'air, orner le
monde en en combattant la monotonie, annoncer les événements
futurs, proclamer la majesté de Dieu; l'arc-en-ciel, la voie lactée,
phénomène aussi intermittent que la comète, les signes de pluie sont
paroles divines;[53] le processus naturel est porteur d'un signe adressé
à l'homme par la Providence; la météoromancie tentait de déchiffrer
ce code divin,[54] et Tyard souligne le rôle révélateur de l'harmonie
universelle conféré par Dieu aux météores: l'arc-en-ciel 'est adjousté
depuis le déluge aux météores par ouvrage divin, pour signe du
traicté de paix faict entre Dieu & les hommes, en cest article qu'il
n'adviendroit plus de déluge'.[55] Pour Tyard, la région élémentaire
des météores est habitée de diverses 'espèces intellectuelles', 'anges
exécutants entre Dieu et les hommes un continuel office' (*Premier
Curieux*, 1578, f. 82 v;). En 1560, Ronsard regrette que la France
n'ait pas prêté une attention suffisante aux pluies prophétiques, à la
comète, à une colonne ardente;[56] pour lui, ce sont des esprits élémentaires, des démons qui, secourables, clignotent dans le feu Saint-
Elme, ou, maléfiques, brûlent sous forme de feux follets, provoquent
séismes, orages, parhélies et pluies monstrueuses;[57] tandis qu'en
1553 il concevait les formes prêtées aux mystérieux nuages comme un
pur jeu de l'imagination poétique,[58] en 1555 il explique la distorsion
du corps aérien des démons par une assimilation aux métamorphoses
de ces mêmes météores;[59] la poésie météorologique ne peut décrire
l'univers sans lui supposer un sens:[60] les *Météores* de Stanhuf (1551)
démontraient que ce n'est pas la fantaisie créatrice des hommes mais
la volonté de Dieu qui confère aux nuées leurs formes lourdement
significatives.[61]

Pour la grande poésie, l'admiration est une préparation à l'adora-
tion; de même que la vision surnaturelle est un substitut de l'expérience physique, de même l'explication logique s'efface devant l'intelligence de l'œuvre divine.[62] Dans le domaine fluent, imprévisible, inquiétant des phénomènes météorologiques, la poésie scientifique
démontre que les mots, à la Renaissance, ne sont pas simplement
emblèmes et signatures marquant les choses, comme le voudrait
M. Foucault:[63] la langue rythmée est un outil précieux pour aider
la déduction logique à inférer un ordre, mais un ordre intérieur,
toujours anxieux de donner un nom au principe de son organisation.[64] Ainsi donc, en ce domaine, chaque poète trouve son originalité non seulement par la puissance évocatrice de ses images, mais

encore par son interprétation personnelle du principe explicatif généralement enseigné en physique, et surtout par la conception d'un *univers* où les météores tiennent un rôle important; c'est dans la tâche de créer un univers que science et poésie se rencontrent; pour l'esprit scientifique, les phénomènes, notamment les météores, ne peuvent être pris en considération que dans la mesure où ils sont perçus dans un système, c'est-à-dire s'ils ont leur place dans un univers en voie d'organisation; pour le poète, d'après les analyses de P. Valéry, l'origine et le but de l'art est 'cette sensation d'univers qui est caractéristique de la poésie, . . . une tendance à percevoir un *monde*, ou système complet de rapports' . . . .[65] Le mathématicien Edouard Le Roy a donné la formule de cette liaison, courante dans la pensée des hommes de la Renaissance, entre la vision du poète et l'explication du savant: 'Lorsque l'artiste exerce librement sa fonction créatrice, n'imaginons pas qu'il s'abandonne à un jeu de fantaisie toute subjective; il *réalise* des virtualités latentes au sein du donné, il fait passer à l'acte des puissances réelles de perception. Il contribue ainsi à nous dévoiler l'implicite richesse de la nature'.[66]

NOTES

1 Voir Henri Chamard, *Histoire de la Pléiade* (Paris 1940) t. III, 164–5; Fr. de Dainville, *La Géographie des humanistes* (Paris 1940); A.-M. Schmidt, *La Poésie scientifique en France au 16ᵉs.* (Paris 1938) (nos références sont empruntées à la réédition des Ed. Rencontre, Lausanne, 1970); Henri Weber, *La Création poétique au 16ᵉs. en France* (Paris 1956) 124–37 et 503–58; Dudley B. Wilson, *Descriptive Poetry in France from Blason to Baroque* (Manchester 1967) et l'introduction au *Premier Livre des Poèmes* de Jean-Antoine de Baïf (Grenoble 1975).

2 *Descriptive Poetry*, 103–22.

3 *Poésie scientifique*, 217.

4 Mathieu Augé-Chiquet, *La Vie, les idées et l'œuvre de J.-A. de Baïf* (Paris 1909) 243.

5 On la confond parfois avec l'astronomie ancienne; Chamard (op. cit., III, 164) pense que les *Météores* de Baïf sont une transposition versifiée de l'*Univers* de Tyard, alors que les deux œuvres n'ont aucun rapport dans l'intention, le ton, la méthode.

6 Sur l'importance et les formes des études météorologiques au 16ᵉs., voir S. K. Heninger, *A Handbook of Renaissance Meteorology, with particular reference to Elizabethan and Jacobean Literature* (Durham 1960).

7 *Tableaux accomplis de tous les arts libéraux* (Paris 1587) signat. A,R et AA.

8 Sur les contacts de Baïf et de Charpentier, voir notamment A. Lefranc, 'La Pléiade au Collège de France en 1567' in *Grands Ecrivains français de la Rennaissance* (Paris 1914) 387–411.

9 Edition Laumonier, STFM XVIII, 457; cf XII, 71 et XV, 25 et I. Silver, *The intellectual evolution of Ronsard*, t. II: *Ronsard's general theory of poetry* (St Louis 1973) 384–6.

10 S. Goulart, annotation à l'édition de 1593 du *Grand Miroir du monde* de Joseph du Chesne, sieur de La Violette, p. 527.

11 Un rayon de feu apparaissait à la Reine quand devait mourir un de ses enfants (Hilarion de Coste, *Eloges*, I, 581), tandis que la colonne étoilée présageait un grand renom (Dorat, éd. Marty-Laveaux, 20); en 1562, un météore figurant une armée en bataille donna à réfléchir (Fr. de Belleforest, *Discours des présages . . . advenuz en la personne du Roy*); en 1565 une étoile diurne parut plus favorable (Brantôme, éd. Lalanne, v, 272); en 1566 une étoile accompagna le roi pendant une procession (De Ruble, *Journal de François Grin* (1894) 34).

12 Cf. les remarques de P. Claudel et de J. Cocteau, cités par G. Demerson, *La Mythologie classique dans l'œuvre lyrique de la 'Pléiade'* (Genève 1972) 10 et 11.

13 Nous n'étudierons pas l'emploi décoratif de la météorologie, qui prouve l'intérêt que suscitait cette science en concurrence avec la mythologie: Dante comparait déjà l'ascension ou la retombée de l'esprit humain à l'exhalaison du feu terrestre vers la lune et à la chute fulgurante du feu issu des nuages (*Paradiso*, chant I, début); de façon plus mièvre, Amadis Jamyn (voir E. Frémy, *Académie des derniers Valois* (1887) 211 n. 1) ou Joachim Blanchon verra son *ardeur* 'figurée' par des lances, des chevrons et autres brandons étincelants, de formes toujours variables, 'comme alors que l'on void les vapeurs s'exhaller' (Blanchon, *Premières Œuvres* (1583) 37).

14 Dans la méthode scientifique, Jacques Grévin demande que l'on distingue la 'raison philosophique', 'explication sommaire de l'essence & nature' des phénomènes, et la 'connoissance historialle . . . submise au jugement des sens', qui considère les différentes espèces et la diversité des choses (*Deux Livres des Venins* (Anvers 1568) 3–5); cf. Wilson, *Descriptive Poetry*, 104 et 134–5.

15 Marcel Raymond, *Vérité et poésie* (Neuchâtel 1964) 272.

16 Début des *Météores, Œuvres*, éd. Ch. Adam (1910) XII, 198.

17 Cf. Sénèque, *Naturales quaestiones*. I, 1, fin.

18 Idée et expression reprises par I. Habert en 1585, *Trois Livres des Météores* (Paris, Jean Richer, privilège de 1584) f. 10 v et 14 v.

19 Cf. D. B. Wilson, 'The Discovery of Nature in the Work of J. P. du Mans' *BHR* XV (1954) 298 et 301. Selon Nicolas de Cues, 'Admiracio stimulus videtur esse omnium quamcumque rem scire querentium' (paroles de l'Orator au début du *De Mente*). Fr. Titelmans achève le livre consacré à la météorologie dans le *De Consideratione* (1530) par un 'Psaume d'admiration au Seigneur admirable'.

20 *Opere Italiane*, éd. Gentile (Bari 1925) I, 119. C'est précisément le génie inventif du système des *Météorologiques* qui explique que cette science n'ait fait aucun véritable progrès avant le XVIIIe s.

21 Voir Hans Strohm, *Untersuchungen zu der Entwickelungsgesch. der Aristotelischen Meteorologie* (Leipzig 1935) 42; Augustin Mansion, *Introduction à la physique aristotélicienne*, 2e éd. (Louvain-Paris 1945) 217–22.

22 C'est ce que veut dire Peletier quand il écrit dans son *Art poétique* éd. Boulanger (1555) 82–3: 'les fez de la Nature se peuvent aussi treter en Poësie'; en effet, ce précepte est immédiatement suivi par l'exemple de l'épicurisme qui animait l'exposé scientifique de Lucrèce et par la mention des emprunts géniaux que lui fit Virgile.

23 *Le Grand Miroir* (1587) L.V.
24 Cf. les excuses adressées à Aristote par Baïf, qui n'accepte pas sa
   théorie (*Météores*, vv. 1001–1016 et les remarques de l'édition citée
   ci-dessus note 1) J. P. de Mesmes, *Institutions astronomiques* (Paris
   1557) 1, 6, *De la Voye laictée ou fumeuse*, Pontus de Tyard, *Deux
   Discours de la nature du monde*, f. 54 v, et W. P. D. Wightman, *Science
   and the Renaissance* (Edimbourg 1962) 122–3,
25 Cf. H. Strohm, *Untersuchungen zu der . . . Meteorologie*, 25; Wilson,
   Descriptive Poetry, 136.
26 'La littérature et la science' *Revue Bleue* 50 (1-10-1892) 437; cf. Cl.
   Bernard, *Introduction à l'étude de la médecine expérimentale* 11, 4: 'Pour les
   arts et les lettres . . . il s'agit . . . d'une création spontanée de l'esprit,
   et cela n'a plus rien de commun avec la constatation des phénomènes
   naturels, dans lesquels notre esprit ne doit rien créer.'
27 Cf. Aristote, *Parties des animaux* 1, 5, 644 b 22: 'Même dans le cas
   d'êtres à l'apparence moins spectaculaire, la nature qui les créa
   accorde des joies indescriptibles à ceux qui parviennent, par une
   contemplation scientifique approfondie, à en discerner les causes, s'ils
   sont d'authentiques chercheurs' et l'allégresse d'Isaac Habert parven-
   ant à une certaine possession de ce monde par l'analyse intellectuelle:
   'les causes ne nous sont de leur estre cachées' (*Météores*, f. 20, *des
   Verges*).
28 Baïf, *Météores*, vv. 330, 243, 348, 353, 461–472, etc.; I. Habert;
   Météores, f. 7–8, 10 v, 16 v, etc.
29 C'est d'ailleurs à propos de la description de météores que se pose le
   problème de l'emploi de mots savants: Baïf et tous les poètes de la
   Pléiade s'éjouissent d'accumuler les savoureux termes populaires (cf.
   Ronsard, *Art poétique*, Laum. XIV, 10–11, 15, 33) et mettent leur point
   d'honneur à rendre des mots comme *antiperistasis* ou *anathymiasis* par
   des périphrases de bonne compagnie, alors que du Bartas pense
   qu'il 'n'y a point danger / De naturaliser quelque mot estranger'
   (*Sepmaine* 1, 2ᵈ jour, vv. 439–40), comme 'antipéristase'; cf. A. E.
   Creore in *BHR* (1959) 131–60; Isaac Habert (*Météores*, f. 27 v) et du
   Chesne (*Grand Miroir*, 191) appliqueront cette maxime.
30 Pour Baïf, voir par exemple les vv. 193–5: 'les tourbillons roüans les
   pierres & la poudre/Font le gast par les chams; souvent l'horrible
   foudre/Rompt la nuë orageuse' . . . Les métamorphoses des vapeurs
   nuageuses sont un thème qui se prête à des effets pittoresques; voir
   p. ex. Ronsard, *Le Nuage* (Laum. v, 47: 'Je vois tout le ciel qui se
   fend . . . Et le chaös qui les menace'), et J. du Chesne, *Grand Miroir*,
   L.v: les 'Nues . . . vont représentant or' quelques gens armés . . . Or'
   des noires Forests, ores quelques Moresques, Des Païsages beaux, des
   plaisantes Crotesques . . . sans que sur ce tableau Nul Peintre ait
   employé ni crayon, ni pinceau, Encores qu'elles soyent par fois toutes
   pourprées, Et de jaune & de rouge & de vert peinturées' . . .
31 *Art poétique*, éd. Boulanger; Wilson, *Descriptive Poetry*, 111.
32 Wolfgang Meurer, *Meteorologia quaestionibus informata* (1587, posthume)
   16.
33 Baïf, vv. 377–92; du Bartas, v. 623 de la 2de journée de la Iᵉʳᵉ
   Sepmaine; du Chesne, *Grand Miroir*, 184; du Monin, *Uranologie*, f. 6v;
   l'origine de cette image est sans doute saint Thomas, *Comm. in
   Meteor.* 1, 6, d'après Aristote, *Météor.* 1, 4, 341 b 25.

34 Augé-Chiquet, *Baïf*, vv. 246–7; cette méthode critique, qui juge les images au nom du bon goût, se retrouve par exemple chez Johanna Lehmann, *Baïfs dichterische Vorstellung von Meer u. Wasser* (Greifswald 1917) 75–7.
35 *Poésie scientifique* 216–17.
36 Voir L. V. Simpson, 'Some unrecorded sources of Baïf's Livre des Météores' *P ML A* 47 (1932) 1012–27.
37 Voir Augé-Chiquet, *Baïf*, 24–9.
38 Lettre à Stanislas Fumet, citée dans S. Fumet, *Claudel* (Paris 1958) 235.
39 Cf. A. Mansion, *Introduction à la physique aristotélicienne*, 251–80.
40 Voir par exemple Ronsard, *Hymne du ciel, Hymne des astres* et Schmidt, *Poésie scientifique* 99–100; cf. Harcourt Brown, 'The Renaissance and historians of science' *Studies in the Renaissance* 7 (1960) 31.
41 Edition du *Liber de Meteoris* (Strasbourg 1539) 223: 'Id genus descriptionum . . . condiunt severitatem harum rerum, ac tedium lectionis levant' . . .
42 *Dialogue contre les nouveaux Académiciens* (1557) 129 (d'après Manilius, *Astr.* IV, 436–40).
43 Cf. Ernst Cassirer, *Individuum u. Kosmos in der Phil. der Renaiss.* (Darmstadt 1963) 131–2; les poètes, sauf I. Habert (*Météores*, f. 12 v: fable des filles d'Atlas; 38: explication rationnelle de Neptune Ebranle-terre), dédaignent les allégories 'physiques' des mythographes qui, de Boccace à N. Conti, en passant par Giraldi, voyaient, à la suite des Stoïciens, en Phaéton l'exhalaison ignée issue de Clymène (c'est-à-dire de l'eau) et d'Apollon-soleil, ou en Typhon un air souterrain comprimé, ou en Python les lourds anneaux de vapeur serpentant à terre comme pour défier le soleil.
44 De semblables voyages cosmiques sont évoqués p. ex. par du Bellay (*Hymne de la Surdité*, vv. 136–8: 'lorsque votre esprit' . . .), par Ronsard (*Hymnes*, Laum. VIII, 85–6; 150), J. P. de Mesmes, *Institutions* (1557) sign. a iij r, du Bartas, *2ᵈ Iour de la I. Sepmaine*, vv. 379–84, etc. On pensait que l'esprit débarrassé de la pesanteur corporelle soit par la *fureur* poétique, soit par la mort, soit par un rêve comateux, parvenait à une vision purifiée de la mécanique cosmique 'que les vapeurs d'en bas n'offusqu*ent* de leurs voilles'; voir par exemple Ronsard, *Hymne triumphal de Marguerite de Valois*, Laum. III, 54 et 74–5 (cf. VIII, 233), d'Aubigné, *Les Fers*, vv. 1195–244. Sur ces élévations intellectuelles, 'typical products of the pre-telescopic age', voir Beverly S. Ridgeley, 'The cosmic voyage in French Sixteenth-century Learned Poetry' *Studies in the Renaissance* 10 (1963) 136–62 et K. Reichenberger, *Untersuchungen zur liter. Stellung der Consolatio Philosophiae* (Cologne 1954) 12–13. Mathurin Régnier a raillé les 'philosophes resveurs' qui, sans bouger de terre, vont au firmament pour connaître les humeurs que le ciel déverse sur les humains (*Sat. 9*, vv. 143–60).
45 'La science primitive, du premier bond, voulait avoir la raison des choses' (Renan, *Avenir de la Science*).
46 Ainsi s'expliquent les prières initiales à Uranie (P. du Val, *Grandeur de Dieu*), à l'Esprit Saint (Baïf, liminaire des *Météores*, *A Caterine de Medicis*, vv. 37–44); Habert (*Météores*, f. 2) demande à Dieu de lui échauffer le cœur pour comprendre les 'corps imparfaits' qui sont constamment créés sous le ciel.

47 Cf. Mansion, *Introduction à la physique aristotélicienne* 38–92; pour Peletier, 'il n'y a chose ni petite ni grande qui ne donne à contampler les divers moyens e intencions de la Nature ... laquele est par tout si providante qu'il n'est an la puissance des hommes de connoêtre à quoe elle tand, jusques à ce que l'efet an soet venu' (*Art poétique*, éd. Boulanger, 169).

48 Par exemple Peletier, *L'Vranie*, l'*Er* (deuxième et troisième str.); Baïf, *Météores*, vv. 25–8, 43; du Bartas, *I. Sepmaine*, 2. Iour, vv. 259–388; Habert, *Météores*, f. 4; du Monin, *Uranologie*, f. 6v.

49 *Microcosme*, ch. I, vv. 409–58; cf. Schmidt, *Poésie scientifique*, 156 et suiv.

50 *Les Antiquitez & singularitez du monde* (1557) 29–54.

51 Ed. de 1586, f. 96; reproduit dans l'éd. Chamard de J. du Bellay, t. II, 282.

52 Ed. de 1586, f. 97 r, 94 r, 98 r. Le *Compendium* du Franciscain Titelmans (1530, 1535, 1545, 1556, 1562, etc.), dont le 6ᵉ livre était consacré à la météorologie, montrait que la considération de la Création prouvait Dieu avec plus de certitude que les démonstrations dialectiques. Cf. Copernic, *De Revolutionibus* (1543) L. I, Prologue, et P. Richeome, *Des Miracles* (premier des *Trois Discours pour la religion catholique* (1597) sur les météores).

53 *Meteorologia*, 25–6; cf. S. Goulart, commentaire du *Grand Miroir* de J. du Chesne, éd. de 1587, p. 525.

54 Voir Cornelius Agrippa, *De occulta Philosophia*, 57; Habert, *Météores*, f. 42 et 67.

55 *Premier Curieux*, éd. de 1578, 79–80.

56 Laum. XI, 24; X, 359; cf. V, 176 et 184; VII, 311; VIII, 63, 158–60; A.-M. Schmidt, *Poésie scientifique*, 122–3; Habert, *Météores*, f. 11–12; d'Aubigné, *Misères*, v. 1005 et suiv. (tempête dans les éléments à la mort du Cardinal de Lorraine).

57 Laum. VIII, 130–2.

58 Laum. V, 48; cf. XI, 163; XIII, 268–9.

59 Laum. VIII, 120.

60 Cf. Schmidt, *Poésie scientifique*, 211: un poème consacré entièrement aux météores confère une grande sérénité d'esprit, alors que des évocations dispersées traduisent l'angoisse; mais on peut remarquer que Ronsard lui-même donne un sens providentiel aux présages maléfiques; un mal défini est moins effrayant qu'une crainte vague.

61 *De Meteoris*, 1562, sign. P3 r–v, P5 r–v, Q5 v.

62 Cf. Wilson, *Descriptive Poetry*, 100, 116, 132–3; du Chesne va jusqu'à demander que, par la repentance l'homme se mette en accord individuellement avec cette harmonie cosmique (*Grand Miroir*, 195).

63 *Les Mots et les choses*, 40–59; cf. le compte-rendu de cet ouvrage donné par J.-C. Margolin in *BHR* 29 (1967) 701.

64 Cf. Rabelais, *Quart L.*, ch. 22: Epistémon domine les terreurs que peuvent causer les feux météorologiques parce qu'il sait les *nommer*.

65 Conférence du 2 décembre 1927, reproduite in *Conferencia* 22, 5-11-1928, p. 466.

66 *La pensée intuitive* (1929) t. I, 48; cf. G. S. Lee, 'La poésie de l'âge des machines' in *La Phalange*, 20 mars 1909: 'La poésie est la découverte de nouveaux rapports; la science est l'admission à contre-cœur de ces rapports; la religion est l'aveu du monde que les poètes ont raison.'

DUDLEY WILSON

The Quadrivium in the Scientific Poetry of Guy Lefèvre de la Boderie

THE MAIN PART OF this paper is devoted to the *Encyclie des secrets de l'éternité* (Antwerp, Plantin, 1571).

As the quadrivium is generally thought of as being a medieval term in the context of the seven liberal arts we will begin by looking at its definition among the medieval encyclopedists. We have chosen to do this in the *Didascalicon* of Hugh of St Victor (composed in Paris in the late 1120s), a work whose popularity is attested by the hundred or so manuscripts which have survived in European libraries. Furthermore, Jerome Taylor, in his introduction to a translation which he published in 1961 (Columbia U.P., p.4), suggests that

> the *Didascalicon* set forth a programme insisting on the indispensability of a whole complex of the traditional arts and on the need for their scientific pursuit in a particular order by all men as a means both of relieving the physical weaknesses of earthly life and of restoring that union with the divine wisdom for which man was made.

We may emphasize this last phrase for, as we shall see, it fits in extremely well with Lefèvre's own views. In addition the treatise itself ends with a few words drawn from a prayer from the Hermetic *Asclepius*.

> Rogemus igitur nunc Sapientiam, ut radiare dignetur in cordibus nostris et illuminare nobis in semitis suis, ut introducat nos 'ad puram et sine animalibus cenam'. (VI,13)

Every field of knowledge has its particular delights and in the innermost secret garden of the Renaissance the most prized and peculiar of flowers is that absurdly inextricable hybrid, the insoluble paradox. For the middle ages at least scientific poetry is just such a growth, especially in its association with the liberal arts. The *Didascalicon*'s attitude is clear and typical. Whereas the quadrivium is certainly the surest and most convenient access to wisdom:

> For these [seven] constitute the best instruments . . . by which the way is prepared for the mind's complete knowledge of philosophic truth. Therefore they are called . . . trivium and

quadrivium, because by them, as by certain ways [viae,] a
quick mind enters into the secret places of wisdom.

On the other hand, poetry itself is envisaged principally as a means
of obscuring wisdom.

There are 2 kinds of writings. The first comprises what are
properly called the arts; the second . . . appendages of the arts
[which are] only tangential to philosophy. Occasionally, it is
true, they touch in a scattered and confused fashion upon some
topics lifted out of the arts, or . . . prepare the way for philosophy. Of this sort are the songs of the poets . . . and the writings
of those fellows whom today we call 'philosophers' and who
are always taking some small matter and dragging it out
through long verbal detours, obscuring a simple meaning in
confused discourses. (III, 3–4, Taylor translation, 87–8)

This perhaps unnecessarily insulting advice to conference-goers is
echoed by an even greater authority; Plato at the beginning of the
Timaeus suggests that, being merely human, we can know nothing:
'Enough if we adduce probabilities as likely as any others, for we
must remember that we are only mortal men and we ought to accept
that tale which is probable and not enquire further.'

The concept of scientific poetry is then a difficult one. By the
1560s however one obvious difficulty is removed. By then, or so we
are told, poetry is no longer a matter of clever versification. Guy
Demerson, in his paper on meteorological poetry, has already hinted
that the secrets of the universe are able to be whispered to the poet
by daimonic messengers and in 1565, in his *Abbregé de l'art poëtique*
(Laum. ed. XIV,4), Ronsard was able to describe as *théologie allé-
gorique* a poetry which was by then firmly rooted in inspiration. Furthermore the esoteric aspects of science are very much established
and, although taken for granted, are actively prized. Indeed, in the
introduction to an anthology of *French Renaissance Scientific Poetry*
published by the Athlone Press in 1974 I have gone so far as to
define scientific poetry as follows:

The science of this age is an amalgam of science, philosophy and
magic and the scientific poet is best seen as the Magus who
interprets a personal vision of these aspects of the universe.
Certain it is that the borderline between science and magic, between interpretation and vision, is by no means clear at this
time—one may perhaps be tempted to suggest that it has become over-clarified in later ages.

Certainly Guy Lefèvre's obsession is not with science as we know it
but rather with the knowledge, the interpretation and even the
justification of God's ways. For, although we must agree with

Plato's suggestion that we are only mortal men, poets have continually sought a way out from their mortality and the temporality and sensuality which limit it, whether their escape be through ritual, drugs, prophecy, dreamings and visions, inspiration, madness, fastings or many another traditional means of putting to sleep and thereafter bypassing the faculty we would nowadays refer to as the 'rational' faculty, in order to transcend the purely sensual aspects of the sublunar universe which surrounds us.

Guy Lefèvre's attitude is made clear in a number of texts. In the dedication to Henri iii of the second edition of his *Hymnes ecclésiastiques* (Paris, R. Le Magnier, 1582) he states that the work is intended as a counterblast to the 'Pseaumes de David traduits en notre vulgaire . . .' for: 'je me suis avisé pour un remède et contrepoison de traduire les hymnes ecclésiastiques et autres cantiques spirituels composés par les saincts docteurs et anciens peres . . .' Several passages in the *Epistre dédicatoire* to the *Encyclie* proclaim a similar aim:

C'est d'un Livre ou Tableau, le plan & simulacre,
Dans lequel sont tracez les mysteres secrets
De l'alme Eternité, que comme chose sacre
Depouille des Hebrieus, des Latins, & des Grecs
A vostre Nom sacré je dedie, & consacre,
Et . . . Je vouë à Dieu, & vous, mes Muses, & moymesme.

(p. 23)

This last passage makes it clear that Guy would have agreed with his brother Nicolas who suggests in his *Introduction* to a translation of Giorgi, *De harmonia mundi* that the universe has progressed and is progressing through a number of stages. The first of these was the age of Jewish Law, the Law of Moses; the second was the Christian age; the third the age of the spirit; the fourth a combination of Hebrew and Greek; the fifth is to interpret the obscurity of Hebrew thought in the light of Roman clarity and will be called Latino-Jewish. The sixth, an amalgam of the second and third, is to be called spiritual-Christian, whereas the seventh is the ultimate age and is described by Nicolas Lefèvre as follows:

Reste la septieme & derniere qui renfermante en son contour les six rondeaux l'un dans l'autre encerclez de ses sœurs & compagnes, merite bien le tiltre & dignité de JERUSALEM nouvelle, attendu qu'en icelle les autres tousjours en eslargissant y viennent accomplir leur course & revolution, ainsi que l'Eglise tant Judaique, Gregeoise, Romaine que spirituelle, ou bien ainsi que les troys estats tant de foys mentionnez tendent au quatrieme qui est en la vision de paix. (fol. ẽ 4 verso)

This point is an important one and we shall return to it. However it is perhaps the moment to return to a more chronological exposition of the work of Lefèvre. Born in 1541, he attended Postel's lectures at the Collège Royal in Paris, and Postel's influence on him, which we shall leave aside completely, has been studied by François Secret in *L'Ésotérisme de Guy Lefèvre de la Boderie* (Geneva 1969). In 1568 he began with his brother Nicolas to collaborate in the Plantin polyglot Bible. The most important result of this collaboration was a translation into Latin of the New Testament from the Syriac and a *Grammatica Chaldaica et Dictionarium Syrio-Chaldaicum* which formed volumes 5 and 6 of the Bible published by Plantin in Antwerp in 1572. Perhaps the best idea of Guy Lefèvre's philosophic and scientific development and training is to be gained from a knowledge of these his oriental studies and the translations from the Latin he produced which included not only Francesco Giorgi, *L'Harmonie du monde, divisee en trois cantiques. Œuvre singulier et plein d'admirable erudition: Premierement composé en latin par François Georges Venitien, & depuis traduict & illustré Par Guy le Fevre de la Boderie Secretaire de Monseigneur Frere unique du Roy, & son Interprete aux langues estrangeres. Plus L'Heptaple de Jean Picus Comte de la Mirandole translaté par Nicolas Le Fevre de la Boderie* (Paris, Jean Macé, 1578), but also the following: Cicero, *De la nature des dieux* (1581); Pico della Mirandola, *Harangue de la dignité de l'homme* (1578) and two works by Ficino: *Traité de la religion chrétienne* (1578) and *Trois livres de la vie* (1581).

Of the two most important of Lefèvre's works, the *Encyclie des secrets de l'éternité* (1571) and the *Galliade, ou de la révolution des arts et des sciences* (Paris, Guillaume Chaudière, 1578; 1582), we shall only have time to deal in any detail with the first which is in many ways a preliminary composition and was indeed meant to have a formal continuation which seems to have been abandoned. In a sense of course, this seems to have been supplied by the *Galliade* which in many ways complemented and indeed superseded the *Encyclie*. In the 1571 edition, the *Encyclie* itself is followed by other shorter poems and we should draw the reader's attention in particular to the *Anagrammatismes*. In his *Introduction* to the Giorgi translation, Nicolas Lefèvre writes at great length on obscure writings and, together with such devices as allegory of various sorts and its more esoteric brother *Anagogie*, he mentions the use of the anagram. Despite the elevated terms of Lefèvre's approach to this genre we cannot help noting that obscurity may result, not in a philosophic and religio-scientific advance but in cleverness and simply in ingenious jingle-jangle. We may well be impressed by the 'fact', insisted upon by Nicolas Lefèvre (Giorgi translation fol. ï 5 recto) that, in

Hebrew, by process of *gematria* the word Serpent has the same value (359) as the word Satan or adversary. We are less impressed when we discover that, although Satan works admirably, being made up of Shîn (300), plus Têth (9), plus Nûn (50), Serpent becomes Nûn (50) + Hêth (8) + Shîn (300) and can presumably only be made to equal 359 by introducing an Aleph (1), and to do this is obviously absurd.

In fact Nicolas Lefèvre is displaying a perhaps understandable ignorance of a cabbalistic commonplace—Numbers xxi, 9 states 'And Moses made a serpent of brass and put it upon a pole, and it came to pass, that if a serpent had bitten any man, when he beheld the serpent of brass, he lived.' This encouraged Christian cabbalists to see the serpent as a prefiguration of Christ on the cross, for Messiah is made up of Mem (= 40) + Shîn (= 300) + Yod (= 10) + Hêth (= 8) which equals 358 which is the numerical value of Serpent.

Even so, the use of gematria associated as it is with the Cabbala is well-known and is in its way acceptable. We are much less likely to be impressed by the thought that, by rearranging the actual letters of the names Charles de Valois, Françoys de Valois, Henri de Valois we arrive at the interesting combinations 'Ce lis d'or a haulsé'; 'De façon suis royal' (not perhaps *too* flattering a reversal); 'Dieu le Harnois'; and that Pierre de Ronsard becomes 'se redorer Pindare'. The whole system can in fact be illustrated by a few lines from an *Ode en faveur de la 'Galliade'* written by Nicolas Lefèvre, brother of Guy, who chooses to sign himself *Le Scerafin vole*:

Le Fèvre en qui les Cieux tournez
Ont formé leur FIGURE ELUE,
Le Fèvre en qui des Arts bornez
L'ENCYCLIE s'est revolue,
Le Fèvre dont l'entendement
Tout encerclant encor embrasse
Des Sciences le fondement
En meint beau CERCLE qu'il nous trace
De sa GALLIADE ou retour,
Où nos Gaules voyent leur attour:
Le Fèvre en qui DAVID revit,
Revit FEU VERGILE & sa Fee,
Et la Lyre qui tout ravit
Revit en L'UN qui GUIDE ORFEE. (fol ẽ 2 recto)

This renaissance of such apparently rhétoriqueur poetic trickeries would seem in many cases to imply the caressing hand of the flatterer rather than the orphic incantations of the prophet.

To return to the quadrivium. Of the four branches of knowledge
or science which make it up (Arithmetic, Music, Geometry, Astronomy) only music is, strangely, neglected in the *Encyclie* and this
neglect is more than made up for in the *Galliade*. All four branches
of the quadrivium are mathematical sciences and 'consider abstract
quantity'. Boethius, noted in the *Didascalicon* (p. 63 of Taylor's
translation), makes the point rather heavily that it is through
mathematics that we may most properly study 'things intellectible'
that is, things which are 'by nature incorporeal and imperceptible to
any of the senses'. As to number itself (dealt with under Arithmetic):
'the power of number is this—that all things have been formed in its
likeness' (Did. p. 67). Or, to quote from Guy Lefèvre's translation
of Giorgi (p. 3):

> Car toutes choses sont disposees par nombres, & pourtant sont
> tellement domestiques & familieres à tous, que rien ne leur
> contrarie: parce qu'estans alliez avec les essences d'enhaut, ils
> montent familierement aux celestes: & derechef besognent
> privement avecques les sensibles, & de là vestent diverses
> natures, & diverses manieres.

The title itself, *Encyclie des secrets de l'éternité*, demonstrates the emphasis Lefèvre wishes to give to movement which, when it is round and
circular, again gives access to the divinity. The same element (which
of course is not an element but belongs to a super-elemental system)
re-appears in the title of the *Galliade* which, according to Lefèvre, is
derived as follows:

> J'emprunte l'etymologie, & deduction de Galliade du verbe
> Hebrieu Galal, qui signifie Reployer & retourner: & pour-
> tant j'ay divisé & distingué l'Œuvre entier en cinq Cercles, au
> reply desquels j'ay mis peine d'encercler brevement l'origine,
> progrez & perfection qu'ont acquis les bonnes lettres au cours
> des Siecles presque par tout le Rond de la Terre, & nommément
> en nostre Gaule. (*Advertissement*, fol. ï 4 recto).

In the first *Cercle* of the *Encyclie*, Lefèvre is mainly concerned with
following Plutarch in much the same way as Montaigne follows him
in the *Apologie de Raimond Sebond* (although of course his conclusions
are widely different), cataloguing anecdotes relating to the intelligence of animals with a view to demonstrating the glory of God and
man's position on the ladder of creation. At least one of the examples
he borrows is strikingly if curiously relevant to mathematics, for he
cites the example of the tunny fish:

> Que diray-je du Thin qui peut l'homme enseigner,
> Et du cours du Soleil les bornes assigner?
> Qui sent bien quand le jour à la nuit il égalle,

Et quand il est si bas que plus il ne devalle?
Car quand il est au point du Chevre-corne entré,
Le Thin demeure au lieu où il s'est rencontré
Sans en partir jamais, jusques à tant qu'il sente
Que dessous le Mouton soit du Soleil la sente.
Or les Thins ne sont pas seulement scrutateurs
Du bel ordre du Ciel, mais grans observateurs
Des Nombres composés, & de l'Arithmetique:
Par grands troupes ils vont d'une forme Cubique
A six costez egaus, dont est environné
De double front nageant leur scadron ordonné;
Si que facilement celui qui les épie
S'il sçait le premier rang, & qu'il le multiplie
Par luy mesmes, aura par le nombre produit
En soy multiplié, tout le conte reduit. (p. 38)

This simple lesson in arithmetic provides us with a neat summary of
the way in which even fish play their part in a mathematical universe
and demonstrate to man the ingenuity of Creation. The emphasis on
the square and the cube reminds us of course of Pythagorean mathematics and the lambda of the *Timaeus*, which concerns directly the
two progressions: 2, 4, 8 and 3, 9, 27.

The second *Cercle* in the *Encyclie* considers quite briefly man himself, his anatomy, reason, senses and soul. The third considers
temperaments, appetites and emotions, and ends with a proof of the
existence of God. The fourth *Cercle* is mainly devoted to human
society and its hierarchies. The fifth begins by defining Nature and
considers the relative places of Nature, God and man with some
details on that most popular of Renaissance gentlemanly diversions,
the art of grafting fruit trees. Its main concern, however, is with
astronomy and the circular movement which it involves. The sixth
circle, relatively brief but extremely diffuse, goes on from Nature,
considering her organization and using the twin images of the organ
and the hydraulic clock with automata, whereas the seventh presents
a series of images and quotations which neatly tie up and involve
one with another the various cultures. Beginning with the cave (or
grotte du monde) from Plato's *Republic*, Lefèvre brings in the black and
white horses of the *Phaedrus* and the *Cercle* has its centre in a long
passage inspired directly by Plato's *Parmenides*, to which we shall
return. Finally, via the *Song of Songs* (p. 121) and the image of the
Minotaur's labyrinth, we arrive at an apostrophe to 'la grandeur du
Nom quatre-lettré' (p. 124) and to the Trinity. Thus Lefèvre com-
pletes his round of the Greek (both platonic and neoplatonic), the
Jewish (and cabbalistic) and the Christian, although one feels that

he omits what his brother Nicolas refers to as the Latin clarity which was to interpret the Jewish obscurities.

It is in the eighth *Cercle* that Lefèvre introduces the *Tabernacle* which does in fact constitute the most important of a number of links between the *Encyclie* and the *Galliade*, links which often depend on Giorgi's work on harmony which, Lefèvre tells us, he had not read before composing the *Encyclie* and in which he was delighted to see so many coincidences with his own attitudes (and possibly also those of Postel). (Cf. his *Epistre* to the Giorgi translation, fol. ã 4 recto.)

Perhaps fortunately, it is no part of our brief to examine *Le Tabernacle* in detail and we propose to return to an examination of the parts of the *Encyclie* which involve the quadrivium.

It is early in the second *Cercle* that Lefèvre lays down that numbers are non-sensual and therefore presumably innate, and yet that they are involved in all creation (p. 54). Archimedes appears in this second circle as the 'typical' mathematician, and it seems certain that Lefèvre has some sort of obsession with him at this time. He appears four times in the *Encyclie* (pp. 15, 56, 71, 101) and, as we shall see later, his sphere forms the basis of one of Lefèvre's *chants royaux*. It is true of course that Archimedes remains an obsession with some people simply as a technological inventor and in the *Times* of 7 November 1973 there was an account of the testing of his solar weapon (a series of polished mirrors by which he is said to have set fire to the warships of the Roman fleet besieging Syracuse in the third century BC) by Dr Joannis Sakkas with the help of the Technical Chamber of Greece.

The third circle presents a further element which increases in importance as Lefèvre's work develops—the use of 'symbolic' numbers, in this case the number four (p. 63). This is of course a commonplace and a great standby of Renaissance mystification. Examples abound in the *Encyclie* (p. 120—number 3; p. 124–4; p. 137–7; p. 143–10) and even more strongly in the *Galliade*.

It is in the fifth *Cercle* that Lefèvre begins to devote the major part of his attention to astronomy and here a basic principle is implied, one which is standard in all medieval treatises which include a definition of the quadrivium. The *Didascalicon* states it with exemplary brevity: (p. 67) 'Geometry holds forth knowledge of immobile magnitude, while astronomy claims knowledge of the mobile'.

Thus Lefèvre celebrates both the perfect roundness (for the sphere is the perfect figure having neither beginning nor end and being totally symmetrical) (pp. 86–7):

Et si cest univers est appellé le Beau,
Le Monde, l'Ornement, luy sied pas le Rondeau ?

Quelle forme vois-tu plus parfaicte ny belle,
Que celle qui contient toute autre forme en elle ? . . .

and also the movement of the universe. Here he deals first with the 'Mouvement Rond' (pp. 88–9):

Aussi le Mouvement qui le premier Ciel porte,
Est tousjours tout-uni, & d'une mesme sorte,
Tournoiant alentour du point égal-distant,
Ne se hastant jamais, jamais ne s'arrestant :
Ains sans estre lasse, ni s'alentir soy-même
Il roue incessamment d'une vistesse extreme,
Que jamais il n'attaint, & que tousjours il suit,
Qu'il ne delaisse point, & qu'en tout temps il fuit
Et si la Rondeur est des Formes l'outre-passe,
Pource est il tout-constant, tout-un, tout-régulier,
Entre-coupé de nul, à luy seul familier.

then with the 'Mouvement Naturel de bas en haut' and finally with the 'Mouvement de haut en bas'. Both these last two are of course firmly attached to the sublunar universe and only the 'mouvement en rond' goes outside its limits.

In the seventh circle the situation becomes more complex as we begin to encroach through the sphere of mathematics on to the sphere of the Unity/Divinity. Lefèvre considers the relationship between the movement of the one and the stability of the other and sees it very largely in terms of the relationship between the circumference and the centre. This paradox is closely followed by that of the balance between the One and Nothing, and both are embodied with Rhétoriqueur ecstasy in the passage directly inspired by Plato's *Parmenides* to which we have already referred.

As is the case with so many of Plato's dialogues, the intellectual atmosphere of the *Parmenides* is difficult to reconstruct, and opinions on it are divided. The standard work on it in English is of course by F. M. Cornford, *Plato and Parmenides* (London 1939) and he summarizes the dilemma on p. vii of his Preface:

At the opposite extreme from the Neoplatonist-Hegelian school stand the modern adherents of the logical interpretation. For some of them the second part of the *Parmenides* is a humorous polemic, designed to reduce the Eleatic doctrine of a One Being to absurdity, through the mouth of its founder. This theory . . . escapes the accusation of anachronism but in its extreme form it charges the prince of philosophers with the most wearisome joke in all literature.

Our own way however is clear. The suggestion that Lefèvre anywhere in his work displayed a sense of humour or a consciousness of possible absurdity is obviously a monstrous one, and there can be little doubt but that he fully accepted Ficino's view (expressed in his translation and commentary on Plato's works), a view to be found also in Plotinus, *Enneads*, v, i, 8, that in the *Parmenides* Plato revealed the innermost mysteries of all theology.

We shall proceed to quote a part of the relevant passage. The platonic adaptation is in fact preceded by eight typically Lefevrian lines:

> Son Centre meut en luy, & il ne se meut point,
> Ce qu'on dit l'Univers de son Centre est le point:
> Et comment est-ce donc que dans soy se replie
> Le non-encerclé Cercle encerclant l'Encyclie?
> Outre luy n'y a rien, outre le Nul il est,
> NUL se retourne en L'UN, de L'UN le nombre naist.
> Si donques L'UN est un, en luy seul il s'assemble,
> Car L'UN ne peut pas estre un & plusieurs ensemble:

The passage from *Parmenides* (some three-score lines) follows, beginning with a couplet that is rather a literary than a literal adaptation:

> Et pource n'est-il point ni son Tout, ni sa Part,
> La part est part du tout, le tout en pars s'espard:
> Reste donc qu'il soit L'UN, or s'il est sans partie,
> Sans entrée est aussi, sans demeure, & sortie:
> Car le commencement, le milieu, & le bout
> Seroient pars d'iceluy, luy non plus L'UN, mais Tout.

> (p. 116, *Parmenides* 137c)

and it is followed by a number of lines celebrating a mathematical trinity based on motion and immobility:

> Car puisqu'il est ainsi que la Machine est meüe
> Et qu'elle n'a de soy ceste puissance émeüe,
> Ne void on pas qu'il faut qu'il y ait un pouvoir
> Qui procede d'ailleurs, & la face mouvoir?
> Trois donc font l'entretien: l'un est la Masse morte
> Qui est meüe, & ne meut: l'autre qui luy apporte
> Le mouvement reglé, meut & est meu aussi
> Et le Tiers, n'est point meu, & si meut cestuy-ci.
> Ce Dernier est premier dont tout l'œuvre commence,
> Il demeure Immobil, toutesfois il avance
> Et agite sans fin le Moteur métoyen
> Tant de l'Eternité que du Temps citoyen:
> Car l'Unité sans plus laquelle est stable & ferme
> Est éternellement, fut & sera sans terme,
> Et à elle s'unit le Moyenneur dispos,
> Qui trouve en l'Infini le point de son repos. (p. 120)

It is obviously difficult to disentangle the patchwork of borrowings which make up much of the *Encyclie*. It is an erudite poem and its basic erudition is accompanied by passages in which the poet gives way to his basic love of the paradox and to his continuing allegiance, which may well have been reinforced by his connection with the Puys at Rouen and Dieppe, to what we must call a Rhétoriqueur style. What in all this is poetic trickery, what is mysticism and what mystification, what the result of a concern with magic in its different manifestations we cannot tell. It is however certain that these passages from the *Encyclie*, despite the eloquence of some of them—and this is particularly true of the passages on movement and the astronomical universe in *Cercles* v and vii—represent at most a groping towards the truth. They are in fact a series of preliminaries which are to be complemented, or at any rate extended by Lefèvre in a number of different ways.

To take a minor example, the preoccupation with Archimedes and his sphere, which originates in Claudian's poem describing the 'orrery' of Archimedes, is continued in one of the *chants royaux* which Lefèvre presented at the Puy de Rouen: *Chant royal. Argumentum ex Claudiano poëta Romano* (*Hymnes ecclésiastiques,* 1578, fol. 238). There is in fact a direct connection between the last stanza of this poem and a passage in the *Encyclie* (p. 71) which also presents a picture of the Persian King Sabor seated in the middle of his own 'orrery' in crystal. Both these passages would appear to have their source in a passage from Jérôme Cardan, *De la subtilité des choses* (Paris, Angelier, 1556, fol. 322 verso).

Again the idea of the Tabernacle, Tente, Pavillon appears in another *Chant royal: Sur la tressainte & pure conception de la Vierge Marie mere de Dieu. Argumentum ex libro Zoharis sive Splendoris* (*Hymnes,* fol. 237). This poem is based on the silk-worm:

> Ce ver divin né de semence pure
> Au tour de soy son Pavillon ombreux
> File et ourdit, de la blanche teinture
> D'une toyson pleine de fils nombreux,
> De plus dougee et subtile fabrique
> Que n'est la ligne en la Mathematique
> Ligne spirale en ses replis divers,
> Plus riche encor' que celle des bois verds
> Que vont cardant les Seres, peuple monde,
> Où les Estez, se cache, et les Yvers
> Le Papillon qui fait sa Tente ronde.

> Le grand Hebrieu, qui trouva l'ouverture

De l'Archetype, où il vid radieux
Dix Sephiroth, qui font la couverture
Du Tabernacle où est le Dieu des Dieux,
Feist le dessein du Tabernacle antique
En imitant le Papillon mystique
Quand sur le mont luy furent découvers
Les grands secrets qu'il raconte aux Desers,
Où la splendeur est tellement féconde,
Qu'œil n'y peut voir souz les nuages pers
Le Papillon qui fait sa Tente ronde.

This last poem is particularly important as it symbolizes, through the image of the silk-worm and its cocoon, the drawing together of threads from Jewish, Greek and Christian sources, together with a reference to the Latin of Pliny. Lefèvre makes it clear in the *Epistre* to his translation of Giorgi's *De harmonia mundi* (fol. ã 4 verso) that the word 'tente, ou pavillon' in Hebrew comes from the same origin as the word for 'Tabernacle'. However, we must not neglect a more pressing—one might say cynically a more material reason—for the choice of this image. In Lefèvre's *Diverses Meslanges poëtiques* (Paris, R. Le Magnier, 1582, fol. 90–91) there is a series of three sonnets under the general title, *Graces au Seigneur Papillon, Prince du Puy à Rouen, en l'an 1576, pour le prix de la Palme, & du Lis, obtenu par l'Autheur*. Is this once again mystification rather than mysticism?

The *Song of Songs* again represents a link between the *Encyclie* in which it appears briefly but unmistakeably (p. 121), the Giorgi treatise, several pages of which are a translation by Lefèvre of an adaptation into Latin by Giorgi (*Ton vii du cantique III* pp. 707 ff. and especially pp. 795 ff.), and the *Galliade*, where a lengthy adaptation appears in the third circle. This poem is of course constantly used by the Cabbala especially in the *Zohar*.

Alas, the Giorgi translation and the *Galliade* are linked in a more melancholy fashion. Both ran into a second edition—the Giorgi in 1588 and the *Galliade* in 1582. Both of these second editions are rare. The Marquis of Lothian (or the National Library of Scotland, depending on which you ask) possesses a copy of both editions of the Giorgi, and the second edition of the *Galliade* is to be found in the municipal library of Trier. Both second editions tell the same sad story. In each case the original sheets (unsold!) have been used again. The publisher of the Giorgi translation shamelessly uses the whole book even including the colophon with the original publication date, adding only a bifolium to the first gathering, which includes a new title page rewritten more sonorously and excitingly and printed in red and black for the delectation of the groundlings. For the *Galliade*, the author has been induced to expand the *Cercle Second*, devoted mainly to architecture, and he has in fact added a matter of 36 pages to the first edition which again uses the original sheets, again adding a new title-page and a conjugate leaf reset line by line.

The main importance of the *Galliade* however from our point of view lies in its exposition of music which occupies almost the whole of the fourth circle. The essentials of the argument used by those early scientists who wished to associate music, mathematics and astronomy are of course a commonplace and are based on the supposedly Pythagorean discovery of a relationship between tones and measurement. In fact, when strings of the same material and gauge are made to vibrate under the same conditions, the relationship between the notes produced by these vibrations will depend on the relationship between the length of the strings, and the relationship can be expressed in simple whole figures. If one is half as long as the other the difference in pitch will be one octave, if the relationship is $2:3$ the result will be a fifth; $4:3$ is a fourth. Thus all the ratios involved in these musical harmonies can be found in the Pythagorean tetractys: $1+2+3+4=10$. These ratios were simply related by Plato in the *Timaeus* to the so-called lambda and to his explanations — if one can call them explanations — that the harmony of the cosmos is based on the squares and cubes of the double and triple proportions starting from one.

It must of course be obvious that all this has very little to do with music as simple-minded persons such as ourselves know it, and the point of the argument is rather to demonstrate an attitude to harmony which is as near as possible non-sensual. As the senses are subject to being deceived, so our judgment regarding the relationship between notes must depend not on these senses but on our reason, working on the science of mathematics, harmony and proportion.

That theories of this nature are not inextricably connected with the old Ptolemaic system—for it is certain that Lefèvre knew of Copernicus: indeed he translates a poem on his *De revolutionibus* (*Divers meslanges poëtiques*, Paris, Le Magnier, 1582, fol. 71, 'Sur la sphere des révolutions de N. Copernic. Du latin de Corneille Gemma.') is easily demonstrated by a reference to Kepler, one of whose main struggles was to rediscover in the Copernican universe similar evidence of proportion and harmony—mathematical evidence—to that which was so amply evident in the Ptolemaic system. This is to be seen in the *Harmonices mundi* (1619) and of course in the famous illustration to his *Cosmographical Mystery* (1596) in which it is

demonstrated that the spaces between the planets are able to be
filled exactly by the insertion of the five recognized 'regular' Platonic
solids, the Dodecahedron (12), the Tetrahedron (4: triangular
pyramid), the Cube (6), the Icosahedron (20) and the Octahedron
(8: triangles).

We are getting into deep waters—and to what profit? What indeed?—as Lefèvre put it in one of the sonnets preliminary to his
translation of Ficino's *De triplici vita* (*Trois livres de la vie*, Paris, 1581).

Helas! que gaignez-vous d'accourcir vostre vie
Sur le livre collez & de jour & de nuit?
Las! vostre chandelier qui pour les autres luit,
Se consumant pour soy sent sa clarté ravie.

Et puis pourquoy doit-on avoir si grand' envie
D'exercer un bel art qu'or tout le monde fuit,
De labourer un champ qui rien ne nous produit
Que langoureux ennuis, & à mort nous convie?

Caterres & froideurs, goutes & mal de dents,
Seront vostre loyer, ô studieux ardents:
Voulez-vous donc mourir pour autruy faire vivre?

A fitting summary of any consideration of Guy Lefèvre's scientific
poetry, especially in its treatment of the quadrivium, is best to be
found in a diagram from Nicolas Lefèvre's introduction to the
Giorgi translation (fol. ẽ 6 verso) which combines the Platonic
lambda, the science of gematria, the tetractys and the largely medieval
idea of the three worlds, Corruptible, Celestial and Angelic. I
reproduce this diagram in the introduction to my anthology of
French Renaissance Scientific Poetry (London 1974, p. 23), together
with an explanation of it by Nicolas Lefèvre. Here is the full flowering of the idea of the scientific poet as Magus, as the prophet of a
new culture and civilization founded on and assimilating ancient
cultures and, in particular, adding Jewish culture to that of the
Greeks, Romans and Christians. And this of course takes us back
to our opening paragraphs and in so doing may indeed be said to
provide a fitting conclusion to a paper chiefly concerned with an
Encyclie and a *Galliade*.

JEAN-CLAUDE MARGOLIN

L'Enseignement des mathématiques en France (1540-70) Charles de Bovelles, Fine, Peletier, Ramus

DANS UN DIALOGUE DE 1528 sur l'éducation et la culture, qu'il a intitulé le *De recta latini graecique sermonis pronuntiatione*[1]—car la philologie constitue le pivot même de la sphère encyclopédique—Erasme en vient à exprimer ses idées sur les mathématiques. Elles tiennent en moins d'une phrase, car l'un des deux personnages qui expriment tour à tour ses idées et ses goûts, Leo—le Lion—se contente de dire: 'Arithmeticen, musicam et astrologiam degustasse sat erit'.[2] Ainsi, dans son cycle d'études, l'adolescent n'aura besoin que de tâter un peu d'arithmétique, de musique et d'astrologie. On sait que l'idiosyncrasie d'Erasme ne le prédisposait guère à l'étude des mathématiques ou de la musique,[3] et que l'astrologie suscitait en lui, comme toutes les sciences mystérieuses, un mélange d'angoisse, d'incrédulité et d'irritation. Que l'on ouvre son *De pueris instituendis*, qui date de 1529,[4] mais qui avait été conçu et rédigé beaucoup plus tôt, ou son *De ratione studii*, qui date de 1511–12: on constatera que l'arithmétique y brille par son absence, ou par une présence qui ne vaut guère mieux. Là, il se contente d'évoquer certains enfants dont les goûts les portent curieusement vers des disciplines telles que la musique, l'arithmétique ou la cosmographie,[5] comme s'il s'agissait de fantaisies ou d'inclinations relevant davantage de l'affectivité que de la raison; ici il n'en est même plus question, car l'étude de la géographie est soutenue davantage par la connaissance des textes littéraires; quant à l'astrologie, 'futile en elle-même'—selon sa propre expression—il n'est pas mauvais de la pratiquer à cause de toutes les allusions poétiques qu'elle contient.[6]

Mais, pourra-t-on objecter, cette ignorance ou ce mépris d'Erasme pour les mathématiques n'est pas la règle générale, et si on lui oppose les noms de quelques humanistes français à peu près contemporains, comme Lefèvre d'Etaples,[7] Clichtove[8] ou Bovelles,[9] on constatera que dans leur enseignement ou dans leurs œuvres, ces philosophes et même ces théologiens ont accordé à l'arithmétique et à la géométrie une place considérable; bien plus, ils ont souvent eu recours, dans des argumentations philosophico-théologiques, à des démonstrations mathématiques ou à des schémas géométriques.[10]

A la vérité, les hommes que je viens de citer constituent plutôt une exception: l'humanisme des années 1510 à 1540 n'a pas donné, ne pouvait pas donner dans le domaine des mathématiques des fruits nombreux et savoureux. Tandis que, loin des Universités traditionnelles comme des Universités nouvelles ou des écoles latines, des mathématiciens poursuivaient isolément et obscurément leurs travaux, ne formant à cette discipline que de rares élèves, les humanistes européens n'avaient pas su intégrer dans leur *cursus* pédagogique ou dans leur programme scientifique—ces fameuses *rationes studiorum*—l'étude systématique des mathématiques grecques (car celles des Arabes étaient alors généralement ignorées des Européens). Pour qu'ils découvrissent quelque intérêt à des questions mathématiques, il fallait que ce fût indirectement, et comme subrepticement, par le canal de Pythagore, de Platon ou de Ptolémée. Ils les connaissaient d'ailleurs mal en tant que mathématiciens, et les 'vers dorés' de Pythagore avaient plus de prix sur le marché humaniste que sa démonstration de la duplication de la surface du carré. Dans la *République* de Platon ou dans le *Timée*, on n'allait guère chercher une théorie des rapports géométriques ou des polyèdres réguliers. Quant à l'édition de la *Géographie* de Ptolémée qu'Erasme lui-même entreprit[11] (sans doute avec l'aide de quelque helléniste plus compétent que lui en ce domaine), elle peut intéresser l'histoire de l'humanisme, mais elle n'a pas fait avancer d'un pas celle de la cosmographie. Même quand un pédagogue humaniste comme Vivès s'intéresse de plus près qu'Erasme aux mathématiques, qu'il en reconnaît le caractère de certitude, qu'il en a compris le mécanisme et l'abstraction, qu'il leur consacre enfin, non pas quelques lignes, mais tout un chapitre (de 5 pages) du livre v de son *De causis corruptarum artium*,[12] et un autre du *De tradendis disciplinis*,[13] qu'il en montre l'intérêt pratique dans la vie de l'homme, qu'il souhaite expressément l'explication en classe des *Eléments* d'Euclide ou qu'il recommande même la lecture et le commentaire de mathématiciens modernes, comme l'Anglais Sacrobosco et sa célèbre *Sphère*,[14] ou l'Allemand Purbach et sa *Théorie des planètes*,[15] il ne fait pas école.[16] En effet, ces questions 'modernes' sont censées relever de techniques appropriées plus directement orientées vers des applications pratiques. Or l'éducation idéale est celle de l'*orator*, et les humanistes pédagogues sont plus soucieux d'apprendre à leurs élèves l'art du bien dire et du bien penser que celui du bien calculer. Ils n'ont pas conscience qu'il n'est peut-être pas de plus haute expression de l'art de penser ou de dire le vrai que la mathématique.

En fait, comme l'a bien montré R. Hooykaas dans son étude sur Ramus qu'il a intitulée *Humanisme, science et réforme*,[17] l'antiscolasticisme des représentants de l'humanisme dans la première partie du seizième siècle leur faisait rejeter dans une même réprobation les 'subtilités' des nominalistes et les 'calculs' (*calculationes*) des dialecticiens qui les conduisaient à discuter des problèmes sur le *maximum* et le *minimum*.[18] Ils ne connaissaient pas—ou fort mal—l'extraordinaire mathématicien que fut Nicolas de Cues (qui fit pourtant aussi des calculs sur le maximum et le minimum), mais ils suivaient celui que l'on peut considérer comme leur chef de file, Rodolphe Agricola qui, en énumérant les inanités de l'Ecole, parle de cette 'verbosa de maximo et minimo et de calculandi (ut aiunt) ratione jactatio'.[19] Ils n'étaient pas en mesure de comprendre les grandes découvertes mathématiques de leur temps ou des générations qui les avaient précédés immédiatement. Ils avaient de l'utilité ou de la pratique sociale ainsi que des finalités éthiques et religieuses de l'éducation, une conception telle qu'ils ne pouvaient pas prendre une distance suffisante pour reconnaître le bien-fondé de spéculations 'mathématiques' pures. Et ils continuaient de s'en prendre aux 'calculs' de Suiseth qu'ils ne comprenaient pas très bien!

C'est pourtant, en France, une institution humaniste, créée par la volonté d'un roi, qui avait su s'entourer des meilleurs esprits de son temps, qui fit jaillir ou, du moins, révéla une génération de savants, parmi lesquels des mathématiciens. Et la sagesse de ceux qui eurent à administrer ce Collège Royal[20] fit créer des chaires de lecteurs de mathématiques: car pour permettre à la science une diffusion certaine, un enracinement et une progression dans les esprits, les livres ne suffisent pas; il lui faut le support d'une institution pédagogique de grand renom; il faut le contact et le dialogue du maître et de l'élève, il faut à un professeur des collaborateurs, des assistants; il faut aussi que les mentalités se transforment, c'est-à-dire, pour le cas qui nous occupe, que les sciences soient intégrées à un programme d'études qui puisse intéresser une bonne partie de la jeunesse cultivée. Un professeur comme Ramus, en s'employant à restaurer le *quadrivium*, permit aux mathématiques de se développer avec harmonie et progression. Nous aurons l'occasion d'y revenir. Mais avant de parler de l'enseignement des professeurs royaux, essentiellement Oronce Fine, Pierre Ramus et Pierre Forcadel, il est bon d'examiner, en dehors de cette institution, la situation des mathématiques en France aux environs de 1540 et à travers des ouvrages d'amateurs éclairés, comme Jacques Peletier du Mans (Peletarius),[21] poète, philosophe, linguiste, homme curieux de tout.

· · ·

JEAN-CLAUDE MARGOLIN

Pour connaitre, vers le début de l'époque qui nous concerne, le bilan de l'enseignement mathématique en France et dans divers pays d'Europe, le plus sûr est encore d'ouvrir les *Scholæ mathematicæ*[22] de Ramus, qui se révèle ici comme historien ou chroniqueur des sciences. Son témoignage rejoint d'ailleurs celui de Mélanchthon qui écrivait, en 1549, à son ami l'imprimeur Johannes Petreius de Nuremberg,[23] que les mathématiques étaient peu pratiquées en France, et qu'il était par conséquent assez facile à de bons étudiants allemands—plusieurs de ses élèves—de gagner leur vie en France en donnant des leçons de mathématiques:[24] ils n'avaient guère à redouter la concurrence! Un autre témoignage, celui de Forcadel, qui révèle que dans les années 1540 à 1550, les Français étaient obligés de 'mendier les ouvrages des Allemands et des Italiens';[25] aussi écrivit-il, pour remédier à cette situation lamentable, un traité d'Arithmétique. Quant à Ramus, il se fait d'abord mettre au courant par ses amis et ses élèves qui voyagent et qui rentrent de l'étranger, de la situation des mathématiques et de leur enseignement en Italie, en Allemagne, en Pologne, en Angleterre.[26] La situation en France est telle, les programmes universitaires sont ainsi conçus que l'on peut devenir maître-ès-arts en ignorant tout des mathématiques, avec deux années de logique et une année de physique.[27] On sait que cette logique était purement formelle, et par conséquent d'une utilité plus que réduite pour l'intelligence et le développement de la pensée mathématique. Dans un passage concernant l'Université de Paris, il se plaint amèrement que les mathématiques ne tiennent aucune place dans les statuts universitaires de la capitale.[28] L'admirateur de Platon—d'un Platon non mutilé de ses passages mathématiques—en souffre particulièrement.[29] Chaque université, pense-t-il, devrait posséder au moins deux chaires de mathématiques.[30] On sait que François Ier créa la première chaire publique de mathématiques en 1532, et que Ramus devait s'y illustrer plus tard. Mais cet enseignement magistral ne devait évidemment pas suffire aux besoins, ou plutôt aux nécessités de l'époque: c'est tout un courant qu'il s'agissait de créer, et les lecteurs publics de mathématiques ne pouvaient que donner de haut une impulsion d'ensemble. Le tour d'Europe et celui des Universités entrepris par Ramus[31] sont pour nous d'un grand intérêt historique, voire philosophique, car le maître ne se contente pas de constater des faits, de signaler ici une pénurie notoire, là une implantation satisfaisante des chaires scientifiques, il s'interroge sur les causes—sociales, religieuses, politiques —de situations aussi variées, ce qui nous conduit nous-mêmes à ne pas séparer ou, du moins, à associer l'histoire des mathématiques, l'histoire de l'enseignement, et l'histoire générale. Au moment où

ses convictions réformées commencent à se faire sentir, Ramus n'est
pas loin d'établir une relation entre la situation plus florissante des
mathématiques dans les pays passés à la Réforme ou à l'intérieur
desquels elle couvait depuis longtemps, et la religion réformée elle-
même.[32] Idée que reprend volontiers à son compte l'historien moderne de Ramus que j'ai déjà cité, R. Hooykaas. Comme toute thèse,
elle mérite un examen aprofondi, que nous ne pouvons évidemment
pas entreprendre ici; comme toute thèse, qui repose sur une hypothèse ou une série d'hypothèses, elle n'est pas à l'abri de la contesta-
tion.[33]

Sur la place de Paris, à l'époque où enseignent Oronce Fine, et un
peu plus tard Ramus lui-même, certains imprimeurs, plus ou moins
spécialisés dans les ouvrages de mathématiques, éditent ou rééditent
des livres plus anciens, souvent traduits du latin, quand ils ne sont
pas écrits directement en français. C'est un signe des temps, auquel
l'humanisme français et l'impulsion donnée à la langue française par
le roi lui-même, ne sont pas étrangers. C'est aussi le temps où de
jeunes poètes, comme Joachim Du Bellay et Peletier du Mans commencent à fourbir leurs armes et à entamer leur croisade en faveur
du français, d'une réforme de la langue (chez le premier), d'une
réforme de l'orthographe[34] (chez le second). Le langage mathématique, et par conséquent son enseignement, n'échapperont pas à
ces mutations culturelles.

Parmi les imprimeurs parisiens, il faut citer Guillaume Cavellat,
imprimeur juré du Roi, chez qui paraissent a l'enseigne de la Poule
grasse, un très grand nombre d'ouvrages de mathématiques entre
1540 et 1570. Et d'abord, la *Géométrie pratique* de Charles de Bovelles,[35]
version française développée de ses feuillets latins de la première
décennie du siècle, époque où l'humaniste picard vivait dans le
cercle amical et érudit de Lefèvre d'Etaples et de Clichtove, cercle
si étroitement refermé que plusieurs opuscules mathématiques de ces
trois auteurs sont imprimés ensemble, et qu'il est même difficile au
bibliographe moderne de rendre à chacun ce qui lui est dû.[36]

On sait que le libraire Geoffroy Tory, de Bourges, avait dans son
Champfleury de 1529, vanté le rôle des langues vulgaires dans l'expression des idées et dans les disciplines scientifiques. Et il cite à l'appui
de sa thèse l'*Aritmetique et Geometrie* d'Estienne de la Roche, dit
Villefranche[37] et la *Géométrie pratique* de Bovelles.[38] A la vérité, si
l'on se reporte à la préface latine que Bovelles a rédigée à l'intention
de Dom Antoine Leuffroy, abbé d'Ourscamp,[39] et datée de Noyon,
novembre 1542, on peut constater que ce n'est pas de son plein gré
qu'il a utilisé la langue française, mais bien pour répondre aux
désirs des praticiens. Lui-même, en dépit d'un long poème français

consacré à Catherine d'Alexandrie,[40] de son étude sur les proverbes français[41] et de celle sur les différents parlers de son pays, appartenait à une génération et était surtout issu d'un milieu où le latin était considéré comme la langue naturellement vouée à l'expression des idées. Qu'on en juge plutôt par les premières lignes de sa préface, que l'on retrouvera dans l'édition Jérôme de Marnef et G. Cavellat de 1566:

> Prié par quelques artisans et ouvriers manuels,[42] vénérable Père . . . de composer à leur intention une Géométrie en langue vulgaire, je n'ai pas opposé à leur sollicitation obstinée une fin de non-recevoir, bien qu'en acceptant de me plier à leur désir, j'aie agi contre mes principes, moi qui jusqu'à présent n'ai pour ainsi dire pas l'habitude de publier un ouvrage dans ma langue maternelle. J'ai donc entièrement réalisé une Introduction à la géométrie en langue française . . .

La suite de la préface nous apprend qu'il a cherché un imprimeur pour ne pas laisser perdre le fruit de son labeur, et que plusieurs graveurs parisiens—il en connaissait un certain nombre—, après lui avoir promis monts et merveilles, n'avaient accouché que d'une ridicule souris.[43] Mais voici qu'Oronce Fine, lecteur royal, en visite à Noyon et à l'abbaye d'Ourscamp, se rend au domicile du chanoine humaniste.[44] Bovelles dépose entre ses mains son tout récent manuscrit pour le confier à des presses parisiennes. Celui-ci s'engage à proposer le texte à un imprimeur, et à se charger lui-même de la gravure des nombreuses figures qui l'illustrent.[44a] Le marché est conclu, et le célèbre professeur de mathématiques tient sa promesse. En dédiant à l'abbé d'Ourscamp sa 'lucubratiuncula', Bovelles pense avoir marqué ce jour d'une pierre plus favorable. Mais il y insiste encore: 'Qu'il ne lui tienne donc pas rigueur de ce cadeau, produit inhabituel de sa fabrication.'[45] Si d'aventure la lecture de ce livre profite à quelques doctes, versés dans la science mathématique (*mysticæ Matheseos scientiæ*),[46] qu'ils en sachent gré aussi à l'excellent travail d'Oronce Fine (allusion vraisemblable au choix de l'imprimeur Cavellat,[47] et à la haute correction technique de l'ouvrage, texte et figures). Et il termine par un 'furtif' distique (*obreptitio disticho*) latin—l'humanisme ne perdant pas ses droits—:

> J'ai pressé le raisin: le vin qu'il faut boire, il le boit!
> J'ai rempli le pressoir: le liquide irrigue son gosier![48]

J'ai insisté sur cette préface pour démentir l'optimisme de Geoffroy Tory: Non, ce n'est pas par les mathématiques que le français a pénétré dans la science. Et l'on pourrait tout aussi bien citer toutes les *Arithmétiques* qui ont suivi celle de Bovelles, et qui d'ailleurs se ressemblent infiniment de l'une à l'autre, celles de Boissière,[49]

Cathalan,[50] P. de Savonne,[51] La Tayssonière,[52] et—si l'on dépasse la date de 1570—celles de Jean Trenchant,[53] Chauvet,[54] Fustel.[55] Réservons la propre Arithmétique de Peletier, car elle présente, comme nous le verrons, ainsi que ses autres ouvrages de mathématiques, des qualités pédagogiques très particulières.

Pour dire quelques mots de la Géométrie de Bovelles, il faut remarquer qu'elle est d'un niveau assez élémentaire, se réduisant aux figures que l'on peut construire avec l'équerre, la règle et le compas, traitant des figures simples comme les angles et les triangles, les polygones, le cercle, mais aussi la superficie d'une 'ronde colonne' (entendons un cylindre) ou la cubication de la sphère. L'Avis au lecteur, placé en tête de l'ouvrage sous forme de 14 décasyllabes, en définit bien l'esprit :

Amy lecteur qui cherches les mesures,
Et quantitez des lignes et figures,
Et de tous corps, par art de Geometrie,
Et plusieurs poincts et secrets d'industrie,
Qui en cest art sont trouvez plus notables,
Et pour les gens d'esperit profitables,
Qui leur scavoir redigent en effect :
Avoir te faut ce livre, qui fut faict
Dedans Noyon, par Charles de Boüelles,
Qui n'est jamais sans faire œuvres nouvelles.
Entens le donc, et si n'oublie pas
L'esquiere droict, la Reigle et le Compas :
Car de ces trois despend l'art et practique,
Et le profit du sçavoir Geometrique. (A2r)

En feuilletant le livre, à la vérité dans les derniers chapitres, on trouve des problèmes, agrémentés de schémas, concernant effectivement la pratique artisanale ou la physique élémentaire : un chariot comporte des roues de dimensions différentes (pp. 165–6), la charge la plus lourde reposant sur les plus grandes roues (comparaison avec les quadrupèdes, dont les membres postérieurs sont plus vigoureux ou plus longs que les membres antérieurs; comparaison avec un homme portant une hotte sur le dos) (p. 167); assimilation grossière des rivières qui s'élargissent en se rapprochant de la mer à une pyramide, 'ayant sa base en la largeur ample de la mer, et le chef supérieur au destroict et source de sa fontaine' (p. 169); assimilation encore de la 'grande encyclie du monde universel' 'qui tient la figure de ronde pyramide renversée, ayant la base au ciel, et le poinct capital en la terre' (p. 171); un inévitable paragraphe sur l'homme géométrique (voir le schéma de la p. 173) la grandeur et la stature de tous les corps humains; des remarques sommaires mi-géométriques, mi-physiques sur le moulin à vent (p. 182) ou le moulin à eau (p. 185) etc.

On peut, sans mépriser le moins du monde un ouvrage de cette sorte, et tous ceux qui s'en inspirent, se demander légitimement, s'il contribua vraiment à la restauration des études mathématiques. Ils me semblent relever davantage d'une histoire des sociétés et des techniques que d'une histoire des mathématiques. Ils fixent toutes sortes de pratiques artisanales ou commerciales, car l'on y trouve effectivement des règles relatives au change des monnaies, aux réductions des mesures les unes aux autres, au régime des foires, et à toutes sortes de calculs. Sans qu'on puisse le vérifier vraiment—car il faudrait disposer de nombreux exemplaires et d'inscriptions marginales très explicites—on imagine sans peine que ces livres étaient davantage entre les mains de 'marchands, financiers, tresoriers, receveurs, affineurs' qu'entre celles d'étudiants. Et la très forte production lyonnaise de ce genre d'ouvrages n'est certainement pas étrangère à cette destination, à ce genre de clientèle.

Entre les années 1540 et 1570, il semble bien que la répartition des ouvrages de mathématiques en latin et en français—et des remarques analogues pourraient convenir à d'autres langues vulgaires—corresponde à une double clientèle: les étudiants des collèges et des Universités où cette discipline du *quadrivium* commence à se répandre, et singulièrement les auditeurs du Collège Royal, annotent copieusement les traités rédigés en latin, ou les traductions latines de Pythagore, d'Archimède ou d'Euclide; au contraire, les traités de perspective, d'architecture, de fortification, qui dérivent de la Géométrie pratique, s'adressent à un public qui ignore le latin.[56] Il faudra le génie et l'obstination d'un Ramus pour bousculer ces lignes de démarcation trop parfaites; et l'on verra que l'utilité pratique des mathématiques, même enseignées en latin, n'est pas incompatible avec leur certitude théorique.

Le cas de Peletier du Mans mérite que l'on s'y arrête tout spécialement.

Car chez ce non-professionnel,[57] dont les qualités pédagogiques et la faculté d'invention ont été bien supérieures à celles de professeurs en titre, l'utilisation concurrentielle ou complémentaire du latin et du français—un français pour lequel il sut d'ailleurs inventer une orthographe spécifique—ne correspond pas nécessairement à une répartition culturelle et sociale de son public, entendons de ses lecteurs.

Rappelons en quelques mots que le 'docte' ou 'fameux' Peletier—comme le désignait Du Bellay[58]—suivit, adolescent, au Collège de

Navarre, les cours de mathématiques et de philosophie de son frère aîné Jean. Les loisirs que lui valut vers 1540 le poste de secrétaire de l'évêque du Mans, lui permirent de cultiver les langues anciennes et modernes, la poésie, les mathématiques. Son goût pour la langue française ne s'exerce pas au détriment de la latine, et il songe à réformer l'orthographe française en la rendant conforme à la prononciation. En 1544 il est à Paris, entouré de doctes amis comme Saint-Gelais et Lancelot Carles, Ronsard, des Masures, Baïf, Dorat, Théodore de Bèze, Denys Sauvage. Ses *Œuvres poétiques*, publiées en 1547, le rendent célèbre. Son goût pour les sciences et ses connaissances approfondies en astronomie, en physique, en médecine, en mathématiques y éclatent presque à chaque vers.[59] Il est à Poitiers, en 1549, quand il publie son *Arithmétique*, dédiée à Théodore de Bèze,[60] alors prieur de Longjumeau. A la différence de Bovelles, qui avait écrit malgré lui son livre de géométrie en français, Peletier se sert de cette langue en toute lucidité et en toute bonne conscience, sans rien sacrifier de la tenue intellectuelle de l'ouvrage. Les frères de Marnef, en partie spécialisés dans ce genre de publications, diffusent rapidement le livre, qui sera réédité à Poitiers en 1551 et 1552, à Lyon en 1554 et 1570. Sans que l'on soit certain qu'il ait exercé à Poitiers le métier de professeur, Peletier put intéresser suffisamment à sa production mathématique professeurs et étudiants, et plus d'un lecteur royal dut utiliser ses écrits. Un exemplaire d'une de ses éditions de l'*Arithmétique*, que possède aujourd'hui la Bibliothèque Nationale,[61] a appartenu au célèbre chirurgien parisien, humaniste et huguenot Rasse des Nœux[62] (ex-libris et date de 1567).[63] Un exemplaire d'une autre de ses œuvres mathématiques, l'*Algèbre*, publiée à Lyon en juillet 1554, faisant également partie du fonds de la Bibliothèque Nationale,[64] a dû servir de manuel de travail d'un lecteur royal, si l'on en juge par l'ex-libris que porte très lisiblement la page de titre et par les innombrables annotations de l'ouvrage. On lit, en tête du livre qu'un certain Henri de Monantheuil, 'professor regius' était propriétaire de l'ouvrage,[65] et deux lignes écrites en latin sur la même page nous apprennent même les dates d'entrée en charge et de retraite de ce professeur royal.[66] Le 16 juin 1586, il cessait ses cours publics, mais conservait le précieux ouvrage, une édition latine datée de 1560, et sortie des presses de G. Cavellat, 'sub pingui Gallina, ex adverso Collegii Cameracensis'. On notera en passant qu'il existe des versions françaises et latines des ouvrages de Peletier, sans qu'il soit toujours aisé de déterminer si la version latine précédait ou suivait la version française : il faudrait se livrer à un travail de bibliographie exhaustive qui, à ma connaissance, n'a jamais été fait. Toujours est-il qu'en ce qui concerne les deux livres du traité d'Algèbre, le texte français est sorti des presses lyonnaises de Jean de Tournes en 1554—comme on l'a vu—et le *De occulta parte numerorum, quam Algebram vocant libri duo* six ans plus tard. Et Pontus de Tyard, dans le discours du *Premier Curieux* fait allusion en mai 1557 au travail de Peletier, qui 'revoyait son Algèbre pour la donner aux Latins'.[67] En fait, il semble bien qu'en abandonnant progressivement le français pour le latin, Peletier ait renoncé, à son corps défendant, à gagner de nouvelles couches sociales à l'étude des mathématiques et qu'il se soit contenté de conserver ou de regagner la faveur des savants patentés.[68] C'est dommage à la fois pour les mathématiques, pour la langue française et pour la 'démocratisation' du savoir.

De l'*Arithmétique* à l'*Algèbre*, c'est aussi le passage de Poitiers à Lyon, par des étapes qui le conduisent successivement à Bordeaux et à Béziers. L'accueil sarcastique que lui valut son projet de réforme de l'orthographe (son *Dialogue de l'ortografe é prononciacion de la langue françoese* date de 1549/50) le fit sans doute se plonger plus avant dans l'exercice de la médecine et dans les mathématiques. Ce qui ne l'empêche naturellement pas, avec une belle suite dans les idées, de rédiger les préfaces (ou *Proèmes*) ainsi que tout le contenu de ses ouvrages scientifiques, selon l'orthographe réformée qui lui paraît conforme à la logique et à une volonté d'unification de la langue: nous ne l'imiterons cependant pas ici dans les citations que nous en ferons, par souci de nous conformer à nos propres usages.[69] C'est à son *Dialogue de l'ortografe* que nous emprunterons une page où Peletier explique avec un sens quasi-prophétique de l'histoire, les raisons qui l'ont déterminé à se servir du français pour traiter des mathématiques. Si le français parvient à conquérir le royaume de ces sciences, où 'la vérité est manifeste, infaillible et constante', il conquerra lui-même ses lettres de noblesse:

> Pensez quelle immortalité elles pourraient apporter à une langue, y étant rédigées en bonne et vraye methode. Regardons même les Arabes, lesquels encores qu'ils soient reculés de nous et quasi comme en un autre monde: toutefois ils s'en sont trouvés en notre Europe qui ont voulu apprendre le langage, en principale considération pour l'astrologie, et autres choses secrètes qu'ils ont traitées en leur vulgaire, combien qu'assez malheureusement. Car on sait quelle sophisterie ils ont mêlée parmi la médecine et les mathématiques mêmes. Et toutefois ils ont rendu leur langue requise, en contemplation de cela. Avisons donc à quoi il peut tenir que nous n'en fassions non pas autant, mais sans comparaison plus de la notre.[70]

Ferdinand Brunot, qui commentait ce même passage dans son

Histoire de la langue française,[71] insistait sur la pénétration et la hardiesse de ces vues, ajoutant: 'rêver de donner l'éternité au français, en l'attachant à une œuvre d'une vérité éternelle, était d'un homme qui pensait.'[72]

A Lyon, où il publia chez l'imprimeur humaniste Jean 1er de Tournes son *Algèbre*,[73] et où il fit aussi connaissance de la 'Belle Cordière' Louise Labé, il put sûrement exercer ses talents pédagogiques. Le 'proème' de l'*Algèbre* est adressé au célèbre maréchal de France, Charles de Cossé-Brissac, lieutenant général du roi en Piémont. On y apprend, toutes flatteries mises à part, que l'habileté du maréchal dans le métier des armes est heureusement associée à son goût des sciences, notamment de la science algébrique dont il fait un éloge qui n'est pas de simple rhétorique. Il semble bien que Peletier ait compris en profondeur la nature des opérations algébriques, qui représentent pour lui la marque la plus évidente de la puissance d'invention de l'esprit humain. Faisant partie de la suite de Cossé-Brissac dans le Piémont, on peut se demander si Peletier fut son conseiller mathématique, son médecin, ou le précepteur de son jeune fils? Comme le pense Paul Laumonier dans sa Notice biographique,[74] il semble bien qu'il ait été à tout le moins précepteur du jeune Timoléon de Cossé, âgé alors de 10 ans environ. D'ailleurs Jean de Tournes publia la même année 1554 un opuscle intitulé *Enseignement de vertu au petit seigneur Timoléon de Cossé*. Comme on voit, les mathématiques ne faisaient pas moins bon ménage avec l'enseignement moral que les *bonæ literæ* et la 'civilité puérile et honnête' de la génération des humanistes de 1520. Nous avons un autre témoignage des leçons de Peletier, mais cette fois, il s'agit de sa grande spécialité, les mathématiques. Ce témoignage est celui de Jean 11 de Tournes le fils et futur successeur de Jean 1er, alors âgé de 14 ans. Dans la préface des *Eléments d'Euclide* qu'il imprimera à Genève en 1611,[75] c'est-à-dire 57 ou 58 ans après ses studieux entretiens avec le familier de son père qu'il admirait tant, il s'adresse ainsi à la 'Noblesse française':[76]

> Je sais, écrit-il, que Forcadel et Errard ont fait voir aux Français l'Euclide ou partie d'iceluy, mais cela ne m'a pas empêché de traduire et imprimer Peletier pour la singulière méthode et merveilleuse facilité qui luy est familière. Ce que je ne commence pas maintenant à congnoistre, l'ayant appris et remarqué dès l'âge de quatorze ans, lorsque ledit Peletier me lisoit, en la maison de mon père, les démonstrations de Théon et de Champagne sur ces six premiers livres.

Ces *Eléments d'Euclide* en français qu'évoque dans ses souvenirs l'imprimeur lyonnais, Peletier les avait publiés d'abord en latin chez son père Jean 1er dans les premiers mois de 1557: *In Euclidis Elementa geometrica Demonstrationum libri sex.* L'emploi du latin n'est pas le fruit de son inconstance.[77] Sans doute répondait-il à deux exigences: l'une, plus contingente, puisqu'il dut apparemment céder aux reproches des savants que n'avait pas encore conquis l'emploi du français et de *son* français; l'autre, qui devait lui être plus personnelle, à savoir son désir de 'tendre à la réputation plus au loin et en vue de plus de monde', comme il l'écrit lui-même dans son Avertissement aux lecteurs, en tête de son *Algèbre*. Dans sa lettre latine adressée en mars 1557 à Pontus de Tyard, que l'on peut lire à la suite des *Demonstrationum libri sex*, et que cite Hauréau dans son *Histoire littéraire du Maine*,[78] Peletier fait un parallèle entre ses productions poétiques, dont il est justement fier, et son œuvre mathématique: les premières, pense-t-il, peuvent lui assurer une longue célébrité, mais ses découvertes scientifiques seront éternelles comme la vérité. Manifestation typique de ce sentiment de la gloire, qu'a si bien analysé Mme Joukovsky,[79] dira-t-on. Mais j'estime que la subjectivité de Peletier n'est pas seulement en cause: il pensait sincèrement que ses traités de mathématiques, même s'ils étaient en partie des commentaires de savants anciens, étaient perdurables de par leur universalité même. C'est dans cette même lettre à Pontus qu'il proclame, avec un dépit non dissimulé: 'Nunc ad Romanos transeo!',[80] lui signifiant par là qu'il abandonne le français, c'est-à-dire son 'enseigne', au moins provisoirement.

Pendant la dizaine d'années qu'il passa à Paris, de 1558 ou 59 jusqu'en 1569, son activité scientifique consista en révisions et additions de ses ouvrages de mathématiques. Les temps étaient difficiles, et l'esprit tolérant de Peletier le maintenait à l'égard des querelles politiques et religieuses. Ce n'est pas la manière de se préserver des ennemis et des détracteurs. Peut-être pour éviter de se battre sur trop de fronts à la fois, peut-être et même sûrement à la suite de l'échec de sa réforme de l'orthographe, il rédigea désormais ses travaux mathématiques en latin, traduisant dans cette langue son Arithmétique, son Algèbre, et composant aussi un ouvrage de géométrie, le *De usu geometriæ liber unus*,[81] à moins que ce dernier ouvrage ne soit légèrement postérieur.

Séjour en Savoie auprès de la duchesse Marguerite de France[82] à laquelle il dédie son poème consacré à ce duché, retour à Paris dans l'été de 1572, nouveau départ pour Bordeaux où il séjourne sept ans. Le voici en 1579 à l'Université de Poitiers où il est chargé d'un cours public de mathématiques.[83] Il l'inaugure par un discours latin,[84] document passionnant car essentiellement autobiographique: il nous révèle notamment qu'au milieu des guerres civiles qui ensanglantèrent la France de 1572 à 1579, Peletier se consolait dans ses travaux mathématiques.[85] Plusieurs sont d'ailleurs restés à l'état de manuscrits. Sa charge d'enseignement des mathématiques à Poitiers ne dura qu'une année, car on le retrouve à Paris en 1580. La rivalité professionnelle, la suffisance des Parisiens à l'égard d'un provincial, l'orgueil presque institutionnel de la plupart des 'professores regii', peut-être aussi d'obscures raisons idéologiques ou religieuses firent que Peletier dut se défendre contre d'âpres attaques, dont on a du mal à saisir les claires raisons. En 1580 il riposte aux attaques d'un professeur royal dans son *Apologia in Mauricium Bressium*.[86] L'année suivante, il est aux prises avec un autre professeur, dont on a déjà rencontré le nom, puisqu'il s'agit d'Henri de Monantheuil, dont la Bibliothèque Nationale possède un exemplaire de l'*Algèbre* latine de Peletier couvert de notes.[87] La controverse porte sur le problème technique de l'angle de contact, Monantheuil ayant écrit une dissertation pour le réfuter: *De angulo contactus ad J. Peletarium*.[88] Peletier termina sans doute sa vie et sa carrière comme principal du Collège du Mans à Paris, en juillet 1582.

Son œuvre de mathématicien et de pédagogue est encore insuffisamment connue. On songe à la déclaration qu'il adressait à ses lecteurs contemporains et futurs, dès le 'proème' de son premier livre d'*Arithmétique* de 1549: 'Ayant désir de laisser au jugement de la Postérité si j'auray esté l'un de ceux par lesquels elle doyve avoir honnorable souvenance de cestuy nostre temps, je me suis délibéré, d'une franche entreprise, luy faire part de tout ce que pourray acquérir par labeur ou industrie. Dont l'un des meilleurs moyens, et duquel je fasse état de lui pouvoir plus gratifier, est la Mathématique. Laquelle j'ai tousjours estimée entre les autres, comme le Soleil entre les étoiles.'[89]

Le grand mérite de Peletier, et son incontestable supériorité sur Bovelles, c'est qu'en combinant les mathématiques spéculatives et les mathématiques pratiques, ou plutôt en vivifiant ou en explicitant les premières non par je ne sais quelle manipulation empirique, mais par un sens aigu de la pratique opératoire, il a contribué à les faire sortir de l'ornière où elles s'étaient assoupies dans les dernières décennies en France. Il réussit à leur faire conquérir leur place propre, hors de la philosophie, même si, par habitude verbale, il continue à les considérer comme une partie de cette philosophie. Il ne craint pas de discuter les travaux des mathématiciens anciens, et surtout leur esprit, comme on peut le voir notamment dans le Proème du livre iv de son *Arithmétique*: 'Ils se sont contentés de l'Arithmétique spéculative, comme vray et propre objet de l'esprit; se proposant qu'il ne doit chaloir à un mathématicien (lequel doit

abstraire ses imaginations des choses maniables et corporelles) de se
mêler de régler les négoces et entremises des hommes.'[90] Et il fait
une utile comparaison avec la musique, dont nul ne pourrait contester que l'extraordinaire développement à l'époque de la Renaissance est dû essentiellement à sa rupture avec les spéculations purement abstraites et théoriques. 'Nous voyons même en la Musique,
qui est un art, de tous le moins actif: que les anciens ne se sont point
addonnés à mettre rien en chant, que sus les instruments, et non par
ecrit, fors long temps après l'Eglise Rommeine introduite.'[91] Mais les
Anciens avaient 'la pratique en main',[92] ce qui pouvait les dispenser
de la mettre par écrit, c'est-à-dire de faire la théorie de cette pratique
dans des traités appropriés. Peut-être avaient-ils également scrupule
à trahir ou à divulguer des secrets (on se souvient de la légende de
la découverte des irrationnelles par les pythagoriciens et la mise à
mort de celui qui en avait divulgué le secret). En fait, Peletier prend
conscience—et nous beaucoup mieux que lui encore—que ses
contemporains sont en train de vivre une véritable mutation culturelle, et que les rapports entre la théorie et la pratique ne pourront
plus se poser comme dans le passé. C'est bien ce que prouvent dans
leurs travaux les historiens des sciences et les historiens des techniques.

En abordant l'œuvre mathématique et pédagogique d'Oronce Fine,[93]
nous allons au rebours de la chronologie, puisque ce mathématicien
dauphinois est né en 1494 (il était de 23 ans l'aîné de Peletier) et est
mort en 1555, soit 27 ans avant le poète, médecin et mathématicien
manceau. Mais il fut le premier titulaire de la chaire de mathématiques
du Collège Royal, et c'est à ce titre que nous le plaçons ici, car dans
l'histoire de l'enseignement des mathématiques entre 1540 et 1570,
l'éclat de cette chaire, et surtout l'éclat que surent lui donner des
hommes comme Fine, Ramus, Forcadel et quelques autres, apparaît
comme prometteur des plus grands développements et des progrès
les plus considérables.[94] De plus, sans que nous soyons renseignés
avec précision sur le nombre et la qualité des auditeurs de ces grands
maîtres, nous pouvons supposer qu'ils devaient constituer un groupe
plus homogène et plus important que ceux des simples collèges
parisiens ou provinciaux, ou des Universités où se pratiquait
l'enseignement des mathématiques.
　　Il faut cependant reconnaître que si la réputation de Fine fut immense et si ses cours publics étaient très fréquentés, il n'a pas laissé
une œuvre de premier plan. L'intervention de Peletier dans la discussion sur l'angle de contingence, et l'égalité entre l'angle rectiligne
et l'angle curviligne, apporta un élément nouveau aux mathéma-

tiques, comme sa méthode pour déterminer les racines rationnelles d'une équation à coefficients rationnels, alors que les démonstrations proposées par Fine pour résoudre certains problèmes célèbres de l'Antiquité, tels que la quadrature du cercle,[95] la duplication du cube, la multisection de l'angle, etc., se sont révélées illusoires, parfois même aux yeux de ses contemporains, comme Pedro Nuñez[96] et Buteo.[97] Mais sa réputation n'en était pas moins considérable à la fois comme professeur, mathématicien, graveur et illustrateur d'ouvrages scientifiques[98] — on se souvient de son intervention dans le travail de Bovelles — , vulgarisateur et constructeur d'instruments scientifiques — astrolabes, quadrants, équatoires, etc.[99] — , en particulier cette fameuse horloge planétaire dont une récente exposition inaugura la remise en place à la Bibliothèque Sainte-Geneviève.

Commençons par laisser la parole à André Thevet, dans son fameux ouvrage illustré paru en 1584 et intitulé: *Les vrais portraits et vies des hommes illustres, grecs, latins et payens, anciens et modernes, recueillis de leurs tableaux, livres, médailles antiques et modernes.*[100] Son portrait physique, qui orne sa biographie, et qui est dû à Jean Janet, peintre de François 1er, est à lui seul tout un programme. Fine est âgé de 36 ou 38 ans, il vient d'être promu à la dignité de 'professor regius': le voici donc coiffé du bonnet professoral, vêtu d'un pourpoint visible sous la toge. En sa main gauche il tient une sphère posée sur deux gros livres; en sa main droite, un compas. Sur une table, devant lui, quelques instruments familiers et symboliques du mathématicien au travail: un cornet d'encre, un parchemin, un papier à demi-déroulé où l'on peut distinguer des figures géométriques. Vu de trois-quarts, le visage tourné à gauche, il se présente à nous avec de longs cheveux, de grands yeux, un nez puissant.[101] Mais ces quelques lignes de Thevet diront encore mieux la gloire du Briançonnais,[102] telle qu'elle était ressentie par ses contemporains:

Les mathémates[103] eussent un fort long temps croupy en un piètre et pitoyable estat (et à notre merveilleux préjudice), si du pays du Dauphiné ne fut sorty un Finé, qui les eut affiné ... Telle peine print-il après elles, que sans précepteur, de soymesmes il s'y façonna si bien, qu'après en avoir faict preuve et en public par des leçons, il fut appelé par ce grand restaurateur des lettres, le Roy François premier, professeur ès-sciences mathématiques. En ceste profession il versa si bien, qu'au gré et contantement des gens de bien et malgré l'envie . . . *il ressuscita en l'université de Paris la splendeur des mathémates qui pour lors estoyent trop abastardies. Mais par ses très doctes et elabourées leçons il leur redonna telle vie qu'il semblait que par luy elles fussent ressuscitées, et que de nouveau l'eschole de Platon fut réveillée dans l'Université de Paris, ou que les mathémates fussent affinées par la dextérité, vigilance et leçons de ce Dauphinois* ...'[104]

L'éloge continue, associant aux leçons et démonstrations orales de Fine, ses multiples écrits et 'l'invention et fabricature de plusieurs beaux instruments et cartes[105] comme ayant la main non moins apte et duite àfabriquer et dresser tels organes, et les peindre, que l'esprit de les inventer'. C'est effectivement à l'association de ses préoccupations scientifiques et pédagogiques—dont la *Protomathesis* porte témoignage—et de sa puissance d'invention technologique, que le mathématicien, astronome et cosmographe dauphinois a dû sa grande renommée à l'époque de la Renaissance. Nous retenons davantage aujourd'hui, comme Gallois dans sa monographie,[106] le talentueux graveur et cartographe. Mais il ne fit pas moins école dans ce domaine, encore assez neuf en France, de la géographie: on en pourra juger à la lecture de l'ouvrage du P. François de Dainville sur les géographes humanistes[107] et les travaux portant sur les aspects mathématiques du globe terrestre. Le P. Possevin, jésuite, qui composait à la fin du siècle sa *Bibliotheca Selecta*,[108] ouvrage énorme dans lequel il passait en revue l'ensemble des disciplines utiles au théologien, et où il traitait notamment (livre xv) '*de Mathematicis* ... *deque Cosmographia et Geographia*',[109] considérait que 'la Sphère la plus estimée de l'époque est celle d'Oronce Finé'.[110] Et il ajoutait qu' 'elle vient d'être surpassée par celle de Gérard Mercator regardée par les gens entendus comme la plus parfaite de toutes'.[111] Ses cartes de France, du Dauphiné, de la Savoie et de la Provence, sa carte de Terre Sainte ou ses deux mappemondes en forme de cœur[112] contribuèrent à le faire passer—aux yeux des autres et à ses propres yeux—comme l'un des plus grands savants du royaume. Parmi les témoignages très nombreux de ses contemporains, on peut encore évoquer le poète soissonnais Hubert Sussanneau ou Sussannée— l'un de ces 'Apollons de collège' ou ces 'bons camarades' dont parle Lucien Febvre[113]—gloire mineure de la *Gallia poetica*. En tête de la *Quadratura circuli* de Fine, il éprouve le besoin d'adresser un éloge versifié en hexamètres, non pas au mathématicien illustre, mais à son épouse, une certaine Dionysia Candida, qu'André Thevet, dans sa biographie (fols. 564-6) traduit par Denise Blanche.[114] Le contenu, comme on peut s'y attendre en pareil cas, est fort banal: heureuse épouse d'avoir un tel mari! Il a su réduire heureusement les cercles en carrés ... Il a enfin réussi ce que des milliers avant lui avaient essayé vainement ... etc. Si Oronce Fine n'avait pas eu d'autres thuriféraires que Sussannée, sa gloire eût été singulièrement obscurcie.[115]

L'abondante liste des ouvrages imprimés d'Oronce Fine, de ceux qu'il a édités, et de ceux qui sont restés à l'état de manuscrit[116] (la plupart se trouvant à la Bibliothèque Nationale et à la Bibliothèque de la Sorbonne)[117] fait apparaître que le latin et le français alternent harmonieusement. Comme avec Peletier du Mans, nous avons affaire ici à un professeur qui s'est posé le problème de la diffusion et de l'utilité de ses écrits, et l'usage du français correspondait chez lui à un souci pédagogique évident. Car en dehors des *Canons d'almanach*[118] et autres pronostications qui pouvaient viser un public plus populaire, plusieurs traités mathématiques, sa *Théorie des planètes*[119] de 1528, sa *Sphère du monde*[120] de 1551, sont écrits et publiés en français de son vivant et par sa volonté. Pour ce qui est de ses traités d'arithmétique (*Arithmetica practica*),[121] de géométrie (*Geometria practica*),[122] ou la partie de son traité de géométrie qui concerne l'instrument nommé *carré géométrique*,[123] ce n'est qu'après sa mort que certains seront publiés en langue vulgaire, encore que pour ce dernier opuscule, un manuscrit de la Bibliothèque Nationale[124] rédigé de la main de Fine nous révèle qu'il était déjà traduit en français par son auteur dès 1538. La géométrie, elle, sera mise en français par l'un de ses successeurs à la chaire de mathématique du Collège Royal, Pierre Forcadel, en 1570,[125] puis rééditée en 1586.[126]

Tout au long de sa carrière professionnelle à Paris—elle dura jusqu'à sa mort, qui survint le 6 octobre 1555—Oronce Fine manifesta sa reconnaissance à l'égard des souverains qui lui permirent de mettre en valeur les sciences qu'il était chargé d'enseigner: il y a là beaucoup plus qu'une manifestation ordinaire de reconnaissance, voire de flatterie. A François 1er, promoteur de sa brillante carrière, il adressait au moment de sa nomination au Collège une *Epistre exhortative* 'touchant la dignité, perfection, et utilité des sciences mathématiques', qui sera rééditée avec la *Sphère du monde* en 1551 et 1552.[127] Ces vers de 10 syllabes groupés par 9 suivant le schéma métrique *aabaabbcc* (en tout 42 groupes, soit 378 vers)[128] ne sont ni meilleurs ni pires que la plupart de ceux des poètes de deuxième ou de troisième rayon, bien qu'Albert-Marie Schmidt ne leur accorde pas le moindre intérêt dans sa *Poésie scientifique au XVIe siècle*.[129] Nous n'en retiendrons que sa présentation comme restaurateur des mathématiques, ce qui n'alla pas sans provoquer l'envie:

Et nonobstant quelques dures attaintes,
Que l'on m'ait fait, je n'en fais mes complaintes,
Mais seulement des arts mathématiques,
Lesquelles sont quasi du tout estaintes,
Et transmuees en sottises trop faintes,

> Par le moyen d'aucuns fort lunatiques,
> Qui ont induit un tas d'arts sophistiques,
> Et divulguez d'une telle maniere,
> Qu'on a du tout les meilleurs mis arriere. (p. 2r, f. 60r)

La strophe suivante résume les trois qualités qu'il est loisible de découvrir dans les mathématiques: leur certitude absolue, leur beauté et leur utilité (même si celle-ci apparaît négativement, comme une réponse possible à un reproche injustifié).

> Sont les clefz de tout perfet sçavoir,
> Oncques vivant ne feit son bon devoir
> A les aimer, qui n'ait eu son desir,
> Ce neantmoins aucuns durs à mouvoir,
> Et lourds d'esprit ont fait tout leur pouvoir
> De les chasser, disans que seul plaisir,
> Lon peult avoir, sans qu'on puisse choisir,
> Quelque support ou quelque profit d'elles,
> En confessant au moins qu'elles sont belles. (p. 2r–v, ff. 60r–v)

Comme un bon écolier, que n'inspirent pas les Muses, Oronce récite sa leçon:

> Il est donc cler que les mathematiques
> Tresnobles sont perfettes, authentiques,
> Et le miroer de toute certitude:
> Car tous les ars nobles ou mechaniques,
> Mesmement ceux qui sont plus magnifiques
> D'elles ont prins leur cours et habitudes
> Ce que voyant Marin homme d'estude,
> Tous autres arts il souhaitta semblables
> Aux dessusdits, tant les trouva feables. (pp. 2v–3r, ff. 60v–61r)

Ou encore cette ingénuité par laquelle nous apprenons que

> Platon qui fut homme de grand memoire
> Laissa souvent le manger et le boire
> Pour contempler ces nobles disciplines . . .
>
> (p. 3r, f. 61r)

Il va donc parler des mathématiques en suivant l'ordre qu'une certaine logique et une certaine chronologie (que nous ne discuterons pas) lui imposent. Tout d'abord, l'Arithmétique, 'le vray chef et pillier/C'est à sçavoir ma fille plus antique'. De Pythagore, Nicomaque, Euclide, Boèce, de l'exaltation de l'unité qui 'fait nombres de grande quantité' (p. 3v), lesquels nombres se résolvent finalement à l'un,[130] à l'évocation de Platon, il passe assez prosaïquement au 'grand seigneur, ou prelat en l'eglise,/Riche bourgeois ou suyvant marchandise, (p. 4r, f. 62r) pour dire cette vérité banale que tous ont besoin de calculer.

La géométrie, qui vient ensuite, compta ses premiers professeurs parmi les Egyptiens, auxquels succédèrent les Grecs, Thalès, Hypocras et Platon.

> Apres survient Euclides en dernier,
> Qui la perfeit et remist en tel ordre,
> Qu'on ne le sceu depuis en cest art mordre. (p. 4r, f. 62r)

L'hommage obligé rendu à Euclide, que tous les mathématiciens de la Renaissance ont traduit, édité ou commenté, est un hommage rendu à la simplicité et à l'évidence des premiers éléments ou fondements de la géométrie elle-même, comme à la certitude rationnelle de ses démonstrations ou à son universelle intelligibilité:

> Il ne fut onc si vraye discipline,
> Veu que ses faux detracteurs extermine
> Par argument et raison invincible:
> Car pour le moins tousiours est reducible
> A ses premiers et certains fondemens,
> Qui sont receus de tous entendemens. (ibid.)

Le professeur souligne la valeur pédagogique incomparable de cette science, dont la 'vacation'

> Est contempler tousiours choses hautaines,
> Et discerner les fausses des certaines. (p. 4v, f. 62v)

En effet:

> Elle nous rend les esprits incitez,
> Doctes, subtils, instruits, habillitez,
> Pour inventer toute chose nouvelle. (ibid.)

Bref, chacun en tire son profit sur le plan de l'intelligence théorique, comme dans la pratique: ne sert-elle pas à la décoration des cités, des églises, des demeures, des chateaux?

N'oublions pas que la musique fait partie des disciplines mathématiques. D'ailleurs Fine avait composé, avant même d'être nommé lecteur royal, en 1529, une introduction pour apprendre à jouer les chansons[131] 'réduites en la tabulature du luth', ainsi qu'un *Epithoma musice instrumentalis*[132] en 1530. Ce qu'il en dit ici en 45 vers (p. 4v–[p. 5v], ff. 62v–63v) correspond aux idées communes à toute son époque, avec un raccourci de mythologie et d'histoire païenne ainsi que d'histoire sacrée (Orphée, Amphion, Hercule, Lucrèce, Platon, Pappus, Apulée, d'une part; saint Augustin, saint Ambroise, le psautier, d'autre part), le rappel de ses vertus thérapeutiques, ou roborifiques.

L'épitre ne pouvait que se clore sur l'astronomie 'laquelle fut des Arabes acquise,/Et puis regna par le pays d'Egypte' ([p. 5v], f. 63v), utile aux médecins comme aux prélats, suivie de ses

> bonnes cousines,
> Tant florissans, tant douces, tant benignes,
> Geographie et sa seur Perspective. ([p. 6r], f. 64r)

dont le mathématicien-géographe va faire un éloge passionné.

En ce temps-là (comme d'ailleurs en d'autres), un tel poème ne pouvait s'achever sans un couplet patriotique, voire nationaliste. La France ne brillait point alors, comme on l'a vu au début, par l'éclat de ses découvertes ou de son enseignement mathématiques (c'est même le sens profond de la politique culturelle de François Ier, quand il introduit cette discipline au Collège Royal). Aussi comprenons-nous ces vers faussement ingénus, mais sincèrement reconnaissants, du sujet à son souverain :

> Plaise toy donc affin que leur cours dure,
> Ordonner un qui jour et nuit procure,
> Les demonstrer à tous publiquement.
> Et ce faisant lon verra briefvement
> France florir et passer en doctrines,
> Les nations et gens circunvoisines. ([p. 6v], f. 64v)

Et la fleur de lys rejoint, dans sa prière, la gloire du 'roy des ciels regnant en paradis'.

Nous avons longuement insisté sur ce poème mineur, car il est très caractéristique de l'état d'esprit d'un homme qui ne manque aucune occasion—généralement en tête de ses ouvrages mathématiques—d'exalter cette science et son enseignement. La référence qu'il fait, une fois de plus, à Platon, au début de son *Arithmetica practica*, n'est pas gratuite, car c'est au Platon pédagogue qu'il songe, à celui qui faisait apprendre les nombres aux enfants,[133] science sans laquelle 'on ne pouvait convenablement administrer ni ses affaires privées ni les affaires publiques'. Quant à l'examen détaillé de ses traités, où sont multipliées des figures de grande qualité technique, on est frappé par le caractère didactique qu'ils présentent—d'un didactisme qui répond à une volonté d'enseignement général, pour ne pas dire populaire—et par le côté pratique qui en est le corollaire. Rien ne le montre mieux que les pages consacrées à la description et à l'expérimentation de ce fameux 'quarré géométrique', dont les principales applications consistent à évaluer des hauteurs ou des largeurs inaccessibles, qu'il s'agisse d'une tour sans échelle, d'une montagne escarpées ou d'un fleuve sans pont.[134]

Oronce Fine n'a pas été sans doute un grand mathématicien : il fut incontestablement un grand professeur et un bon diffuseur des mathématiques.

S'il est un homme, un professeur, réformateur dans l'âme, qui sut donner en France un éclat aux mathématiques, ou tout au moins à leur enseignement, ce fut bien Pierre Ramus.[135]

On a vu à quel point, en dehors de l'école de Mélanchthon, cet enseignement—qui faisait pourtant partie intégrante des arts libéraux—avait été négligé par l'humanisme pédagogique. Il faudra que les mathématiciens commencent par démontrer que leur science n'est pas impie, et que Dieu se satisfait aussi bien de l'arithmétique et de la géométrie[136] que des langues anciennes ou de la grammaire: ils s'y emploieront à la faveur des préfaces, dont l'intérêt est souvent aussi grand, voire supérieur, à celui des traités de mathématiques eux-mêmes. Esprit religieux autant que professeur combatif, philosophe qui plaçait la vérité au-dessus de toute considération d'opportunité, dialecticien redoutable, Ramus, qui connaît bien les ressources de la rhétorique, commence à répandre l'idée que l'étude des mathématiques est un devoir religieux. Ne recherchent-elles pas une vérité intangible et universelle? Son amour pour Platon lui fait évoquer sans cesse la célèbre inscription que le philosophe grec avait fait graver au fronton de l'Académie: 'Que nul n'entre ici s'il n'est géomètre'. On songe au frontispice du grand traité de géométrie et de balistique que l'illustre Tartaglia avait publié en 1537 à Venise[137] sous le titre-programme de *Nova Scientia*: A la porte extérieure d'une sorte d'arène circulaire entourée d'un mur, un étudiant est accueilli par Euclide en personne. A l'intérieur il trouve Tartaglia entouré des disciplines mathématiques, Arithmétique, Géométrie, Astronomie, Astrologie, etc. Sur la gauche, un canon tire, montrant la trajectoire parabolique du projectile. A la porte du fond, donnant accès à une plus petite arène, se tiennent Aristote et Platon, pour introduire l'étudiant en présence de la Philosophie qui siège sur son trône. Platon tient une banderole portant l'inscription latine: 'Nemo hic geometriae expers ingrediatur'. Dans la préface latine de son traité d'arithmétique, imprimé à Paris chez André Wechel,[138] qu'il dédie au Cardinal Charles de Lorraine,[139] puissant protecteur des lettres et des arts, et pour lui un appui politique de première grandeur, Ramus va même jusqu'à attribuer à tous les peuples de l'antiquité une part du génie mathématique. On peut se demander si c'est l'esprit humaniste ou l'esprit religieux qui le fait ainsi ranger les Hébreux aux côtés des Egyptiens, des Grecs et des Romains: 'Les éléments des mathématiques, ô Mécène, jouirent jadis d'un incroyable prestige chez les Hébreux, les Egyptiens, les Grecs et les Romains: ce sont elles, en effet, qui constituèrent pour les premiers parents du genre humain, Adam, Seth et Noé, des occupations divines, par leurs contemplations des ouvrages mathématiques de Dieu, très bon et très grand'.[140] De là, par Abraham et

JEAN-CLAUDE MARGOLIN

par d'autres savants Hébreux, la 'translatio studiorum' se fit en direction de l'Egypte, dont le préfacier souligne le caractère sacré : les mathématiciens étaient les prêtres. Les noms des mathématiciens grecs abondent, mais Ramus indique très vite le caractère pratique de certains traités, toujours utilisables par les peintres et les architectes, ceux de Vitruve en particulier.[141] Dans ses *Scholæ mathematicæ*,[142] Ramus reviendra plus tard sur les liaisons qu'il pense avoir découvertes entre les mathématiques et les desseins de Dieu. Non seulement il n'oppose pas aux devoirs sacrés de la religion ce qu'en d'autres temps certains esprits eussent considéré comme des occupations purement mondaines, mais il pense et il proclame que l'Ecriture Sainte nous incite aux études mathématiques. Le prophète Ezéchiel ne donne-t-il pas les dimensions exactes de la cité sainte ? Ne trouvonsnous pas dans l'Ecriture des textes à l'appui de la géographie, de l'optique ? Le vrai Dieu est mathématicien (on connait le succès de la future formule leibnizienne 'Dum Deus calculat fit mundus'), les vrais mathématiciens sont d'authentiques croyants. C'est chez Ramus une affaire de conviction, et les *Scholæ mathematicæ* multiplient les formules à l'envi, sur lesquelles R. Hooykaas revient, tant dans l'étude que nous avons déjà citée[143] que dans son ouvrage *Science and theology in the Middle Ages*.[144] La formation mathématique, sans se substituer pour autant à l'éducation religieuse, est la meilleure école pour le néophyte ou apprenti chrétien, car l'harmonie géométrique et la certitude des démonstrations mathématiques rappellent irrésistiblement que 'les cieux racontent la gloire de Dieu'. Les mathématiques sont un véritable instrument de décryptage de l'obscurité de certains passages de l'Ecriture, la vérité est une, et un théologien serait mal venu à taxer cette science, d'inutile, voire d'impie.[145]

Si j'insiste sur ce soubassement philosophico-religieux de la pensée de Ramus, mathématicien et professeur, c'est qu'en dehors de son importance dans l'économie de son propre système de pensée, il commençait à orienter les esprits dans une voie nouvelle : en cette seconde moitié du XVIe siècle, où les arts mécaniques ont fait de grands progrès, où les engins utilisables dans les activités de guerre comme dans les œuvres pacifiques de l'industrie, du commerce, de la navigation, de l'architecture, etc., requièrent constamment des modèles mathématiques, l'opposition de la théorie et de la pratique ne conserve toute sa rigueur que dans le cerveau de quelques professeurs traditionalistes ou rétrogrades, comme ce Jacques Charpentier l'adversaire acharné de Ramus.[146] On peut constater à quel point notre auteur manifeste son indépendance intellectuelle, et quel est son sens de l'esprit du temps' et même, en général, son sens de l'histoire. En effet lui aussi pratique l''amicus Plato', et il sait se séparer de son maître, quand celui-ci oppose d'une façon trop rigoureuse les sciences théorétiques ou contemplatives et leurs applications pratiques. 'Platon, écrit-il dans ses *Scholæ mathematicæ*,[147] se réjouissait autant des *contemplations* mathématiques qu'il méprisait leur emploi populaire et vulgaire, et il croyait qu'Eudoxe et Archytas se souilleraient par des travaux mathématiques manuels.'[148] Il quittera donc Platon sur ce point. Et réciproquement, lui que l'on a coutume de représenter comme l'adversaire inconditionné d'Aristote en raison de la fougueuse diatribe de sa jeunesse[149] et des graves ennuis que lui causèrent les Aristotéliciens scolastiques de l'Université de Paris, n'éprouve aucune gêne à louer le philosophe du Lycée pour son enseignement de la mécanique et la publication d'un livre à ce sujet. C'est une constante de l'esprit de Ramus, et il va sans dire que ses idées, il les applique aussi bien dans ses cours que dans ses livres : en unissant la pureté contemplative des vérités mathématiques à l'efficacité pratique des applications techniques, il fait franchir un pas considérable à cette science et fait virer l'humanisme traditionnel en un humanisme que l'on peut qualifier de moderne. C'est d'ailleurs l'expression qu'utilisait dans son célèbre ouvrage de 1940[150] le Père F. de Dainville pour désigner le nouveau cours des lettres et des sciences que les Jésuites parvinrent à instituer progressivement dans la seconde moitié du xvιe siècle. Cet humanisme moderne dans lequel les mathématiques occupent une place importante et où l'on n'oppose plus aux pures idées platoniciennes les nécessités opératoires et techniques, on peut en trouver des échos dans tel passage de la *Ratio studiorum*[151] de 1586, qui se proposait d'ailleurs dans son exposé des motifs, d'argumenter contre les trop nombreux Jésuites conservateurs qui se faisaient encore les détracteurs des mathématiques :

Elles apprennent aux poètes le lever et le coucher des astres ; aux historiens la situation et les distances des divers lieux ; aux philosophes, des exemples de démonstrations solides ; aux politiques des méthodes vraiment admirables pour conduire les affaires dans le privé et à la guerre ; aux physiciens, les modes et les diversités des mouvements célestes, de la lumière, des couleurs, des corps diaphanes, des sons ; aux métaphysiciens le nombre des sphères et des intelligences ; aux théologiens les principales parties de la création divine ; aux juristes et aux canonistes le comput, sans parler des services rendus par le travail des mathématiciens à l'Etat, à la médecine, à la navigation et à l'agriculture. *Il faut donc faire effort pour que les mathématiques fleurissent dans nos collèges aussi bien que les autres disciplines.*[152]

Précieuse convergence pour l'historien des idées que celle de ce programme des rédacteurs Jésuites de la charte scolaire de 1586 avec les arguments proclamés une trentaine d'années plus tôt par un homme auquel son destin réservait de mourir victime en juillet 1572 des massacreurs de la Saint-Barthélemy.

Les *Scholæ mathematicæ* sont à lire attentivement, car il n'est pas de texte où apparait avec plus de clarté l'esprit de l'enseignement des mathématiques de Ramus. Qu'il s'agisse d'Archimède, dont il déplore qu'il n'ait pas reconnu 'que la fin des arts est dans l'usage, non pas dans la contemplation',[153] ou encore une fois, de Platon, dont il va jusqu'à dénoncer la 'jalousie'[154] ou la 'partialité aveugle' qui 'a failli faire périr non seulement l'*usage* de la géométrie, mais cette science elle-même', Ramus ne mâche pas ses mots;[155] mais il n'a pas non plus son pareil pour dénicher chez ces grands hommes les passages de leurs œuvres où il pense avoir trouvé des alliés pour son entreprise: Archimède n'a-t-il pas écrit quelques ouvrages de mécanique, et Platon ne proclame-t-il pas quelque part l'*utilité* du calcul dans le domaine de la stratégie? C'est alors que ce philosophe est 'le vrai Platon, animé par l'esprit platonicien'.[156] Les mathématiques sont la nécessaire propédeutique aux fonctions de gardiénage de la Cité comme à celles de gouvernement de la République.

L'enseignement des mathématiques de Ramus, tel qu'il apparaît à la fois par les nombreuses préfaces de ses ouvrages, ses *Scholæ*, sa correspondance, et quelques manuscrits ou notes de cours (la Bibliothèque de la Sorbonne en possède) est donc un enseignement positif et pratique,[157] sans préjudice de la rigueur théorique des définitions et des démonstrations. Il prend violemment parti contre toutes les sortes de spéculations mystiques sur les nombres et les proportions, issues du courant néo-pythagoricien ou du courant néo-platonicien, dont la Renaissance s'était tellement nourrie.[158] Dans son esprit, cette sorte de 'métamathématique' rejoint les spéculations des scolastiques concernant les diverses quiddités ou essences des choses. Autant il ne veut pas séparer la pratique des mathématiques de l'exercice de la foi — entendons de la foi véritable — autant il rejette dans le même discrédit toutes les formes d'arithmomancie ou de géométrolâtrie, et toutes les variétés de superstition à résonance religieuse: le croyant et l'homme de sciences nettoient d'un même coup de balai ces écuries d'Augias. Il poursuit d'ailleurs, ce faisant, la tradition d'un Lefèvre d'Etaples ou d'un Bovelles, celle de Peletier et de Fine, dont on a souligné l'intérêt des Arithmétiques et Géométries *pratiques*. Tradition que l'on pourrait faire remonter encore plus haut, si l'on songe à la *Practica Geometriæ*[159] de Hugues de St Victor, qui date de 1130.

La réforme des études et de l'enseignement mathématiques entreprise par Ramus fait partie intégrante de son programme de réformes de l'Université, mais elle en constitue certainement l'une des pièces maîtresses, car la promotion de cette discipline marquait *ipso facto* le déclin de la logique et de la dialectique traditionnelles. D'autre part, en un temps où l'on ne pouvait pas enseigner proprement la géométrie si l'on ignorait le grec, puisque les cours consistaient pour une bonne part en commentaires d'Euclide, sa défense conjointe des mathématiques et des langues anciennes (sans préjudice pour le français), et ses efforts courageux pour interdire par l'institution d'un examen préalable l'entrée du Collège Royal à des ignorants comme le sicilien Dampestre Cosel[160] en octobre 1565, ou le trop célèbre Jacques Charpentier[161] en mars 1566, sont à verser à son actif. Mais il n'était guère suivi par ses collègues ou par le Parlement, dont Waddington a reproduit le curieux arrêt du 11 mars 1566,[162] aux termes duquel Charpentier—qui reconnaissait lui-même son ignorance du grec et des mathématiques[163]—devait faire la preuve pendant trois mois qu'il était capable d'enseigner les *Eléments* d'Euclide. Ce qu'avec une superbe impudence l'homme qui déclarait que cette science était un jeu d'enfants, sinon une fange où ne pouvaient se complaire que des porcs,[164] inaugura son cours public dans une chaire de mathématiques par la lecture d'Aristote[165] en latin! Les péripéties de la bataille de Ramus et de Charpentier sont trop connues pour que l'on y insiste ici, et une communication[166] sur la réforme ramusienne de l'Université me dispense de longs discours. Rappelons que pour Ramus, comme on le voit au début du livre IV des *Scholæ mathematicæ*,[167] la division courante du *quadrivium* en arithmétique, géométrie, astronomie et musique—division à laquelle sacrifiaient les mathématiciens dont nous avons déjà parlé, et notamment Oronce Fine dans son Epître à François Ier[168]—est contestable; il préfère une division fondée sur l'opposition des *intelligibilia* et des *sensibilia*, et il tend à rejeter dans le domaine de la physique— ou, comme nous dirions aujourd'hui, de la physique mathématique —l'astronomie, l'optique et la physique. Ce travail d'épuration nous paraît d'autant plus remarquable qu'il est fait par un homme qui n'a sous la plume ou à la bouche que l'idée d'une arithmétique ou d'une géométrie *pratiques* et qu'il avait à faire front contre ses ennemis qui le traitaient d'*usuarius*.[169] Mais nous saisissons mieux la distinction qu'il fait entre des séparations de type logique, notionnel ou classificatoire, et des complémentarités d'ordre pratique. L'application d'une discipline à une autre ne doit pas permettre la confusion entre les objets distincts qu'elles visent l'une et l'autre. D'autre part, un logicien peut parfaitement appliquer ses facultés et sa méthode à l'examen de phénomènes physiques, s'il les considère d'un certain point de vue général, s'il s'intéresse aux principes mis en jeu dans la recherche de la causalité; de même un physicien peut faire des mathématiques en réduisant les 'realia' observés à des figures, lignes ou courbes, et en leur appliquant des méthodes de calcul. C'est là vraiment une manière moderne de penser, qui ne doit pas plus à Platon qu'à Aristote.

Ainsi les arts mathématiques ne comprennent-ils en propre que deux branches, l'arithmétique et la géométrie, la première s'occupant des quantités discrètes, la seconde des quantités continues. La pensée de Ramus s'exprime ici, comme toujours, avec une netteté et une rigueur qui devaient faire merveille auprès des étudiants: 'Mathematica igitur est arithmetica in numero, geometria in magnitudine; musica autem, astrologia, caeteraque illa *physicotera* non sunt artes mathematicae'.[170] En effet ces dernières sciences ne portent ni sur le nombre ni sur la grandeur, mais sur une *chose* physique nombrée ou sur une *chose* physique quantifiée.[171] Idée importante, qui n'est sans doute pas nouvelle puisqu'on la trouve déjà exprimée au Moyen Age par Pierre d'Ailly,[172] et assez récemment par Tartaglia,[173] mais qui était passablement oubliée.

La lecture intelligente des mathématiciens grecs, et notamment du géomètre Euclide—dont on n'éditait, traduisait ou commentait généralement que les six premiers livres—est révélatrice de cette complémentarité bien comprise de la théorie et de la pratique: en effet, bien que, pour des raisons qui tiennent autant au génie mathématique d'Euclide qu'à la philosophie contemplative d'inspiration platonicienne dont il était nourri, les *Eléments* ne traitent effectivement que des axiomes, des définitions, des notions purement rationnelles, que leurs figures soient idéales, et qu'en dehors des démonstrations fondées sur un petit nombre de principes logiques, l'évidence intuitive soit le seul recours, ils ouvrent la voie à toutes les applications de la vie pratique. La règle et le compas, seules pièces de la panoplie euclidienne, sont-ils concevables en dehors de leur réalisation? Entre l'enseignement, objet propre de la géométrie théorique, et l'action, objet de la géométrie pratique, il n'y a pas de médiation, pas plus qu'entre l'*agent* (ou *artifex*) qui fait ses cours au Collège Royal, et les *artisans* de la Rue St-Denis ou du Pont des Orfèvres[174] 'qui repose moins sur des poutres et des solives que sur une masse d'or et d'argent'. On connaît le célèbre passage des *Scholæ mathematicæ* dans lequel le professeur, nous prenant comme par la main, nous fait faire un tour de la ville, 'la plus grande et la plus opulente de toutes les cités', pour nous montrer, non par démonstration mathématique, mais par une évidence pratique, l'importance de l'arithmétique dans la vie quotidienne, commerciale et artisanale de Paris.[175] Nous renvoyons, pour l'ensemble des rapports entre les arts libéraux et les arts mécaniques, et pour l'étude des propres rapports de Ramus avec les artisans de la capitale sur le terrain qui nous occupe, à l'étude bien documentée de Hooykaas, dont la source principale est cette histoire vivante et personnelle de l'enseignement des sciences et des techniques que constituent les premiers livres des *Scholæ mathematicæ*. Une traduction française—ou en quelque autre langue moderne—serait la bienvenue.

C'est dans son Arithmétique et dans sa Géométrie, ouvrages intégrés dans ses *Scholæ mathematicæ*, que Ramus fit preuve à la fois de qualités d'invention, mais aussi—il faut bien le dire—d'un certain esprit rétrograde. Ce qu'il écrit sur les grandeurs ou les lignes rationnelles et irrationnelles constitue, si l'on peut dire, un état de la question, du moins dans l'enseignement français. Il a parfaitement intégré la plupart des notations et abréviations de l'arithmétique. L'un des livres les plus intéressants des *Scholæ* est ce livre xxiiii dans lequel il exprime avec netteté cette vérité mathématique devenue depuis fort banale, mais qui faisait alors figure de nouveauté: la multiplication d'un nombre négatif (l'expression n'est pas encore née) par un nombre négatif donne un nombre positif, autrement dit deux négations équivalent à une affirmation (ou plutôt à une *position*). On pourra examiner les opérations qu'il dispose à la page 275 de ses *Scholæ*.[176] On peut par contre, regretter que trop souvent la description tienne lieu de démonstration, en arithmétique comme en géométrie. Ce qu'il y a de plus intéressant dans l'œuvre mathématique de Ramus—et sans doute, dans son enseignement dont elle est le reflet ou la préparation—c'est, à propos d'un problème ou d'une démonstration, son souci de références historiques, son désir de nous faire comprendre, qu'en dépit du caractère universel et intemporel des vérités mathématiques, cette science a un passé, par rapport auquel le mathématicien moderne doit se définir. Peut-être eût-il été théoriquement quand même préférable (si je me place du point de vue du lecteur et de l'historien modernes) que ces deux ordres de préoccupations se soient trouvés séparés dans le texte imprimé. Dans son livre xxi des *Scholæ*,[177] il en vient à critiquer le livre x d'Euclide ou plutôt ses démonstrations qu'il juge trop subtiles ou obscures, et qui portent sur l'unité de mesure, puis sur l'incommensurabilité, les grandeurs symétriques ou asymétriques. Il n'a, dit-il, rien lu de plus obscur,[178] non qu'Euclide soit difficile à comprendre, même pour des gens peu savants et sans culture (ce qui est pour le moins contradictoire), mais ce livre est difficile à approfondir.[179] Il reproche au géomètre grec l'absence de démonstration dans sa théorie des figures planes ou des volumes incommensurables (*irrationales*),[180] mais il oublie lui-même d'en proposer de véritables. En tout cas, même si ses reproches sont discutables, il fait preuve, une fois de plus, d'indépendance d'esprit en portant sur Euclide, comme il l'a fait sur Platon—ne parlons-pas d'Aristote—un regard hypercritique. N'est-ce pas à ces 'obscurités' ou à ces 'subtilités' du géomètre théoricien qu'il songeait, quand il proposait en 1562 dans son fameux 'Advertissement sur la Réforme de l'Université de Paris'[181] au roi Charles IX (ou plutôt à la reine-mère Catherine de Médicis) une réforme donnant aux mathématiques une place importante, mais sans accorder un monopole aux *Eléments* d'Euclide? 'Mettez au premier honneur et degré de l'estude publique, écrivait-il, les artz mathematiques qui anciennement n'apartenoyent qu'aux Roys et nobles Seigneurs de ceste savante escrime'.[182] Et le nom d'Archimède lui vient ensuite plus facilement sous la plume que celui d'Euclide.[183] Peletier du Mans, dans son ultime ouvrage, *De l'Usage de géométrie*,[184] ou plutôt dans l'épître dédicatoire de la version française adressée à Messire Albert Degondy, comte de Rets, rejoignait Ramus quand il déclarait: 'Et de ma part je suis bien loing de l'opinion de ceux qui n'apellent géométrie sinon celle Elementaire, traittée par Euclide, non pas celle usagère d'Archimède, d'Apoloine, de Tolemee et des autres auteurs excellens qui ont si ingenieusement conjoint l'artifice avec l'expérience.'[185] Mais nous avons déjà vu que, sauf en des heures d'abattement, Ramus faisait des 'théoriciens' et des 'praticiens' ou 'usagers' les artisans également nécessaires des mathématiques.

Nul ne pourra en tout cas contester le zèle désintéressé de ce professeur devenu un exilé, un persécuté—et qui mourra sous le couteau des assassins sans avoir pu achever son œuvre—, lui qui avait fondé par testament, en date du 1er août 1568, une chaire de mathématiques au Collège de France en y consacrant la plus grande partie de ses rentes de l'Hôtel de Ville.[186] Il voulait en même temps assurer sa succession, ce qui est l'un des gestes auxquels se reconnaissent généralement les véritables maîtres. Rappelons quelques lignes de ce testament:

> Sur ma rente annuelle de sept cents livres à l'hôtel de ville de Paris, j'en lègue cinq cents pour le traitement d'un professeur de mathématiques qui, dans l'espace de trois ans, enseignera au collège royal l'arithmétique, la musique, la géométrie, l'optique, la mécanique, la géographie et l'astronomie, non selon l'opinion des hommes, mais selon la raison et la vérité. Je nomme et établis comme professeur, pour les trois premières années, Frédéric Reisner, afin qu'il achève les travaux que nous avons commencé ensemble, spécialement en optique et en astronomie.[187]

Et il revenait sur l'idée qui lui était chère, d'un concours ouvert à tous les candidats, sans distinction de pays, et d'un examen public et impartial qui devait désigner le plus compétent. La chaire de Ramus devait être illustrée jusqu'à la Révolution française par quelques grands noms de l'histoire des mathématiques.

Au nom de Pierre Ramus il faut associer celui de son principal collaborateur des années 1560–1565, qui obtint, sur ses instances, une chaire de mathématiques, Pierre Forcadel de Béziers.[188] Il faut souligner le fait qu'il n'appartenait pas aux 'doctes et érudits en latin et grec'[189] et qu'il n'écrivait pas le latin, faute de le savoir suffisamment. Ainsi, dans les années 1560–1570, un professeur de mathématiques peut enseigner sa discipline et écrire des livres directement en français. Et Ramus l'humaniste n'a pas de préjugés à cet égard. On peut affirmer que, dans ce domaine tout au moins, l'enseignement humaniste traditionnnel a vécu. Ce qui n'empêche pas notre mathématicien de publier des traductions françaises des neuf premiers livres d'Euclide en 1564, ainsi que de plusieurs autres œuvres mathématiques et astronomiques de savants anciens ou modernes, comme Archimède, Proclus, Théodose, Autolycus, Fine, Gemma Frisius, etc. Il a pu utiliser des traductions latines, peut-être même, pour certains, des traductions françaises; mais il devait quand même savoir assez de grec et de latin pour *traduire* en français ces œuvres.

A la vérité, le professeur Forcadel ne se contente pas de donner le texte d'Euclide, le commentaire explicatif est de lui, ou plutôt il réalise une synthèse des démonstrations que l'on peut lire dans le texte grec d'Euclide et de ses propres explications. L'ouvrage est abondamment illustré, avec quelques artifices typographiques dans la confection des figures. Plusieurs exemplaires de plusieurs éditions consultés à la Bibliothèque Nationale[190] montrent que l'ouvrage était soigneusement lu et annoté (remarques marginales, astérisques, *notae*, etc.). Ici encore, quelques extraits des préfaces qu'il a adressées pour chacun des neuf livres, à de hauts personnages du royaume, sont révélateurs à la fois des milieux sur lesquels il a besoin de s'appuyer, et de la popularité de l'enseignement des mathématiques en français. Ces personnages ont nom Gaspart de Coligny,[191] Amiral de France (livre II), Charles de Thelligny, gentilhomme ordinaire de la Chambre du Roi (livre III), Maistre Pierre de Mont Doré, conseiller du Roi et maistre de sa librairie (livre V), M. Guetauld, docteur en médecine en la ville d'Orléans (livre VI), le livre VII étant dédié à l'illustre Cardinal de Châtillon, le livre VIII au médecin du Roi Chappelain, le dernier livre à Monsieur De Belesbat, conseiller et maistre de requêtes ordinaire de l'Hostel du Roi. Nous sommes en avril 1564 pour les six premiers livres, en janvier 1565 pour les trois suivants. On apprend que l'Amiral de Coligny, fervent de mathématiques, encourage ceux qui s'y adonnent et qui en font profession.[192] Ramus et Forcadel sont protestants, le premier depuis 1562. Le Cardinal de Lorraine est devenu l'une des 'bêtes noires' du parti réformé. Il est loin, le temps où lui étaient adressées de glorieuses dédicaces! Le livre (III) des cercles, des droites et des angles, est présenté par un rapprochement classique entre les sphères célestes et la sphère terrestre, le macrocosme et le microcosme. La préface à Pierre de Mont Doré rappelle que l'auteur enseigne les mathématiques depuis quatorze ans (donc depuis 1550) et que ses travaux ne visent qu'à profiter au bien public (rappel qui n'est pas inutile en ces temps de guerre civile et religieuse): c'est la raison qui l'a poussé à faire des traductions, pensant qu'ainsi il pourra étendre son enseignement à un plus grand nombre d'esprits. Avec le non-humaniste Forcadel, nous sommes loin d'un autre collaborateur de Ramus, ce Jean Péna auquel son maître avait fait obtenir une chaire de mathématiques à l'âge de 23 ans, en 1555 et à propos duquel il écrivait dans ses *Actiones duæ mathematicæ* (1566): 'Parmi les savants érudits en latin et en grec, Jean Péna a été pour nous un assistant de premier ordre dans les sciences mathématiques; et c'est avec notre assistance qu'il s'éleva jusqu'à la chaire royale.'[193] Un autre témoignage de Ramus, dans la *Math. præf. quarta* (*Collect.* p. 188), nous dépeint ce jeune homme—qui devait mourir à 26 ans—comme également doué dans les lettres gréco-latines, en philosophie et en mathématiques. Mais revenons à Forcadel, et à son souci proclamé d'instruire la jeunesse: ses commentaires du livre d'Euclide qui traite de 'la perfection des raisons et proportions' en feront foi. La préface du livre VI qui parle principalement de figures rectilignes, souligne leur intérêt pratique pour l'étude de la perspective et de l'architecture: nouvelle manifestation, assez discrète, du caractère d'utilité des mathématiques, telles qu'il faut les enseigner. La faveur du Cardinal de Châtillon dans les années 1564–5 lui est précieuse, et ce n'est pas sans un certain orgueil accompagné de flatterie qu'il souligne, dans la préface du livre VII, que sa traduction des trois nouveaux livres d'Euclide est une œuvre de pionnier, puisqu' 'aucun n'y a mis la main' jusqu'à présent.[194] Ainsi récompensera-t-il le souverain qui lui a fait la grâce de le nommer lecteur royal.

Mais plus encore qu'avec les *Eléments* d'Euclide, c'est avec son *Arithmétique*[195] française en trois livres, qui date de 1556–7, que Forcadel fait preuve d'originalité. Dans cette première édition—qui sera suivie de plusieurs autres tout au long du siècle, dont l'édition de 1573, datée du 10 juillet[196] et adressée au nouveau roi, Henri III, au 'Roy de Pologne esleu, fils et frere de Roys de France'—il utilise les abréviations usuelles, la notation mise au point par Chuquet pour les racines, ainsi que les signes + et —. On remarquera à cet égard qu'il y renonce dans les éditions ultérieures: ainsi en 1573, dans l'édition de Jérôme de Marnef et Guillaume Cavellat, il écrit: 4 *plus* 9, au lieu de 4 + 9, et il écrit les racines en toutes lettres, abandonnant le symbole $\sqrt{}$. Est-ce un réflexe de conservation? Avait-il eu des déboires avec des auditeurs ou des lecteurs? Il ne s'explique pas à ce sujet.

La préface à l'édition de 1573 a ceci d'intéressant qu'outre les flatteries conventionnelles adressées au nouveau souverain et le rappel de la faveur dont il jouissait auprès du feu-roi Charles ix (qui l'a nommé 'l'un de ses lecteurs ordinaires esdictes sciences mathé-matiques'), l'auteur insiste sur le caractère original de son travail: cet 'art de bien et seurement supputer' . . . n' 'a été mis en lumière d'autre que de moy'. On notera en particulier l'insistance avec laquelle il parle des fractions.[197] On notera les nombreux exemples concrets qui lui servent à faire mieux comprendre la théorie des opérations: utilisation des lieues, des écus, des livres. En fait, on peut se demander si tous ses développements sont utiles: il semble qu'il y ait des redondances, et si l'on compare l'Arithmétique de Peletier du Mans à celle de Forcadel, la palme revient, à notre sens, à l'amateur éclairé qui ne fut jamais lecteur royal, mais dont les ouvrages étaient largement utilisés par les enseignants. On notera encore un certain flottement dans le vocabulaire français désignant les termes techniques: le *multiplicande* de Peletier devient le *multipli-cant* chez Forcadel, mais tous deux désignent notre multiplicateur par le terme de *multipliant*. Ramus, lui, utilisait le mot latin *multi-plicator*. Dans l'édition de l'Arithmétique de Forcadel de 1573, une main postérieure (mais de combien postérieure?) a écrit: '*multi-plicable*' (en place de *multiplicande*), et *multiplicateur* (selon l'usage moderne). Forcadel préfère le terme de *partiteur* à celui de *diviseur*, mais *quotient* lui est familier à lui aussi.[198] Les preuves de la multi-plication ou de la division sont surabondamment développées, avec toujours cette même insistance sur le caractère pratique des opéra-tions.

On a l'impression que le lecteur royal, en écrivant ses livres, s'adresse à un public moins lettré et moins savant que celui de Ramus ou celui de Peletier, voire de Fine. Et pourtant, il n'y aurait à cela aucune raison objective. C'est aussi l'impression qu'on retire en examinant son *Arithmétique par les gects* (c'est-à-dire par les jetons) de 1558,[199] dont J. Fontès, dans son Mémoire sur Forcadel,[200] nous assure que c'était une méthode de calcul à la portée de gens peu instruits. Ne serait-ce pas, tout au moins dans l'esprit de Forcadel, l'une des destinations du Collège Royal, ce haut lieu de l'instruction ouvert à tous, et par conséquent aux personnes désireuses de s'instruire, mais n'en ayant pas encore acquis les moyens intellectuels? Les travaux d'Abel Lefranc et les archives du Collège de France ne nous permettent pas de savoir quelle était la proportion d'auditeurs 'motivés' et d'auditeurs 'populaires' aux cours de mathématiques. Mais l'insistance de Forcadel et ses intentions déclarées fournissent une indication que l'on aurait tort de négliger.

Si nous voulons maintenant, en guise de conclusion, faire un bilan de l'enseignement des mathématiques en France entre les années 1540 et 1570 environ, il faut commencer par nous tourner vers le reste de l'Europe. Nous sommes amenés à reconnaître, avec tous les historiens des sciences, que l'école allemande et l'école italienne notamment avaient produit, bien avant cette époque ou durant ces années des savants et des maîtres qui firent progresser la science mathématique comme aucun de nos professeurs français ne l'a fait. Il suffit d'évoquer d'une part les noms de Werner, de Riese, mais surtout de Rudolff et de Stifel, et d'autre part ceux de Luca Pacioli, Tartaglia, Cardan et Bombelli.[201] Quand on songe à leurs travaux sur l'équation du 3e degré, qui aboutit à de remarquables découvertes, sur les notations algébriques, l'étude des progressions arithmétiques ou géométriques, les proportions, les irrationnelles quadratiques ou cubiques, etc., nous sommes loin des traités d'arithmétique, de géométrie ou d'algèbre de Bovelles, de Peletier, de Fine, et même de Ramus, en dépit de telle ou telle invention ou de telle amélioration dans l'exposé des problèmes classiques que nous avons signalées au passage. Certes, même un Michaël Stifel est encore préoccupé par le problème de la quadrature du cercle, mais ses travaux algébriques et arithmétiques[202] compensent largement cette concession à un passé ou à une tradition stérile, alors qu'Oronce Fine a consacré à ce faux problème tout un ouvrage et que, dans ses autres traités, il ne fait guère que répéter les mathématiciens grecs et arabes. Ramus lui-même, dont on a souligné le rôle immense dans la réforme de l'enseignement des mathématiques et son importance comme historien de cette science, n'a pas fortement contribué à son progrès. En dehors de son traitement du nombre négatif dans son traité d'arithmétique, il n'a pas manifesté dans la connaissance de la science de son temps la même volonté de progresser que dans la pratique des méthodes universitaires.

C'est là précisément où je veux en venir. Sans que l'on puisse, pas plus au xvie siècle que de nos jours, séparer radicalement l'enseignement et la recherche, il semble que le niveau des recherches mathématiques en France comme leur degré de considération étaient si faibles dans les années 1535-40 que la première tâche était bien de les réintroduire ou de les introduire dans le cycle de l'enseignement normal des arts libéraux, et de redorer en quelque sorte leur blason, que l'humanisme philologique avait largement contribué à ternir. Certes, nos professeurs et mathématiciens français sont un peu en retard dans leurs propres informations, et les découvertes des Allemands et des Italiens mettent trop longtemps avant de vivifier leur propre enseignement. Mais en sont-ils les seuls responsables? N'est-ce pas plutôt aux conditions générales de la transmission du savoir— surtout dans ce domaine—qu'il faudrait s'en prendre? N'oublions pas que certaines découvertes, comme celle de la résolution de l'équation du 3e degré, ont fait l'objet de controverses épiques ou comiques entre Cardan, Tartaglia et quelques autres, pour savoir qui devrait s'en attribuer le mérite: des années seront donc nécessaires avant que la vérité mathématique ou la certitude des démonstrations ne s'impose, par-delà les péripéties individuelles. Et il n'existe pas à cette époque, en dépit des efforts d'un Ramus pour collecter le maximum d'informations des Universités européennes, de rencontres ou de congrès internationaux où l'on échange informations, méthodes, résultats de recherches.

D'après tout ce que nous avons dit, et surtout d'après des travaux de recherches actuellement entrepris, comme la découverte de ce cahier d'étudiant que Peter Sharratt a faite il y a quelques années,[203] nous pouvons estimer que l'effort pédagogique entrepris par ces mathématiciens qui furent pour la plupart professeurs, a porté ses fruits, et qu'il contribua à modifier le panorama culturel des Universités françaises. A cet égard le Collège Royal exerça, surtout sous l'impulsion de Pierre Ramus, une influence exemplaire. En insistant comme ils l'ont fait—peut-être un peu trop, pensera-t-on, mais ceci n'était qu'un juste retour des choses—à l'aspect pratique, voire pragmatique des différentes branches des mathématiques, ils ont contribué à dissiper le préjugé suivant lequel ces sciences sont mystérieuses, subtiles, purement abstraites ou 'philosophiques'. Certes, un mathématicien ou un logicien moderne estimera qu'en écrivant les mathématiques de façon à ce qu'elles fussent utilisables par les marchands de la rue Saint-Denis (si tant est que ces marchands aient souvent utilisé les traités de Ramus!), le professeur royal a retardé le moment nécessaire de leur formalisation, donc de leur progrès ou de leur fécondité. Mais quoi! Malherbe lui aussi, voulait que ses poèmes fussent compris des marchands du Port-au-foin, et il n'en a pas été moins l'objet, depuis près de quatre siècles, des soins attentifs des universitaires. Quand nous parcourons ces arithmétiques, ces algèbres ou ces géométries *pratiques*, nous constatons qu'elles ne négligent ni les définitions théoriques, ni les démonstrations générales, et que les constructions indiquées ressemblent davantage à celles qui s'appliquent aux problèmes que nous trouvons dans les traités des anciens grecs ('je tire un trait, j'abaisse une perpendiculaire, je dispose tel chiffre sous tel autre', etc.) qu'à des constructions purement empiriques. Et, malgré une tradition ininterrompue depuis le Moyen Age, cette mise en pratique des données mathématiques constituait alors un puissant et nécessaire antidote contre l'invasion stérilisante et mortelle de la rhétorique scolastique dans tous les domaines du savoir.

Nous avons assisté enfin au débat, sinon au combat du français et du latin. Reconnaissons que ce problème de l'emploi de la langue vernaculaire dans les ouvrages scientifiques n'est pas propre à la France, et que la plupart des traités de mathématiques des savants allemands ou italiens que nous avons évoqués ont été rédigés dans leur langue nationale (raison supplémentaire de la lenteur de leur diffusion). Mais pour nous en tenir aux quelques traités signalés dans cet exposé, nous remarquerons l'effort heureux—du point de vue scientifique comme du point de vue linguistique—entrepris par des auteurs bilingues pour choisir et souvent pour inventer l'expression juste et le discours plus ou moins concis que de nouvelles couches d'écoliers ou d'étudiants répèteraient et transmettraient peut-être aux générations futures. Nous avons assisté, dans les années 1555– 1570 à un retour en force du latin, mais le mouvement amorcé par Bovelles, Fine et Peletier n'était pas abandonné puisque dans le dernier tiers du siècle, on revient au français, comme dans la traduction de la *Géométrie* de Fine par Forcadel. Cela est à mettre au profit de nos mathématiciens français. Viète et Fermat publieront encore en latin, mais la *Géométrie* de Descartes et les *Côniques* de Pascal seront en français. Ainsi, le bilan de ces années 1540–70 est-il plus pédagogique et culturel que proprement scientifique, mais, en dépit de leurs modestes inventions et—pour certains—de quelques aberrations, ces hommes n'ont pas peu contribué à l'avènement d'un humanisme moderne.

NOTES

1 Voir *Erasmi Opera omnia* (Amsterdam 1973) 1–4, 1–103.
2 Ibid., 31, 564–5.
3 Voir à ce propos notre ouvrage, *Erasme et la musique* (Paris 1965) (De Pétrarque à Descartes, ix)
4 Voir nos deux éditions: Genève (=Droz) 1966 (Travaux d'Humanisme et Renaissance, n° LXXVII), et Amsterdam (= *ASD*), 1–2, 1971.
5 'Mais voici que se révèle déjà, même chez les petits enfants, certaine inclination particulière vers des disciplines déterminées, telles que la musique, l'arithmétique ou la cosmographie' (*ASD*, 1–2, 67, 7 8, et Droz, p. 445). Il ajoute aussitôt: 'J'ai moi-même connu directement des individus qui, extrêmement lents à s'éveiller aux règles de la grammaire et de la rhétorique, se sont révélés très doués pour ces sciences plus subtiles' (*ASD*, 1–2, ibid., 8–10).
6 'Non ignoranda astrologia, quod hanc passim suis figmentis aspergunt poetae, praesertim Higini' (*ASD* 1–2, 123, 10–11).
7 Pour Lefèvre d'Etaples, on pourra recourir aux travaux de Renaudet, notamment *Préréforme et humanisme à Paris pendant les premières guerres d'Italie, 1494–1517* (Paris 1916) 2e éd. (Paris 1953), de M. Mann Philipps, notamment *Erasme et les débuts de la Réforme française, 1517–1536* (Paris 1934) au livre d'E. Rice Jr., *The Prefatory Epistles of Lefèvre d'Etaples and related Letters* (New York 1972) et à la thèse (inédite) de Guy Bedouelle, *Lefèvre d'Etaples et l'intelligence des Ecritures* (Université de Paris-I, 1973).
8 Pour Clichtove, on se reportera essentiellement à l'important ouvrage de Jean-Pierre Massaut, *Josse Clichtove, l'Humanisme et la réforme du clergé*, Bibl. de la Faculté de Philo. et Lettres de l'Univ. de Liège, fasc. CLXXXIII, 2 vols. (Paris 1968). Il comporte une abondante bibliographie; voir aussi E. Rice, op. cit.
9 Pour Bovelles, on consultera parmi les travaux (partiels) les plus récents: H. de Lubac, 'Le Sage d'après Ch. de Bovelles' dans *Mélanges offerts* à M. D. Chenu (Paris 1967) 385–97; C. Dumont-Demaizière, *Ch. de Bovelles: la différence des langues vulgaires et la variété de la langue française . . .* (Amiens 1972) (Société de linguistique picarde, t. XIV); B. S. Kunda, 'Introduction à l'anthropologie philosophique de Ch. de Bovelles' (en polonais) *Acta Universitatis Wratislaviensis*, n. 136, *Prace Filozofiozne*, VII, 15–33; M. Laporte, 'Charles de Bovelles (1479–1566). Apport de quelques sources noyonnaises, contribution à une étude sur son séjour à Noyon', *Moreana* 41 (mars 1974) 37–47.
10 Voir notamment l'édition Henri Estienne (Paris 1500–01 et 1510) des différents opuscles de Bovelles, dont le *Liber de intellectu*, le *Liber de sensu*, le *Liber de nihilo*, et le *Liber de sapiente*.
11 Ed. de 1533, Bâle, H. Frobenius et N. Episcopius.
12 *Opera omnia*, ed. Mayans (Valence 1785) (reprod. Londres, 1964), t. VI, 203–7.
13 Ibid., IV, c. 5, 369–73 (*De scientiis mathematicis; quot sint, quaeque uniuscujusque materia . . .*).
14 'Nec minus de Geometria praecipit, quin sphaeram quoque conscripsit ad eam, quae extat Joannis a Sacrobosco' (ibid., 373).
15 '*Theorica* item *Planetarum* idem Faber [il s'agit de Lefèvre d'Etaples] quae discipulus ejus Jodocus Clichtoveus elucidavit [v. plus haut]

commentariis; argumentum et fundamentum totius operis ex Georgio Purbachio est sumtum' (ibid., 373).

16 Sur les idées pédagogiques de Vivès, voir, parmi d'autres, le livre—déjà ancien—de Foster Watson, *Vives on Education* (Cambridge 1913).

17 *Humanisme, science et réforme, Pierre de la Ramée, 1515–1572* (Leyde 1958).

18 Voir aussi de R. Hooykaas, *Science and theology in the Middle Ages*, F.U.Q. 3, 1954, *passim*. Dans *Humanisme, science et réforme*, il fait allusion en note (p. 28, n. 33) à Rodolphe Agricola, Vivès et Ramus, tous adversaires farouches des nominalistes et des 'calculateurs'.

19 Cité par Hooykaas, p. 28, n. 33. Cf. *De inventione dialectica libri tres* d'Agricola, ed. de 1539, et Hartfelder, *Philipp Melanchthon als preceptor Germaniae* (Nieuwkoop 1964) (réimpression de l'édition de Berlin 1889) 218.

20 Voir la monographie d'Abel Lefranc, *Histoire du Collège de France* (Paris 1913) et son article, 'Nicolas Clénard humaniste belge et les commencements du Collège de France', *Humanisme et Renaissance* 7 (1940) 253–69.

21 Voir la notice biographique de Paul Laumonier en tête de son édition des *Œuvres poétiques*, Paris, Revue de la Renaissance, 1904. Voir aussi l'édition plus récente de M. Françon, Rochecorbon, Gay, 1958.

22 P. *Rami Scholarum mathematicarum libri unus et triginta*, Basileae, per Euseb. Episcopium et Nicolai fratris haeredes. Anno MDLXIX, in – 4°, 320 p. Au verso du titre on lit: *Argumentum Scholarum mathematicarum. Tres primi libri continent Proœmium mathematicum, id est exhortationem ad mathematicas artes, ad Catharinam Medicæam, reginam, matrem regis . . .* Voir aussi les éditions de 1578 (Bâle), 1599 (Francfort) et 1627 (Francfort).

23 Voir Hooykaas, op. cit., 84.

24 'In Gallia non tanta sunt studia Mathematum. Imo aliqui ex nostris Auditoribus, in Gallia docentes Mathemata, hoc labore se sustentarunt' (*Corp. Ref.* VII. Epist. 4639, col. 514). La lettre est adressée 'Johanni Petreio civi ac Typographo Noribergensi, amico suo colendo', 16 déc. 1549.

25 J. Fontès, Mém. Acad. Sc. Toulouse, 9eme série, t. VI (1894) 287 (cité par Hooykaas, p. 85, n. 56).

26 *Scholæ physicæ præfatio*, 1565 (Collect. p. 75). Voir aussi *Scholæ mathematicæ*, lib. I–III, *passim.*, et lettre du 14. Cal. 1565 (*Collect.* p. 205). Les *Collectaneæ præfationes, epistolæ, orationes* (ed. Parisiis, ap. Dionysium Vallensem, 1577) contiennent, entre autres opuscules, toute une série de préfaces, dont les *Physicæ præfationes tres*, et quinze lettres.

27 *Scholæ mathematicæ* I, 12.

28 Voir Hooykaas, op. cit., 85 et Ramus, *Proœmium reform. Academ. Paris.* (*Collect.* p. 476).

29 Voir aussi *Scholæ mathematicæ* I, 12.

30 Une pour l'arithmétique, la musique, la géométrie et l'optique; une autre pour les sciences astronomiques et la géographie (cf. *Scholæ mathematicæ* II, 67).

31 Hooykaas, op. cit., 85 sq.

32 Ibid., 86–7.

33 Peut-on vraiment affirmer, comme le fait Ramus dans son discours 'Basilea', que la terre bâloise n'a rien produit avant l'arrivée de l'Evangile, rien avant Œcolampade et Calvin? D'ailleurs, avant la visite qu'il rendit à Bâle en 1568-9, Ramus mentionnait à peine cette cité dans les *Scholæ mathematicæ*. Comment avait-il pu oublier de bonne foi l'un des deux centres de l'humanisme rhénan?

34 Le *Dialogue de l'ortografe é prononciacion de la langue françoese* date de 1549. Il est contemporain de la *Défense et illustration de la langue française* (ed. princ. 1549).

35 *Livre singulier et utile touchant l'art et practique de Geometrie*, composé en François, par maistre Charles de Boüelles, Chanoine de Noyon. Voir aussi, de la même année, l'édition S. de Colines: *Géométrie pratique composée par le noble philosophe Maître Charles de Bouelles et nouvellement par lui revue, augmentée et grandement enrichie.*

36 Voir notamment le *Mathematicum opus quadripartitum*, édité par H. Estienne en 1500-01 et 1510 dans le même volume (énorme) in f° que le *Liber de intellectu*, ainsi que les *Geometricæ introductionis libri sex*, auxquels sont adjoints des opuscules sur la quadrature du cercle, la cubication de la sphère et l'introduction à la perspective, tous ouvrages qui se trouvent réunis dans un recueil intitulé: *Arithmetica Severini Boetii in compendium redacta sive introductio in Arithmeticam speculativam Boetii, cum Jodoci Clichtovei commentario et astronomico libro Jacobi Fabri Stapulensis, quibusdam Caroli Bovilli lucubrationibus* (Paris, Henri Estienne, 1503).

37 Edit. princ. Lyon, C. Fradin, 1520 (BN *Rés.* v. 899), in 4°, pièces lim., 230 ff. Il y a une réédition en 1538 à Lyon, chez Gilles et Jacques Huguetan.

38 Tory avait vu l'ouvrage publié en 1511 et 1514 par Henri Estienne sous le titre: *L'art et science de géométrie avec les figures sur chacune règle par lesquelles on peut facilement comprendre la dite science*. Les termes de *Géométrie pratique* ne sont pas antérieurs à 1542.

39 *Carolus Bovillus V. P. Do. Antonio Leufredo, Abbati Vrsicampi dignissimo S. A.* Leuffroy fut abbé d'Ourscamp de 1520-1556 (*Gallia christiana*).

40 *Vie de Madame Sainte Catherine*, texte manuscrit de 784 vers contenu dans le Ms. 1134 de la Bibliothèque de la Sorbonne (que nous nous proposons d'éditer avec une introduction, un commentaire et des notes).

41 Il est vrai qu'ils étaient expliqués en latin: voir son ouvrage *Proverbiorum vulgarium libri tres* (Paris, Galiot du Pré, 1531). En tout, 650 proverbes qui étaient usités en France au début du xvᵉ siècle.

42 'Auturgis manuve operariis' (a3r).

43 Ibid. 'Quidam ex Parisiensibus chalcographis, in istius excussione aureos polliciti montes, ridiculum murem peperissent' (a3v).

44 '... adfuit tandem Orontius Regius Mathematicus, qui quum visendi tui causa Noviodunum ventitasset, meque etiam domi oportunus Phanio convenisset ...' (a3v).

44a '... [se] figurarum quoque quas ibidem frequentius inscripsi, futurum ligneis in tabellis pictorem' (a3v).

45 'Dicatum igitur tibi vulgata lingua libellum, pro insueto nostrae officinae xenio, ne flocci habe' (a4r).

46 L'adjectif *mysticæ* est assez surprenant, car bien que Bovelles ne
répugnât pas personnellement à des considérations sur la 'mystique'
des nombres, le traité de Géométrie qu'il publie en français est très
éloigné de toute arithmologie.

47 Le second des imprimeurs dont il était question ('Duo protinus
ingenue spopondit') est vraisemblablement Simon de Colines, qui
avait déjà imprimé Bovelles.

48 *Uvas expressi, vina ille bibenda propinat:*
Torcular implevi, guttura at ille rigat.

49 *L'art d'Arytmétique contenant toute dimension singulière et commode tant
pour l'art militaire que pour autres calculations* (Paris, Annet Brière, 1554)
in – 4°.

50 *Arithmetique et manière d'apprendre à chiffrer* . . . (Lyon, Th. Payen,
1555).

51 *Arithmetique* (Paris, Nic. de Chemin, 1565).

52 *Compost arithmetical* (Lyon, Benoît Rigaud, 1567); *Briefve arithmetique,*
ibid., 1570; *Les principaux fondemens d'arithmetique,* ibid., 1571.

53 *Arithmetique: Ensemble un discours des changes* (Lyon, M. Jove, 1571) in
– 8°.

54 *Les Institutions d'arithmetique* . . . (Paris, Hier. de Marnef, 1578), in–8°.

55 *L'arithmetique abregée coniointe a l'unité des nombres* (Paris 1588) in–f°.
Un certain nombre d'autres ouvrages sont indiqués par F. Buisson
dans son *Répertoire des ouvrages pédagogiques du XVIe siècle* (Paris 1886).
Voir, à l'Index rerum, la liste des mathématiciens (dans les sections
Arithmétique, Musique, Géométrie, Astronomie et Cosmographie,
pp. 731–2).

56 On peut rappeler que Dürer avait inauguré le mouvement en publiant
en allemand en 1525 son *Instruction sur la manière de mesurer,* et en 1528
son *Traité des proportions.* Lui aussi visait à l'utilité pratique et
s'adressait aux apprentis peintres, architectes, charpentiers, et autres
artisans ou artistes.

57 A la vérité, il enseigna assez souvent les mathématiques au cours de sa
carrière; mais sa personnalité était multiple, assez ondoyante, et la
postérité a retenu davantage le poète que le mathématicien. Même
dans les préfaces de ses ouvrages de mathématiques, le poète semble
supplanter l'homme de science. Ecoutons-le par exemple, dans le
Proeme sur le second livre de son Algèbre proférer un véritable hymne à la
gloire du nombre Un, où il rivalise avec Ausone: 'Qui sera celui qui
pourra antrer an assez grande admiracion s'il veut prandre pie sus la
grande perfeccion de cet Vn, premiere e seule source des Nombres?
Au milieu dequez il demeure comme souuerain Gouuerneur:
Denominateur des nombres Antiers: e (affin qu'il soèt par tout)
Numérateur des nombres Rompuz: Vrey image de la Diuinite: de
laquele je peu chanter ici après Virgile,

> Ce grand Esprit qui antretient e guide
> Le Ciel, la Terre e la Pleine liquide,
> Du haut Titan la lampe tousjours clere,
> Et de sa Seur, qui par amprunt eclere
> Parmi les feuz d'vne beaute confuse:
> Ame, qui ét par les mambres diffuse
> Et fèt mouuoer ce grand Cors uniuers,
> Inspirant vie aux Animans diuers.'

Voir A.-M. Schmidt, *La poésie scientifique en France au XVIe siècle* (Paris 1938) 21.

58 Voir notamment la pièce *Contre les envieux Poètes* et la seconde *Préface de l'Olive* (Ed. Marty-Laveaux, I, 72, 145, 506; II, 206, 241, 257).

59 On connaît la célèbre pièce *A ceulx qui blament les Mathematiques* (éd. Laumonier, p. 104), qui se termine par une profession de foi religieuse où les mathématiques ont leur grande part:

> Ceste science l'homme cueille
> Alors qu'il imagine
> La facture et grande merveille
> De la ronde machine.
> C'est celle par qui mieux s'apprenne
> L'immense Deité
> Et qui des Athées reprenne
> L'erreur et vanité.

60 Cette dédicace disparaîtra dans l'édition lyonnaise de 1554.

61 BN V20137.

62 Cet exemplaire n'est pas signalé par Mme J. Veyrin-Forrer dans son article, pourtant si documenté, sur Rasse des Nœux (*Le collectionneur François Rasse des Neux*), paru dans les *Studia bibliographica in honorem Herman de la Fontaine Verwey* (Amsterdam 1968) 389–417.

63 Cette date semble avoir été particulièrement favorable à l'acquisition de livres et documents par Rasse des Nœux, si l'on en juge par l'article de J. Veyrin-Forrer (notamment 402–3). On y voit qu'il rassembla toute une série de pièces ayant trait à l'activité de Ramus et à ses démêlés avec la Sorbonne et le Parlement, et à son conflit avec Jacques Charpentier. Rasse possédait apparemment de nombreux ouvrages de mathématiques contemporains: cf. son *ex-libris* de 1551 sur un exemplaire de la *Practica arithmetica* de Cardan (1539), reproduit dans l'art. cité, pl. 5, et celui du 9 déc. 1542 (avec notes de cours) sur un exemplaire de l'*Arithmetica practica* d'Oronce Fine, 1542 (art. cité, pl. 1).

64 BN V6743.

65 'Henrici de Monantheuil professoris regii'.

66 'Incipi legere publice die Martis 5. Aprilis. Absolvi legere die Lunae 16 Junii ann. 1586' (tout en haut de la page).

67 'Jacques Peletier estant icy, [c'est-à-dire au château de Bissy, dans le Mâconnais], écrit Pontus, pour en m'honorant de sa gracieuse familiarité, se rafraischir après le travail qu'il avait presté à son Euclide, partie revoyant son Algèbre pour la donner aux Latins, partie se recréant avec moy selon qu'infinis sujetz se présentaient à nous pour filosofer ensemble; le 24e de May MDLVII, après la minuict ... apperceut Jupiter esclairant de raiz si lumineux que l'ombre apparaissoit' (texte cité par Laumonier, op. cit., p. XXII).

68 C'est le sens de son 'Nunc ad Romanos transeo!' (lettre à Pontus de mars 1557).

69 Voir cependant celle que nous avons faite à la note 57.

70 *Dialogue de l'ortografe é prononciacion françoese* (Poitiers, J. et E. de Marnef, 1550), p. 17.

71 Tome II, *Le XVIe siècle*, éd. Colin, revue et augmentée (1967) 57.

72 Ibid., 57.

73 Le privilège est daté du 15 juin 1554, l'avertissement aux lecteurs 'de Lion, ce xxviii de Juillet M.D.LIIII'.

74 p. xx.

75 Voir l'exemplaire de la Bibl. Nat. (v 6071) qui a appartenu à des Augustins de Paris.

76 Texte imprimé en caractères de civilité.

77 Voir plus haut, note 68.

78 (Paris 1852) t. iv.

79 Dans son livre *La gloire dans la poésie française et néo-latine du XVIe siècle* (Paris, Genève 1969).

80 Voir note 68.

81 Les historiens des mathématiques en retiennent les très subtiles et très originales considérations sur l'angle de contact ou de contingence. La date de l'édition originale de ce dernier ouvrage est incertaine. La Bibliothèque Nationale possède une édition latine de 1572 (Parisiis, Aegid. Gorbinus) et une édition française (*De l'usage de géométrie par Jacques Peletier, méd. et mathématicien*) de 1573 (Paris, Gilles Gourbin) [BN. *Rés.* v 824, et 3 autres ex.].

82 Voir l'ensemble des communications présentées à l'occasion du 4e centenaire de Marguerite de Savoie au Colloque de mai 1974 organisé par les Centres Universitaires d'Annecy et de Chambéry, et par l'Université de Turin. Il y fut question plus d'une fois de Peletier du Mans.

83 Il devient alors vraiment professionnel.

84 *Jacobi Peletarii, Medici et Mathematici oratio Pictavii habita in prælectiones Mathematicas* (Pictavii, ex officina Bochetorum, 1579). Ce discours latin de trente pages, qui est resté souvent ignoré des biographes de Peletier, a été publié par Paul Laumonier dans la *Revue de la Renaissance*, oct.– déc. 1904.

85 Voir la Notice de Laumonier, p. xxviii.

86 Paris, J. Richer, 1580, in–8º.

87 Voir notes 64–6.

88 (Paris, Mettayer, 1581) in–4º.

89 Cité par Laumonier, pp. xxx–xxxi.

90 Ed. J. de Tournes (1554) 213.

91 Ibid.

92 'Ils avaient la Pratique si a main . . .' (p. 214).

93 Sur Oronce Fine, voir la thèse latine de L. Gallois, *De Orontio Finaeo gallico geographo* (Paris 1890) et plusieurs articles cités dans l'étude de D. Hillard et E. Poulle signalée à la note 95. Voir aussi la biographie que son ami Antoine Mizault ajouta peu de temps après sa mort au 'tombeau' poétique de Fine, connu sous le nom de *Funebre symbolum virorum aliquot illustrium de optimo et doctissimo viro Orontio Finæo . . .* (Paris 1555) in–8º (12 ff.).

94 Même si, comme on l'a dit, le Collège Royal ne représentait pas la totalité ou la quintessence des études mathématiques qui se pratiquaient alors en France.

95 Voir en particulier son traité de la *Quadratura circuli*, suivi de *De circuli mensura et ratione circumferentiæ ad diametrum demonstrationes duæ* . . ., Lutetiae Parisiorum, apud S. Colinaeum, 1544, in–fol., pièces lim., 107 ff. (cf. exempl. de la BN: v.1431, provenant de la Bibl. du couvent de S. Bernard à Paris). Voir aussi l'ouvrage récapitulatif

de ses travaux *De rebus mathematicis hactenus desideratis libri* IIII, *quibus inter cœtera circuli quadratura centum modis et supra* ... *demonstratur*, Lutetiae Parisiorum, ex. off. M. Vascosani, 1556, in–fol. Voir enfin la bibliographie de Fine dans l'Appendice de l'article de D. Hillard et E. Poulle, 'Oronce Fine et l'horloge planétaire de la Bibliothèque Sainte-Geneviève,' *BHR* XXXIII–2 (1971) 345–9.

96 Voir l'ouvrage intitulé *De erratis Orontii Finæi* ... *qui putavit inter duas datas lineas, binas medias proportionales sub continua proportione invenisse, circulum quadrasse, cubum duplicasse, multangulum quodcunque rectilineum in circulo describendi artem tradidisse et longitudinis locorum differentias aliter quam per eclipses lunares, etiam dato quovis tempore manifestas fecisse, Petri Nonii* ... *liber unus* (Conimbricae 1546) in–fol.

97 Ou Jean Borrel, chanoine de St Antoine des environs de Valence (1492?–1572), dont la réfutation est imprimée à la suite de la *Quadratura circuli* de Fine dans l'exemplaire de la Bibl. Nat. A la page II du traité de Fine, une note manuscrite renvoie d'ailleurs à Buteo. Outre l'article (cité) de D. Hillard et E. Poulle, voir les notices du Catalogue de l'*Exposition de la Bibliothèque Sainte-Geneviève* (22 novembre–22 décembre 1971), établi par Jacqueline Linet, Denise Hillard et Emmanuel Poulle (Préfaces d'E. Dennery et M. Bois) à l'occasion de la réinstallation de l'horloge astronomique construite à l'intention du Cardinal Charles de Lorraine (dont on a déjà rencontré le nom dans maintes dédicaces des poètes et mathématiciens de l'époque). Voir aussi, à la fin des *Opera geometrica* de Buteo (Lyon, Bertellus, 1554) deux vers laudatifs d'un certain Philippe Cantor 'ad confutationem quadraturae circuli': 'Antiquos fines corrupit Orontius orbem/ Quadrato mutans, Buteo restituit' (p. 155).

98 Cf. A. F. Johnson, *Oronce Finé as an illustrator of books*, in *Gutenberg Jahrbuch* (1928) 107–9. Voir aussi R. Brun, *Le livre français illustré de la Renaissance* (Paris 1969) 143, et, du même auteur. 'Maquettes d'éditions d'Oronce Finé', dans *Studia bibliographica* ... *La Fontaine Verwey* (op. cit.) 36–42. La page de titre du *Protomathesis* de Fine (qui comprend ses ouvrages d'arithmétique, de géométrie, de cosmographie et de gnomonique) est illustrée par une admirable gravure, toute symbolique, dont il est lui-même l'auteur.

99 Voir le Catalogue de l'Exposition Oronce Fine et l'article (cité) de D. Hillard et E. Poulle.

100 Paris, Vve J. Kerver et G. Chaudière, 2 tom. en I vol. in–f⁰, 664 ff. (BN G.1493).

101 Voir la courte brochure d'Emile Escallier consacrée à notre auteur, *Aspects d'Oronce Fine* (Gap 1957) 5.

102 'philosophe excellent et accomply au reste en la connaissance des mathemates' [*sic*].

103 On notera cette expression—calquée sur le grec *mathemata*—qui n'est pas très fréquente dans le vocabulaire scientifique français du XVIe siècle.

104 C'est nous qui soulignons.

105 Voir le Catalogue de l'Exposition de la Bibl.Ste-Geneviève.

106 Voir plus haut, note 93.

107 *La géographie des humanistes* (Paris 1940) (notamment pp. 12, 13, 36, 37 41, 56, 57, 105, 111, 124, 155).

108 *Biblioteca selecta qua agitur De ratione Studiorum*, Romae ex typis Apost. Vaticanis, 2 vol. in–folio, 1593.

109 Publié à part sous le titre: *Apparatus ad omnium gentium et Methodus ad geographiam tradendam* (Venise, J.-B. Ciotti, 1597 et Rome 1597).

110 *Monumenta Ignatiana*, XII, 110.

111 *Biblioteca selecta*, Coloniae Agrippinae (1607), t. 11, 257.—Ces deux dernières références, d'après F. de Dainville, op. cit., 41 (et notes).

112 Voir L. Gallois et D. Hillard et E. Poulle, art. cit. p. 323 et notes 39–42 (notamment sur la redécouverte récente à la Bibliothèque Nationale de sa carte de Terre Sainte).

113 *Le problème de l'incroyance au 16e siècle* (Paris 1968) (nouv. édit), livre 1, ch. 1. Sur Sussannée, voir dans ce livre les pages 32, 42, 56, 64, 71, 72, 92, 93, 95, 106, et 481–482 (bibliographie).

114 Voir aussi A. Mizauld, *Funebre symbolum* (op. cit.), fol. cl^{vo}: 'conjugem Dionysiam cognomine vero Candidam'.

115 Nous donnerons ici quelques-uns de ces vers:
Nemo Mathematicas exactius addocet arteis,
Expolit, inventis amplificatque novis.
In quadram redigi monstrat fœliciter orbes,
Tentatum multis hactenus illud opus.
Tentarunt multi, nullus perfecit: ad istam
Fata reservabant talia dona diem.
Monstrat ad haec, loca quid distent, ut scribere uno
Circum multiplex angulum orbe queat ...
Felix tam raro Candida nupta viro!

116 La liste la plus complète paraît bien être celle qu'en ont dressée D. Hillard et E. Poulle (art. cit.).

117 Ibid., 346–7.

118 (Paris, Simon de Colines, 1543) réédités en 1551, 1556, 1557; (Paris, R. Chaudière, 1551) première édition en 1543, rééditions en 1556 et 1557; trad. anglaise c. 1558; (Paris, G. Cavellat, 1556) (réédition du texte paru en 1543 et 1551; réédité en 1557; trad. anglaise c. 1558); (Paris, G. Cavellat, 1557); (Londres, Thomas Marshe, c. 1558), ouvrage anonyme.

119 *La théorique des cielz, mouvemens et termes practiques des sept planètes ... rédigée en langaige françois*, (Paris, J. Pierre, 1528) in–fol., 45 ff. (édit. anonyme, mais comprenant la devise de Fine: 'Virescit vulnere virtus'; rééditions: 1557, 1558, 1607, 1619).

120 *La sphère du monde, proprement dite cosmographie, composée nouvellement en françois ... par Oronce Fine* (Paris, M. de Vascosan 1551) in–4°, 64 ff. Le texte latin a paru la même année, peut-être même simultanément chez le même imprimeur.

121 *Orontii Finæi ... Arithmetica practica libris quatuor absoluta*, Parisiis, ex off. S. Colinaei, 1535, in–fol. ,66 ff. (première partie de la *Protomathesis*, rééditée en 1542, 1544 et en 1555).

122 *Orontii Finei liber de geometria practica ...*, Argentorati, ex off. Knoblochiana per G. Machæropoeum, 1544, in–4°, 134 pp.

123 *La composition et usage du quarré géométrique, par lequel on peut mesurer fidèlement toutes longueurs, hauteurs et profunditez ... par Oronce Fine ...* (Paris, G. Gourbin, 1556) in–4°, 28 ff.

124 Ms. de 17 ff. sur vélin (manuscrit de dédicace offert à François Ier) (Ms. fr. 1334)).

125 *La practique de géométrie d'Oronce* [*Fine*] . . . *en laquelle est comprins l'usage du quarré géométrique* . . . *traduit par Pierre Forcadel* . . . (Paris, G. Gourbin, 1570) in–4°, 118 pp.
126 Paris, G. Gourbin, in–4°, 127 pp. C'est en cette même année 1586 que le texte latin parut pour la dernière fois chez le même imprimeur.
127 Cf. Hillard et Poulle, Appendice bibliographique (cité), p. 336, n° 7, et p. 339, n° 27. Le texte original, imprimé à Paris, chez P. Leber en 1532 (in–8°, 8 ff.) porte un titre légèrement différent de celui que l'on trouve à la suite de l'édition de la *Sphère du monde* de 1551. Le titre de 1532 est: *Epistre exhortative, touchant la perfection et commodité des ars libéraulx mathématiques, composée soulz le nom et tiltre de la très antienne et noble princesse dame Philosophie* . . . A la fin: *Hanc epistolam* . . . *dictabat Orontius* F[*ineus*] *Delph* . . .
128 Dans l'édition de la *Sphère* de 1551 dont nous disposons (BN: V 7643), cette Epître occupe les 6 ff. 59–64 (ou P1–P4 + 2 ff. n. s.).
129 Il est vrai qu'ils ne sont pas proprement scientifiques.
130 Cette exaltation mathématico-philosophique de l'Unité est un thème constant chez les poètes scientifiques, et même chez les autres. Elle a pour elle une tradition antique.
131 *Très brève et familière introduction pour entendre et apprendre par soy mesmes à jouer toutes les chansons réduictes en la tabulature du lutz avec la manière d'accorder ledict lutz* . . . (Paris, Attaingnant, 1529) in–4° oblong (Deutschen Staatsbibl. de Berlin, en dépôt à Tübingen).
132 *Epithoma musice instrumentalis ad omnimodam hemispherii luthine et theoricam et practicam per Orontium Finæum.* (Paris, Attaingnant 1530) in–4° oblong (Deutschen Staatsbibl. de Berlin, en dépôt à Tübingen et Vienne, Ö.N.Bl.).
133 'Merito igitur Plato, primum numeros mandat pueros esse docendos . . .' (A3v).
134 Cf. par exemple les 17 chapitres du livre I de la *Practique de la géométrie*, trad. Forcadel, éd. de 1586.
135 La littérature sur Ramus est immense, et l'on ne saurait—même succinctement—donner une idée des travaux utiles à notre sujet. On renverra à l'excellente et récente mise au point de Peter Sharratt, 'The Present State of Studies on Ramus', *Studi Francesi*, N. 47–8, an. XVI–2/3 (mai–déc. 1972) 201–13. En ce qui concerne Ramus mathématicien, il signale l'ouvrage—que nous avons déjà utilisé—de R. Hooykaas, *Humanisme, science et réforme, Pierre de la Ramée* (Leyde 1958) et la thèse (en néerlandais) de Johannes Jakobus Verdonk, *Petrus Ramus en de wiskunde* (Assen 1966) x–455 pp.) Ce dernier ouvrage distingue entre l'enseignement des mathématiques de Ramus, ses rapports avec ses élèves dont plusieurs devinrent ses collègues ou ses successeurs, et les travaux proprement scientifiques du professeur royal (cf. Sharratt, p. 205). Du même Verdonk on signalera l'article 'Uber die Geometrie des Petrus Ramus' '*Sudhoffs Archif* 52 (1968) 371–81, et de P. Sharratt lui-même, 'La Ramée's Early Mathematical Teaching', *BHR* (1966) 605–14. Ce dernier article touche au cœur de notre sujet: en effet, outre un exemplaire inconnu d'un *Euclide* de 1545 que l'auteur a découvert à la Bibliothèque de la Sorbonne, il y est fait état d'un manuscrit de 11 pages (non signalé dans le fichier de la Sorbonne), notes d'étudiant prises au cours de leçons de Ramus traitant de l'arithmétique de Fine.

JEAN-CLAUDE MARGOLIN

136 Cf. la fin de l'*Epître exhortative* de Fine.
137 *Nova scientia* inventa da Nicolò Tartalea ... In Vinegia, per
  Stephano da Sabio (BN *Rés*. v. 887).
138 P. *Rami, eloquentiæ et philosophiæ professoris regii, Arithmeticæ libri tres,
  ad Carolum Lotharingum cardinalem* (Paris, apud Andream Wechelum,
  1555) cum privilegio regis (Idib. sept.), in–4°, 110 p.
139 On retrouve encore ici ce puissant personnage. Son nom sera
  naturellement supprimé des éditions ultérieures de Ramus.
140 Cf. *Præfatio mathematica secunda* (*Collectaneæ præfationes*, p. 169).
141 *Collect.*, p. 170.
142 L'édition que nous utilisons est l'édition originale de 1569 (Basileæ,
  per Eusebium Episcopium et Nicolai Fratris haeredes), in–4, 320 pp.
  Dans le recueil factice de la B.N. (v. 6202–I et 2) ont été ajoutés
  Buteonis Delphinatici Opera geometrica (160 pages) (voir la fin de la note
  97).
143 p. 74.
144 *F.U.Q.* 3 (1954) 147 sq.
145 *Scholæ mathematicæ*, 52 (éd. 1569).
146 Qui fera tout pour lui interdire l'accès du Collège Royal et
  l'obtention d'une chaire de mathématiques.
147 L. 11, p. 53; (cf. Hooykaas, op. cit., 77).
148 'Sic enim Platonem mathematicis contemplationibus delectatum
  diximus, ut usum vulgarem et popularem contemneret, Archytamque
  et Eudoxum velut opere atque opificio mathematico commaculari et
  coinquinari crederet', *Scholæ mathematicæ*, 11, 53; et encore ceci:
  'Fructum geometriae mirabilem afferunt mechanica et organica, et
  sine his humana vita ferarum non hominum vita esset, ut secundo
  libro percipietur. Mechanicam et organicam Archytas et Eudoxus
  adamarunt...' (ibid., 1, 18–19).
149 Voir ses *Aristotelicæ animadversiones* (in Ch. Waddington, *Ramus*, 1855,
  pp. 444–5, et surtout dans la bibliographie de Walter J. Ong
  Cambridge, Mass. 1968).
150 *La naissance de l'humanisme moderne* (Paris 1940).
151 *Ratio atque institutio studiorum*, Romae 1586, texte publié dans Pachtler,
  Mon. germ. paed., t. 11.
152 Pachtler, 11, 141—Le P. de Dainville, dans une note de la p. 60 de son
  livre, renvoie à Quintilien (*Inst. orat.*, 1, 10), Cicéron (*De oratore*, 1,
  187).
153 Cité par Hooykaas, p. 77. Cf. *Scholæ mathematicæ* 1, p. 29 (éd. 1569):
  'Atqui utinam Archimedi potius in mentem venisset, *artium finem esse
  usum, non contemplationem*, maximeque hominum ac certissimae utilitati
  consulere maluisset.'
154 *Scholæ mathematicæ*, p. 53.
155 Il reconnaît avec ce souci d'indépendance intellectuelle que nous
  avons déjà caractérisé: 'Deque Platone idem quod de Aristotele saepe
  alias sentiamus, in utriusque philosophi libris varias de variis rebus ac
  discrepantes sententias deprehendi: *neque Platonem semper Platonem,
  neque Aristotelem semper Aristotelem esse*' (c'est nous qui soulignons),
  Scholæ mathematicæ 11, 55.
156 'Plato igitur verus et Platonico spiritu animatus audiatur' (ibid. 11,
  p. 55).
157 'Statui mathematicam non solum ad philosophandum in physica et

L'Enseignement des mathématiques

politica, sed ad agendum et quidvis domi militiaeque fabricandum pertinere' (*Scholæ mathematicæ* 11, p. 54)—Hooykaas donne de nombreuses références à un Platon favorable à l'utilisation 'mécanique' des mathématiques, dans sa note 17 des pages 77–8 de son livre.

158 'Mathematici etiam quidem scriptores auxere hanc mathematum infamiam, qui contemplationum et demonstrationum illecebris capti, usum omnem incredibiliter aspernantur, mathematicumque subjectum in phantasticis et ab omni sensu abstractis mathematis constituunt ... Sic Pythagorei musicam ratione tantum metiebantur, spreto auditus sensu atque judicio ...' (*Scholæ mathematicæ* 11, p. 53).

159 Cf. R. Baron, 'Sur l'introduction en Occident des termes "geometria theoretica et practica" ', *Revue d'Histoire des Sciences* 8 (1955) 298–302.

160 Voir Waddington, op. cit., 168 sq.

161 Ibid., 173 sq.

162 Ibid., 176–8.

163 'Sum *analphabètos, agéometrètos*, agnosco hoc quoque' (cité par Waddington, 175).

164 Cf. *Scholæ mathematicæ* 1, 21, et *Jacobi Carpentarii ad Expositionem de methodo, contra Thessalum Ossatum*, etc., 1564, fol. 11v.

165 Le *De Cælo* (Waddington, 179 sq.).

166 Celle de Peter Sharratt sur Ramus et la Réforme de l'Université, notamment dans les sciences mathématiques.

167 pp. 108–9.

168 Voir plus haut, op. cit., p. 111 v.

169 C'est-à-dire 'usager' (comme il parle de la géométrie 'usagère' d'Archimède).

170 *Scholæ mathematicæ* 1v, 114.

171 'Nihil enim praecipiunt de quantitate, nihil de numero, nihil de magnitudine, sed de re physica numerata, de re physica magna' (ibid., 114).

172 Cité par Tartaglia (cf. Hooykaas, op. cit., 41 n. 35).

173 'Euclide Megarense acutissimo philosopho, solo introduttore delle scientie mathematice' (Tartaglia, Venetia 1569, 11, 3).

174 Cf. *Scholæ mathematicæ* 11, 54–5.

175 'Romam et antiquitatem omnem missam faciamus, et pro urbibus omnibus Lutetiam unam urbium omnium longe maximam et opulentissimam urbem circumspiciamus, et mathematicae utilitatis testem producamus. Dionysiaca via est urbis illa regalis ditissimis mercatoribus frequentissima. Hoc hominum genus non modo cum provinciis amplissimi regni omnibus, sed cum mercatoribus Italis, Hispanis, Germanis, Flandris, Britannis quotidiana commercia exercet, varietate magna prorsus et dissimilitudine numismatum, ponderum, mensurarum. ... Reperies Arithmeticae primas et summas subtilitates in commutationibus et comparationibus illis adhiberi et exerceri, mercaturamque totam Arithmeticam esse ... Progredere vero a regali illa via Palatium versus, occurret pons aurificum non tam tignis et trabibus solidus, quam auri atque argenti pondere gravis. Interroga hoc divitum hominum genus, qua scientia aurum cum argento ... Jam propius in ipsam Palatii arcem ascendito, et honoriaeque abacos et calculos introspicito, nil nisi Arithmeticam quandam in toto illo splendore, nil nisi Arithmeticos magistros recognosces. Verum si in regis aerarium penitus introieris, in eoque divisores, quaestores,

judices attente animadverteris ... mirabere Arithmeticae artificio tantas utilitates et commoditates in hominum vita comprehendi ...' (ibid.)

176 *Multiplicationis exemplum* (*Scholæ mathematicæ* XXIV, 275)

$$\begin{array}{r} 8 - 9 \\ 8 - 9 \\ \hline -72 + 81 \\ 64 - 72 \\ \hline 64 - 144 + 81 \end{array}$$

'E duobus negatis fit affirmatus, quia multiplicator non est integer'.

177 p. 257 sq.
178 'Nihil unquam tam confusum vel involutum legi vel audivi' (258).
179 'Non ad intelligendum ... sed ad perspiciendum penitus (257).
180 Ibid., 258.
181 Paris, Wechel (l'ouvrage ne porte pas de nom d'auteur).
182 op. cit., 50.
183 '... Vous ferez naistre et sortir d'autres Archites, d'autres Archimèdes, du labeur et industrie desquelz (estans nez et instruitz en vostre royaume) pourrez user à vostre honneur et proufit ...'.
184 A Paris, chez Gilles Gourbin, 'à lenseigne de l'Esperance, devant le College de Cambray'.
185 A rapprocher du sonnet de P. Demay, de Chastelleraud, secrétaire du Duc de Savoie, au verso de la page de titre:
  Si ce grand Archimede, honneur de Syracuse,
  La foudre et la terreur des Rommains assaillans,
  Pour son divin savoir fut prisé des vaillans ...
186 Cf. Waddington, 326–8.
187 Op. cit., 326.
188 Son nom figure assez honorablement dans les Histoires des mathématiques; il mériterait une monographie. On citera néanmoins le mémoire de J. Fontès (voir note 25).
189 Selon les propres expressions de Ramus.
190 Notamment ed. de 1565, in 4° (V. 6746–3), de 1566, in-8° (V. 18185, V. 18271), s.l.n.d., in–4° (V. 6746–2).
191 On notera la liaison fréquente de mathématiciens protestants (de plus ou moins longue date) avec de grands personnages de la religion réformée.
192 Op. cit., f. 41r.
193 Voir Waddington 176.
194 C'est un fait que les six premiers livres d'Euclide étaient généralement présentés et commentés.
195 '... en laquelle sont traictées quatre reigles briefves qui contiennent les deux cents quarante anciennes et plusieurs autres reigles pour l'exercice des nombres entiers ...', Paris, G. Cavellat (BN *Rés.* v. 900).
196 Paris, H. de Marnef et G. Cavellat (BN v. 6747).
197 L'une des conséquences de la découverte et de l'exploitation des nombres irrationnels.
198 Une étude systématique du vocabulaire français et du vocabulaire latin de ces traités de mathématiques serait des plus fructueuses pour l'histoire de la langue comme pour l'histoire des idées.
199 Paris, pour G. Cavellat, in–8°, 67 ff. (BN *Rés.* p. v. 407).

200 Voir note 188.
201 Pour tous ces noms—bien connus—, voir, dans un premier temps, la *Bibliographie (Histoire des sciences et des techniques)* de F. Russo, Paris, Hermann, 1954; suppl. ronéotypé, 1955.
202 Voir notamment son *Arithmetica integra*.
203 Art. cit. p. 153, n. 135.

M. A. SCREECH

Medicine and Literature : Aspects of Rabelais and Montaigne (with a glance at the Law)

'TANT EMBRASSE ON QUE chet la prise'. I have chosen a wide subject to talk on, since it deals with both Rabelais and Montaigne; wider still because it deals with some of their relationships to Renaissance medicine, which itself requires a glance at Renaissance Law and Renaissance philosophy. But there are times when it is pleasant to stand back from the detail and look for the pattern. A paper read before a group of learned colleagues and friends is perhaps an appropriate occasion.

In Rabelais and Montaigne we have two men who seem almost as different as possible: the one, dependent on patronage, a professional *savant*, a committed comic dogmatist of quite unnerving certainty; the other, Montaigne: the independent gentleman, with the gentleman's contempt for professional learning; a man whose writings have little to do with comic certainty, much to do with sceptical humour. But I suggest it might be wise to note at times how much they have in common, not least because this will throw into relief the quality of their differences.

These two authors were brought closer together by the very nature of their writings: Rabelais, if he wanted to be understood by other than the most formally erudite of readers, had to leave aside all those squabbles amongst doctors and amongst lawyers which were no more than that. He had to select his material from amongst those quarrels which had left the scholarly cell and entered into the public domain. Montaigne too, because of the fact that he was presenting himself as an amateur not a professional, also naturally drew much of his material—not least where medicine and law were concerned—from the same public domain of shared and accessible knowledge. It would not be either a long or a difficult assignment to draw up a quite impressive list of material, sources and assumptions common to them both. That is why it is not an impossible task to make comparisons between their critical comments on the Renaissance assumptions of knowledge.

. . .

Rabelais of course was a doctor. He finds his place readily in the libraries of the history of Medicine. In histories of the Law, and law libraries, the place he occupies is small. That his medical work was honoured in his day is shown by the quality of his patrons, the judgments of his contemporaries and (what I have only recently discovered, in the work that Miss Gwyneth Tootill, Miss Anne Reeve, Mr Stephen Rawles, Mr Stephen Bamforth, myself and other colleagues have devoted towards a new Rabelaisian Bibliography) by the wide diffusion of his medical books. His *Hippocratis ac Galeni libri aliquot* turns up all over the place. There is no doubt that the editions of this work were widely appreciated and seriously used. But Rabelais's professional standing as a committed Platonic doctor should not blind us to the fact—and it is a fact—that he writes less as a doctor than as a student of law. Well before he had acquired his medical credentials, Budé had dubbed him 'juris studiosissimus'. His commitment to humanist law was, to judge from his books, a deeper and more passionate one than his commitment to his 'art'. Nowhere in his novels is there anything quite so blistering where medicine is concerned as his scornful dismissal of the glossists of the *Pandects*, that 'belle robbe d'or, triumphante et precieuse à merveille' which thanks to Accursius and his tribe is now 'brodée de merde'. This carefully contrived outburst in *Pantagruel* (Textes Littéraires Français viii *bis*, 58–9) is clear propaganda in favour of Budé and the *mos gallicus*. The editions imprudently correct Rabelais here, asserting that his citing as authority 'Ulpian, *l. posteriori, De origine juris*' is an error for 'Pomponius, *De origine juris*'. But it is nothing of the sort! He is clearly inspired by Budé's annotation on *Ex lege posteriori, De origine juris*, where, in fact, Pomponius is censured—'hoc in loco hallucinatus est Pomponius'. Budé—like Rabelais—considered Ulpian to be 'omnis antiquitatis peritissimus' and his insistence on the close interrelationship of law and moral philosophy is warmly cited by Budé (*Ex lege prima, De justitia et jure*). He cites Ulpian many times in his commentary on *Ex lege posteriori, De origine juris*. Rabelais was a keen student of law (closer I believe in some ways to Budé even than to Tiraqueau, to whom he clearly owes much). He places his most developed philosophical work, the *Tiers Livre*, within a legal framework; it starts off with a *Prologue* deeply indebted to Budé's *Prefatio* to the *Annotationes in Pandectas*, and reaches its essential conclusion (after much legal jesting) in Christian Folly as understood by a Christian humanist who was deeply indebted to Budé's glosses. We should not be blinded to this great debt to legal studies. Naturally we associate 'Christian Folly' today primarily with Erasmus's *Moriae encomium*.

Rabelais's debt to that work may, or may not, be real. At all events the debt to legal sources and preoccupations is detailed and demonstrable.

There is nothing like this detailed and sustainedly partisan commitment where medicine is concerned except—and the exception is important—in the *Tiers Livre*. There medicine takes its weighty but not primary place in the Renaissance encyclopedia. Law, on the other hand, not only supplies a great deal of the matter of the novels from the outset, it also shapes some of Rabelais's suasive and dissuasive rhetoric, leading him to write with all the legal tricks of the advocate in the law-court, arranging whole episodes in accordance with the maxim, *Contraria juxta se posita, et minora: meliora, et pejora appareant*, and being guided by its canons in the overall construction of a whole book.

Rabelais clearly took seriously the claims of Ulpian—and scholars such as Budé—that 'Jurisprudentia est divinarum atque humanarum notitia, justi et injusti scientia'.

Where law and medicine meet and clash—as they often did—Rabelais gives the priority to law, as virtually any Renaissance *lawyer* would have done, but few doctors, at least willingly. One might note that Rabelais in his writings was helped by the clear inference that legal knowledge had wider currency amongst general readers than medical knowledge (except in certain definite fields) a fact which enabled him to make his points (both serious and comic) in pages which today can appear appallingly erudite. This point has been recently strengthened by Dr Michael Freeman in his note on 'Les éditions anciennes de Coquillart' (*BHR*, 1974, 87).

In law, Rabelais's position is clear and consistent. He prefers Roman law to canon law (where they clash) and has no time at all for the decretals, forged or genuine. The great texts of Roman law he treats with the utmost reverence. In medicine his task was much less easy. There were already clashes amongst the great Classical doctors themselves, Galen for example writing partly against Hippocrates. To contrast the tribe of later legal commentators and glossists, unfavourably, with the majesty of the texts they were expounding was a relatively straight-forward job—until one got down to detail. Where medicine was concerned, authority was opposed to authority. But, where medical authorities clashed, Rabelais rushes into the fray, inevitably championing one side against all comers.

Montaigne avoided any suggestion that he had studied law (or indeed any other subject) professionally. But it is wise to remember that, in *Des Livres* his denial of study is heavily qualified: 'ou, si j'estudie, je n'y cherche que la science qui traicte de la connaissance de moy mesmes, et qui m'instruise à bien mourrir et à bien vivre' (II, 10). Not a bad syllabus that! Any Renaissance man who took that seriously *must* have gone into law. There are signs of some genuine legal and medical learning hiding behind the assumption and parade of merely amateurish knowledge. When Montaigne writes (*Des Prognostications*, I, XI): 'J'aimerois bien mieulx regler mes affaires par le sort des dez que par ces songes', one is entitled to see not only the rejection of *Prognostications*—legally the specialized preserve of doctors in France—but also the Classical legal notion (championed by Rabelais with a due display of the appropriate authorities and by Sir Thomas More with lighter legal acumen), that one can and should have recourse to the dice, in *casus perplexus*, when there is 'no other way'.

Rabelais and Montaigne, indeed, meet textually over the harm done to Roman law by the meddling of Tribonian, Justinian the First's legal adviser known as the 'architect of the *Pandects*'. Rabelais attacked Tribonian at length in the *Tiers Livre*, in a passage indebted to Budé's annotation on *Ex lege ultima, De edilitio edictio*: 'Attendu mesmement que tout leur directoire en judicature usuale a esté baillé par un Tribunian [. . . qui . . .] *leurs a taillé leurs morceaulx* par ces petits boutz et eschantillons des loix qu'ilz ont en usaige.' Montaigne writes with less passion, but falls upon the same phrase: 'L'opinion de celuy-la ne me plaist guieres, qui pensoit par la multitude des loix brider, l'authorite des juges, *en leur taillant leurs morceaux*.' The common phrase—*tailler leurs morceaux*—enables us to be certain that the opinion Montaigne dislikes is that of Tribonian (not of Justinian as the notes say). *Tailler leurs morceaux* is doubtless a legal common-place, going back at least to Budé who bitterly attacked Tribonian and his colleagues for being like bad surgeons who 'ad vivum *ressecans, accisas* nobis Pandectas verius quam compendiosas dederunt'. (*Ex. tit. II, De origine juris, in verbo Vindicias filiae suae*).

But whereas Rabelais's scepticism in legal matters and legal con-tradictions is coloured by a strong religious indignation, which leads him to turn to God, the *Justus Judex* for the resolution of the insol-uble, Montaigne turns for the resolution of his problems to total subordination to the Roman Catholic Church and, in human terms, goes in quest of the laws of Nature. He is as insistent as Rabelais in his rejection of the glossists, but he has no respect for the great Roman *corpus* either—or indeed, for any other human system of laws. The only 'fondement mystique de leur authorité' is that they *are* laws. But laws are made by men: 'autheurs vains et irresolus' (III, 13).

Rabelais is never sceptical in this way about the 'belle robe d'or, triumphante et precieuse à merveille'. But, in the *Tiers Livre* he has a scepticism of his own, one based upon a sober awareness of the intervention of the Devil in the processes of law; the Devil he saw (through a literal understanding of the words of the Vulgate) as not only transfiguring himself as an angel of light, but specifically working injustice through his ministers, the corrupt legal officials (TLF, XLIIII, 299). He also saw clearly something he had held to be a comic perversion of the ignorant in *Pantagruel*: that the law contains its own 'antinomies et contrarietez'.

This legal scepticism in Montaigne and Rabelais has a long history and is influenced at least to some degree by the third of the famous Delphic triad: 'Comes aeris alieni et litis est miseria'. Both Rabelais and Montaigne pay more than lip-service to Nature and her laws. But precisely because he sees the Devil at work perverting justice, Rabelais has recourse to the author of Nature, through various ways, including the casting of dice, a process approved of by the Law itself. Montaigne is well aware of Evil. I suppose he accepted the Church's teaching about the Father of Lies. But the Devil as a person simply does not figure in the *Essais* (which is doubtless one of the qualities which make the *Essais* seem more 'modern' than Rabelais's novels). Rabelais would I suspect see this as a ruse, Satan having convinced most men that he does not exist. Montaigne sees no remedy for human problems in human knowledge either, preferring, in passages heavily indebted to the much-criticized Cicero, to seek out and follow the *vestigia Naturae*. But in the last resort, Rabelais seems to know what Nature requires (cf. his chapters in the *Quart Livre* on *Physis* and *Antiphysis*). Montaigne does not —yet; except that life and its conditions are a gift from God.

If this seems a lot of law in a paper on medicine, I do apologize, but both Rabelais and Montaigne saw medicine as part of the standard trilogy: theology for the soul; law for property, and medicine for the body. Both were also fully committed to the standard Christian notion that Man is body-and-soul conjoined when alive, and that death is precisely the separation of the soul from the body. These three 'subjects' (as we tend to think of them) were in a definite hierarchy but had delimitation disputes. On the whole, medicine worked with 'natural' knowledge and had the body as its domain. This is stressed by Rabelais in the consultation with Rondibilis in the *Tiers Livre*. When Montaigne refers to 'nos medecins spirituels et corporels' he means of course theologians and doctors. Psychology, the study of the soul, was a theological matter; at the other extreme, surgery was distinguished from medicine to such an extent indeed that Montaigne, who has little good to say for medicine itself, can give it qualified approval, 'parce qu'elle voit et manie ce qu'elle fait . . . là où les medecins n'ont point de *speculum matris* qui leur descouvre nos cerveaux, nostre poulmon et nostre foye' (II, 37). Montaigne dissociates himself completely from medicine. It is, over and over again, a matter of 'leur art'. The *leur* detaches it from himself; the *art* contrasts it with that natural knowledge which doctors were thought to be specially concerned with, and with Nature's 'simples' (which anyway for Montaigne, make up some two-thirds of the effective medical pharmacopoeia). Yet despite this rejection of the very 'art' to which Rabelais owed his professional life, the domain of publicly accessible knowledge in which they both placed part of their writings often brought them together here too, only to emphasize what a gulf separated them.

Montaigne certainly had more than a smattering of medical knowledge, but little inclination to go into medical detail. He can play the doctors at their own game when needs be—by showing, for example, that curing a nasty illness with nasty medicine is hardly in conformity with Hippocrates's authoritative medical axiom: *contraria contrariis curantur*! (I, 30). But he goes far beyond this, of course, dubbing the whole approach of the medical 'art' towards health and illness as unnatural.

The constant use of 'art' for medicine explains I believe why he attacks it so strongly in *De l'experience*, which openly sets out on its long and delightful quest for Nature from a clearly Aristotelian standpoint—soon to be left behind. The *Metaphysics* starts by dealing with those areas where we must use experience rather than reason, and indeed makes 'experience produce art'. When Montaigne read these words, in whatever language, I suspect he saw in τέχνη, *ars*, 'art', a direct allusion to medicine, which ought to be based on experience and yet can so rarely assemble and control its knowledge. (τέχνη, *ars*, was the normal word for medicine).

Of all medical questions widely and publicly debated in the Renaissance, and so often quarrelled about, no subject was more popular than that dealing with theories of generation and birth. Books on the subject are legion: I have been ploughing through them, on and off, for years. It is precisely because these subjects formed part of the public domain—for how can a society be indifferent to ideas about sexuality and, say, legitimacy—that both Rabelais and Montaigne seem to me to be at their most revealing when dealing with these topics.

Both saw the seminal propagation of the species as one of the supreme gifts of God to Man. The famous chapter VIII *bis* of *Pantagruel* springs to mind, with death compensated for by 'une espece de immortalité', achieved by means of 'propagation seminale'. Yet here—as in the *Tiers Livre*—the treatment of sex as such is curiously detached. Where Pantagruel, in the *Tiers Livre*, is invited by his father to think about marrying, he treats the matter as one of 'indifference', as one of the *adiaphora*. Nowhere in the novels is sexuality discussed seriously except in relation to theology, medicine or progeny. Even in that liberal passage of the *Tiers Livre* where a case is made out for the re-marriage of the widow of proven barrenness, the role of sex is avoided as though Pantagruel were a maiden aunt; men may marry such widows 'pour leurs vertus, sçavoir, bonnes graces, seulement en consolation domesticque et entretenement de mesnaige' (*TL*,VI). Sexual desire in Rabelais is essentially comic, unless severely controlled and subordinated to a greater purpose. There are no sexual complications in the Abbey of Thelema; no love complications in the *Tiers Livre*. Montaigne's delight in his God-given sexuality is as far removed from the learned humour of the ex-monk as it is possible to get. It would of course be an error to attribute this attitude in Rabelais to medicine as such. Indeed Rabelais's attitude to the fertile marriage is close to that of the canon lawyers, who, for example, conceded that marriage was an honourable estate in the *Authenticae* (*Collatio 4, tit. I, De nuptiis*): 'sic est honestum, ut humano generi videatur immortalitatem artificiose introducere, et ex filiorum procreatione renovata genera manent jugiter, Dei clementia quantum est possibile, nostra immortalitate damnatae naturae' and so on.

I am not of course suggesting that Rabelais took this idea from this source. On the vexed question of the maximum length of a pregnancy, one might have expected Rabelais to write as a doctor, but he does not. When seeking his material for the chapter in *Gargantua* dealing with eleven-month pregnancies he turns not to the doctors but to Tiraqueau's learned and unreadable study entitled *L.Si unquam, c. de revoc. donat.*, published in 1535. On this matter of prolonged pregnancies, the doctors of the Renaissance were overwhelmingly in favour of the longer periods of eleven—or even thirteen—months. Still in 1630, Alphonso À Carranza can claim that doctors in general accept eleven months as a provenly reasonable pregnancy, on the authority of [Pseudo-] Hippocrates. It was the humanist school of lawyers—not, on the whole, doctors—who took a stand, as Rabelais did, in favour of the limit of nine months or at the most ten. Rabelais's humour in this episode requires one to accept that nine months is obviously correct. It is this which makes the medical and legal disputes on this subject so comic, allowing as they do the merry widow two months' grace to father off her bastard on her dead husband's estate. Montaigne will have none of this. He believes in eleven-month pregnancies for the good and solid reason that he was an eleven-month child himself. 'Et moy, je secours, par l'exemple de moy-mesme, ceux d'entre eux qui maintiennent la grossesse de onze moys. Le monde est basty de ceste experience: il n'est si simple femmelette qui ne puisse dire son advis sur toutes ces contestations, et si, nous n'en sçaurions estre d'accord (11, 12).' Our reaction to this will either be a sage nodding of the head, or else some variation on the reflexion that it's a wise child who knows his own father. But within its context we should note that Montaigne presents this as a question dividing the professions (in the plural): 'Voylà les medecins, les philosophes, les jurisconsultes et les theologiens aux prises, pesle mesle avecques nos femmes, sur la dispute à quels termes les femmes portent leur fruict.' I think he must have known that in general he was siding with medical opinion here against the new legal schools. Book after book dealt with this subject. It is a question treated after all by Joubert in a work that Montaigne is known to have read: *Erreurs populaires au fait de la medecine* (iii, chap. 2). Joubert comes down strongly for the traditional medical opinions, including eleven-month pregnancies. It occurs also in Henri Estienne, (in another book Montaigne had read): the *Apologie pour Herodote*. But he prefers to give his reasons on the grounds of natural, unlearned, untutored experience, since no doubt, 'l'experience est proprement sur son fumier au sujet de la medecine, où la raison luy quite toute la place'. (iii, 13). Was Montaigne so hostile to medicine that he could not bring himself to confess to an agreement with the doctors on *any* point?

This notion that experience is the basis of most medical knowledge would not have been denied by most doctors of the time. Whilst in practice working from authority, they frequently appealed to conclusions which their authorities claimed to have reached experimentally. But Montaigne wants untutored experience—hence doubtless his rejection of the allegedly experimental Paracelsus. Judging from Rabelais's own excursions into experimental medicine, Montaigne was right. Much play is made by scholars on Rabelais's dissections. It would be wrong to think they were truly experimental. Rabelais knew for example that some of the new schools of medicine, including Vesalius and his followers, denied the existence of the *rete mirabilis*—that fine network of blood-vessels in the cranium which distilled the 'animal spirits', the spirits, that is, of the soul. Vesalius was correct. There is no such thing. But

Rabelais makes his good doctor Rondibilis (*Tiers Livre,* TLF, XXXI, 104 ff) refer to 'les conduitz *manifestes en anatomie* sus la fin du retz admirable'. In the following chapter (XXXII, 74) the interconnection of the wandering womb with 'toutes les parties principales du corps' is again said to be 'evident en l'anatomie'. Paré, incidentally agreed with Rabelais, finding out experimentally that the *rete mirabilis* was where the authorities said it was. But 'nous avons changé tout cela'.

Renaissance theories of human generation were dominated by the clashes of opinion about how semen was produced and whether woman had a secondary semen. Nobody had yet thought of a human egg. Since classical times, controversies on this subject were legion. It is highly revealing how our two authors treat this clash of opinion. Montaigne sees it as food for his scepticism about medical notions, as H. C. Agrippa had done before him. Rabelais, with the full creative partisanship of the comic propagandist, tackles the question in quite the opposite way. He isolates the Hippocratic ideas he approves of and attributes them to the 'good' doctor. The (largely Galenic) ideas he disapproves of he attributes to Panurge, so emphasizing both the clash of opinion and the acceptance of one school in preference to the others. Panurge accepts the Galenic-Arabic opinions in the Praise of Debts and Debtors; he goes on to make a praise of the testicles in full Galenic manner in the Praise of the Codpiece. You may remember that Galen, like Panurge, said that it would be better to have no heart than to have no testicles. When Rabelais comes to Rondibilis, he selects from the Hippocratic *corpus* precisely those parts of his doctrine, and the alleged experiments by which it was verified, which appear side by side with the Galenic ones in the compendia of medical controversies. The opposite views are then seen in complete contrast, the erroneous ones elaborated by empty sophistry, the 'correct' Hippocratic ones by careful suasive rhetoric. Was Rabelais one of those who considered Hippocrates to have had Nature's secrets of the formation of semen in the brain revealed to him by a special revelation? I suspect he was. Rabelaisian dogmatism, in the presence of increasingly chaotic knowledge and opinion, seems inevitably led towards placing ultimate trust in divinely-revealed authority. The question of how semen was produced was of basic importance to Rabelais, affecting as it did his ideas on celibacy, continence and indeed the entire dignity of man as an individual person. Galen's ideas he saw as lessening the dignity of the person in the interests of the species.

Montaigne's sceptical by-passing of the medical authors can have exciting results. Doctors, busy men then as now no doubt, were prepared to go on quoting their great Classical authorities at second or third hand for century after century, without ever being led apparently to verify their quotations against their original sources. One of the most frequently cited sources on sexual matters, long before Montaigne wrote and for many years afterwards, was Plato in the *Timaeus* (91 AD). On this authority, doctors had for over a millennium taken this *locus classicus* to prove that woman was more subordinated than man to her sexuality, being at the mercy of a mobile womb, an *animal avidum generandi*, which when not satisfied would produce hysteria (*sensu stricto*) that is, a state virtually indistinguishable from death. On the alleged authority of Plato, woman was therefore cast into the rôle of a human being who was less personally individual than man, a creature probably created more especially for the propagation of the race than for the perfection of her individual womanhood. Rabelais presents this opinion (*TL* XXXII) exactly as the elder John Riolanus is still to do a full generation later in his *Generalis Methodus Medendi* (III, 4–1: *de utero*). Having expounded his allegedly Platonic idea, he rounds on Galen who (whilst accepting the general contention of Plato, as the doctors read him) quibbled about whether the womb was really an 'animal' or not, according to approved definitions.

All this Montaigne by-passes. He quietly went back to Plato himself. And there he found that Plato in the very same passage had not only made woman subject to her sexuality, but man equally to his: 'Les Dieux, dict Platon, nous ont fourni d'un membre inobedient et tyrranique, qui, comme un animal furieux, entreprend, par la violence de son appetit, sousmettre tout à soy. De mesmes aux femmes, un animal glouton et avide, auquel si on refuse aliments en la saison, il forcene, impatient du délai.' The effect of this on theories about woman cannot be exaggerated. Gone completely is the medical profession's allegedly Platonic belief in the natural inferiority of woman. Gone is the entire edifice of female subordination to her sexual role, whilst man cultivates—or may cultivate—his individual dignity as a man. Plato as read correctly by Montaigne leads straight to a different conclusion indeed: 'les masles et les femelles sont jettez en mesme moule; sauf l'institution et l'usage, la difference n'est pas grande'. A conclusion diametrically opposed to traditional and authoritative medical ideas.

Here I have stressed a diametrical opposition. But in fact Rabelais and Montaigne are often in verbal agreement at the very moments they are just as opposed. Both these catholic Christians accept the ideal of *Nosce teipsum*; of the golden mean; of the primacy of Nature

($Φύσις$). But Montaigne gave these words deeper and more Ancient meanings. For Rabelais, *Nosce teipsum* is not an almost impossible precept requiring years of reflection. It is an important part of that bundle of precepts condemning self-love, $φιλαυτία$, that blinding source of evil and ignorance. He exploits it as such when Panurge encounters Her Trippa. Rabelais, like Molière at least at times, seems to need certainty against which he can provoke the laughter caused by manifest error. — Am I the only one whose breath is taken away every time I hear Cléante say with Socrates in *Le Tartuffe*:

> Mais en un mot, je sais, pour toute ma science
> Du faux avec le vrai faire la différence?

We find the same unnerving certainty in Pantagruel himself. Rabelais seeks, in domain after domain, absolute certainty. This certainty he finds increasingly in revelation. All sound learning is for him a *manne celeste*. Printing was an invention inspired by the Holy Ghost just as gunpowder was the work of the Devil. He turns most readily for his certainty to Holy Writ or to the great Classical authors. In the *Tiers Livre* we are fully in the domain of revealed knowledge, both in the course of the quest and in its artistic conclusion in Bridoye and Trouillogan, both Fools who can be inspired by a God who exalts the humble and meek. Pantagruel, it is stressed, 'has the gift of wisdom from the Father of Lights'.

The treatment of Socrates by Rabelais and Montaigne can teach us a lot. For Montaigne, Socrates is the master of masters—of Montaigne as of Plato himself, a great but purely human being. So, in his *ultima linea rerum*, the closing pages of *De l'experience*, he writes: 'rien ne m'est à digerer fascheux en la vie de Socrates que ses ecstases et ses demoneries'. He had taken care, in *Des Prognostications,* to demythologize Socrates's *daemon*: it was perhaps 'une certaine impulsion de volonté'. We all have experience of it; it can be so strong that it could seem like inspiration. Rabelais, on the other hand, reaches what seems to be in retrospect, the inevitable end for Pantagruel: he gives his hero, in his *ultima linea rerum* (the end of the *Quart Livre*) a fully Socratic *daemon*, just as he gave to Langey an essentially superhuman, heroic status. The superhuman status of Socrates he stressed with great emphasis in the prologue to *Gargantua*.

Rabelais clung to what were for him the great certainties of evangelical religion, law and medicine. All these certainties were authorized by majestic authority; departures from them could bring down upon those silly enough to hold erroneous views the full light of his comic vision.

But Montaigne saw no certainty in these sources. He detested the easy habit of denigrating the great men of the past, but he placed even the greatest in the context of opinion and basic human uncertainty. Outside the authority of the Catholic Church, he saw nothing at all but flux: 'Ou il faut se submettre du tout à l'authorité de nostre police ecclesiastique, ou du tout s'en dispenser. Ce n'est pas à nous à establir la part que nous lui devons d'obeïssance' (1, 28). In fact over the question of ultimate truth both Rabelais and Montaigne are very close. Both are able to draw the standard Christian notion from the same pre-christian text. Montaigne's last chapter—like how many treatises before him, over how many centuries —starts off with the great Aristotelian text, which forms the first sentence of the *Metaphysics*: 'Il n'est desir plus naturel que le desir de connoisance. πάντες ἄνθρωποι τοῦ εἰδέναι ὀρέγονται φύσει' which was usually latinized as 'omnes homines naturâ scire (*or* cognoscere) desiderant.' Starting from this fundamental Aristotelian tenet, Montaigne soon reaches the conclusion which I believe to be in this context a standard one in his day, and for many centuries before him: 'Il n'y a pas de fin à nos inquisitions; notre fin est en l'autre monde'. An excellent commentary on this, is Rabelais's Almanac for 1535, part of which has come down to us:

Les anciens Philosophes qui ont conclu à l'immortalité de nos ames, n'ont eu argument plus valable à la prouver et persuader que l'advertissement d'une affection qui est en nous; laquelle descrit Aristoteles (*lib. i. Metaph.*) disant que tous humains naturellement desirent sçavoir [...] Parce doncques qu'en ceste vie transitoire ne peuvent venir à la perfection de ce sçavoir ('car l'entendement n'est jamais rassasié d'entendre, comme l'œil n'est jamais sans convoitise de voir, ny l'oreille de ouyr,' (*Eccl.* i) et Nature n'a rien fait sans cause, ny donné appetit ou desir de chose qu'on ne peut quelquefois obtenir, autrement seroit iceluy appetit ou frustratoire ou depravé), s'ensuit qu'une autre vie est aprez cette-cy, en laquelle ce desir sera assouvi. Et reputeriez en gaing mirifique, si certainement on vous en predisoit la verité. Mais si à cettuy fervent desir voulez satisfaire entierement, vous convient souhaiter (comme saint Pol disoit *Philipp.* i) '*Cupio dissolvi et esse cum Christo*'). [...]
Autrement en predire seroit legereté à moy, comme à vous simplesse d'y adjouter foy. Et n'est encores depuis la creation d'Adam né homme qui en ait traité ou baillé chose à quoy l'on deust acquiescer et arrester en asseurance.

I have read out only a part of the work. But the whole of this Almanac adopts a position which ought really, I suppose, to lead directly to full Christian scepticism of the kind Montaigne embraced. Within the context it is limited above all to astrological uncertainty. I think that in the *Tiers Livre* (the next work he wrote, no doubt, after this Almanac), he does get close to total Christian scepticism, but a scepticism about *unaided* human knowledge; divine revelation and inspired knowledge is another matter: and that he sees all over the place, in the Bible (of course) but also in the great *Auctoritates* of law, philosophy and medicine.

Montaigne is sceptical about all unaided human endeavour and also fastened on to the great *Cupio dissolvi* of St Paul, in the *Apologie*: 'Ces grandes promesses de la beatitude eternelle, si nous les recevons de pareille authorité qu'un discours philosophique, nous n'aurions pas la mort en telle horreur que nous avons . . . Je veuil estre dissout, dirions nous, et estre avec Jesus-Christ (11, 12).' And previously (11, 3): 'Mais on desire aussi quelque fois la mort pour l'esperance d'un plus grand bien. "Je desire, dict Saint Paul, estre dissoult pour estre avec Jesus-Christ."' This is of course the cry of one of those 'venerable ames' to whom is vouchsafed 'un estude privilegé'. The 'marmaille d'hommes que nous sommes' can simply rejoice in the gift of life—of body and soul conjoined in the rich union of a close 'marriage'—and leave authoritative interpretations to God, who is his own interpreter and who will make it plain: 'C'est à Dieu seul . . . d'interpreter son ouvrage' (11, 12). Montaigne's attack on medicine is not primarily a mockery of its failure to effect cures; it goes hand in hand with his mockery of all human—as distinct from revealed— knowledge. It is only after he has reviewed the chaos of human opinions on the soul that he passes on to the chaos of human opinions about the body (which are of course dominated by medicine). 'En voylà assez pour verifier que l'homme n'est non plus instruit de la connoissance de soy en la partie corporelle qu'en la spirituelle.' But Rabelais works within the context of a much wider series of revelations, revelations partially vouchsafed even to Pagan Sages and mirrored however darkly in the authoritative sources of law and medicine as well as philosophy. Rabelais, as the *Tiers Livre* shows, held out to those of his readers who were good, wise and religious the hope of access to direct and indirect revelation.

Was Rabelais one of those doctors such as Manardi who believed Hippocrates incapable of making a mistake, incapable of misleading others? Was he one of those who believed him to have been the subject of a special revelation? I believe he was.

In the case of both Rabelais *and* Montaigne, in fact, only revelation seems to stand between man and complete uncertainty in all things. 'La participation que nous avons à la connoissance de la verité, quelle qu'elle soit, ce n'est par nos propres forces que nous l'avons acquise . . . c'est un pur present de la liberalité d'autruy [God]' (11, 12). These words could be applied directly, and without shuffling, to Rabelais's works. Rabelais does not (I suspect) give absolute and ultimate authority to medicine because he does not give ultimate importance to the body. He does not give ultimate authority (as Montaigne did) to the Roman Catholic Church but to the Holy Scriptures by which the Church itself must be judged. An important element in this (not of course the only one, or even the primary one) was this respect for civil law. To hand the last word to the Church would have been to hand the ultimate questions of law to the canon lawyers. This he will not do. In the *Tiers Livre* he subordinates canon law to civil law. In the *Quart Livre* he judges the papimaniacs' parody of the Church of Christ against God as revealed at the Burning Bush. The parody of the Holy Scriptures which these papimaniacs swear by is, most tellingly, the books of decretaline law, the bastion of the parodied Church.

In these great matters Rabelais's medical art played little or no part. His legal studies did.

Rabelais's thought in his books is the essentially orthodox religion of a turbulent ex-monk (duly absolved for his apostasy), who knew his civil law.

But he is pre-Tridentine up to his teeth. Montaigne is superbly at his ease with his head on the pillow of the post-Tridentine Church.

A. H. T. LEVI

Ethics and the Encyclopedia
in the Sixteenth Century

THIS PAPER SETS OUT from the hypothesis that the sixteenth-century Renaissance in northern Europe witnessed, if it was not constituted by, a considerable and comparatively sudden value-shift in western European society. The humanists, who were certainly the agents of this value-shift, seem more likely to have been its product than its cause. But to correspond with the importance attached by the humanists to interior moral sentiment, there emerged from the crucible of educational reform the clear, if short-lived, view that ethics held primacy of esteem among the disciplines. The humanists, interested in reorganizing the curriculum, from time to time had recourse to the ideal, or the image, of the encyclopedia, understood literally as the circular or logically interdependent organization of the disciplines. Did the encyclopedic reorganization of the disciplines in fact take place, or was it no more than a dream? If it did take place, by what process was ethics promoted to become the chief fruit of all intellectual endeavour, and hence queen of the curriculum disciplines where formerly had reigned philosophy or theology? How did ethics relate to the other encyclopedically organized disciplines, and how did it emerge with primatial status?

There is a difficulty in interpreting Renaissance references to the encyclopedia, since the linguistic register of these references is not easy to detect and certainly changes as the century progresses. Appeals to the antique ideal of the encyclopedia vary in tone from the adventitious to the programmatic by way of the hermetic. The encyclopedic ideal could aim at the restructuring of the curriculum disciplines into a logically interdependent new whole, but it can also be encountered in texts whose register is frankly mythological and in which, for instance, it serves merely to underline the spiritual importance of the arts of poetry and music.

The context in which explicit references to the encyclopedic ideal are found changes from the consideration of educational reform in the first half of the century to esoteric practices for the achievement of spiritual perfection by penetrating the secrets of the cosmos later on. Concern for the organization of the knowable into a new logical system endured, but explicit references to the encyclopedia which we must attempt to trace cross the threshold into the realms of neo-platonist mysticism shortly after the mid-century, and are thereafter seldom found in the more practical treatises on educational theory, or even in the context of the ambitious attempts to draw up compendia of or guides to the whole field of available knowledge. We shall therefore have to consider an elusive ideal, one which was in fact almost realized, but which changes, one might almost say evaporates, into something unrealizable before the aim in pursuit of which it was first deployed was actually achieved.

The only imaginatively powerful and logically rigorous realization of the encyclopedic dream is due to Descartes. It was only completed with the publication in 1649 of the posthumous *Les Passions de l'âme* which contained as much of the definitive Cartesian ethic as Descartes ever published. The original scheme for a logical organization of the disciplines had been modified after being originally laid down in the *Discours de la méthode*. Ethics, originally conceived as deducible from the medicine which itself depended on the physics, later became itself directly dependent on the physics, a parallel branch of the tree of knowledge with mechanics and medicine rather than a derivative of medicine.

Descartes was of course far too powerful a thinker to have followed deliberately any antique or modern paradigm in the elaboration of his philosophy. But if his organization of the knowable goes beyond the liberal arts to include mechanics, medicine, physics and ethics, it none the less represents a true and important effort logically to organize the non-revealed and non-empirical regions of the knowable, and so centres on the propedeutical liberal arts contained in the quadrivium and the trivium, omitting such revealed, positive or empirical disciplines as law, oratory, history, poetry and theology. If Descartes does not formally adopt the sixteenth-century fashion of regarding any one technique, rhetorical, architectural, musical or poetic, as capable of being imposed on all the disciplines and hence as being in itself a resumé of the whole encyclopedia, he is not far from regarding mathematical method as fundamental to any logical organization of what is certainly knowable. The reduction of the arts to mathematical method is at least prefigured in the sixteenth century by such figures as Jacques Peletier du Mans.

The metaphysics contained in the *Discours de la méthode* was reworked in the *Meditationes* of 1641. The *Principia philosophiæ* of 1644, republished in French with an important new preface in 1647, contained a further book of metaphysics and three books of general physics, making four in all. Descartes had projected a fifth book on the physics of animals and plants and a sixth book on the physics of the body-soul union in man, but he did not write either of them. The preface talks of metaphysics as the root of knowledge, with physics the trunk and medicine, mechanics and ethics now equally branches of the tree of knowledge. But in 1649 the first part of *Les Passions de l'âme* deals with the special psycho-physics of the body-soul union and is offered as a substitute for the missing sixth book of the *Principia*. The remainder of the work is largely devoted to the definitive ethic which from the beginning had been the aim of the whole Cartesian enterprise. Descartes therefore did not quite realize the encyclopedic ideal, since he omitted the physics of animals and plants together with all but early sketches for the medicine and the mechanics. But he did attempt to organize the knowable into a single logical system, and his attempt is the most powerful and rigorous we have. In the end the etymologically circular encyclopedia turned out to be as tree-shaped for Descartes as it had been for Porphyry and Lull, but its final fruit was now an ethic which purported to be logically derived from the apodictically certain foundations of metaphysics.

Like Descartes, Gassendi too believed that the whole of philosophy, including physics, was merely a stepping-stone to the all-important ethic established in moral philosophy, a view which Gassendi believed he shared with Pythagoras, Socrates, the Cynics and the Stoics. Both Gassendi and Descartes took a severely practical view of ethics, regarding it not as an abstract discipline but as a practical guide to good living. Indeed, virtually the whole of the northern Renaissance accepted Seneca's view, 'facere docet philosophia, non dicere'.[1]

Attempts to reorganize all that is knowable into a single logical system had already been made in antiquity. In the high middle ages they were renewed not only by the thirteenth-century scholastics, but notably also by Lull. And if Lull's adepts exercised only a surreptitious influence on an orthodoxy of which they were increasingly subversive, Lull's doctrine, suitably transformed, can still be discovered behind some of the bolder intellectual adventures of the optimistic first half of the sixteenth century in France. In a famous chapter Montaigne, writing during the wars of religion, distances himself from the work of Raimond Sebond which he had translated, but Sebond's *Theologia Naturalis* is at least partly Lullian in inspiration.[2]

The problem of reorganizing knowledge into logically interconnected disciplines reached its climax in the sixteenth century. The seven liberal arts of the quadrivium and the trivium had always been regarded as a propedeutic, to philosophy in the ancient world and to the graduate disciplines of medicine, theology, civil and canon law in the middle ages. In the sixteenth century there arose a clear demand to add other disciplines to the seven, and hence the need for a new unifying principle and a reorganization of the liberal arts. For a moment it seemed credible that there could be elaborated an encyclopedia, an ἐγκύκλιος παιδεία or ἐγκυκλοπαιδεία, an 'orbiculata series disciplinarum' with a properly logical structure. Some attempts to link the disciplines were of course merely pedagogical devices, akin to the application of 'method' and aimed at making the knowable more easily and superficially learnable. They could set out to promote rhetorical skills, or they could be vulgarizing initiatives to render knowledge more easily available to others than professional scholars.

In the strict sense the encyclopedic ideal intent on a logical reorganization of the relationships between the disciplines must be distinguished from the compendia of information, the pedagogical and scientific methods, the mnemonic techniques and the attempts to promote rhetoric to union with or primacy over dialectic, although each of these phenomena was related to the encyclopedic ideal in its consequences for the logical reorganization of the disciplines.[3] The idea of the ἐγκύκλιος παιδεία or 'orbis doctrinae' was derived in the Renaissance largely from Quintilian, who uses both Greek and Latin terms in the first book of the *Institutio oratoria* (I,x,i). It is mentioned again by Martianus Capella in the late fourth-century *De nuptiis Philologiæ et Mercurii* in which the seven liberal arts, led before Philologia by Apollo, are referred to as 'disciplinæ cyclicæ'. It reappears in the Renaissance as a specifically humanist concept, by which time the seven liberal arts had finally been transformed from techniques into distinct and defined areas of subject matter.

What the Lullian tradition contributed to the encyclopedic dream in the sixteenth century was the notion that the trees of science were more than simple classifications of knowledge and corresponded in some way with the realities of the cosmos. Lull's legacy, interpreted in the middle of the sixteenth century with the aid of a neoplatonist psychology on the Cusan pattern, could lead to the belief that the principle uniting the disciplines was the mind's ability to reconstitute within itself the structure of the cosmos. Both Pierre de la Ramée and Jacques Peletier du Mans sometimes speak in terms which suggest that the mind's knowledge is necessarily formed into a logical or encyclopedic system which reflects the real relationships in cosmic reality, although it is possible that each grasped at this intellectual calculus in order to justify views that he already held.

Other attempts to organize the whole field of knowledge, not tight enough in logical organization to warrant the title 'encyclopedia', were as frequent in the Renaissance as they had been in the middle ages. The most obvious example is the 900 theses of Pico della Mirandola which in 1486 attempted to reduce the knowable to a series of discrete propositions which were however not logically linked to one another. But the term 'encyclopedia' was in fact used of equally loose collections of knowledge from different disciplines. Remigius Rufus Candidus refers in the preface of his *In rhetoricen isagoge* (Paris 1515) to the influence of Bernard Lavinheta 'amicus noster Raimundi studiosissimus' on his desire to publish the rhetoric, 'ut in eo, tanquam in nitidissimo speculo, omnium disciplinarum imaginem contemplari vel potius mirari liceat'. Rhetoric here, as music later, is thought to comprehend the whole encyclopedia of disciplines. Rufus, following Quintilian, goes on to explain that the orator needs to know the rules of all the disciplines, to 'percellere diligenter orbem illum disciplinarum quem encyclopediam vocant'. The rhetoric is offered as a brief compendium of those things 'quæ uniuscuiusque disciplinæ perceptionem concernunt'.[4] The disciplines, in so far as they are unified by rhetoric, form an encyclopedia not in the sense of any logical connection between them but in the sense of being unified through the application of a single art.

However, the great humanist treatises of the earlier part of the sixteenth century do not often go farther than a mere reference to the encyclopedic ideal, and most do not even go so far as that. Neither the generation of Hegius and Rudolf Agricola, nor that of Erasmus, Vives, Sadoleto and Melanchthon was interested in it, perhaps because of its association with Lull.[5] The major educational reformers of the sixteenth century certainly linked their suspicions of Lull to their mistrust of the Cabbala. Rudolf Agricola has no doubts at all of the superiority of his scheme of dialectical invention over Lull's art, which he considers beneficial to the orator solely for his 'Copia'. Agricola says of Lull in the opening chapter of the second book of the *De inventione dialectica*, 'non literas sciebat', 'obscuritas ergo ingens est in discendo et horror incultus', while Erasmus's *De copia* ignores Lull altogether.[6]

Rabelais, who does use the term 'encyclopedie' in *Pantagruel*, thereby attesting to its currency in 1532, follows Erasmus in his contempt for divination and the art of Lull. The famous humanist manifesto contained in Gargantua's letter to his son in the eighth chapter of *Pantagruel* recommends the study of the liberal arts, but concludes, 'Laisse-moy l'astrologie divinatrice, et l'art de Lullius, comme abuz et vanitez'. Both Sadoleto and Vives remained solidly attached to the importance of rhetoric, to the study of ancient authors, and to the sort of educational reform movement of which Erasmus was to become the definitive spokesman, although Vives is aware of the *De nuptiis* of Martianus Capella, and refers to Crinitus's *De honesta disciplina* as an attempt to fulfil the ideal of unified knowledge laid down by Aulus Gellius. Melanchthon, intent on assuring the primacy of moral philosophy, goes so far as to suggest that ethics could be a 'rivulus ex Physicis manans', which is one step forward towards the Cartesian encyclopedia.[7] Melanchthon refers to Quintilian and the ἐγκυκλοπαιδεία and, in the 1537 prefatory epistle to the *Epitome philosophiæ moralis* makes it quite clear that, in his view, the organization of the disciplines ought to confer the primacy on moral philosophy.[8]

Budé was perhaps the first northern European humanist seriously to envisage the strict encyclopedic ideal. He regards the liberal arts as accomplishing that which Aulus Gellius had identified with 'humanitas' and defined as 'eruditio institutioque in bonas artes'.[9] Budé however goes beyond Aulus Gellius in seeing the liberal arts, which determine man's total relationship with the Muses, as an 'orbicularis doctrina', an 'eruditio circularis', and an ἐγκυκλοπαιδεία or 'orbiculata series disciplinarum'.[10] Budé was clearly thinking in the 1529 *Commentarii linguæ graecæ* of Martianus Capella's *De nuptiis* which was itself published in 1533 by an anonymous editor who may well have drawn on Budé's work for his introductory interpretation.[11] Budé's innovation was to put the Renaissance humanist 'Philologia' in the place of Cicero's 'Philosophy' as the source from which the other disciplines derive. For Budé 'Philologia' was itself a discipline, as was philosophy for Cicero, rather than an art or method applicable to all the disciplines, so that the encyclopedia momentarily envisaged by Budé was truly a logically organized system of the disciplines. The dependence of the other disciplines is not however totally logical, so that in the end Budé envisages little more than the primacy of philology, which should combine with the other disciplines into a harmoniously or, as he says, architecturally structured unity. The reference to architecture is perhaps inspired by the description of architecture as an 'encyclios disciplina' by Vitruvius. In the *De transitu*, Budé does refer to the encyclopedia in his effort to justify the 'dogmata . . . philosophiæ secularis et priscæ' as containing the 'vestigia sapientiæ' and as serving for a propedeutic for 'studia sanctiora', but any reference to the encyclopedia in the context of Budé's justification of Greek studies must be counted as special pleading rather than any committed view about the reorganization of the syllabus.[12] In the end Budé, like Erasmus, was concerned to emphasize the importance of rhetoric, understood as including a knowledge of the antique and particularly the Greek texts, as a prerequisite for a proper study of all the disciplines. It is for this reason that Budé promotes philology to the place reserved by Cicero for philosophy and by the scholastics for theology.

If Budé appealed to the encyclopedia in order to establish the primacy of rhetoric over scholastic dialectic, there are two other mid-century exponents of the encyclopedic ideal, Mario Nizolio and Pierre de la Ramée, whose final intention seems to have been much the same. Nizolio had produced his Ciceronian lexicon, the *Observationes in M. T. Ciceronem*, in 1535. Nearly seventy editions of this work appeared in the following hundred years. In 1553 Nizolio published his four volumes *De veris principiis et vera ratione philosophandi contra pseudophilosophos*, a work of educational reform in which Nizolio argues the usual humanist case for reuniting philosophy and eloquence and holds that without a knowledge of the precepts of rhetoric, all learning is ignorance.[13] He reproaches Agricola for allowing to dialectic the function of discovering truth, although he also admires him, and he regards rhetoric as the only universal art. Philosophy and rhetoric are not two disciplines but one, constituted by the mutual dependence of thought and language.[14] The discipline resulting from 'Philosophia et sapientia cum Oratoria et eloquentia conjuncta' is described by Nizolio as nothing other than 'omnia literarum studia et universa res literaria'. It is in fact the encyclopedia, 'tota ea facultas et professio, quam Græci ἐγκυκλοπαιδείαν, Latini vero circulum omnium doctrinarum vocant'.[15]

Having made his point about the unity of knowledge and its encyclopedic organization, Nizolio immediately distinguishes 'duas illas dimidias et maximas totius encyclopædiae partes' into 'sapientia' and 'eloquentia'. There is some confusion in Nizolio's subdivisions under these two headings, since rhetoric appears both as another name for 'Logica sive Oratoria sive Eloquentia', and as a subordinate category to it, along with grammar, poetry and history.[16] In the end it is however clear that the encyclopedia for Nizolio is merely a name for the unified field of knowledge resulting from the humanist ideal of the union of eloquence and philosophy as symbolized by the marriage of Mercury and Philology. The field of knowledge is subdivided into 'Physics' which discusses the nature of things, including divine things, 'Politics' which comprises the practical arts and sciences including ethics, and 'Logic' which stands for the major parts of the arts syllabus such as grammar, rhetoric, poetry and history. Nizolio represents another stage in the progress to the grand vision of Descartes, but he does not hierarchically organize the speculative and practical ends of philosophy. He simply co-ordinates them in the statement that the function of philosophy is 'vere cognoscere et scire, et recte agere ac facere'.[17] Nizolio in the end comes much nearer to regarding rhetoric as an art applicable to all the disciplines than to constructing a true encyclopedia in which the disciplines depend logically on one another.

Pierre de la Ramée, in spite of his interest in the pedagogical organization of knowledge and his programmatic insistence on the union of philosophy and eloquence, neither attaches importance to the properly encyclopedic ideal nor allots any particular primacy to ethics. His writings suggest that his recourse to the encyclopedic ideal was merely metaphorical, an attempt by a pedagogical theorist to cover a projected reform he was trying to defend with ancient and fashionable authority. It has been amply demonstrated that Pierre de la Ramée was more concerned with the organization of the teachable than with the logical interdependence of the knowable.[18] His failure to attach any particular importance to ethics separates him from those Renaissance humanists concerned with the inter-relation of the disciplines on a level deeper than the merely peda-gogical. The humanists, hitherto primarily concerned with poetry and rhetoric, had after all taken over chairs of moral philosophy from the early fifteenth century, so indicating the mainstream humanist concern with ethics among the philosophical disciplines at a very early date.[19] Pierre de la Ramée seems to have been a merely marginal figure whose pedagogical interest in the reorganization of the disciplines is not really relevant to the realization of the encyclo-pedic ideal.

As the century draws on, the encyclopedic ideal diverges farther and farther from any serious or realistic attempt to reform the sylla-bus and becomes more and more clearly associated with the mytho-logical register in which the neoplatonist humanists of the northern Renaissance expressed their confidence in the power of universal knowledge. The change from a practical reformatory to a mytho-logical and symbolic register can almost be charted by measuring the frequency of allusions to the Cusan image of the circle. Jacques Peletier du Mans is, for instance, driven relatively early by the desire to establish the possibility of knowing all that is knowable, princi-pally by arguing the mind's power, based on the memory, to re-constitute within itself the whole structure of the cosmos.[20] His ambition is clearly related to some forms of expression of the encyclopedic ideal, since he accepts the mathematical proportions residing in the memory as identical with the mathematical proportions which underlie the physical laws of the cosmos, just as the musical encyclopedia regards the mathematical proportions underlying musical harmonies as those which are inherent in the universe itself. Both can therefore plausibly suggest that the individual achieves harmony with the cosmos and its creator, that is to say spiritual perfection, by reconstituting within himself the mathematically conceived structure of the cosmos itself.

It is easy to see how Peletier's psychology provides both for progress towards the full ambition of Descartes himself and for a calculus which makes the poetic and scientific mental reconstitution of the universe promote in the individual a life-enhancing likeness to God. Only through numbers and proportions can man know nature in the circular progress through which God communicates himself to the world and the world returns to him.[21] Peletier is drawing on Nicolas of Cusa, probably as transmitted by Charles de Bouelles, but he provides a link with Ronsard not only in his insistence on the vernacular, but more importantly in his conception of the learned vocation of poetry. He insists on encyclopedic knowledge as a source of the poet's mastery of nature. The aim of the poet is to reach 'perfeccion d'esprit', to embrace 'par cogitacion l'univers¢ structure des choses'. He must possess 'la connoessanc¢ d'Astrologi¢, Cosmografi¢, Geometri¢, Phisiqu¢, brief d¢ tout¢ la Filosofi¢'. He must be familiar with the mechanical arts as well.[22]

Scève, too, attempts to encapsulate the sum of what is knowable in the spherically organized *Microcosme*. His inspiration is strongly neoplatonist, although his dependence on Charles de Bouelles and Reisch's *Margarita philosophica* take him away from the encyclopedic reorganization of the disciplines towards more arid and mnemotechnical pursuits. It is as if, alongside a legitimate humanist ambition to reorganize the disciplines of the curriculum, which snatched for its justification at the antique ideal of the encyclopedia and gave preeminent importance to ethics because *bonæ literæ* led to moral improvement, there grew up a desire to explain the psychology of spiritual perfectibility through the practice of the arts and sciences. Inevitably, the various sorts of neoplatonism developed by Ficino, Bouelles, Cusa and even Postel presented the paradigm. Instead of a humanist reorganization of the disciplines, which had sometimes referred to the encyclopedia as a model, and in which the spiritually perfective aspects of humanist study were given prominence with the primacy attached to ethics, we are confronted with a fundamentally more excited vision of human perfectibility which loses interest in the reorganization of the disciplines, encyclopedic or not, and in the primacy of ethics, to shore up the plausibility of its optimism by anchoring it in the only philosophical framework which could be created to support it. Whenever this necessarily neoplatonist framework itself referred to the encyclopedic ideal, it understood it in the quasi-mystical terms of the musical encyclopedia whose adepts achieved their spiritual perfection by recreating through poetry and music their harmony with the universe itself.

This seems clear from the work of two further sixteenth-century French authors who at least refer to the encyclopedic ideal, Pontus de Tyard and Guy Le Fèvre de la Boderie. Pontus de Tyard was one of many sixteenth-century French authors who attempted to express at least the essentials of human knowledge in artistic form. Such attempts had been frequent in antiquity and even more frequent in the middle ages. The sixteenth century saw a whole spate of handbooks and collections of what we should now call essays on historical and moral themes which sought to set out in compendious form some or all of what was knowable. Montaigne started out to some extent with a related attempt, although he developed a much more interesting ambition than to achieve comprehensive coverage of even the odd facts and opinions he delighted in contrasting.

Tyard however does refer to the authentically encyclopedic ideal of a spherical, that is interlocking and interdependent, organization of the disciplines. His original ambition was clearly to include in the *Discours philosophiques* a comprehensive treatment of the disciplines.[23] His ambition evaporates, with his neoplatonism, as in the late 1550s France was engulfed in the crisis of optimism which foresaw bankruptcy and the wars of religion and after which neoplatonism was to go sharply out of fashion, except possibly at court and where, among the magistracy, it was transposed into a more severe and defensive stoicism. The introduction to Tyard's *Solitaire premier* of 1552 announces however the original vision of the possibility of achieving 'la difficile cognoissance de la divinité'. The acquisition of 'l'intelligence des choses celestes et divines' is shown as the path to 'l'eternelle felicité'. The 'parfait studieux' seeks now not glory but virtue. The sciences are steps to the summit, and the summit is 'la Spherique Enciclopedie, et plus haute imagination'.[24]

For Guy Le Fèvre de la Boderie, the encyclopedia is an esoteric guide to hermetic truth, firmly neoplatonist in origin and no longer relevant to educational reform in general or to the position of ethics in particular. The *Encyclie des secrets de l'éternité* of 1571 is predominantly a work of youth in which the mysteries of heaven and earth are treated in eight 'circles' and which is clearly indebted to Postel.[25]

La Galliade ou de la révolution des arts et des sciences of 1578 comes after the translation of Ficino's *Symposium* commentary and its interpretation by La Boderie in the orthodox terms of Christian mysticism. Its inspiration is patriotic, and it sets out to declare the Gallic origins of the arts and sciences in five circles, still under the influence of Postel. The Ramist notion of 'invention' as the rediscovery of existing truth and Peletier's views about the mathematical nature of the memory, also discernible behind the first chapter of Sebillet's *Art poëtique* of 1548, are clearly related to one another and to the encyclopedic ideal as it developed on the neoplatonist wing of the northern Renaissance in the second half of the sixteenth century.

The encyclopedia had preserved its relevance to a logical organization of the disciplines until as late as 1559, the date of Paul Scaliger's *Encyclopediæ seu orbis disciplinarum tam sacrarum quam prophanarum Epistemon*, but even at this date the organization of the disciplines was becoming engulfed in considerations of 'method', and the individual academies were beginning to make the logical connections between the disciplines seem brittle. Already in 1548 Gyraldi's *De deis gentium*, a principal source for Tyard, had held that the relationship between the Muses symbolized that between the disciplines and referred to the 'cyclicæ scientiæ' of Martianus Capella. Gyraldi refers both to the Greek encyclopedic ideal and to its mention by Vitruvius.[26] Once the encyclopedic ideal becomes capable of symbolic representation, however, it inevitably loses its force as a basis for a systematic proposal to reform the curriculum. The projected primacy of ethics becomes dissipated into the general moral and even religious aims of Tyard, whose Pasithée is herself a symbol of the encyclopedia, since her music is the 'image de toute l'Encyclopedie', or into the moral and religious aims of Baïf's Academy according at any rate to Mersenne's account.[27] Music, after rhetoric, becomes the universal art or method, and it leads to spiritual perfection.

By the end of the century the encyclopedic guides to knowledge and the philosophical handbooks were more important in the context of curriculum reform than the neoplatonist efforts to reconstitute in the mind the structure of the universe which had preempted the title of encyclopedias. La Primaudaye's *L'Académie Françoise*, published between 1577 and 1590 and completed by *La philosophie chrestienne* of 1594, indicates in its very title how the encyclopedic compilation was to disintegrate on the threshold of the seventeenth century into a proliferation of different academies, as the logical interdependence of the disciplines became more and more tenuous before the great Cartesian reaction. What by that date had been established was the primacy of ethics among the disciplines, which is quite clear in La Primaudaye's text.

Music had been the connecting thread for the neoplatonists of the high Renaissance. It remained important for Rivault and Mersenne. But those seventeenth-century authors primarily concerned with the logical reorganization of the disciplines, Possevino and Alstedt for instance, like Descartes and Gassendi, were increasingly to emphasize that the fruit of learning was an ethic. Mersenne, the inheritor of the sixteenth-century ideal, was primarily interested in the physical sciences. But for Gassendi, as for Descartes, ethics was the fruit of the tree of knowledge.

The encyclopedia was invoked, if only occasionally, by the educational reformers of the early sixteenth century. Their work on the logical reorganization of the disciplines resulted, among other things, in the promotion of ethics to the queen of the disciplines, a position occupied by ethics well before the end of the sixteenth century as illustrated in the many attempts to provide handbooks to knowledge. But explicit reference to the encyclopedia lost contact with any attempt to reorganize the disciplines about the middle of the century or shortly thereafter. The encyclopedic ideal was now invoked in an hermetic pursuit as a means of penetrating the secrets of the cosmos, and it was linked to a strongly neoplatonist psychology which gave credibility to the increasingly strident claims that poetry and music were, in certain conditions, life-enhancing, morally improving and spiritually perfective. The educational reform, purged of references to a now neoplatonist encyclopedic ideal, which was forced by the wars of religion into what was at best a fringe cult, continued through the compilations and the applications of method until it surrendered any residual claim to be the basis for the logical interdependence of the disciplines. When Amyot comes to translate Plutarch's treatise on music, he does not even retain the term ἐγκύκλιος παιδεία, and renders merely 'toute science et litterature liberale'.[28]

The history of the encyclopedic ideal from Budé to Descartes highlights the sense in which the northern Renaissance was a reaction against medieval codes of behaviour. The whole educational reform of the sixteenth century had a moral and religious aim in view, and the gradual emergence of the primacy of ethics over all the other disciplines in Gassendi and Descartes itself sums up the fruit of the efforts of even the early sixteenth-century humanists. The 'encyclopedia' became a chimera, irretrievably linked to a neoplatonist and mythological view of man and his activities, recruited to upgrade the importance of certain sorts of music and poetry and now only tenuously linked to learning and not at all linked to the logical interdependence of the curriculum disciplines.

The attempt at a logical organization of the disciplines was optimistic, and optimism was eclipsed in France during the wars of religion. But optimism revived in France during the first decades of the seventeenth century, and it is not surprising that we find Mersenne preoccupied with Baïf, or Gassendi proclaiming the primacy of ethics, or Descartes very nearly successful in constructing on rigorously deductive principles the encyclopedia of which Budé had dreamed. The final fruit of the Renaissance attempt to reorganize the disciplines on a logically deductive basis is to be found in the logical and rigorous Cartesian system, irrefutable on its own premises. The final product of that system was to be a doctrine of behaviour, a path to happiness, an ethic.

NOTES

1 Ep. 20, §2. On the status of the ethic contained in *Les Passions de l'âme* within the Cartesian system, the original intentions of Descartes and their subsequent modifications, see A. H. T. Levi, *French Moralists: the Theory of the Passions: 1585–1649* (Oxford 1964). Gassendi points out that, together with Pythagoras, Socrates, the Cynics and the Stoics, 'Epicurum tanti fecisse Moralem Philosophiam, ut Physicam eatenus solum esse curandum censuerit, quatenus utilis quibusdam perturbationibus eximendis, ad ipsam proinde Moralem, illiusve finem conducit' (*Petri Gassendi Animadversiones in decimum librum Diogenis Laertii . . .*, (Lyons 1649) vol. 3, 1183).

2 On the Lullian inspiration of the encyclopedic tradition in the sixteenth century, see François Secret, 'La tradition de "de omni re scibili" à la renaissance: l'œuvre de Paul Scaliger', *Convivium* 23 (1955) 492–7, and Paolo Rossi, 'The Legacy of Ramon Lull in Sixteenth-century Thought' *Medieval and Renaissance Studies* 5 (1961) 182–213. On Montaigne's attitude to Sebond, see J. Coppin, *Montaigne, traducteur de Raymond Sebond* (Paris 1924) 65–71.

3 In his essay on 'The Transformation of the Liberal Arts in the Renaissance' in *Developments in the Early Renaissance*, ed. Bernard S. Levy (Albany 1972) 158–223, Richard McKeon, for instance, uses the encyclopedic umbrella to cover too many phenomena which cannot be referred to attempts to construct an encyclopedia in the strict renaissance sense of the term.

4 On Rufus, see Paolo Rossi, *The Legacy of Ramon Lull . . .*, Lavinheta was a Franciscan active in publishing texts of Lull from 1514 to 1523, during which period he lectured on Lull at Cologne.

5 Erasmus does refer in passing to the 'cyclopedia' in the 1529 *De pueris . . .* (ed. J.-C. Margolin (Geneva 1966) 459), but he uses the humanist term merely as an elegant way of referring to the whole of the curriculum.

6 For Agricola's view, see p. 181 of the Cologne 1539 edition. This allegation is taken up from that made by the Dominican Nicholas Eymerc (1320–1399). Jacques Lefèvre d'Etaples defends Lull in the preface to the edition of four of his works in April 1499, 'Neque vos quicquam deterreat quod vir ille idiota fuerit et illiteratus, horridæ rupis et vastæ solitudinis assiduus accola; nam et creditus quadam superna infusione dignatus, qua sapientes huius saeculi longe præcellaret' (*The Prefatory Epistles of Jacques Lefèvre d'Etaples and Related Texts*, ed. Eugene F. Rice (New York 1972) 77).

7 Vives refers to Martianus Capella in the *De corruptis artibus*, Book 2, ch. 1 (*Opera omnia*, t. 6 (Valentia 1785) 78), and to Aulus Gellius in the *Prælectio in convivia Francisci Philosophi* (*Opera omnia*, t. 2, 84). For the Melanchthon quotation, see the *Epitome philosophiæ moralis* (1541) 4.

8 See *Melanchthons Werke in Auswahl*, Band 3, ed. Richard Nürnberger (Gütersloh 1961) 17, and the *Epitome philosophiæ moralis* (1541) 3–13. See also Quirinus Breen, 'The Subordination of Rhetoric to Philosophy in Melanchthon', *Archiv für Reformationsgeschichte* 43 (1952).

9 See Aulus Gellius, *Noctes Atticæ*, xiii, 17, and for Budé, J. Bohatec, *Budé und Calvin, Studien zur Gedankenwelt des französischen Frühhumanismus* (Graz 1950) 13.

10 See for instance the 1527 *Annotationes priores in Pandectas*, 9, and the references in Bohatec, *Budé und Calvin*, 13–14. When Bohatec links Budé's dependence on Aulus Gellius for his concept of 'humanitas' with the 'orbicularis doctrina', he may be going too far. Henri Chamard, in his edition of Du Bellay's *La Deffence et illustration de la langue françoyse* (Paris 1961) 58, quotes two other references in Budé to the encyclopedia, and suggests as a source Plutarch's *De la musique* §13. It seems unlikely that Budé was influenced by this passage, although Plutarch's treatise was to exercise a massive influence a little later in the century. In §13 Lysias ends his speech by referring to Soterichus as a student not only of music, but also περὶ τὴν ἄλλην ἐγκύκλιον παιδείαν.

11 This is suggested, but not proved, with reference to Budé's 1530 *Philologia* by Bohatec, *Budé und Calvin*, 14. Bohatec also finds a reference to the encyclopedia in Cicero's *De oratore* (i, xlix, 212).

12 On the *De transitu*, see L. Delaruelle, *Guillaume Budé, les origines, les débuts, les idées maîtresses* (Paris 1907) 194.

13 See the introduction by Quirinus Breen to his edition of Nizolio, *De veris principiis . . .*, 2 vols. (Rome 1956).

14 The mutual dependence of thought and language was a point already made by Budé, who supported it with reference to the twin meanings of 'reason' and 'word' for λόγος and to the cognate Latin words 'ratio' and 'oratio'. For the dual sense of λόγος in Nizolio, see C. Vasoli, *La dialettica e la retorica dell'Umanesimo. 'Invenzione' e 'Metodo' nella cultura del XV e XVI secolo* (Milan 1968) 624–5.

15 *De veris principiis*, ed. Q. Breen, Book 3, ch. 3, vol. 2, p. 34.

16 Ibid., Book 3, ch. 3 and ch. 4, vol. 2, pp. 35–7 and p. 45.

17 Ibid., Book 3, ch. 3, vol. 2, p. 36.

18 See especially W. J. Ong, *Ramus, Method and the Decay of Dialogue* (Cambridge, Mass. 1958).

19 See P. O. Kristeller, 'Humanism and Scholasticism in the Italian Renaissance', *Byzantion* 17 (1944–5) 365–6.

20 On Peletier, see especially Hans Staub, *Le curieux désir, Scève et Peletier du Mans, poètes de la connaissance* (Geneva 1967).

21 See Staub, op. cit., 11–20, and Peletier's *Louange de la Science* in the Paris 1581 *Œuvres poétiques intitulés Louanges* (Staub p. 19), ff. 52v–53r, 'Des Choses de ce Monde, de leurs portions,/L'Homme ne cherche rien que les Proportions./Car c'est le haut savoir, qui Nature conserve,/Que Dieu à lui tout seul, en elle se réserve.'

22 Jacques Peletier du Mans, *L'Art poëtique*, ed. André Boulanger (Paris 1930) 216–17.

23 See on Pontus de Tyard, Kathleen M. Hall, *Pontus de Tyard and his 'Discours philosophiques'* (Oxford 1963).

24 Pontus de Tyard, *Solitaire premier*, ed. Silvio F. Baridon (Geneva 1950) 3–4. See also page 73.

25 See François Secret, *L'Esotérisme de Guy Le Fèvre de la Boderie* (Geneva 1969).

26 *Omnia opera* (Leiden 1696) col. 560. See Frances A. Yates, *The French Academies of the Sixteenth Century* (London 1947) 83–4 and 191. Apollo and the Muses symbolize the encyclopedic ideal in the decorations of the château of Ancy-le-Franc (Frances Yates, *French Academies*, 138).

27 See Mersenne's *Quæstiones celeberrimæ in Genesim* (Paris 1623) cols. 1683–4, Frances Yates, *French Academies*, 25, 133 and 325–6, and A.-M. Schmidt, *La poésie scientifique en France au XVIe siècle* (Paris 1938) 154.

28 *Les Œuvres morales et meslees* (Lyon 1592) vol. 2, 668 verso.

KATHLEEN M. HALL

Pontus de Tyard:
a reply to a recent article

TYARD BY NOW NEEDS no introduction. It will be remembered that he was born in Burgundy, according to my calculations,[1] in 1522; he published four volumes of Neoplatonic and Petrarchist poetry between 1549 and 1555, and prose treatises on various aspects of the encyclopedia. These started with the *Solitaire premier, ou, prose des Muses, et de la fureur poëtique* of 1552, his nearest approach to covering the Trivium, neglecting grammar and logic but concentrating on rhetoric. There followed the *Solitaire second* on music, probably in 1555; it is being edited by Professor McClelland and M. Vaccaro, whose absence we deeply regret. In 1556 appeared the *Discours du temps,* on methods of reckoning time and chronology; in these two treatises and in the 1558 *Mantice* on astrology may be seen relics of the Quadrivium. In 1557 came *L'Univers,* later republished as the *Premier* and *Second Curieux,* on cosmology, geography, the soul, God, and whether the world will end. All this is not the whole of Tyard's work, but the most important and the encyclopedic part. In the last twenty years he has been acquiring more and more readers, once they had shaken off the prejudiced nineteenth-century belief that he was obscure and unreadable. Once one knows the language of the Renaissance, his work is easy to read; it is not so easy to interpret the author's aims and personality.

In the twenty years since I completed my thesis on him and the ten since I published a compressed and corrected version of it, much important work has been done on Tyard, often better than mine. I recognize in my book mistakes and immature approaches and opinions; many were pointed out in a review by Wallace Kirsop.[2] Tyard has featured in Grahame Castor's fine *Pléiade Poetics;*[3] Professor Lapp and Professor McClelland have published editions of his poetry[4] which would be perfect if they could be rolled into one; and Dr Eva Kushner of Carleton University has started work which promises to make her the greatest expert on him yet. The article of hers with which I am particularly concerned appeared in the *Revue belge de philologie et d'histoire:*[5] 'Le "Solitaire premier" de Pontus de Tyard: prolégomènes à une interprétation.'

185

Dr Kushner begins by indicating in Tyard studies 'un certain
désaccord qui incite à tenter de faire le point', and I shall interrupt
to say how true that is. There is the problem of how far he was in
and of the Pléiade: for Dr Kushner 'ce serait absurde' to question it;
I pointed out in my book[6] that there is no authentic record that he
met Ronsard before 1575. There is evidence that he met Du Bellay
and Peletier but not in Paris, and I look forward to such new evidence as Dr Kushner can produce. There is the problem of his use
of the dialogue form in his prose discourses: he repeats his sources
slavishly, so that one must ask how far his views are theirs, and yet
divides up his source-material freely between imaginary characters
(or characters with real counterparts and in one case with a real
name, that of Maurice Scève), so that one must ask whether all or
any of these characters reflect his views. Busson and Lapp used to
class him as a rationalist; Lapp is less inclined to do so in his edition
of the poems. I recognize my own portrait of Tyard in a pretty
caricature by Dr Kushner, 'un aimable compilateur sans conscience
profonde de tout ce qui s'entre-choque dans ses compilations'; and
I admit my book underestimates an aspect of Tyard's style observed
by Du Perron in 1578 in his introduction to the second edition of
L'Univers: 'Souvent il y couche à la haste . . . un mot cachant mys-
terieusement tout le reste . . .'. Frances Yates stressed Tyard's Neoplatonism, and Dr Kushner in this article does the same, though
elsewhere she agrees with Professor Levi and me that it weakens
from 1556 on. For the moment, however, I shall imitate her approach
of returning to the 1552 text of the Solitaire premier and taking it as
representing Tyard's views at that time, whatever its sources. Dr
Kushner wishes to 'faire le point sur le rôle du Solitaire premier . . .
microcosme de toute la pensée de Pontus de Tyard . . .' For her, and
for me, what Tyard says makes sense and fits in with what he says
elsewhere and with experience; but I think it adds up to a slightly
different total from hers.

She properly points out in Tyard what in a passion for source-
hunting I may have undervalued, 'une certaine originalité à la
mesure de son talent'. On his poetry she quotes Vianey:[7] 'je n'ai pas
encore reconnu chez lui un seul plagiat véritable . . .' As I have said,
she could also have argued more strongly Tyard's independence of
the Pléiade. Where I collected the influences on his poetry and prose
noted by various critics, and tried to arrange these influences in
chronological order, she rightly emphasizes his ability to 'les
dominer à sa façon'. The heart of her article is the statement: 'Le
Solitaire premier traite de la nature et du rôle de la pensée; mais cette
enquête s'ouvre sur une enquête plus vaste concernant la connais-

sance, enquête dont on sait qu'elle débouchera par la suite, dans les discours suivants, sur une exploration de l'univers auquel l'homme est lié par cette connaissance'; and once again I agree and applaud.

But Dr Kushner passes straight to an attack on my theory that Tyard was losing interest in Neoplatonism already in 1552, that the *Solitaires* drift off into mere encyclopedism in the sense of parrot-like repetitions of classical commonplaces unrelated to a central theme. I concede that I gravely underestimated the extent to which Tyard's sources in the second half of the *Solitaire premier* and in the *Solitaire second*, Giraldi, Boethius, Gafori and Glareanus, were themselves Neoplatonists. But I still think I am right to say that in the *Solitaire premier*, which treats firstly of the four divine frenzies together and then of the poetic frenzy, Tyard hints that he will later treat also of the mystical and prophetic frenzies, 'faire tant qu'encores les autres trois fureurs, ne . . . demeurent incogneües';[8] and he never does so. At the end of the *Solitaire second*, Tyard recalls his promise 'd'en faire plus expresse description';[9] a marginal note reads 'Ocasion du troisieme Solitaire'; no such work is extant. Dr Kushner and I agree about the fourth frenzy, the erotic: 'si Pontus de Tyard n'a pas consacré une partie du plan à l'amour, c'est parce que l'amour occupe tout l'espace du texte'; 'je n'ay autre travail . . .', says Tyard, 'que de la vous representer devant les yeux'.[10] The *Solitaire premier*, like so many Renaissance dialogues and especially those of Leo Hebræus, is a conversation with a woman depicted at once as pupil and Neoplatonic mistress.

However, to my claim that Tyard breaks his promise to describe the second and third frenzies, or does so in the completely transformed shape of *L'Univers* and *Mantice*, Dr Kushner replies:

Si Pontus de Tyard pèche contre la lettre de l'art d'écrire . . . il s'est abondamment acquitté de l'esprit de sa tâche. En effet, la fureur poétique suffit à rendre compte de la disposition psychologique commune aux quatre fureurs . . . puisqu'aussi bien les Muses . . . président à toute l'encyclopédie du savoir . . . et que, chose très importante, les symboles de ce savoir peuvent emprunter les voies de la théologie *ou* celles de l'étude de l'univers.

In other words, no distinction is to be made between the first three *furores*, perhaps between any of the four; they all merely symbolize ways of exploring different aspects of the universe by means of contemplative thought. Dr Kushner does see and attempt to solve a difficulty:

Dans le schéma . . . la fureur religieuse . . . occupe le second degré dans la remontée de l'âme vers la lumière. Selon une optique chrétienne, cela pourrait signifier une place inférieure. Toutefois, il faut se souvenir que . . . 'philosophica ingenia ad Christum perveniunt per Platonem' . . . Si donc il est possible de parvenir au Christ à travers une philosophie et des mystères non chrétiens, il n'y a plus de hiérarchie qui tienne parmi les degrés de l'ascension . . . N'importe lequel des quatre degrés peut servir de symbole à la pensée chrétienne . . .

She does not in fact show in the *Solitaire premier* anything particularly Christian, as distinct from theistic, unless she means that love is the way to comprehend *l'Amor che muove il sole e l'altre stelle*.

I find it difficult to dismiss as lightly as she does Tyard's numerous references to an *order* governing psychological processes, references which to me make it clear that for him there is no 'disposition psychologique commune aux quatre fureurs'. To begin generally: over and over in Tyard's work it appears evident that for him an order is not a mere matter of expository convenience; it represents a real, interesting and often important sequence in space, time or quality. His statement in *L'Univers* 'que l'unité est premiere que la pluralité, et le simple premier que le composé'[11] may refer less to chronology than to primacy; but *L'Univers* also names the nine orders of angels, in order,[12] and considers why the Zodiac is taken to begin with the sign of Aries: it is because the year really does begin when the sun is in that sign, 'car la creation requiert une chaleur moderee'.[13] The *Discours du temps* treats similarly the subject of when the day begins, and the reasons for the order of the days of the week.[14] By the final edition of the *Discours philosophiques* three passages,[15] totalling more than three sides in folio, are devoted to determining the order of the planetary spheres; and, given this order and that each planet emits a musical sound, the *Solitaire second*[16] asks whether the highest note is emitted by the highest or the lowest. The *Solitaire premier* holds back the names of the Muses deliberately until it is stated that each is associated with a sphere; Calliope has 'le premier et plus honorable lieu', and the others follow 'suivant le nombre selon le rang que je leur donneray'.[17]

Still more important, 'sous l'ordre . . . des noms des Muses est subtilement celée la maniere, et l'ordre parfait, moyennant lesquels l'on parvient à l'intelligence accomplie des doctrines et sciences'.[18] Dr Kushner quotes this only to argue that the Muses lead one to all knowledge; but the order is clear and precise, with a pedigree going back to Fulgentius, psychologically sound and unalterable. '*Premierement* il faut vouloir sçavoir, et *puis* se delecter en celle volonté:' a constrained or grudging will is no basis for education; '*en apres* estre en instante meditation, songneux poursuivant de la chose qui delecte, laquelle *consequemment* il faut apprendre', grasp intellectually. One must fifthly memorize, sixthly 's'exercer à augmenter et renouveller de ses inventions ce dont l'on se souvient', seventhly evaluate these 'inventions', eighthly select from among them, and ninthly publish. To Tyard, order means order.

What he says about the divine frenzies is all from Ficino, except for some clarification and emphasis, again often emphasis on order. Any human soul, in the fall from heaven which brings it to birth in this world, 'passe par quatre degrez':[19] first it loses its unique perception of God and concentration on that perception, 'l'unité tant estimée, qui la rendoit cognoissante, et jouissante du souverain UN, qui est Dieu', to become aware of the Platonic Ideas: 'elle contemple en stable et immuable action les Idées de toutes choses' which yet are not God. Next it begins to reason about the Ideas (the, tone of distrust of reason anticipates Montaigne's): 'elle contemple les universelles raisons des choses, et par les ratiocinations discourt depuis les principes jusques aux conclusions . . . elle a diminué sa premiere grandeur d'un second degré'. It then becomes involved in a 'multitude d'imaginations diverses', sensuous impressions which are neither directly perceptive of God or the Ideas, nor even rational; and finally it becomes absorbed in bodily activity, 'dispersant sa force à la generation, accroissement, et norriture des corps.' The fall is pre-natal and instantaneous, so that its stages cannot be attested experientially; but the final state is reflected in the picture in *L'Univers* of the 'grossiers et ignorans, qui . . . s'addonnent du tout aux choses fortuites et transitoires . . . les voluptez sensuelles, les richesses, les estats et honneurs, la gloire, et autres telles choses, lesquelles les hommes circonvenus par decevantes opinions, se depeignent et imaginent eux-mesmes . . .'[20]

Tyard is just as systematic about the process of cure. In its fallen state the soul is divided, in part paralyzed and in part deeply disturbed:

> la superieure partie de soy est endormie, et (comme on pourroit dire) estonnée de si lourde cheute: et l'inferieure toute agitée et elancée des perturbations, d'où s'engendre un horrible discord et desordre disposé en trop improportionné proportion.[21]

The poetic frenzy, or any enjoyment of music and song, is precisely destined to remedy this. The sleeping part of the soul is aroused, 'resveillant par les tons de Musique l'ame en ce, qu'elle est endormie'; later we see the Solitaire by his own singing moving his 'ame à se passionner',[22] and in the *Solitaire second* another auditor 'd'une bouche entr'ouverte et des yeus plus qu'à demi desclos, se clouant (ust on jugé) aus cordes'.[23] Meanwhile the lower part of the soul is calmed 'par la suavité et douceur de l'harmonie', united within itself (though not yet to the higher part) by 'Musiciens accords', and brought to temperance by 'vers compassez en curieuse observance de nombres et de mesures'. Similar views are expressed by Peletier in his *Art poëtique*.[24]

'Encor toutefois n'est-ce rien': that this is an imperfect cure is proved by the picture of the audience in the *Solitaire second* as sad, taciturn, 'privez de tout sentiment, ormis de l'ouïe',[25] and of the Solitaire himself, after his singing, as 'moins disposé à tout entretien, qu'avant . . .'[26] The two parts of the soul, still separated, have to be united by the mystical frenzy, and withdrawn from the excessive attention to terrestrial objects and images that forms a part of poetic sensitivity: 'il faut effacer l'inconstante solicitude des diverses opinions . . . les purifications, et devotieux offices, incitent l'Ame à se rassembler en soy-mesme.' This is so normal and obvious a preparation for worship that Tyard does not specify it elsewhere, but St François de Sales does so: 'nous enfermons notre esprit dans le mystère que nous voulons méditer, afin qu'il n'aille pas courant çà et là, ni plus ni moins que l'on enferme un oiseau dans une cage.'[27] Meditation is still an excessively rational activity and to suppress it, the prophetic frenzy is necessary, 's'eslevant haut outre toute apprehension d'humaine et naturelle raison'; Montaigne describes this ironically: 'par la privation de nostre raison, et son assoupissement . . . nous devenons prophetes et divins'.[28] Then and not before then can the soul rejoin God: 'quand tout ce qui est en l'essence, et en la nature de l'Ame, est fait un, il faut . . . que soudain elle se revoque en ce souverain UN'. Certainly poetic frenzy alone will not achieve this. Grahame Castor agrees: 'poetry is taken [by Tyard] to be merely a means to an end, and not an end in itself . . . poetry was something which one discarded or grew out of . . .'[29]

But if the frenzies are not all different versions of the same experience, if they have to be experienced in sequence, some other questions arise. Tyard does not answer them explicitly, but a few phrases here and there perhaps permit a guess at what his answer would be. The soul's descent into the body is instantaneous, or almost, yet it takes a lifetime to make one's way back: 'une laborieuse constance . . . ne coulans la vie perissable de ce corps en autre dessein, que d'aquerir une meilleur vie immortelle . . .'[30] Does this mean that during life the soul evolves through stages, first the corporeal, then the poetic, then the mystic, then the prophetic, remaining at any given stage until the next experience promotes it? No; that is disproved by the *Solitaire premier*'s statement that poetic frenzy can pass off:

le Poëte admire (j'ose dire travaille à comprendre) la gravité, et le sens de ses vers, que l'intervallaire fureur divine luy a dictez alors, que las, et remis il s'est allenti et retiré du labeur, ainsi que le Dieu l'a laissé . . .[31]

That Tyard is here taking up a definite position on one side of a controversy is proved by the disagreement voiced by Le Caron's Jodelle:

Ce n'est ainsi qu'on doit juger de la puissance des Muses: depuis qu'une fois ravissent l'esprit à elles, tousjours l'entretiennent en une grandeur digne de leur divinité . . . Quant à ceux, lesquelz se feignent par moments estre époints d'une celeste et violante agitation, et incontinent à eux revenus se mescognoissent, ilz me semblent miserablement tourmentez de quelque maladie . . .[32]

Montaigne, however, comes back to Tyard's view:

Les saillies poëtiques, qui emportent leur autheur et le ravissent hors de soy . . . surpassent sa suffisance et ses forces . . .[33]

Then must one hope that at some times when one is in the state of *furor poeticus* the mystic frenzy may descend, at some of those still rarer times the prophetic frenzy may follow—as in some board games one may throw three sixes in succession and win—so that one day one may experience all four frenzies consecutively and die happy? No; for it is clear from Tyard's previously mentioned statement about erotic frenzy that it can be experienced without being either accompanied or preceded by the second and third frenzies. Ronsard even seems to hint that erotic frenzy can cause poetic frenzy: 'Par luy mon cœur premierement s'aisla . . .'[34] I can only conclude that each *furor* is a valuable exercise for the soul; as it becomes more practised in submitting to poetic and perhaps erotic frenzy, it will find the other two frenzies accessible also—just as a student of the Trivium would find logic and rhetoric being fed into his course when enough grammar had been acquired. The more often the soul experiences any and every *furor*, the more easily and frequently they will come; the soul's normal, average state will become one of less insensitivity, less perturbation, less division, less rationalism; it will reach the serenity attributed to Scève in the *Discours du temps*:

Je ne say (reprint Sceve) quelle particuliere ocasion vous fait . . . tenir le vivre en un si grand mespris: mais quant à moy, j'estime la vie m'estre donnee de Dieu, comme un depost en garde: et vrayment je la garderay tant et si cherement qu'il me sera possible, atendant qu'il plaise au Signeur, duquel j'en ay la charge, de la r'avoir de moy . . .[35]

That was written in 1556; if Scève was already working on the *Microcosme* (which according to Saulnier was completed in 1559)[36] Tyard would be in no doubt that his friend could be credited with having experienced the mystical and prophetic frenzies as well as the poetic and erotic, that Scève was well on the way to being, was almost ready to be reunited with God.

NOTES

1 Kathleen M. Hall, 'En quelle année naquit Pontus de Tyard?' *Revue des sciences humaines*, nouvelle série, fasc. 91 (1958).
2 *Aumla*, XX (1963) 384–6.
3 Grahame Castor, *Pléiade Poetics* (Cambridge 1964).
4 Pontus de Tyard, *Œuvres poétiques complètes*, ed. J. C. Lapp (Paris 1966); Pontus de Tyard, *Erreurs amoureuses*, ed. J. McClelland (Geneva 1967).
5 *Revue belge de philologie et d'histoire*, L (1972) 760–7.
6 Kathleen M. Hall, *Pontus de Tyard and his 'Discours philosophiques'* (Oxford 1963).
7 Joseph Vianey, *Le Pétrarquisme en France au seizième siècle* (Montpellier 1909) 123.
8 Pontus de Tyard, *Solitaire premier*, ed. S. F. Baridon (Geneva 1950) 74; *Discours philosophiques* (Paris 1587), f. 36. Other references will be to Baridon's edition, with the 1587 foliation in parentheses.
9 *Solitaire second* (Lyons 1555), p. 156 (1587, f. 129).
10 *Solitaire premier*, p. 74 (f. 36).
11 *The Universe of Pontus de Tyard*, ed. J. C. Lapp (Ithaca, N.Y. 1950) p. 8 (1587, f. 202). Other references will be to Lapp's edition, with the 1587 foliation in parentheses.
12 Ibid., p. 125 (f. 284 v).
13 Ibid., p. 18 (f. 209).
14 *Discours du temps* (Lyons 1556), pp. 18 and 33 (1587, ff. 342 and 347v).
15 *Discours philosophiques*, ff. 212v–213, 216v–217, 223.
16 *Solitaire second*, p. 140 (f. 119).
17 *Solitaire premier*, p. 40 (f. 20).
18 Ibid., p. 54 (f. 26). The italics are mine.
19 Ibid., pp. 12–16 (ff. 6v–8).
20 *The Universe*, p. 133 (f. 290v).
21 *Solitaire premier*, p. 18 (f. 9). Unannotated quotations in this paragraph and the next come from pp. 19–20 (ff. 9v–10).
22 Ibid., p. 77 (f. 37).
23 *Solitaire second*, p. 114 (f. 103v).
24 Jacques Peletier du Mans, *L'Art poëtique*, ed. A. Boulanger (Paris 1930), pp. 65–7.
25 *Solitaire second*, p. 114 (f. 103v).
26 *Solitaire premier*, p. 77 (f. 37).
27 Saint François de Sales, *Introduction à la vie dévote*, ed. H. Bordeaux (Paris 1939) 80.

28 Montaigne, *Essais*, ed. P. Villey (Paris 1922), 11, 323.
29 *Pléiade Poetics*, pp. 1 and 196.
30 *The Universe*, p. 134 (f. 291).
31 *Solitaire premier*, p. 26 (f. 13).
32 Louis Le Caron, *Les Dialogues* (Paris 1556), f. 137.
33 Montaigne, *ed. cit.*, 1, 162–3.
34 Ronsard, *Œuvres complètes*, Laumonier 1v, 64.
35 *Discours du temps*, p. 80 (f. 368).
36 Saulnier, V.-L., *Maurice Scève* (Paris 1948), 1, 406.

The History of George Buchanan's Sphæra

THE TALE OF THE *Sphæra* is a strange one: never completed, it engaged Buchanan's attention, off and on, for the best part of thirty years, and even after his death strenuous efforts were made by admirers to publish a work, which was soon to be discredited in its fundamental attitudes. In recent years the poem has attracted some critical interest: a quarter of a century ago, Professor J.R.Naiden completed a thesis built round an English version,[1] the only one apart from an anonymous translation preserved in manuscript in the Harleian collection.[2] In the last few years further information has come to light; and the Edinburgh colloquium affords an excellent opportunity of bringing this information together, of briefly reconsidering the value of the poem and of showing how much still remains to be done to fill the gaps in its history.

I

The origins of the *Sphæra* are traditionally associated with Buchanan's appointment as tutor to Timoléon, son of the maréchal de Cossé-Brissac, probably c. 1554. There is no doubt that the poem was designed in part for pedagogic ends: there are references to the author's pupil in four out of the five books,[3] and one line suggests that a portion was written during his stay in Italy.[4] Still, other factors were at work, and it is highly probable that Buchanan's interest in mathematics and astronomy went back further in his career. When he was arrested in Coimbra, the Inquisitors found among his books the *Arithmetica integra* of M.Stifelius (Nurenberg 1544), and this was the copy he was later to bequeath to the University of St Andrews.[5] Other relevant books he possessed, though we cannot ascertain their dates of purchase or acquisition, were: *Euclides cum commentariis Procli græce, Diui Seuerini Boethii Arithmetica* and Jakob Ziegler's *Commentarii Pliniani*.[6] During his Coimbra days Buchanan enjoyed, for a while, the company of Elie Vinet, already at work on a school edition of the Sacrobosco; Vinet, a friend until death parted them, never ceased to encourage him to complete the *Sphæra*.[7] Also in Coimbra was the celebrated mathematician Petrus Nonnius (Pedro Nuñez), from whom Vinet extracted the *Annotationes* that were later to grace his edition of Sacrobosco and who appears to have been on friendly terms with Buchanan as well.

Among the *barbistes* who were recruited for the reform of the College of Arts at Coimbra was another lifelong friend of the Scotsman: Nicolas de Grouchy. These men had been singled out in part because of their competence in Aristotelian studies,[8] and Grouchy, who like Vinet left Portugal well before Buchanan, was soon back at work on his edition of Aristotle, based on the Latin version of Joachim Périon. When Buchanan, released by the Inquisition, had finally made his way to Paris, Grouchy was bringing out volumes relevant to his friend's concerns: from 1552 to 1554 are printed the *De Cælo*, the *De Generatione et corruptione* and the *Meteorologica*, a work which was to be closely commented by Vicomercato, the Royal Reader. Buchanan returns to Paris when the Aristotelian debate is still very vigorous. Moreover, many of his friends and colleagues were taking an interest, not only in Aristotle, but in mathematics and astronomy, as a brief perusal of the milieux he frequented will suggest, milieux which naturally are not split up into watertight compartments: (i) the distinguished classical scholars Adrien Turnèbe, Jean Dorat and Denis Lambin, the future editor of Lucretius; (ii) friends interested in mathematics and often connected with the *officina* of Michel Vascosan: Elie Vinet, Pierre de la Ramée,[9] Pierre de Montdoré; and though proof positive is still lacking, it would be very strange if the paths of Buchanan and Peletier du Mans did not cross at some point. In 1554, Vascosan publishes the second edition of Oronce Finé's *De mundi sphæra libri V*, and here again one wonders whether Buchanan had not, at some period, come into contact with this humanist, prominent in Paris since his student days; (iii) links with the circle of Henri de Mesmes, though we are still poorly informed about their nature and dates; (iv) the connections with the Pléiade, many of whose members are known to Buchanan and are taking or will take some interest in astronomy and 'scientific' poetry—Ronsard, Baïf, Pontus de Tyard, Belleau. During this time, too, great emphasis is laid on the relations between learning and poetry—and a concomitant feature of the literary scene will be the emergence of the *dialogue* as a genre in which scientific as well as other matters will come under scrutiny. Nor is there lack of stimulus from the Neo-latin sector: quite apart from the current prestige of earlier writers such as Pontano, one should mention Jean Lyège (Lygæus) whose *De humani corporis harmonia libri IIII* is brought out by Vascosan in 1555, and especially Antoine Mizault (Mizaldus) now well launched on his series of popularizing works (in prose and verse) on astronomy and cosmology.[10] Mizault

was patronized by Marguerite de France to whom Buchanan was
beholden at this time; it is therefore very likely that the two men
knew each other, but at all events Buchanan was acquainted with his
writings.

It is in this intellectual climate that Buchanan puts pen to paper,
though we cannot be sure just how much of the *Sphæra* was composed before his return to Scotland: a reasonable guess might be
that at least the first two books were fairly fully sketched out by
then, but Buchanan was a busy man, often on his travels and enjoying
only irregular hours of leisure. On the other hand, one gains the
impression, if nothing more, that he had done enough for friends
and colleagues to have their appetites whetted. The early years of
his return to Scotland are poorly documented and only in the mid-
1560s do we come on to more solid ground. In 1565, Buchanan
composed a Latin poem to celebrate the wedding of Mary Queen of
Scots and Darnley, and some lines uttered by Apollo and the Muses
suggest that the subject of the *Sphæra* was still close to his heart:

Digna coli cœlo, terras cole: sidera nosse
  Si iuuet, hîc duce me, sidera nosse potes.
Metior hoc radio terras, mare, sidera: monstro
  Quam paruo humanus ludat in orbe labor.[11]

The last line, in another register, echoes Buchanan's development of
the Earth's insignificant size towards the end of the third Book.
More substantial is a sentence from a letter to Pierre Daniel in 1566,
giving an account of the state of play of various poetic compositions:
'De Sphæra mundi nondum vacauit absoluere secundum librum,
ideoque primum nondum descripsi: ut quodque erit absolutum, ad
te mittam.'[12] Though this promise was never kept, Buchanan shows
a serious concern for his poem and indicates that the first two books
seem to have reached a fairly advanced stage, but it is difficult to
decide whether 'completion' implies the finishing of something still
being worked out, or the proper revision of something pretty fully
written out at an earlier stage; Buchanan was often anxious to revise
texts that had been printed, how much more might he tinker with
an unpublished work lying so long on his desk? In the following
year, van Giffen (Gifanius), who often acted as an agent for the
house of Plantin, tried in vain to extract some texts, no doubt including the *Sphæra*, out of Buchanan;[13] and notes for a letter from
Pierre Daniel to the Scotsman, written perhaps in February 1567,
show that Pierre de Montdoré in particular was anxious to get hold
of the poem.[14] By now, of course, Buchanan was becoming increasingly involved in matters of state; and the death of Timoléon in 1569
might possibly have removed another spur to composition, though

there were other motives to keep the poem in play. There are certainly enough friends around to give him the feeling that his posthumous fame might owe much to the completion of such a work.

There were further stimuli to come. In the first place, Buchanan was appointed, together with Peter Young, tutor to James VI; and there is evidence that mathematics and astronomy were to form a significant aspect of the young King's training; so that the text, originally intended for Timoléon, might be put to further use in the royal context. On the one hand, the lines added at a later date to the King's *Genethliacon* (1566) stress the importance of astronomical studies;[15] and on the other, the Royal library contained a number of relevant works, many of which had been acquired on the recommendation of the two tutors:[16] the *Ephemerides* and *Elucidatio, fabrica ususque Astrolabi* of Stoffler; the *Sphæra* and other works by Piccolomini; R. Gemma's *Principes d'astronomie et cosmographie auec l'usage du globe*, in the French version of C. de Boissières; A. Mizault's *Cosmographie*; and finally, the *Astronomia* or *Astronomique discours* by Buchanan's compatriot J. Bassantin (or Bassendean).[17]

Secondly, there seem to be various pressures emanating from the Low Countries, with which Buchanan had developed strong humanist ties, partly through connections established during his years in France,[18] partly through the activities of English friends in the Cecil and Sidney circles.[19] More needs to be discovered about these Dutch connections: so far as the *Sphæra* is concerned, it is known that Jan van Hout, secretary to the town Council of Leiden, had undertaken a translation of the poem c. 1574–6; and it may well be that he had access to a manuscript, a copy of which Dousa the elder had managed to lay hands on, probably during his sojourn in London in 1572 and had brought home in the following year. In 1575 he wrote to his friend Daniel Rogers, whose part in the transmission and publication of Buchanan's poems is far from negligible: 'mihique exscribenda dedisti. Atque inter cætera magni illius Buchanani de Sphera opusculum, cuius exemplum Migrodio me acceptum referre par est, qui illud mei honoris gratia tuo permissu, manu sua accuratissime excepit.'[20] Unfortunately, no trace of van Hout's version has survived, and more's the pity, not only because of its intrinsic interest, but because it would have shed light on the state of the poem some ten years before the author's death. Dousa's letter, as well as a list of Buchanan's works drawn up, probably, in the mid-1570s,[21] talk as if the poem was complete, which seems unlikely. Nevertheless, the attention paid by the Leiden humanists both to astronomical studies and to Buchanan's literary activity, may well have helped him to remain at work on the *Sphæra*: it is during these years that J.-J. Scaliger will bring out his masterly edition of Manilius, and his passion for ancient writings on astronomy was wide-ranging.[22] Daniel Rogers, the cultural go-between, was himself familiar with these fields of study;[23] and Dousa's son was to make use of Buchanan's poem in order to enrich his own poetic treatise.[24]

A third stimulus during these years was the epistolary exchange with Tycho Brahe. How this began is something of a mystery; Brahe sent the Scotsman a copy of his book the *De nova stella*, describing the phenomenon of 1572 and published two years later,[25] but it is not clear what prompted him to the gift or how he had come to know about Buchanan's astronomical interests. There is a persistent legend that the Scotsman had Danish connections, but material proof of this has yet to come to hand; all we have is the Scotsman's reference, in the First Defence before the Inquisition, to a rich Danish widow, whom he claims as his *avita*, a vague enough term. In two important aspects, Buchanan and Brahe differed: the implications of the discovery of the *nova stella* and the role of astrology. It may be going rather far to see in the fifth Book of the *Sphæra* a specific attack on Brahe;[26] Buchanan had other targets on the astrological score, and from the scientific point of view, the two men probably agreed more than they differed; and though Brahe was critical of certain views expressed by Buchanan, he maintained a lifelong admiration for the Scotsman, to the extent of having his portrait adorning his study in the company of other celebrities.[27] In short, such encouragement as Brahe may have given Buchanan to complete his poem may not be explained in terms of reaction exclusively.

Yet, for all these useful pressures, little headway seems to have been made in the middle years of the decade. Daniel Rogers was still pestering him: 'Sphæricorum tuorum ut nobis copiam facias, etiam atque etiam peto'[28] and Pierre Daniel also joined the queue for more poetic material from Buchanan's pen.[29] However, the latter had been too ill during 1575–6 or so to get down to work, as he informed Brahe in the autumn of 1576;[30] and when he was somewhat restored in health, he had other fish to fry: the *Baptistes* was due to appear in 1577,[31] he was under pressure to put the finishing touches to the *Rerum scoticarum historia*,[32] and friends were urging him to commit the *De Jure Regni* to print.[33] We shall find evidence of his dictating portions of the *Sphæra* in his last years,[34] but he seems to have lost his taste for composition, let alone publication. It has been conjectured that Canter's edition of Stobæus (Plantin, 1575) may have spurred him on,[35] but one does begin to wonder to what extent

Buchanan amplified his text during the last decade of his life. By
1579 he had more or less given up the unequal struggle, as a letter to
the irrepressible Daniel Rogers makes evident: 'Astronomica non
tam abieci quam extorqueri invitus tuli, neque enim aut nunc libet
nugari, aut si maxime vellem, per ætatem licet.'[36] Elie Vinet, faithful
as ever, continued to press him: 'Sphæram tuam desiderant solam
multi, ego imprimis',[37] but Buchanan was now at the threshold of
death and the work had come to look like the project in Henry
James's *The Coxon Fund*, never to be brought to its fitting conclusion.

II

The *Sphæra*, to use the title generally accepted, is composed of five
books, of which the fourth remains unfinished (119 pp.) and the
fifth lacks, in all probability, a few dozen lines.[38] Book I describes
the sublunar and supralunar parts of the universe and concerns itself
particularly with the sphericity and the immobility of the earth. In
Book II, Buchanan asserts the sphericity of the whole universe and
firmly espouses the geocentric conception of the scheme of things.
He attacks Epicurean theories, and discusses views on the movements of the planets and on the quintessence. The third Book
describes the sky, the Zodiac, the horizon, the Milky Way, the zones
of the Earth. The fourth was seemingly to deal with more technical
matters, such as the courses of the stars and the planets, and the last
Book, after a condemnation of astrology and an eulogy of true
science, is devoted to the matter of eclipses, discussed through the
persona of Sulpicius Gallus who emerges as a true, empirical seeker
after truth, but serves also to dramatize the presentation of the
material.

This sketch of a summary shows that Buchanan has, for the most
part, adhered to the stock subject-matter of such treatises, though
Hume Brown and Du Monin oversimplified the position by seeing
in the *Sphæra* a versified elaboration of Sacrobosco,[39] whose material
overlaps with Buchanan's to the extent of rather less than half, though
there are grounds for thinking that Book IV might have followed
Sacrobosco more closely.[40] Obviously Buchanan had no intention of
providing the verse equivalent of a text which his friend Vinet was
editing for use in schoolrooms; and the scientific poem had developed its own conventions, which he would not wish to ignore. At
the same time he would hardly dismiss a stock text-book, written
by a compatriot[41] and edited by humanists whose work he warmly
admired—Lefèvre d'Etaples, Melanchthon and of course Vinet. For
various reasons he would wish to introduce new views and information, determined in considerable measure by the humanist climate of
the 1550s.

It is during these years of contact with the Pléiade and Parisian humanism that Buchanan's Muse undergoes rejuvenation: his output then is abundant and varied, and the idea of writing a scientific poem would come to him easily in such an ambience, though his reluctance to finish the most technical of the books suggests greater sympathy with the way in which, say, Ronsard was moving in his *Hymnes*, with which the *Sphæra* occasionally offers thematic resemblances. Then there is the humanist awareness of recent additions to knowledge,[42] and Buchanan is sensitive to the claims of experience and observation, especially in Book v, and concerned to provide a reasoned exposition of his case: there is little sign that he was much attracted by neo-platonist or 'occultist' explorations of phenomena, indeed in the matter of presentation the *Sphæra* often gives more of an Aristotelian ring. However, there are limits to his espousal of the experimental approach, for he is inhibited by an unconscious conservatism, shared by many contemporaries in certain areas of enquiry, but also, I suspect, by his recent experiences in Portugal. The *Sphæra* develops in some detail the theme of the Divine Plan, the presence of a Christian God behind the universe, which is destined to sing his praises.[43] Buchanan also makes a point of attacking Epicurean theories, like other humanists in the 1550s who refer, in rather imprecise terms, to the presence of 'epicureans' and 'atheists'.[44] He not merely adopts the geometric conception of the universe, he specifically refers to the 'erroneous' views of those who favour heliocentrism—in this case, naturally, Copernicus is under fire.[45] His attack on astrologers may, to some extent, belong to a later stage of composition, but he is after all touching on a hotly disputed issue of the times, since there are areas where prophesy may threaten the freedom of the Divine Will. When Buchanan returns from Portugal, he is very careful to avoid suspicion in a France committed to the *chambre ardente*, he makes advances to noble families of proven orthodoxy and he inserts in certain poems an indication of his fidelity to the Roman Catholic Church. Though it would be going beyond the evidence to see in passages of the *Sphæra* an explicit statement of orthodox faith, Buchanan does not miss the opportunity of expressing his law-abiding attitude to matters which have a certain relevance to contemporary debate. We know, of course, that Buchanan has not abandoned his evangelical outlook or friendships and that, on his return home, he will declare his Calvinist principles; but while he was still in France, such evidence as we possess suggests that, like other humanists and friends, he was not willing to leave the Catholic Church so long as he thought compromise was possible and apparently had no intention of leaving the country for good.

Whatever the final truth of the matter, the *Sphæra* does emphasize the Divine pattern of the Universe, and this also allows the poem to move away from the purely technical to a wider, more poetic treatment of themes. There are passages on divers aspects of the human condition,[46] praise of human reason,[47] the wonders of nature,[48] the Golden Age,[49] mythological development,[50] attacks on greed[51] and warfare,[52] and each book ends on a note of moral reflection. To some extent, Buchanan is following conventions of the Neo-latin scientific poem, but many of these themes have their counterpart in Ronsard's cosmic poetry, and marginally in some of Du Bellay's later poems.[53] Which brings us to a consideration of his principal sources.[54]

So far as the scientific content is concerned, Buchanan draws extensively on classical sources, as long as they do not conflict with his Christian outlook or his awareness of recent discoveries (up to a point!) We have seen that Sacrobosco was a convenient, but not overriding, source of basic material; and I am inclined to think that the Scotsman made considerable use of Aristotle, especially in the first two books, where he discusses the sphericity of the earth and universe, expounds the geocentric view, but adopts a different attitude to the question of the *primum mobile* and of the plurality of movements.[55] Particularly important is the influence of Cleomedes, rightly indicated by Naiden,[56] but now ascertainable beyond doubt. The Bodleian possesses a copy of the 1539 edition printed by Neobarius in Paris;[57] this copy belonged at one time to J. Furdin, who was later to edit Adrien Turnèbe's *Animadversaria*. One owner purchased it in 1552, and it contains on the inside cover the following inscription:

Hic libellus emendatus est ad exemplar Geo. Buccanani Scoti doctiss.

Cor. significat codicem Coronæi professoris regij.

This proves not only that Buchanan was acquainted with Cleomedes, but that he owned the Greek text and was seriously interested in matters of textual criticism. Proof of this concern in the Latin field is already to hand, but this volume gives further evidence of his activity and standing in the Greek domain. There are many ideas and views in Cleomedes that he could have borrowed with profit;[58] one valuable feature was the transmission of Posidonius's theories on the habitability of the tropical zones—which Cleomedes himself does not share; the lively attack on Epicurean views about the size of the world may also have struck him; other themes, of course, overlap with several sources.[59] Buchanan was certainly acquainted with the writings of Ptolemy,[60] Proclus,[61] Stobæus,[62] and he derived

important themes from the second Book of Pliny's *Natural History*
—not only scientific material, but the idea he developed on Endymion and the introduction of Sulpicius Gallus.[63] And for the description of the Zodiac, he is clearly indebted to Hyginus.[64]

Some of these last names bring us nearer the more poetic aspects
of the *Sphæra*; and Buchanan was bound to read the classical poets
who displayed astronomical interests. One obvious source is Manilius, so frequently published in the first half of the sixteenth century
and studied with particular distinction by the Scotsman's friend
Joseph Scaliger. There are suggestions that at the very least Manilius (especially Book 1) provided him with poetic formulae and
perhaps encouraged him in the use of some mnemonic tricks of
style.[65] Lucretius too is important, and I cannot follow Naiden in
his denial of any influence from that quarter,[66] and all the more so
as he has himself tracked down more Lucretian echoes than tags from
any other poet.[67] Of course, Buchanan rejects the philosophical
assumptions underlying the *De rerum natura*, but he resembles
Lucretius in some measure in his harmonization of science and
poetry,[68] and he develops certain Lucretian themes of a more
general nature, but in a Christian *caisse de résonance*—the praise of
reason, the attacks on greed and cruelty. No Parisian humanist could
ignore the Latin poet at that time; we saw that Buchanan was a
friend of Lambin, the future editor of Lucretius, and the textual
reminiscences are even more numerous than Naiden suggested.[69]
Among the earlier writers to whom the Scotsman is beholden are:
Aratus (in Avienus' Latin version, though he is aware of the
Ciceronian tradition too),[70] Martianus Capellanus for the occasional
detail,[71] and among the moderns Mantuan,[72] Pontano,[73] Mizault,[74]
and possibly Palingenius.[75] Very occasionally Buchanan, like Corneille, seems to have remembered himself.[76] Finally, there are the
classical authors for whom Buchanan had a lasting affection, who
greatly influence his language and style and who come in handy here
because either they touch on strictly scientific matters from time to
time or provide stylistic patterns for the passages of more wide-
ranging reflection and description: Vergil,[77] Ovid,[78] Statius[79] and
Lucan.[80] It would, none the less, be a mistake to see in the *Sphæra* a
mere patchwork quilt of thematic and stylistic reminiscences:
Buchanan is well in control of his material and impresses his poetic
personality on the text.

III

Buchanan was hardly in his grave (1582) when his admirers set
busily to work in the hope of rescuing the *Sphæra* from oblivion; for
the next forty years a series of *états* will find their way into print,

nearly all claiming manuscript authority. The first episode, though
a non-starter, is of some interest. Jean-Edouard Du Monin, the
eccentric author of an *Uranologie* (1583), tells us that a young Scotsman, Alexander Levinstone[81] arrived in Paris with a manuscript of
the poem, given him by Buchanan. He allowed Du Monin to see it,
but the latter finding it not suitable for the composition of his own
poem, handed it back; his account is however valuable because of
his description of this manuscript, though it raises problems:

> Icelui, comme fait heritier par la bouche du souverain testateur de
> quelque 2500. vers Latins quités sur le métier par fu M. Bucanan
> en la Sphere: apres auoir pieusement soigné la tutelle de cet
> enfant posthume m'auoit désiré que de iuger seul digne pere
> adoptif de cette rare mince orpheline . . . Mais en ces deus mille
> ou tant de vers, ie n'y voiois pas grande approche de la somme
> qui m'estoit necessaire au parement de mon edifice. Car bien
> que, sur ma méme modelle, assauoir sur Sacro Bosco il avoit
> desseigné les diagrammes des 5. livres, toutefois le premier
> estoit estropié, le second saignoit au milieu de son trac, le
> quatrieme estoit tout en blanc, & le cinquieme n'auoit que la
> teste, sans conter que le troisieme me sembloit etre trop a ieun,
> non pas en la poesie (laquelle ie ne me facherai iamais conceder
> aus seuls Bucanan, & Dorat, & non à autre) mais aus nerfs de
> la Science: si que il me faloit presque totalement viure sur le
> mien, comme la confluence t'en fera foi . . . J'ai donc à ma
> liberté couru à vau de routes par les Cirques du Ciel: attendant
> que par plus meur aduis des letterés, i'enrichisse ces echantil-
> hons de Bucanan de mes 6. ou 7. milles vers Latins, que ie
> vetirai de sa parure Latine, plus proprement croi-ie, que ne
> feroit autre que moi en mon ieune age: Ce que deia i'eusse
> fourni, si la copie des lambeaux de ce diuin Poëte, eussent
> demeurez chez moi.[82]

On Du Monin's reckoning, one book is missing (iv, which was
never finished anyhow) and the others (except iii, it seems) are
incomplete, and yet we have roughly as many lines as the poem in
the state in which it has come down to us; but perhaps Du Monin
was rough and ready in his calculation. The phrase 'si que il me
faloit presque totalement viure sur le mien' hints that Du Monin
perhaps did incorporate some bits and pieces of the manuscript
into his own elucubration, though the return of the text obviously
nullified the more ambitious use he had in mind; but we have no
means of checking, since the manuscript is no longer extant.

In 1584 Daniel Rogers re-enters the stage, as he appears to have
some connection with the Heidelberg edition of Buchanan's poems

in that year, an edition which contained a *Fragmentum* of the *Sphæra*.[83] Whether this was part of the manuscript of which Dousa had knowledge a decade or so earlier, cannot be established, but Naiden reasonably suggests that the number and nature of the variants point to an early state of the poem. A year later, Féderic Morel printed a so-called complete edition, *Sphæra . . . in quinque libros distributa*, based on two unspecified manuscript sources: the second manuscript (*alius codex*) had reached him after the type had been set up, so that its variants had to be added to the end of each book. The edition remains puzzling, in that all that is known to be left of it are: the first book, preserved in the Bibliothèque Nationale,[84] and the second, which forms part of the David Murray collection in Glasgow University Library.[85] This edition served as a model for the one brought out by Prévosteau (without date), the son-in-law of Féderic Morel: as a secondary production, it adds nothing to the manuscript tradition.[86]

The next episode takes us across the Rhine. In 1584, John Johnston and Robert Howie, having completed their studies at Aberdeen, turned up in Rostock, each with a different manuscript of the *Sphæra*, which it has been reasonably conjectured might have been transmitted to them by Alexander Arbuthnet, a friend of Buchanan's and at one time Principal of Aberdeen University.[87] In Rostock there was a fervent admirer of the Scots humanist, Nathan Chytræus, but though he was to play a cardinal role in the diffusion of the Psalm paraphrases,[88] he does not seem, on present evidence, to have had a hand in the saga of the *Sphæra*. The young Scotsmen planned to leave Rostock for Heidelberg within the year, but in the event they parted company. Johnston made his way to Helmstädt where he was to spend two years, while Howie betook himself to Herborn. There he became friendly with Johann Pincier, professor of medicine at the recently established *gymnasium illustre* and a devotee of the Neo-latin Muse. He and Howie published the latter's manuscript;[89] they probably knew of the earlier, partial editions, since they refer to *nonnullis exemplaribus* they had consulted, but the text suffered from gaps and illegible patches in their source. In his preface, Howie had mentioned the existence of the manuscript owned by Johnston, who soon despatched it to Herborn, so that Pincier was able to use it for his 1587 edition.[90] In both editions he had inserted *argumenta* for each book, and in the 1587 edition he added his *Supplementa*, providing a hypothetical conclusion to Books IV and V.

Apart from the Prévosteau edition, the *Sphæra* will appear henceforth in the more or less complete *poemata* of Buchanan, beginning with the 1594 and 1609 editions.[91] The manuscript sources have, however, still not dried up. About 1612–15 Adam King based his unpublished edition and commentary upon a manuscript which offered a few variants.[92] Then, in 1615, John Ray published, through Andrew Hart, the most complete edition to date of the poems.[93] He too claimed to have worked from an autograph manuscript, though few new variants came to hand: the first book is very reminiscent of Morel's text, and the other books run close to King's source. Finally, there is the Saumur edition of 1620–1, which appears to be fairly rare,[94] but is important because the text of the *Sphæra* brings together variants from earlier editions and adds new ones from a manuscript dictated by Buchanan to his domestic John Geddy, as we learn from the notice of the *Typographus Lectori beneuolo S.*:

> . . . Cum autem audiuissem multa varijs in editionibus variè legi, nonnulla etiam corrupta videri, ad opem viri cuiusdam docti confugi; qui quanquam erat occupatissimus, tamen pro suo in remp. litterariam amore, horis subcisiuis, varias lectiones collatis inter se varijs exemplaribus notauit, & coniecturas quasdam suas addidit, in libris de Sphæra emendandis plurimum operæ posuit, cum quod in ijs multa essent vindice digna, tum quod ad eam rem haberet adiumenta; ut pote præter exemplaria typis impressa (in quibus Edinburgense facile primas tenet) optimum manuscriptum à Doctiss. viro Gul. Geddeo nactus, quod eius frater Ioan. Geddeus dictante ipso Buchanano olim exarauerat. Quæ in editione Edinburgensi ex authoris autographo emendata sunt manuscriptum penè omnia confirmat, quædam etiam in melius mutat, & 22. versibus in fine libri quinti auctius est, quos licet ipsi operi adjiciendos non censuerit, tamen post varias lectiones tuo iudicio subjecit. Vale.[95]

These last 22 lines have rightly been viewed with suspicion by later critics and they certainly do not seem to have found their proper place. At the end of the second volume of the Saumur edition, there is provided a list of variants collected by the *vir doctus*, some 128 of which the 'new' manuscript source offered 34 hitherto unknown. Naiden's collation led him to suspect that the Geddy manuscript lacked Book 1.[96]

From this time on, momentum fades: the last generation of friends and colleagues who had known Buchanan personally was on the way out; the scientific presuppositions of the *Sphæra* were losing ground, and its incomplete state was an increasing liability. It possesses undoubted literary merit,[97] but for the scholar who ventures into this maze, in the hope of providing a respectable edition, a host of traps and disappointments lie ahead. The chronology of

composition we have seen to be sketchy in the extreme, the manuscripts have all disappeared and the author never gave any hint as
to whether this or that one might command more authority; indeed
how could he, since the poem was still far from the finishing post?[98]
We may be rather baffled by the enthusiasm with which the *Sphæra*
was posthumously pursued, but it was certainly a yardstick of the
reputation which its author continued to enjoy. The history of this
poem is an interesting example of international collaboration in the
field of scholarship, and above all, the text still remains relevant to
our understanding of French humanism in the mid-sixteenth century.

NOTES

1 James R. Naiden, *The Sphera of George Buchanan (1506–1582)* (1952)
   privately printed. Though more recent information and a different
   approach may lead me to disagree with Dr Naiden on occasion, it is a
   pleasure to acknowledge his pioneer work in this field.
2 British Museum, Harleian ms. 4628 (15). The version is signed J.C.
3 *Sphæra*, I, 16 (and exordium generally); II, 1 ff.; III, 1 ff.; V, 80 ff.
   I use the 1725 Ruddiman-Burmann edition of the *Opera omnia*, II,
   427–507. Though the presentation of the text is not above reproach
   it has the advantage of having the lines numbered. Hereafter the
   abbreviation *OO* is used.
4 I, 25–9.
5 This is shown by the inscription on the last board: 'de m^e Jorge
   bucanano'. On the books given to St Andrews by Buchanan see D.
   Irving, *Memoirs of the Life and Writings of George Buchanan*, 2nd
   edition (Edinburgh 1817), Appendix by Professor Lee, the source for
   later references; see also *Munimenta Almæ Universitatis Glasguensis*
   (1854) III, 407 for a list of books presented to Glasgow by Buchanan
   in 1578.
6 As described in the earlier lists. The Euclid (Glasgow University) was
   printed in Basel, 1533; the Boethius by Simon de Colines, 1521, and
   the Ziegler at Basel, 1531. These two books were presented to St
   Andrews.
7 See below, p. 199.
8 *Vita*, in *OO*, I, f. h 2 r.
9 Later Ramus was to ask Buchanan to do what he could to further the
   study of mathematics in St Andrews, *Prooemium mathematicum* (Paris
   Wechel, 1567) 60.
10 See the catalogues of the BM and BN.
11 *OO*, II, 400.
12 *OO*, II, 724. The letter is dated *Edinburgi 24 die Julii, 1566.*
13 *OO*, II, 724–6. The letter, dated *17 Cal. Feb. 1567*, does not specifically
    mention the *Sphæra*.
14 'Salutat te imprimis Montaureus et libros de Sphera mundi præ
    omnibus desiderat . . .', Notes for a letter by Pierre Daniel to

Buchanan (Berne, Burgerbibliothek, ms. 141, f. 164 v), reproduced by John Durkan, 'George Buchanan: some French connections', *The Bibliotheck*, IV (1963) 71.

15 *Silva* VII, ll. 104–5; *OO*, 11, 343.

16 'The Library of James VI, 1573–83', *Miscellany of the Scottish Historical Society* (First volume), Edinburgh, 1893; see also T. W. Baldwin, *William Shakspere's Small Latine & lesse Greeke*, 2 vols. (Urbana 1944) especially vol. 1, 532 ff.

17 Bassendean seems to have been an eccentric autodidact who taught for a time in Paris, though it is said that he knew neither Latin nor French. He returned to Scotland in 1563 and died four years later. The French translation of his work appeared in 1557; there was also a Latin version, of which a later edition appeared in Cologne in 1613. The BN holds a copy of his *Astronomique discours* bound with the arms of Catherine de Medici. It is highly probable, though not proved, that Buchanan knew this mathematician.

18 It seems that Buchanan got to know Dousa and Fruter during his mysterious journey to France in 1565–6; the Scaliger connection probably goes back further, since Buchanan knew the father in his Bordeaux days. Fréderic Jamot also knew Buchanan.

19 See James E. Phillips, 'George Buchanan and the Sidney Circle', *Huntingdon Library Quarterly* XII (1948) 23–56; Jan van Dorsten, *Poets, Patrons and Professors—Sir Philip Sidney, Daniel Rogers and the Leiden Humanists* (Leiden-London 1962).

20 On all this see J. A. van Dorsten, op. cit., 43–4, and for the text of the letter, 202–3.

21 Cotton Collection, British Museum, Caligula v, f. 261 v. This list, for all its interest, poses a number of problems.

22 The Bodleian possesses two volumes, bound together, of Greek authors including Empedocles (1573), with Scaliger's signature; also his copy of the Basel Manilius of 1551, with marginal notes by his hand.

23 The Bodleian also possesses a composite volume containing, among other texts, a Latin translation of *Theodosii Tripolitae Sphæricorum libri tres*, Aratus in Greek and in Latin, and Hyginus, and bearing the signature *Daniel Rogerus Anglus* (press-mark: Savile T.10).

24 See J. A. van Dorsten, op. cit., 43.

25 Fuller details in Naiden, op. cit., 56–60.

26 Ibid., 59. This leads Naiden to suppose that a substantial portion of Book v was composed very late; I am not sure that the evidence is sufficiently unambiguous to admit this interpretation, but a new look at the problem is desirable.

27 Ibid., 62.

28 *OO*, 11, 737. The letter is dated *3 Cal. Sept. 1576.*

29 Ibid., 734. The letter is undated, but seems to belong to this period.

30 Ibid., 738. This is the letter in which Buchanan also informs Brahe that William Lummisdale had earlier been the agent in the delivery of the Dane's book. The letter is dated *postridie Nonas Sept. 1576.*

31 Not 1578 as is sometimes thought. T. Vautrollier brought out the first edition at London in 1577 (copies in BM and Bodleian), but the following year saw an outcrop of re-issues or editions: (i) *Londini, Et prostant Antuerpiæ apud Iacobum Henricium* (St Andrews, BN, BM,

Glasgow University); (ii) London, T. Vautrollier (Cambridge University, Huntingdon Library, Bordeaux Municipal Library); (iii) *Edinburgi, Apud Henricum Charteris* (BM, with Thomas Ruddiman's bookplate); (iv) Frankfort, A. Wechel, with a liminary poem by Daniel Rogers (BM). In 1579 a re-issue(?) by A. Wechel at Frankfort (St Andrews, National Library of Scotland). A proper bibliographical examination of these volumes would be desirable.

32 See H. R. Trevor-Roper, 'George Buchanan and the Ancient Scottish Constitution', *English Historical Review*, Supplement 3, 1966.
33 Daniel Rogers had read the work in manuscript in 1576, *OO*, 11, 737.
34 See below, p. 205.
35 Naiden, op. cit., 75.
36 *OO*, 11, 756.
37 Ibid., 767.
38 These two books were 'completed' by Johann Pincier and Adam King; the *supplementa* may be read in *OO*, 11, 485–96 and 508–27.
39 P. Hume Brown, *George Buchanan, Humanist and Reformer* (Edinburgh 1890) 163–4; on Du Monin, see below, p. 203.
40 On Buchanan's indebtedness to Sacrobosco, see Naiden, op. cit., 40–3 and 63–5.
41 As was pointed out by P. Sandys in his poem *In tres Sphæræ Scriptores Scotos*, *OO*, 11, 534.
42 Especially the findings of travellers, of which his colleagues Teyve, Nuñez and Vinet were also conscious.
43 See particularly 11, 280 ff., 332 ff. and 616–54, where Buchanan asserts the creation of the universe.
44 See especially 11, 198 ff.
45 11, 141 ff.
46 1, 661 ff.
47 11, 15 ff., where the mind is mentioned in relation to its divine origin.
48 111, 452 ff.
49 Not in a set piece, but the concept underlies references to times when Nature and innocence were not affected by the darker sides of man's character; this comes to the surface in the passage on Virgo (Zodiac), 111, 198 ff. where reference is made to the ages of bronze and iron.
50 111, 120–277 (the Zodiac); v, 99–196 (Endymion).
51 1, 181 ff., where Buchanan indulges a hatred of the Portuguese that shows itself in other writings too.
52 111, 463 ff. Buchanan may praise man's mind, but the cumulative impression he gives of his nature is a sombre one.
53 In their edition of Du Bellay's *Les Regrets et autres Œuvres poëtiques*, *TLF* (Geneva 1966) J. Jolliffe and M. A. Screech note a few resemblances to the *Sphæra* (e.g. 282 and 295–6).
54 Naiden has gone into these problems in far more detail than can be discussed here.
55 The *De Cælo* is of course the most important source here; Buchanan may owe something to the *Meteorologica* for his discussion of the origin of the Milky Way, 111, 383–412, but he also looked elsewhere.
56 Naiden, op. cit., 55–6 and 70–2, where he concludes that 170 ll. of Book I and some 25 ll. of Book 11 remind one persuasively of Cleomedes, though here and there he accepts possible overlap with other sources. Nonetheless, we have here a major influence on the *Sphæra*.

57 *ΚΛΕΟΜΗΔΟΥΣ ΚΥΚΛΙΚΗ ΘΕΩΡΙΑ ΕΙΣ ΒΙΒΛΙΑ Β', Nunc
primùm typis excusa prodit, cum Regio priuilegio in quinquennium.* Parisiis
per Conradum Neobarium, Regium in Græcis Typographum.
M. D. XXXIX. The Bodleian possesses no less than four copies of
this edition; it is the fourth in the Catalogue that concerns us here
(Press-mark: Auct. S. 6. 25).

58 E.g. reflections on the smallness of the Earth (1, 593 ff.), on methods
for measuring it (1, 563 ff.), the theory that mountains do not affect the
argument about the sphericity of the Earth.

59 Naiden lists: arguments favouring the sphericity of the Earth, the
concentric spheres of the elements air and fire, the view that the
sphere is a perfect figure, op. cit., 71. But there is also overlap with
Aristotle.

60 Cf. the reference in 11, 138.

61 This emerges from our knowledge of the books Buchanan possessed;
but his friend Elie Vinet also translated Proclus into French (1573).

62 See Naiden, op. cit., 75. Gifanius refers to Canter, the editor of
Stobæus *Eclogarum libri*, in an earlier context, when writing to
Buchanan in 1567, OO, 11, 726.

63 v, 99 ff. and 197 until the 'end'.

64 The debt is analyzed by Naiden, op. cit., 73–5, but I think that
Buchanan has also turned to Aratus and Pontano for stylistic effects
in this section.

65 1, 5–6 fulgentia ... templa, cf. *Astr.* 1, 447 (but also Lucr. v, 491); 1, 278
inferne se circinat orbem, cf. *Astr.* 638 supra se circinat orbem; v, 92
decircinat is a word apparently only used by Manilius (*Astr.* 1, 296).
Naiden, op. cit., pp. 36–7, gives a selection of poetic echoes from
divers authors; the ones I suggest are additional.

66 'There is no resemblance, philosophical or poetic, to Lucretius in
language, content, or manner', op. cit., 79.

67 Ibid., 36.

68 Probably at first and at second hand.

69 1, 102 stratis e mollibus; cf. Lucr. IV, 849 lecti mollia strata; 111, 466
Exercent canos vasto cum murmure fluctus; cf. Lucr. 11, 767 Vertitur
in canos candenti marmore fluctus.

70 111, 161 cubile/Sisyphium lateat Merope; cf. Avienus 597; v, 295
ignicomans, cf. Avienus 8.

71 Tags such as conspicuum ... ignem (111, 21 cf. Mart. Cap. perspicui
ignis), fulgentia sidera (v, 431) or furvae ... caliginis (v, 452) may be
remembered from this author, but other sources are possible.

72 In other poems, Buchanan shows familiarity with Baptista Spagnuoli
and there are various phrases here that could conceivably be traced
back to him: 111, 11 reuolubilis æther, 111, 100 labentia tempora,
111, 178 Ditisque seueri, 111, 262 Borealibus auris, v, 142 salutiferum
... medicamen.

73 A cluster of echoes occur in 111, 128–34 (Naiden mentions l. 131):
111, 128 Aurato ... villo Pont. ostentatque Auratum Aries de
corpore villum; 111, 134 quia vel Phryxum avexit Phryxique
sororem, cf. Pont. Vectabat Phryxumque una Phryxique sororem;
111, 537 cæruleum ... in alueum, cf. Pont. Dum cæruleo prouectus
ab alueo; v, 220 nubes pluuios modo soluat in imbres; cf.
Pont. Soluitur & pluuij rumpunt de nubibus imbres.

74 III, 199 sinuosæ . . . tunicæ, cf. Miz. sinuosa volumina pallæ; v, 4
penetralia cœli, same phrase in Mizault.

75 v, 230 lapidosi grandinis Paling. lapidosaue grando.

76 v, 45 magicis . . . susurris echoes magicisque susurris, *Franciscanus*,
793; this may, of course, be a reminiscence from Mantuan.

77 I, 7 audacibus annue cœptis, taken from *Georg.* iv, 40; i, 55 glomeran-
tur in orbem, taken from *Georg.* iv, 79; i, 296 Humentesque bibit rores
fumosque volucres, cf. *Georg.* ii, 217–8; iii, 68 Tum male pubentes
defendit pampinus uuas, cf. *Ecl.* i, 448 Heu, male tum mitis defendet
pampinus uuas; v, 125 & flauam per lactea colla refusæ, cf. *Aen.*
viii, 660 lactea colla auro innectuntur; v, 346 liquidam deiectus in
undam, cf. *Aen.* v, 859 liquidas proiecit in undas.

78 I, 195 In vigiles ne blanda quies irrepat ocellos, cf. *Fasti*, iii, 19 blanda
quies furtim victis obrepsit ocellis; i, 268 curuum sinuatur in arcum,
cf. *Met.* xiv, 51 curuos sinuatur in arcus; iii, 46 lanigeri pecoris, cf.
Fasti, i, 384 lanigerumque pecus; iii, 230 Lernæi tabe veneni, same
phrase in *Met.* ix, 130; v, 37 elisus fulsit si nubibus ignis, cf. *Met.* vi,
696 elisi nubibus ignes; v, 93 pleno cum tota recanduit orbe, cf. *Met.*
vii, 78 totoque recanduit ore; v, 130 Spectat inexpleto fugientem
lumine, cf. *Met.* iii, 439, Spectat inexpleto mendacem lumine for-
mam; v, 335–6 spectando . . ./conscelerare oculos, cf. *Met.* vii, 34–5
oculosque videndo/conscelero.

79 Statius (not mentioned by Naiden).
I, 39–40 contain two echoes: *Th.* ii, 400 *Astriferum* iam uelox
circulus *orbem* and *Sil.* iii, 3, 36 nitido . . . cœlo; i, 57 puluereumque
globum, cf. puluereo . . . globo, *Sil.* i, 7, 124; ii, non expugnabile
cœlum, cf. *Th.* vi non expugnabile robur; iii, 166 poplite flexo, cf.
Th. x, 590 poplite nunc sedunt flexo; v, 352 per multa foramina, cf.
Th. xii, 776 per mille foramina; v 372 occidui Phœbi, also *Th.* v, 477.

80 I, 161 summo apparent carchesia malo, cf. Luc. v, 418 Hic utinam
summi curuet carchesia mali; ii, 106 sub nocte sopora, Luc. ii, 236,
sed nocte sopora; ii, 116 trepida formidine, cf. Luc. viii, 44 trepida
. . . formidine; iv, 87 Assyria scrutari sidera cura, cf. Luc. vi, 429
Assyria scrutetur sidera cura; v, 358 Fama est saxificæ faciem vidisse
Medusæ, cf. Luc. ix, 670 In quo saxificam iussit spectare Medusam;
v, 361 Babylona superbam, cf. Luc. viii, 299–300 superbam . . .
Babylona.

81 The Christian name is given, not in this text, but in a Latin poem
Lectissimo Iuueni Alexandro Leuinstonio . . ., *L'Uranologie ou le Ciel* de Ian
Edouard Du Monin . . . Paris, Guillaume Julien, 1583, fol. 188 v.
This would seem to refer to Alexander, 2nd Earl of Linlithgow, the
grandson of William Livingston and Agnes Fleming; his father, also
Alexander, would be too old to fit the pattern.

82 Ibid., f. 205 v–207 r. I have quoted the passage at some length as the
book appears to be fairly uncommon (copies in BM and BN). Naiden
was unable to consult it, and was under the impression that Du
Monin had provided a paraphrase, but the text hardly supports this
view.

83 *Georgii/Buchanani/Scoti/Franciscanus et Fratres./Elegiarum Liber I./*
Siluarum Liber I./Hendecasyllabωn Liber I./Epigrammatωn Libri III/
*De Sphaera Fragmentum./*Device/Anno/cIↃ. IↃ. xxcIv. 223 + 1
blank p. 8°. The *De Sphera Libri I. Fragmentum* will be found on

207–17. Fuller bibliographical descriptions of the 1584, 1594, 1609 and 1615 editions will be found in my article, 'George Buchanan's Latin Poems from script to print: a preliminary Survey', *The Library*, Fifth Series, XXIV (1969), especially 321 ff. The 1584 edition is fairly common: St Andrews, BM, National Library of Scotland, Aberdeen University, Glasgow University, King's College and Corpus Christi College, Cambridge, Worcester College, Oxford.

84 *Sphaera Georgii|Buchanani Scoti|Poetæ Clarisssimi:|In quinque libros distributa, tam eleganter & |accuratè scriptos, ut cum antiqua poësi certare| posse videantur.|*Device/Lutetiæ,/Apud Federicum Morellum/Typographum Regium/M.D. LXXXV./Ex Privilegio Regis. A–C^{iv}, D^{ii}: foliated.
Copy of Book I in BN (Press-mark. *Rés.* V. 1038). With it is bound a commentary: *In|Sphæram Georgij|Bucanani Scotj|Commentarius Joan. Grangerij Regij Professoris|Eloquentiæ Collegij Præleo Bellouaci Primarij an° 1623.*

85 Copy of Book II in Glasgow University, Murray Collection (pressmark: Mu. 50. e. 33).

86 Described in Naiden, op. cit., 159: the only known copy is in the Bibliothèque Sainte-Geneviève, Paris.

87 On all this see James K. Cameron, *Letters of John Johnston and Robert Howie*, St Andrews University Publications LIV (Edinburgh and London 1963).

88 See my article 'Notes on the composition and reception of George Buchanan's Psalm Paraphrases', in *Renaissance Studies*, Six Essays ed. I. D. McFarlane, A. H. Ashe and D. D. R. Owen, Scottish Academic Press (Edinburgh and London 1972).

89 *Sphæra|Georgii Bu-|chanani Scoti,|poëtarum nostri seculi facilè principis:| Quinque libris descripta:|Nunc primùm è tenebris eruta & luce donata.|*Device/Herbornæ,/Apud Christophorum Coruinum./CIↃ IↃ XXCVI. xii + 94 + 6 unnum. pp. 8°. Copies: St Andrews (the title-page carries the autograph *Robertus Stephanus|1586.|Prid. Cal. Iunias.*), Glasgow University (Murray Collection), Edinburgh University (Robert Howie's copy), BN, Toulouse (Bibl. Municipale), Emmanuel College, Cambridge, Bodleian. Naiden, op. cit., 158 mentions one or two other locations.

90 *Sphæra;|À Georgio|Buchanano Sco-|to, Poëtarum nostri|seculi facilè principe, quinque libris de-|scripta, multisáque in locis ex colla-|tione aliorum exemplorum in-|tegritati restituta.|Cui accessere libri quar-|ti & quinti, quos autor non absoluerat, supplementa.|*Autore Iohanne Pinciero, aulæ Dil-/lebergensis medico./Device/Herbornæ,/Ex officina Christophori Coruini./CIↃ IↃ XXCVII. 6 + 113 + 3 unnumb. pp. 8°. Copies: St Andrews, Bodleian, Cambridge University, Emmanuel College, Cambridge, Aberdeen University, BM, BN, National Library of Scotland.
Pincier republished his *Argumenta* and *Supplementa* in his *Parerga . . .* (Herborn 1617) (Copy in BM).

91 Described in the article mentioned in note 83. These editions are not based on manuscript tradition.

92 The manuscript of King's edition and commentary is preserved in Edinburgh University Library. See Naiden, op. cit., 154.

93 *Georgii|Buchanani|Scoti.|Poemata|omnia innumeris penè|locis, ex ipsius*

autographo/castigata & aucta/ . . . Edinburgi,/Ex Officina Andreæ Hart,/Anno 1615./. 12⁰.

This edition is in two parts, separately foliated. The *Sphæra* will be found in the second part, f. 13r–M 4 v, followed by Pincier's *Supplementa*.

Copies: National Library of Scotland, Cambridge University, B M, Huntingdon Library, Glasgow University, New College, Oxford. Naiden, op. cit., 160, lists further locations, but St Andrews does not possess either of the two copies he mentions.

94 *Georgii/Buchanani/Scoti,/Poetarum sui sæculi/facilè principis, poëmata quæ super-/sunt omnia, in tres partes diui-/sa, multò quàm antehac/ emendatiora* . . . /Device/Salmurii,/Sumpt. Cl. Girardi, Dan. Lerpinerii. Ioan. Burelli./Anno M.D C.XXI.

This edition is composed of two volumes, separately paginated, 316 + 4 blank pp., and 376 pp. The *Sphæra* will be found in the second volume (which has its own title-page, dated M . D C.XX.), but with a separate title-page, p. [205], dated M . D C. XXI. The text runs from p. 207 top. 278, including Pincier's *Supplementa*.

Copies: to Naiden's list (op. cit., 161), Aberdeen University, St Andrews, Bordeaux, Marburg, should be added: B N, Versailles, Toulouse (Bibl. Municipale).

95 *Typographus Lectori beneuolo S.*, vol. I, p. 363 (wrongly printed 633). The *vir doctus* is assumed to be John Cameron.

96 Naiden, op. cit., 154–5.

97 Favourable critics include O. Borch (Borrichius), Irving and Hallam.

98 Moreover, Johann Pincier has been suspected of inserting conjectures without proper warning.

ANDRÉ STEGMANN

Un Thème Majeur du Second Humanisme Français (1540–70) : l'Orateur et le Citoyen.
De l'Humanisme à la Réalité Vécue

L'APPARITION DE LA QUERELLE ramiste en 1543, sa violence et son éclat, sa poursuite durant trente années est un phénomène assez exceptionnel pour qu'on s'interroge sur sa signification profonde.

La réduire à une lutte philosophique—et par là plus ou moins marginale—sur le primat d'Aristote ou de Platon—serait en méconnaître à la fois la nature et l'importance.

On sait bien sans doute que, derrière l'attaque d'Aristote par Ramus il y a la scolastique, derrière l'élaboration d'une *Dialectique* nouvelle un souci d'unification de la connaissance et de la vulgarisation de la culture.

Ainsi posés brutalement et clairement par Ramus, ces problèmes en soulèvent beaucoup d'autres qui leur sont liés directement, mais c'est parfois indirectement qu'ils s'y rattachent, sans qu'il soit toujours facile pour nous d'en saisir le lien, clair pourtant pour les contemporains.

D'autre part, la France de 1540 a forgé son propre humanisme, tourné vers l'utilité et l'efficacité: humanisme vécu, où l'enjeu de la culture—appelée tour à tour *bonæ litteræ, humaniores litteræ, philologia, rhetorica*—vise à la fois à la transformation de la conscience individuelle et à des réformes pratiques en tous domaines, pédagogique, politique, social.

La rencontre de ces deux phénomènes explique pourquoi, dans la France de 1540, la bataille ramiste se présente plutôt comme un noyau de fixation, autour duquel gravitèrent repensés plus clairement, les problèmes du langage, de la rhétorique, de l'histoire et du droit, et leurs applications au domaine politique. Néanmoins, la tâche de l'humanisme reste de former l'orateur et le citoyen.

Ainsi posée, la question change de sens et les deux camps apparaissent moins brutalement opposés. Tout en attaquant Ramus sur sa méthode, bien des adversaires ne sont pas loin de ses principes. Ramus, pour sa part, sans la moindre palinodie, semblera souvent accorder plus qu'il ne semble à ses ennemis.

L'héritage du premier humanisme

Si Lefèvre d'Etaples, qui demeurera le maître et le guide incontesté de cette époque, se souciera essentiellement de restaurer la *Théologie vivifiante*[1] du pseudo-Denys (1498), et de ramener, dans la primauté du sacré, l'humanisme à ses sources chrétiennes, il n'en reste pas moins le défenseur constant d'Aristote, qu'il ne cessera de rééditer de 1492 à 1534. Les *Œuvres morales* et la *Politique* brièvement introduites et commentées[2] sont pour lui parmi les premières en date et en importance, parce qu'elles fondent la vie civile sur des principes cohérents et solides, où s'accordent nature et raison.

En 1506, les *Hécatonomies*,[3] édités avec la *Politique* et les *Economiques* de Xénophon, qui s'en prennent assez durement à la *République* de Platon, mais suivent en partie les *Lois*, étudient concrètement l'organisation de la Cité, en une véritable 'architecture intelligible' (J. Boisset): l'éducation, les magistrats, le rôle des lois et l'urbanisme sont particulièrement étudiés.

L'éducation du citoyen l'emporte ici sur celle de l''orateur', dont la formation pratique n'est pas clairement définie.[4] Un de ses disciples, G. Jouenneaux[5] qui enseigne les lettres à Paris dès 1490, semble s'être chargé de ce rôle. Il publie successivement en 1492 un Commentaire aux *Elegantiæ*, puis un *Traité d'éloquence* d'A. Dati, dédié à Briçonnet, enfin du même Dati un *Libellus isagogicus*, qui introduisent en France la réforme rhétorique italienne.[6]

Vers la même époque Denys Lefèvre (< 1488–1538) explique à Coqueret directement les auteurs grecs et latins, et notamment Quintilien et Cicéron. Dans son *Traité de l'origine des choses*,[7] compendium encyclopédique qui deviendra vite l'un des best-sellers de la Renaissance, P. Vergil consacre le premier livre aux disciplines libérales. Au chapitre 12, consacré à l'histoire, il lance une idée qui fera fortune: se fondant sur le *De oratore* de Cicéron, il lui assigne une place privilégiée. Même nouveauté sur la rhétorique (ch. 13): elle est affaire d'expérience, comme la médecine et comme le prouvent Démosthène et Cicéron: il oppose le rhéteur à l'*orateur*, formé par sa culture à toutes les fonctions sociales.

Mais c'est avec Budé que le thème prend son unité et son ampleur. Dès les longues digressions du *De asse*,[8] il part en guerre contre les enseignements à la fois vagues et étroits des Facultés de théologie, de médecine et de droit, orientés à la fois vers la pratique et le gain. A cette technicité inculte il oppose l'*orateur*, qui s'interroge sur les problèmes—test philologique de l'homme nouveau—compare les activités du voisin et s'enrichit à leur approche, cherche dans l'expression l'exactitude et l'élégance, qui sont pour lui complémentaires. Cet 'orateur-philologue', qui fera passer le bien public avant son intérêt, partagera son temps entre l'étude, la réflexion et son activité sociale. Le terrain privilégié des *humaniores litteræ* est l'histoire, supérieure au droit même.[9] Ces vues seront reprises, condensées à l'usage des enfants royaux dans le *De studio litterarum* (1527) et le *De philologia* (1530). La 'philologie' englobe toute la culture: elle n'est pas une technique, mais conjoint dons naturels, effort, droiture morale. Budé la résume dans la formule *facundia, humanitas, candor*. La *facundia* est l'éloquence fondée sur la philosophie, enseignée par Aristote, Platon et Cicéron. Ce sont les vertus chrétiennes qui vivifieront *candor* et *humanitas*. C'est au Roi lui-même qu'il adresse l'*Institution du Prince*: trois chapitres sont consacrés au rôle privilégié de l'histoire, un à l'*orateur* (ch. 13) et Budé va jusqu'à émettre le vœu—non réalisé—d'une Faculté d'éloquence à Paris.

Le *De transitu* (1534) semble marquer un recul, sinon un reniement.[10] Mais si Budé souligne la distance qui sépare la philosophie du Christ des lettres profanes, la philologie conserve sa fonction propédeutique et peut contribuer à libérer l'homme de ses appétits trop mondains. Il n'y en avait pas moins là un risque certain pour l'engagement humaniste.

Autour de ces œuvres majeures, on pourrait en associer beaucoup qui, moins nettement exprimées, participent du même esprit.

On ne s'étonnera pas que les dizaines de préfaces de J. Bade,[11] insistent sur les rapports entre rhétorique et sagesse, et notamment celles qui introduisent des textes de Gaguin, Pic, Politien, P. Crinito, Cicéron, Isocrate, Plutarque, Quintilien, Thucydide:[12] son officine était le rendez-vous des humanistes qui y échangeaient leurs vues. Certains—J. Toussain, P. Danès—formeront le lien vivant avec la génération suivante.

Curieusement, un autre courant, qui n'interfère que rarement avec l'humanisme,[13] celui des rhétoriqueurs, rejoint et renforce l'aspect qui nous occupe. Dans son tardif traité, le *Grand et vrai art de pleine rhétorique* (1521), P. Fabri ne se contente pas d'exposer en détail, en les illustrant, les multiples règles de l'école (c'est le livre II, consacré à la poésie) il expose,[14] en s'appuyant sur Platon et Cicéron[15], les règles oratoires, qu'il déclare nettement 'science politique'. Cette œuvre maintenant encore méconnue connut un succès certain, avec six rééditions, de 1521 à 1544.

Les facteurs de changement

L'importance prise par la querelle ramiste et ses implications intellectuelles et politiques tient aussi à de nombreux facteurs de changement, et en premier lieu, l'essor de la Réforme calviniste; la dédicace à François Ier de l'*Institution de la religion chrétienne*, les répercussions en France de la diète de Ratisbonne (1541) puis de l'intérim d'Augsbourg (1548); la prolongation des persécutions individuelles et la répression des Vaudois d'Avignon (1545) créent de nouveaux problèmes et de nouveaux rapports entre pouvoir et conscience individuelle. Comment convaincre par la Parole et rester fidèle sujet, sans trahir sa foi : drame de conscience que Calvin vivra, avant que son successeur, Théodore de Bèze, ne le résolve dans le sens de la révolte armée; drame vécu et payé du bûcher pour Dolet, avant que celui de Servet, à son tour, ne pose le problème en termes différents. Le *De hereticis* de Castellion le formule clairement à la conscience européenne.

En France, le Collège de France, enfin réalisé, devient le lieu privilégié des grands débats : la réalisation du programme humaniste, la qualité des premiers professeurs transformèrent le climat intellectuel.

En province la création de Facultés de droit, ou leur renouvellement firent d'Orléans, Bourges, Toulouse des foyers nouveaux, orientés vers les problèmes politiques immédiats.

La diffusion accrue du livre,[16] et notamment dans des villes comme Lyon, favorables à la libre expression, amorcèrent le grand essor de l'opinion publique.

C'est en toutes directions que s'accroissent les publications, mais tout spécialement éditions et rééditions, traductions d'œuvres antiques à portée sociale immédiate (Plutarque, Xénophon, Pline, Columelle), les historiens considérés comme les plus formateurs politiquement (Dion, Appien, Diodore),[17] les commentaires aux œuvres majeures, les modernes élargissant les horizons géographiques et intellectuels (P. Jove, Cuspinien, Olaus Magnus, Cromer, J. Funck, Munster),[18] les œuvres d'histoire engageant une nouvelle saisie politique (Sleidan, S. Fox, J. Carion).

Mais l'auteur qui passe incontestablement au premier plan est Cicéron, héritier à la fois de Platon et d'Aristote, bon philosophe autant que dialecticien, praticien et théoricien, avant tout *orateur* et *citoyen*, capable d'asseoir à la fois les principes juridiques, moraux et esthétiques et marquer la diversité des liens.[19] Nous aurons bien des occasions de l'évoquer par la suite.

Les changements politiques seront, eux, nombreux et profonds. Le long règne de François Ier marque une nouvelle phase après 1540.[20] Jean et Guillaume Du Bellay prennent un rôle politique important. Le premier protège Rabelais et Sleidan, le rôle de doyen du Sacré Collège du second modifie la politique internationale.

La France observe les multiples tentatives iréniques de Charles-Quint, qui aboutissent à l'*Intérim* d'Augsbourg (1548): des échos en passeront en France, avec F. Baudouin et Cassander.[21]

Le durcissement marqué par le règne d'Henri II ne modifiera pas foncièrement sur le plan intellectuel les problèmes, désormais ouverts, des transformations mentales posées à l'égard du pouvoir et les rapports entre philosophie, philologie, histoire et attitude civique.

De 1547 à 1559 se poursuit la querelle ramiste, l'organisation des groupes réformés, qui touchent de plus en plus l'Eglise et la noblesse, et l'organisation de cercles iréniques, notamment en 1550 à Bourges autour de la nouvelle duchesse de Berry, Marguerite de France, qui donne naissance à une nouvelle école juridique avec Cujas, Baudouin, Duaren.

Le résultat s'en fait sentir au niveau national avec le renversement de politique opéré par Catherine de Médicis, à la mort d'Henri II et l'avènement de M. de L'Hôpital, autour duquel se grouperont des prélats pacifiques, J. de Morvilliers, Jean de Monluc, Marillac, et des juristes qui formeront tôt le parti des politiques, Hotman, Du Moulin, Doneau, Pithou, Bodin — enfin, dont la *Méthode de l'histoire* fixe dès 1566 les bases d'un nouveau concept de l'histoire et les assises politiques de la *République*, formulation cohérente des rapports de l'orateur et du citoyen.

Malgré la renaissance inlassable de l'hydre de la guerre civile, le pouvoir tentera patiemment, à chaque sursaut, de l'étouffer. Du moins ces guerres seront-elles l'occasion d'un épanouissement inégalé de l'opinion publique. Par delà l'événement, la plupart des écrivains chercheront des bases intellectuelles solides : jamais l'orateur et le citoyen ne seront plus étroitement associés.

Ce long préambule était nécessaire pour mesurer à la fois les transformations du thème par rapport au premier humanisme, les liens divers qui naissent des courants, apparemment distincts sur le plan strictement littéraire, et le nouveau caractère de réalisme et d'urgence qu'il prendra par instants à la lumière de l'histoire. Toutefois, par delà les vicissitudes du moment, la plupart des auteurs visent à une action plus profonde et plus durable. Les deux courants se mêlent, sans qu'il soit toujours possible de distinguer la part de l'occasion, celle de la permanence.

Les transformations pédagogiques

A côté de sa double action polémique et théologique, le calvinisme s'efforce de fonder un humanisme plus profondément nourri de l'Ecriture.

M. Cordier, poursuit l'œuvre pédagogique qu'il avait commencée avant sa conversion.[22] Dès 1541, à son *Commentarius . . . de quotidiano sermone*, il adjoint un *Carmen paræneticum*, dont le titre précise clairement les intentions : 'ut ad Christum pueri statim accedant'. Les

Sententiæ proverbiales . . . gallico-latinæ (1547),[23] le *Miroir de la Jeunesse* (1559) aboutiront aux *Colloquia* (1564) son œuvre la plus populaire. En cicéronien fidèle,[24] mais cicéronien chrétien , il associe les préceptes historiques aux préceptes moraux. Bien qu'il vise surtout à l'éducation de la première enfance, il ne renonce pas à nourrir la mémoire de l'enfant de principes fidèles au *De oratore*.[25]

Cl. Baduel, autre converti, cherche lui aussi une *'ratio christiana'*. Dans son *De ratione studii . . . in matrimonio* (1544) il se propose de montrer l'équilibre de l'intellectuel dans le mariage. Mais les définitions éparses sur la finalité de l'étude sont l'écho fidèle du *De oratore*.

Les deux règles sont *ratio* et *oratio* (pp. 21, 24 et 107), le but l'*utilitas communis*, la *Respublica*, qui annule la 'philautia' ou le cadre trop étroit de la famille (p. 27 et 77). Pour cultiver les arts utilement, il faut 'neglectis rationibus privatis . . . utilitatibus publicis inservire atque consulere' . . . (106) et la même expression est reprise à quelques lignes de la page finale (109).

Pour y parvenir, il suffit de l'*Orationis elegantia et rerum cognitio*—En effet, 'nihil est ad societatem accommodatius' (pp. 22–23). Si le nom de Christ résonne douze fois dans le traité, si la défense de la vérité est la fin de la connaissance, c'est encore à former, par l'orateur, le citoyen, que s'applique Baduel.[26]

Il n'y a rien là de bien nouveau: on a reconnu l'esprit et les termes mêmes de l'école strasbourgeoise, quand Sturm venait de reformuler le programme dans son *De literarum ludis . . .* (1538).

Le traité de 1542, *De amissa dicendi ratione* allait être plus explicite encore et renforcer les liens entre orateur et citoyen. Les multiples dédicataires de l'ouvrage sont qualifiés non seulement d'*ornatissimi viri*, mais d'*optimi cives*.

Si la tradition mélanchthonienne[27] se poursuivra en pays protestant—et par delà les frontières germaniques—elle se retrouve dans les préoccupations des humanistes de toute tendance. Charles-Quint lui-même en donnera la formulation lapidaire à la diète d'Augsbourg (1549): 'Scholæ seminaria sunt, non Prælatorum tantum et Ministrorum Ecclesiæ, sed etiam Magistratuum et eorum qui consiliis suis Respublicas gubernant'.

Le problème de la rhétorique

Dans une telle perspective de rénovation pédagogique, on conçoit que la nature et la place de la rhétorique présente une grande ambiguité. Aussi les batailles engagées à son propos sont-elles souvent en porte-à-faux.

Prôner l' 'orateur', c'est défendre et définir les préceptes rigoureux de l'art oratoire, partie de la rhétorique. Former l'orateur à l'utilité publique, c'est combattre une certaine rhétorique sophistique, à la fois trop technique et dépourvue de sens moral, et une autre forme de rhétorique, purement esthétique, qui a sa fin en soi.

De plus, quels liens exacts la rhétorique entretient-elle avec la recherche du vrai, c'est-à-dire la Dialectique, et d'autre part, avec la Politique et, à travers elle, l'Ethique ? C'est dans ce concept monolithique qu'Aristote servait toujours de base, Platon, plutôt de complément nécessaire, atténuant la rigidité du système, orientant l'imagination poétique, restituant le sens de la parole. Cicéron enfin apparaissait comme la pierre de touche et le conciliateur.

Ce postulat admis, bien des querelles sur la rhétorique s'éclairent et des positions, apparemment radicalement opposées, se rapprochent, au delà des *paradoxes* soutenus par les adversaires.

En prolégomènes à la question et la période qui nous intéressent, la querelle du *Ciceronianus* (1 5 2 8 – 1 5 4 0) avait préparé la bataille ramiste.

Erasme avait attaqué les cicéroniens hypercritiques et purs esthètes, insoucieux de substance et de doctrine,[28] mais pour mettre à la place . . . *le vrai cicéronien,* c'est-à-dire celui qui 'réserve à Cicéron la première place et la principale', mais en devenant son *émule,* en le servant 'dans ses idées, ses pensées, . . . non dans ses mots'. Quel est alors le rôle de la rhétorique proprement dite ? Erasme avait répondu en lui assignant un rôle propédeutique : 'Je m'oppose à ce qu'on entraîne personne à l'imitation rigoureuse de Cicéron avant de lui avoir appris les préceptes de la rhétorique.'[29]

Toutefois, dans sa revue des bons guides, si R. Agricola reçoit un bel éloge pour son style 'solide, nerveux, élégant' . . . 'sa rhétorique [qui] rappelle un peu Quintilien pour l'éloquence et Isocrate pour la composition' . . ., si Zazius le juriste est loué comme orateur, Thomas More ou Melanchthon, jugés, il est vrai, par le sourcilleux Nosopon, ne reçoivent que des éloges mitigés pour avoir délaissé l'étude de l'éloquence[30] et l'on hésite en outre sur les oppositions dressées entre Isocrate, Quintilien ou Cicéron.

En attaquant Aristote et en concentrant toutes ses forces au problème d'une Dialectique unifiée, Ramus n'a pas d'autre idéal que d'élargir, par l' 'orateur' que chacun peut devenir, le citoyen qu'il doit être.

Il importe peu, au premier abord, qu'il ait tort ou raison, sur les problèmes particuliers qu'il pose.

Jeune encore et mal rompu à la philosophie, il sera en fait assez facile à ses adversaires de montrer qu'il est mauvais dialecticien ou infidèle aristotélicien.[31]

Lorsque, la première bataille livrée, il fait le point dans son discours parisien du *De studiis philosophiæ et eloquentiæ conjugendis* (1 5 4 6), il sait où il veut aller: les jeunes gens qui le suivent doivent devenir 'grammairiens, orateurs, philosophes' pour se préparer pleinement 'à la religion et à la vie politique'. Rompus à la base aux auteurs et particulièrement à Cicéron, ils consacreront la quatrième année à la rhétorique, la cinquième à la dialectique . . . Libérés de l'école, ils laisseront les règles et associeront dans la vie la finesse et l'élégance du discours et la raison critique.

Son principal biographe, N. de Nancel résume fort bien son action: 'Septem artes liberales instituit, informavit, perpolivit'.[32] Informavit: la portée nouvelle—c'est là sa seule nouveauté—[33] c'est, malgré certaines faiblesses du système la finalité donnée à l'éloquence liée à la philosophie: former le plus immédiatement à la vie civile, sans spécialisation propre, des hommes droits, efficaces et habiles, par la culture de la Ratio et de l'Oratio.

C'est à juste titre que Nancel note les maîtres avoués par Ramus lui-même: Latomus, Sturm et Lefèvre.[34] Nous sommes ici au cœur du problème, au delà des querelles philosophiques et religieuses, dont même la critique moderne ne s'est pas toujours dégagée. Lefèvre, suspect aux 'ultras' catholiques n'a jamais été tenté par la Réforme; il fut en outre le plus fidèle des aristotéliciens. B. Latomus, premier professeur d'éloquence au Collège de France, qu'il enseignait, comme le fera Ramus, avec les Discours de Cicéron, suivit et vulgarisa la Dialectique de R. Agricola: il demeura, par ailleurs, dans la stricte orthodoxie romaine. Quant à J. Sturm, son irénisme explique sa sympathie aux Réformés, les éloges de grands prélats libéraux, Bembo, Sadolet, et la fureur des doctrinaires luthériens . . .

Ce qui soutient Ramus, c'est son sentiment profond du progrès radical accompli depuis cinquante ans par l'humanisme.[35] C'est plus encore, et il l'avoue dans son ultime ouvrage, trop peu cité, qu l'on peut considérer comme son testament spirituel, la Defensio pro Aristotele, contre Schegkius (1571), la certitude qu'il est fidèle à l'esprit véritable d'Aristote, déformé par la scolastique: plus qu'à des règles strictes, mais compliquées, Aristote a voulu essentiellement former l'exercice de la raison et du jugement.[36] Sur la dialectique, telle que lui, Ramus l'entend, Platon l'a 'portée à son zénith', sans qu'il soit légitime, comme le font les scolastiques, de s'en tenir au seul Aristote, et particulièrement pour la rhétorique, où ils se complètent. Mais Ramus et ses modèles sont tous cicéroniens: c'est pourquoi, entre autres, ils associent Platon à Aristote. Il leur a fallu toutefois atténuer les attaques de Cicéron contre une certaine rhétorique: celle des rhéteurs et des avocats. Sans renier la finalité politique et morale de la rhétorique cicéronienne,[37] s'ils ont bien retenu la conception large de l'éloquence, formulée par Crassus, ils n'ont pas mis assez l'accent sur la formation de ce praticien politique que demeure Cicéron. Pour lui, l'*omni laude cumulatus orator*, se forme par l'histoire, le droit et la philosophie politique.

C'est pourquoi, malgré l'importance et le tumulte de la bataille ramiste, il faut chercher ailleurs des 'cicéroniens', sur ce point plus attentifs.

Plutôt que de refaire avec plus ou moins de bonheur, des traités antérieurs, on se contente de les rééditer et on assiste à une véritable *renaissance* des grands pédagogues du xvème siècle, parallèle aux nombreuses rééditions commentées des maîtres antiques; à côté des théoriciens, les praticiens, Démosthène, Isocrate[38] et, aux frontières de l'art oratoire, beaucoup d'historiens, considérés comme complets, et utilisés aussi à cette fin pédagogique: nous y viendrons.

Qu'il suffise de rappeler ici le rôle capital joué par E. Dolet. Défenseur de Longueil en 1535 contre les attaques d'Erasme, il rappelle que, malgré la minceur de l'œuvre (mais Longueil avait-il eu le temps?) il avait clairement formulé dès 1514 le lien entre orateur et sagesse civile. Cette invitation cicéronienne à la finalité civique qu'il redéfinit contre Erasme, Dolet va en restituer les textes, en soulignant par les dédicaces les liens qui l'unissent aux autres restaurateurs de la bonne orientation pédagogique, Sadolet, G. du Bellay, L. de Baïf, Boyssonné. C'est en 1537–8, le gros *Commentaire de la langue latine*; en 1538, le *Cato christianus*; en 1540 une nouvelle *Imitatio ciceroniana* et outre les innombrables rééditions des plus importants classiques, les traductions des *Epîtres* et des *Tusculanes*, et les implications civiles avec le *De officio legati* de 1541. S'il insiste, dans la double tradition des réformateurs catholiques et protestants, sur la primauté des *Saintes lettres*, le texte de 1544 souligne l'intention de vulgarisation civile: *Bref discours de la république française*.

Le successeur de J. Toussain dans la chaire de grec au Collège de France (1547) Adrien Turnèbe, qui donna une traduction latine des *Moralia* de Plutarque en 1570[39] et diverses éditions princeps de textes grecs, ne cessa de s'intéresser à Cicéron, comme maître privilégié de pédagogie civique. Il reste aussi non seulement dans la ligne de ses maîtres Budé et Toussain, mais aussi le continuateur de Dolet.

Il commente en 1553 le *Pro Rabirio*, en 1554 le deuxième livre du *De oratore*, sous le titre de *Joci Ciceronis*, puis, attaqué par Ramus, compose sur le *De fato* un long libelle *Adversus quendam qui non solum logicus esse, verum etiam dialecticus haberi vult*. Il y relève contre Ramus, sans le nommer, des erreurs de traduction, mais surtout une déviation générale profonde, qui consiste à orienter tout le texte vers la 'dialectique', non vers la philosophie morale, et à rattacher le *De fato* (Du destin) aux Περὶ δυνατῶν (sur les actes possibles), sans voir que Cicéron s'en prend à Chrysippe.

Par delà ces questions techniques, Turnèbe montre qu'en jetant à tort—faute de le comprendre—un discrédit sur la pensée de Cicéron[40] défenseur avec Diodore de la nature humaine, du libre arbitre, de la justice, oser parler à son propos—comme d'Aristote—d'impiété, cette nouvelle trahison fait que cette nouvelle Académie prônée par Ramus, retourne contre elle l'accusation.[41]

Le terme de cette diatribe violente, c'est que, pour Turnèbe, Ramus substitue 'à l'éloquence une vide diarrhée verbale, à la modestie de la philosophie l'arrogance et l'intolérance . . . à la connaissance philosophique une gaucherie qu'une légèreté de sophiste rend insolente . . .'[42]

Sa bile jetée, il revient à l'œuvre la plus politique de Cicéron dans une édition commentée du *De legibus* (1557).

Malgré des positions personnelles différentes, son successeur Denis Lambin conserve le même esprit, mais revient plus expressément aux rapports entre orateur et citoyen. Dans la chaire de grec, ses cours vont plus souvent qu'aux poètes, à Démosthène, Isocrate, à l'Aristote de l'*Ethique* et de la *Politique*. Il compose une *Vie de Cicéron*, dont il refait en 1566 une édition monumentale. Ses discours publics ne sont que des variations sur le même thème, rendu plus actuel par les guerres civiles: conjoindre *Ratio* et *Oratio*, l'orateur et le citoyen: 1564, *De laudibus litterarum*—1565, *De philosophiæ moralis laudibus*—1566, *De rationis principatu et recta institutione*—1568, le titre le plus explicite: *De philosophia cum arte dicendi conjungenda* . . .[43] Le problème des rapports entre dialectique et rhétorique semble alors résolu—par l'oubli.

La querelle contre Ramus s'était pourtant poursuivie, sans relâche durant trente années, sur le seul problème de l'interprétation de l'*Organon* d'Aristote, avec des champions divers, scandalisés surtout de la nomination de Ramus au Collège de France en 1551. Son plus sérieux adversaire, J.Périon, cesse alors ses attaques et se contente de poursuivre son édition d'Aristote, à la lumière de Cicéron, reprise par un pillard indiscret, contre lequel proteste Périon, Nicolas de Grouchy. Les médecins J.Charpentier et Riolan reprennent l'attaque sur le plan épistémologique et métaphysique: les écrits brefs et précis du second sont d'une extrême importance pour l'interprétation d'Aristote. Mais c'était là désormais querelle d'école et jeux de prince.

Le sens de l'histoire

En grande partie en dehors d'elle, mais liée aux mêmes centres d'intérêt se développe une autre querelle de première importance, celle du sens de l'histoire.[44]

Aristote et Cicéron se trouvent, comme par hasard, ici encore au cœur du problème. Si les Italiens en ont été le plus souvent les protagonistes, la France, qui en a suivi l'évolution particulièrement décisive de 1540 à 1550, aboutit avec Baudouin et surtout Jean Bodin, à des solutions particulièrement heureuses, d'où sortira l'énorme littérature ultérieure de la raison d'Etat, déplaçant le problème des rapports entre rhétorique et civisme vers ceux liés à la pratique, à l'histoire et au droit.

Pour comprendre, en France, le processus de cette évolution, il faut ajouter à la présence des théoriciens italiens comme Patrizzi, Speroni ou Robortello, l'évolution critique sur les historiens anciens et modernes, dont la *Methodus* de Bodin n'est que l'aboutissement et la synthèse.

Bodin fait le plus grand cas de Suétone: il avait fait l'objet d'une réédition à Lyon en 1548 avec les commentaires de Sabellico, Ph. Béroalde, Erasme et B. Ignazio. Fl. Josèphe a 'une écrasante supériorité dans la connaissance de l'antiquité grecque' . . . 'il y confirme les assertions de Moïse'. Outre les rééditions et traductions du texte (notamment de Fr. Bourgoing en 1558), il fait l'objet d'un livre destiné aux enfants pour comprendre l'*institutio respublicæ*, de la part de Castellion (Bâle, 1546). Diodore dont Seyssel avait donné une traduction partielle en 1530 est réédité par H. Estienne en 1559, après une traduction intégrale d'Amyot en 1554. La préface en définit l'intérêt: '[Diodore expose] les affaires du monde, en matière d'état, liées entre elles et reste très utile pour la conduite de la vie.' Le même Seyssel présente en 1544 une traduction complète d'Appien, dont Bodin louera la conception 'moderne', fondée sur les documents et l'histoire économique et sociale. Polybe, pour Bodin, est l'un des seuls qui fournisse 'une étude approfondie de toute la vie romaine (M. 48) qui discute avec abondance sur la politique et s'étend sur le devoir de l'historien (M. 44) et blâme souvent l'ignorance des historiens antérieurs (M. 45).' Une traduction de 1542 précède l'édition bâloise du texte grec en 1549. A cet égard, l'œuvre de traducteur de L. Meigret, connu surtout comme réformateur de l'orthographe, est exemplaire. De 1541 à 1547, il donne successivement deux éditions complétées de Polybe (1542 et 1545), le *discours* 'royal' à Nicoclès d'Isocrate (1544), Salluste, 'avec la harangue de Cicéron contre lui' (1547) et le *De officiis* 'ou devoir de bien vivre'.

Ce choix d'auteurs complémentaires dispense Meigret de s'étendre longuement dans ses préfaces sur ses intentions: ce primat de deux historiens exemplaires associés à deux classiques de la philosophie civile, prépare modestement, mais efficacement la transformation qui s'opère à la fois dans l'élargissement de la vision historique et le concept même d'histoire.

Ces matériaux patiemment accumulés, Bodin les assemblera génialement dans sa *Méthode de l'histoire* (1566), en définissant successivement les critères de classement des historiens, selon des règles philologiques et comparatistes, puis la manière de les exploiter en philosophie politique et non plus en historien, enfin en dressant les linéaments de son système, approfondis plus tard dans la *République*.[45]

Ce qui nous intéresse ici, c'est la visée pédagogique avouée de Bodin. Par des voies bien différentes et avec un but limité, celui de la formation pratique du citoyen, il rejoint sous cet angle ce désir de vulgarisation que toute son époque répète. Ramus, seul, a cru pouvoir offrir une clé universelle et permettre l'accès de toutes les connaissances. Bodin, lui, ne voit plus seulement dans l'histoire une section privilégiée de l'éducation, mais une science autonome 'accessible à tous' 'au dessus des autres disciplines, sans aucun autre concours' (préface). Quant à son rôle, l'histoire suffit à tout: 'Elle se chargera de nous révéler non seulement les techniques nécessaires à notre existence, mais les préceptes de la vie morale ... l'assiette qui convient aux lois, la meilleure forme de la république et le moyen d'être heureux' (préf. XLIII). Ses lecteurs sont toutefois 'non les solitaires, mais ceux qui participent à la vie sociale' (ch. 1, p. 4).

Tout pour le citoyen: la loi civile, la philosophie morale, les règles domestiques 'toutes les actions des hommes conspirent à défendre la société' (p. 17). Mais le problème, qu'Aristote a vu sans pouvoir le résoudre, consiste à trouver une définition commune au bonheur individuel et à celui de la cité, le premier étant aussi repos et contemplation, 'cette droite conversion vers Dieu d'un cœur purifié' (p. 20).

Bodin ne donne pas seulement à l'histoire son autonomie et sa primauté absolue, il modifie les rapports traditionnels d'*orateur* et de *citoyen*, semble biffer la rhétorique et retourner le problème des rapports entre philosophie morale et politique.

Sa position est plus complexe. Dans les longs parcours détaillés des chap. 5 et 6, la nature universelle et sa connaissance, l'analyse des données psychologiques de la nature humaine, le plaisir esthétique et les arts retrouvent une place discrètement évoquée ici, puisqu'ils n'entrent pas dans le propos de Bodin, encore qu'il laisse échapper au chapitre 7 un hymne aux temps modernes, bien proche de ceux de Rabelais ou de Ramus.

Bodin a fait subir une autre mutation à l'histoire, destinée à la formation civique. La méthode philologique comparative qu'il transporte à l'histoire toute entière est celle du juriste. Il avait été précédé dans cette voie par F. Baudouin[46] que ses multiples expériences de professeur de droit à Genève, Bourges, Strasbourg, Heidelberg, ses applications pratiques de droit romain à des problèmes concrets (droit rural, héritage, conflit de juridiction entre l'Eglise et l'Etat) et la détérioration de la situation politique[47] incitent à formuler, cinq ans avant Bodin, sa théorie de l'histoire (*De institutione historiæ universæ et ejus cum jurisprudentia conjunctione*, 1561).

Le but de Baudouin n'est ni de soumettre l'histoire à l'histoire du droit, ni d'intégrer celle-ci dans le concept de l'histoire, mais au contraire, de rendre possible l'histoire du droit à la lumière de l'histoire universelle. Mais cette histoire est moins celle de l'historiographie que celle des documents de tous ordres, chartes, inscriptions et médailles, littérature folklorique et chansons. Propos tout modernes? Baudouin les tire de Varron, du traité des *origines* de Caton... à travers le *Brutus* de Cicéron.

Voici donc une nouvelle lecture de Cicéron: Périon y cherchait la Logique d'Aristote, les pédagogues une rhétorique, les orateurs des règles culturelles et techniques, avec Baudouin il rénove l'histoire.

Ce serait trahir Baudouin que de le limiter à ce rôle de théoricien, si important soit-il. Il s'était exprimé, dès 1556, avec le *Constantinus*, pour une politique chrétienne, de tendance irénique, qu'il tentera d'introduire en France à la demande expresse de Condé, pour concilier les tendances des partis, sur la base de l'Intérim d'Augsbourg. Mais Calvin et Bèze veillaient. Condé (ou plutôt son porte-parole, Bèze) répliqua privément avec sévérité au programme envoyé, cependant que le texte du *De officio pii ac publicæ tranquillitatis vere amantis viri*... de Cassander (mais que Calvin crut l'œuvre de Baudouin) entraînait une réplique injurieuse de Genève.[48]

Ainsi le rejet théorique de l'orateur' dans la thèse de Baudouin se trouvait infirmé dans la pratique, de même qu'à sa laïcisation théorique de l'histoire en 1561 succédait en 1563 un irénique *Discours sur le fait de la réformation de l'Eglise*, à propos duquel Calvin et Bèze reprirent leur plume acérée contre le 'Triplapostat'. A la séparation fictive de l'orateur et du citoyen répondait leur étroite liaison dans l'action politique. En fait, l'opposition est moins entière qu'elle ne semble, puisque la préface de 1561 définissait la fonction des hommes dans l'histoire 'd'abord comme spectateurs, puis comme acteurs, comme juges enfin'... En ce sens, l'histoire est bien cette *historia integra* qu'annonce le titre de l'ouvrage.

L'ascension des juristes humanistes

Cette nouvelle définition de l'histoire, ce sont en France, des juristes qui la font. La leçon de Budé a porté et l'enseignement d'Alciat et de Cujas a préparé les voies à leurs successeurs, qui ont pu choisir leurs horizons et formuler des synthèses, sans rien perdre de leur technicité.

Malgré son admiration pour Polybe, Bodin le critique en juriste: 'les lois Portia, Valeria et Sempronia montrent l'erreur de Polybe en matière capitale'.[49] F. Baudouin étudie et publie pendant vingt ans sur le droit romain avant d'écrire le *De institutione historiæ*. Il recherche, à travers les cas particuliers antiques et modernes, les rapports institutionnels fondamentaux et leurs conséquences sociales.[50] C'est moins par 'instabilité mentale'[51] que par droiture morale et approfondissement historique qu'il cherche sa voie religieuse pour revenir, après trois brèves années d'expériences réformées, à l'orthodoxie.

Dans ses deux traités pédagogiques de 1555 et 1557, il prépare la formulation définitive de la thèse du *De institutione* en associant lois, histoire et philosophie morale. Mais celle-ci a pris un autre visage: elle est essentiellement la résultante des mœurs pratiquées à une certaine époque, plutôt que l'objet idéal de la conscience individuelle: on retrouve ici l'historicisme foncier de Baudouin. Mais contrairement à toute attente ce constat objectif le rejette plus fortement dans le camp humaniste. Cette histoire des mœurs, qu'elle soit de la grande époque romaine, ou du Bas-Empire, avec l'histoire des donatistes de Carthage, souligne les dangers des habitudes collectives et de la rigidité des lois. Le problème reste donc tout entier de faire passer *de la conscience individuelle à l'opinion publique* les mutations nécessaires: c'est toute la dialectique des rapports de l'orateur et du citoyen, bien que Baudouin ne privilègie pas expressément ces deux termes.[52] Tout son enseignement tient dans cette formule: 'aperiri ludum civilium studiorum, ex quo prudentes eruditi non ad privatam modo jurisdictionem, sed et ad majorem tuendæ Reipublicæ facultatem et imperiorum relationem prodeant.'[53]

De l'immense activité juridique des années 1545-70 qui, avec Hotman, Cujas, Duaren, L. Du Chesne, Ch. Du Moulin, G. Cousin (l'un des derniers 'famuli' d'Erasme), Ph. Bugnyon, étudie souvent, non sans querelles intestines, les mêmes problèmes théoriques de droit romain (lois des douze tables, histoire critique du Code Justinien) ou pratiques (usure, mariage, abréviation des procès), dégageons ce qu'ils ont en commun: le souci d'une nouvelle pédagogie du droit, les relations de leur science avec la philosophie et l'histoire.

Hotman, après dix ans d'écrits techniques, donne son *Jurisconsultus*

(1559), mais c'est après avoir longuement commenté les *Discours* de Cicéron.[54] En 1560 G. Cousin rédige quelques épitres *sur l'étude du droit*.[55] Certains juristes préfèrent aborder indirectement cette formation politique: J. Brèche en 1541 et Ch. Du Moulin en 1546 traduisent deux opuscules moraux de Plutarque (*De la doctrine du prince* et *De l'usure*), Jean Colin, obscur châlonnais, 'licencié en lois', après avoir réédité trois textes de Cicéron, traduit en 1548 la *Vraie Sapience* de Vivès.[56] En 1554, un pur praticien, Jean Papon s'attache à comparer les deux princes de l'éloquence grecque et latine, Démosthène et Cicéron. Les textes les plus intéressants pour notre propos sont les discours d'ouverture au Collège de France du juriste Léger Du Chesne, de 1558 et de 1561.[57] Cicéronien, on ne s'étonne pas de le voir faire l'éloge funèbre de Turnèbe en 1566, après avoir polémiqué à son tour contre Ramus en 1553.

Un dernier aspect, encore méconnu de nos jours,[58] de ce caractère profondément engagé du droit dans les années cruciales qui précédent les guerres de religion, c'est la bataille ouverte sur le problème du pouvoir de l'Eglise aux premiers siècles.

Ce n'est pas par hasard si ces traités paraissent entre les deux textes de Castellion, le *De hereticis* de 1554 et la *lettre à Calvin* de 1562. On a déjà évoqué le *Constantinus* de F. Baudouin en 1556. Il semble bien qu'il réponde à un texte de Hotman de 1553, publié à Genève (Hieropolis) le *De statu primitivæ ecclesiæ ejusque sacerdotiis*.

A leur tour, Duaren en 1557, édite le *De sacris ecclesiæ ministeriis ac beneficiis* Baudouin, la même année, les *Edicta veterum principum de Christianis*, et G. Cousin, chanoine de Nozeroy, en 1562, un *De iis qui Romæ jus dicebant olim deque eorum origine et potestate*, qui répond indirectement et en pur droit romain, au problème brûlant engagé depuis huit ans.

Nous voici, semble-t-il, loin du problème théorique de l'histoire intégrale et de la réforme pédagogique de droit. En fait, tous ces aspects apparaissent complémentaires: la force des choses entraîna les hommes de science à une praxis de plus en plus prégnante.

Engagement et désengagement (1560–70)

1560 est une date et peut-être la fin d'une époque. Avec l'avènement de Catherine, le colloque de Poissy, les Etats-Généraux et l'édit de Saint Germain qui multiplièrent les chances de la paix, puis la soudaine et terrible première guerre civile, les problèmes théologiques et les appels à l'opinion publique passèrent au premier plan.

En contrepartie—et parfois comme contre-poison volontaire, chez les citoyens les plus engagés, on assiste à un retour de la littérature en quête de contemplation ou de philosophie générale, voire de simple évasion.

La littérature engagée issue de la première guerre civile révèle à la fois le caractère fictif des oppositions théoriques de jadis et inversement, l'illusion de l'accord des cicéroniens des bords opposés. Le réel, comme toujours, agit comme révélateur. A Toulouse, J. de Coras tente de livrer la ville aux réformés; de Bâle, Castellion et Cassander lancent leurs appels iréniques, déchaînant la colère de Bèze et de Calvin. G. Postel, entrant dans la mêlée, propose un accord qui entraîne la réplique immédiate de Matthieu d'Antoine, ministre lyonnais. Turnèbe, lié à M. de L'Hôpital, suit la même voie modératrice et diffuse, en français, un discours du chancelier *Sur les moyens d'obvier aux troubles* (1564), puis se réfugie dans l'étude érudite : il en sortira les trois gros volumes d'*Adversaria*. Sa mort en 1566 provoque une vraie bataille littéraire, à laquelle la politique n'est pas étrangère.[59] Avec une ténacité candide, L. Le Roy multiplie les longs ou petits traités historiques[60] continuant à chercher les analogies de la terre et du corps humain pour défendre l'autorité royale et 'par delà les causes naturelles la divine Providence!' Il continue à chercher, en 1567 'à accommoder les Politiques de Platon et d'Aristote aux mœurs et négoces de ce temps'. La veille de sa mort, en 1575, il prononce deux discours significatifs; l'un analyse les troubles du royaume, l'autre est un *De jungenda sapienter sentiendi scientia cum ornate dicendi facultate*. Comme ce cicéronianisme intempestif sonne amèrement!

La parole est désormais à l'actualité. Les deux camps multiplient la publication de textes officiels[61] pour se gagner l'opinion publique et les pamphlets se font plus rares. L'histoire du passé vient à l'appui des thèses soutenues. Dans le camp calviniste les uns s'impatientent de l'inaction des princes et demandent bien plus que la liberté de conscience, d'autres (Calvin, Viret, La Planche) espèrent encore dans une paix juste.

Beaucoup s'éloignent de la bataille et trouvent dans l'érudition ou la méditation un remède personnel à leur échec. Certains agissent sans plus écrire. J. Sturm à Strasbourg,[62] D. Lambin au Collège de France[63] poursuivent leurs savantes éditions. Seuls, Riolan, de sa chaire de médecine et Charpentier, de celle de philosophie, continuent à harceler Ramus.

Si H. Estienne, que son métier d'imprimeur contraindrait à lui seul à poursuivre son aide aux réformés, réédite, entre autres, les *Colloques* de M. Cordier et les *Rudimenta Fidei* de Calvin, Hotman se tait jusqu'à la Saint Barthélémy et accepte des missions en Allemagne pour Jeanne d'Albret et Condé. Mais il compose, dans sa retraite de Sancerre en 1564 une *Consolation* tirée des Saintes Ecritures.[64]

Le bénédictin J. Périon, autre adversaire de Ramus, s'était consacré depuis 1553 à des œuvres chrétiennes. La publication, post-hume, en 1565, des œuvres complètes du pseudo-Denys prenait le double visage d'un anachronisme et d'un appel à la sérénité contemplative. Castellion édite à Bâle l'*Imitation de Jésus Christ* (1563).

Michel de L'Hôpital, après un dernier appel à la tolérance en 1567 et sa retraite forcée, multiplie dans ses lettres versifiées les appels à la vie des champs et à la vie contemplative. Sa conversion va jusqu'au reniement: 'Je regretterai toujours que les meilleures années de ma vie aient été employées à l'étude des mots plutôt qu'à celle des choses . . . Les commentaires m'ennuient et me fatiguent, la vraie philosophie est aux cieux'.[65]

S'il renie l'orateur, le citoyen ne renonce pas à ses devoirs: 'Nous nous devons à Dieu d'abord, ensuite à la patrie. Si tu te consacres à ce dernier culte, supportes-en les charges. Quand l'Etat ne voudra plus de toi . . ., pars sans regret. Ton nom restera pur et honoré et tu auras en partage le bien suprême, la conscience d'une noble vie.'

Ainsi évolue en trente ans ce thème majeur. Héritage du premier humanisme, la réforme et la révolte intellectuelle de Ramus l'actualisent fortement. L'éclat du Collège de France et l'intensification de l'impression lui donnent très tôt une portée européenne. Autour du rapport entre orateur et citoyen s'agglutine l'essentiel de la production philosophique, historique, pédagogique, littéraire même. S'il semble que le débat reste au plan intellectuel, il est en fait constamment sous-tendu par les problèmes politiques et sociaux.

A cet égard, le principal résultat, que nous n'avons fait qu'esquisser, est l'essor de la philosophie politique, avec un accent plus fort sur le rôle de l'histoire. C'est l'heure des juristes qui, dans la tradition souhaitée par Budé, associent les vues pédagogiques et les problèmes philologiques et stylistiques aux questions propres au praticien.

La figure qui domine tous les débats, l'auteur qui les rassemble tous, dans un commun respect, sinon dans une totale admiration, c'est Cicéron. Intense et bref apogée, de 1535 à 1560, éclipse quasi totale de 1560 à 1575, bref occident de 1575 à 1580, avant un déclin définitif.

La guerre civile met les idées à l'épreuve, durement. L' 'orateur' entre dans la mêlée ou se réfugie dans la méditation. L'illusion cicéronienne a vécu. Le citoyen demeure, avec une conscience où la part intellectuelle et morale demeure l'affaire de chacun.

NOTES

1 Cf. la récente mise au point d'E. Rice: 'J. Lefèvre and his circle' dans *Humanism in France* (Congrès de Warwick, 1969) éd. par A. H. T. Levi (Manchester 1970).
2 Cf. mon article 'La politique de Lefèvre d'Etaples' dans l'*Humanisme français au début de la Renaissance* (xivème Colloque international de Tours, Vrin 1973).
3 Dans les *Actes* ci-dessus: J. Boisset, 'Les Hécatonomies de Lefèvre d'Etaples'.
4 Cicéron et Quintilien sont encore peu connus et peu exploités. De Cicéron, c'est le moraliste du *De officiis* qui intéresse alors. L'humanisme français s'est assigné alors des tâches plus générales. Sur cette évolution voir J. Massaut, *J. Clichtove* (Liège-Paris 1965) où les réformes philosophique et réligieuse dominent.
5 Il sera le premier des 'fabristes' à entrer au monastère bénédictin de Chezal-Benoît où le suivront plus tard les frères Gernand. Ses traités eurent trente ans de succès.
6 Avec Dati, Perotti, Guarino de Verone ... cf. E. Garin, *Il pensiero pedagogico dell'Umanesimo*. Tr. fse. (Paris 1968) et F. Simone, *Il Rinascimento francese* (Turin 1965).
7 Ière édition, 1499—Ière édition complète, Bâle 1521—28 rééditions au xvième siècle, outre les traductions en toutes langues: l'un des best-sellers de la Renaissance dont il est traditionnel—à tort—de se moquer, depuis Rabelais et Cervantès.
8 Ière édition en 1515—édition abrégée en 1520—Cf. L. Delaruelle, *G. Budé* (Paris 1907).
9 Dédicace et préface.
10 Les jugements modernes diffèrent, selon l'accent mis sur les affirmations antérieures de Budé (en particulier dès le *De asse*: primat et autonomie de la sagesse chrétienne). Cf. R. R. Bolgar, 'Humanism as a value system' (Actes de Warwick, cf. n. 1) et Mme de la Garanderie, 'Le style figuré de Budé' (Actes de Tours, cf. n. 2).
11 Cf. Ph. Renouard, *Bibliographie des impressions de J. Bade* (Paris 1908).
12 Présentation de la traduction de Claude Seyssel (1514). Ce dernier, traducteur officiel infatigable, souligne lui-même à la fois le rôle politique et littéraire de la traduction—et ce même rôle dans le contenu des auteurs qu'il choisit, Appien, Justin, Diodore. Bodin, dans sa *Méthode de l'histoire* explicitera les intentions de Seyssel.
13 Peu de relations personnelles—du moins à notre connaissance—entre Lemaire de Belges, Gringore ou Marot et les humanistes latinisants; quelques influences communes: Boccace, Pétrarque ou les auteurs latins, Cicéron en particulier; quelques visées analogues, mais plutôt par rencontre, sur les réformes politiques et sociales. P. Jodogne, 'Les rhétoriqueurs et l'humanisme' (Actes de Warwick) le rapprochement maximum (le reste faible)—à propos surtout d'O. de Saint Gelais et Molinet—166–7.
14 Au livre I, double de celui consacré à la poésie (295 pages contre 133).
15 Et occasionnellement Quintilien.
16 Cf. les statistiques dans L. Febvre et H. J. Martin—L'*apparition du livre* et H. J. Martin: *Livre, pouvoirs et société à Paris au XVIIème siècle*, 2 vol. (Genève 1969).

17 Diodore (1539) Dion Cassius (1548 et 1551) Appien (1551) Diodore (1559), le Plutarque latin complet de Xylander (1560).

18 P. Jove (1540 et 1549) Munster (1544) Olaus Magnus (1550) Funck (1550) M. Cromer (1552) Sleidan (1548) Seb. Fox (1555).

19 Cf. les éloges convergents de Longueil, Melanchthon, Sturm, Latomus vers les années 1530. Le petit condensé de N. Goulu paru en 1564, qui rassemble en 40 pages toutes les notions philosophiques essentielles à partir du seul Cicéron: *Epitome in universam Ciceronis philosophiam* montre non seulement la permanence de l'image, mais le progrès vulgarisateur accompli. L'accent y est bien mis sur le thème qui nous occupe: *'Cum ad civilem societatem natus sit homu . . ., perpetua oratione quà regat populos, stabilitat leges, castiget improbos'*.

20 Effets de l'édit de Villers-Cotterets (1539) législation anti-ouvrière renforcée (art. 191)—1544: serfs de domaine affranchis—1542: création d'une banque publique et catastrophe financière des fonds d'Etat; difficiles fluctuations de la politique extérieure et invasions toujours menaçantes . . .

21 Cf. mon article: 'Cassander, victime des orthodoxes'. Colloque de Montpellier, 1973 (Vrin 1974).

22 Successivement aux collèges parisiens de Lisieux, de La Marche où il eut Calvin pour élève, puis à celui de Bordeaux.

23 Extraites pour le plupart des *Adages* d'Erasme.

24 E. Chappuys les traduit en français en 1576.

25 Il commente les *Epitres* de Cicéron (1553) et en fournit des extraits en 1556, à l'usage des jeunes élèves.

26 Il sera, lui aussi, traducteur de Cicéron et d'Isocrate.

27 Baduel est d'ailleurs en correspondance avec Melanchthon en 1550.

28 Cf. Erasme, *La philosophie chrétienne*, Ed. P. Mesnard (Vrin 1970) 355-6.

29 Ibid., 356-7.

30 Ibid., 338-40 et 336, respectivement.

31 Cf. mes 'Observations sur Aristote du bénédictin Périon' dans *Aristote et Platon à la Renaissance*, xvième Colloque de Tours (Vrin 1974). Périon oppose à Ramus un Aristote cicéronisé. Celui-ci d'ailleurs, dans sa dernière œuvre, *Defensio pro Aristotele* montre que ce n'est pas Aristote, mais les aristotéliciens maniaques du xvième siècle et selon lui, d'ailleurs infidèles—qu'il avait attaqués. Cf. *infra* n. 36.

32 Nancel, *Petri Rami vita* (Paris 1599) 43.

33 Cf. Ong, *Ramus* (Harvard 1958) livre I, chap. 1.

34 Nancel, op. cit., 90.

35 Garin, op. cit., Extrait du *Discours* de Ramus en 1536, p. 184.

36 *Defensio pro Aristotele* (1571) contre Schegkius, en 16 points. '*Aristotele est mens, non tuus*' (p. 32). La conjonction de l' 'orateur' et du citoyen est clairement affirmée: *'ut logica sit omnibus in otio, in negotio domi forisque, in pace et bello dux cogitandi et judicandi regulaque formandæ rationis'* (p. 7).

37 Cf. Pichon, *Histoire de la littérature latine* (Paris 1897).

38 La traduction d'Isocrate par Macault 1544 est conjointe en 1548 à celle des *Philippiques*.

39 Cf. R. Aulotte, *Amyot et Plutarque* (Genève 1965) 182-3.

40 Turnèbe résume ainsi l'attitude de Ramus: *'Ciceronem inane et individuum novasse'* (p. 11).

41 Turnèbe.—*Adversus* . . . 26, in fine.
42   „   .—*Adversus* . . . 51, verso.
43 Tous ces textes seront réunis après sa mort (1572) et associés à ceux de Muret et de Le Roy en 1579.—BN, Paris, z.13958.
44 Le plus récent ouvrage sur cet important problème est celui de G. Cotroneo, *I trattatisti dell' Ars historica* (Naples 1971). Les pages qui suivent apportent à cette excellente étude quelques compléments et peut-être, pour les années 1540–70, une nouvelle perspective.
45 *Méthode de l'histoire*, éd. P. Mesnard (Paris 1941): Suétone (p. 57), Polybe (48) Denys d'Halicarnasse (47). Cf. mon étude: 'L'apport antique dans la réflexion de Bodin sur l'Etat'. Congrès de Rome, 1973 (à paraître aux Belles-Lettres, 1974).
46 G. Cotroneo, pp. 343–83, après D. R. Kelley, *JHI* 25 (1964) restitue toute sa dimension à ce méconnu.
47 L'échec du Colloque de Poissy et la détérioration des rapports avec Genève (1560–1).
48 Cf. l'article cité en note 21.
49 *Méthode de l'histoire* . . . 168.
50 Cf. *infra*—sa recherche sur les décrets des empereurs romains sur les chrétiens (1557), complément au *Constantinus* (1556).
51 Selon des formules, souvent répétées par la critique moderne, épousant le seul point de vue calviniste.
52 Cf. pourtant par ex. '*res utiles* . . . *ut orationis luce commendentur*'. *De inst.*, 162.
53 *De inst.*, 150.
54 En particulier la lettre de Cicéron à Quintus: *De provincia recte administranda* (Lyon 1564).
55 *De legali studio epistolæ* (1560) qui reprend une brève étude de 1543: *Epistola de legalis studii ratione*.
56 Aulotte, op. cit., 115: La tendance de Cousin à la vie contemplative apparait parallèlement dans son autre traduction de Plutarque: *De la tranquillité d'esprit*.
57 Cf. Lefranc, *Histoire du Collège de France*.
58 On le conçoit, devant la rareté des études modernes d'histoire du droit, qui fait encore l'objet de quelques travaux de spécialistes, eux-mêmes peu engagés vers la synthèse historique. Reconnaissons que les gros in–folios ne sont pas d'abord facile.
59 On trouvera dans la *Bibliographie de la littérature française* d'A. Cioranescu (nº 21404–21417) les auteurs de ce 'tombeau'. Turnèbe venait juste de prendre parti sur la guerre civile dans son *Bref Discours sur l'occasion des troubles de ce temps* et la vigueur de ses attaques contre Ramus n'était pas oubliée.
60 *De l'origine, antiquité, progrès, excellence et utilité de l'art politique* (1567)— *Les monarchiques* (1570)—Dans son *Excellence du gouvernement royal* (1575) il regrette '*l'impossibilité de la naturelle république universelle*'. Ses appels pacifiques de 1563, 1567 et 1570 ont la même rhétorique vague et justifient le sévère jugement de son biographe, H. Becker (*L. Leroy*, Paris, 1896) '*bavardages de pédant*'.
61 La Place: *Histoire de notre temps* (1560)—*Mémoires de Condé* (1564) et toutes les rééditions accrues—J. Crespin: *Actes des martyrs* (1564)— Bèze: *Histoire ecclésiastique* (1560)—pour ne citer que les grandes synthèses.

62 Non sans le désenchantement et l'angoisse manifestés dans la correspondance. En 1574 et 1576, Sturm n'hésite pas pourtant à reparler de l'orateur: *De imitatione oratoria—De universa ratione elocutionis rhetoricæ*: survie anachronique.

63 Discours d'ouverture de 1563, 64, 65 et édition glosée des *Politiques* d'Aristote en 1567. La France est en paix de 1562 à 1567 et l'éloge des lettres, de la philosophie morale et de la raison peuvent paraître un retour nécessaire aux grands principes, tout en désamorçant les passions que continuent d'exciter les récits de la première guerre.

64 Les contemporains ne l'ont, hélas! pas connue (Ière édition, 1595). La figure et le rôle d'Hotman en eussent été grandis.

65 Lettre à Corbinelli composée entre 1567 et 1572. Cf. *Poésies complètes* traduction de Louis Bardy de Nalèche (Paris 1857) 330 et 351–2.

FRANCO SIMONE

La Notion d'Encyclopédie:
Élément caractéristique de la Renaissance française

L A PERSPECTIVE GÉNÉRALE DES études et des recherches sur
l'Humanisme et sur la Renaissance en France a changé pendant
les dernières années d'une façon qui ne pourrait être plus significa-
tive. Il est indéniable que, encore il y a une vingtaine d'années, les
préoccupations principales des critiques et des historiens étaient de
souligner la rupture ou la continuité entre la civilisation du Moyen
Age et celle de la Renaissance. Ensuite, cette tendance pour des
motifs assez compréhensibles a été remplacée par la volonté de
mettre en relief comment et dans quelle mesure la France de l'Humanisme et de la Renaissance est à l'origine de nombreuses caractéristiques fondamentales de la pensée moderne.[1] Ce n'est pas un
hasard si, en 1970, le prof. Eugenio Garin a libellé *De la renaissance
à l'âge des lumières*, une nouvelle série d'études et de recherches.[2] En
présentant son livre, l'historien a souligné que sa véritable intention
était justement celle d' 'attirer notre attention sur la continuité, bien
que dans la diversité, de quelques thèmes constants du xve au
xviiie siècle'.[3] On pourrait facilement faire remarquer que M.
Garin dans sa présentation pensait au xve siècle italien. Néanmoins,
on ne peut croire que la fonction médiatrice de la culture française
de la Renaissance, et tout particulièrement du 'libertinage érudit'
entre le xvie et le xviiie siècle, ait pû échapper à l'auteur de
l'important ouvrage sur *L'Educazione in Europa* (1957). Par ailleurs,
comment peut-on penser qu'une semblable perspective, si utile et
fructueuse, pouvait être amorcée et interprétée historiquement sans
avoir présent à l'esprit dans ses solutions fondamentales, déjà
acquises, le problème capital des rapports entre le Moyen Age et la
Renaissance?
Je suis convaincu que l'on peut éclairer et justifier l'ampleur des
études les plus récentes sur la Renaissance française seulement si
l'on a bien présent à l'esprit la fonction d'opposition vitale exercée
par la culture du Moyen Age sur la culture française du xve et du
xvie siècle. C'est ainsi que, pour démontrer jusqu'à quel point la
réaction provoquée par la présence active de la tradition médiévale
est indispensable pour comprendre les nouvelles idées de la Renais-

sance, j'ai choisi comme exemple typique et comme témoignage fondamental, l'histoire, riche et assez complexe, du mot et de la notion d'"Encyclopédie'. Je crois que cette histoire est utile pour éclairer les doutes encore nombreux qui entravent nos recherches. De même, je crois cette histoire indispensable pour confirmer que les auteurs français de la Renaissance ont trouvé de nouvelles solutions aux problèmes moraux et culturels qui ont été transmis et résolus, par les représentants les plus qualifiés du Moyen Age. En outre, je considère cette histoire nécessaire pour expliquer la fonction médiatrice des humanistes français entre la pensée italienne et l'Europe; enfin, je crois cette histoire très utile pour saisir l'aspect fondamental de l'Humanisme engagé, plus que jamais, dans l'effort qui lui appartient en propre, de 'laïciser', c'est à dire 'séculariser' ou, du moins, 'humaniser' les solutions médiévales de problèmes finalement interprétés selon les exigences d'une vie civile et concrète.

1. Pour bien comprendre toute la portée de l'effort que la culture française de l'Humanisme et de la Renaissance a manifesté en assimilant la notion d' 'Encyclopédie', il est indispensable, en premier lieu, de rappeler, même sommairement, comment les auteurs grecs et latins et, après eux, les auteurs du Moyen Age ont créé et utilisé cette notion.

A ce propos, il faut tout de suite remarquer que, pendant les dernières années, les études sur cet argument ont fait des progrès considérables. Les travaux de plusieurs éminents collègues nous ont donné une histoire suffisamment claire de l'évolution à travers les siècles de l'antiquité et du Moyen Age de la notion qui nous intéresse. En ce qui concerne la période gréco-latine nous sommes renseignés par les travaux de R. Collison[4] et de L.M.De Rijk;[5] pour les siècles de la patristique par H.I.Marrou;[6] pour Isidore de Séville par J.Fontaine;[7] pour les autres siècles du Moyen Age par M. de Gandillac et ses collaborateurs.[8] Je résumerai, donc, jusqu'au xiie siècle, je dirais même jusqu'à Saint Bonaventure, les résultats obtenus, en ayant soin de les intégrer dans un panorama plus vaste[9] que j'estime indispensable pour justifier les développements humanistes qui représentent l'objet principal de ma recherche.

Celle-ci, bien entendu, mettra volontairement de côté, même si elle est intéressante et importante, l'histoire des manuels encyclopédiques depuis l'antiquité jusqu'au *Didascalion* de Hugues de Saint-Victor, du *Speculum Maius* de Vincent de Beauvais (1264) au *Speculum universale* de Raoul Ardent et jusqu'à tous les ouvrages encyclopédiques des siècles suivants. Dans mon exposé une attention exclusive sera réservée à la notion d'*Encyclopédie* en tant qu'idéal éducatif qui, pendant des siècles a été adapté aux différentes exigences de l'évolution culturelle pour triompher finalement à l''Age des lumières' avec le *Discours préliminaire à l'Encyclopédie* de D'Alembert. Pour bien préciser dans quelle perspective j'entends me placer, je dirai en synthèse que mon intention est celle de répondre à la question suivante: que veut affirmer Rabelais quand, dans le chapitre xx du *Pantagruel*, il fait prononcer par Thaumaste l'éloge suivant du protagoniste: 'En quoy je vous puisse asseurer qu'il m'a ouvert le vrays puys et abisme de encyclopédie?'[10] De même, que veulent dire ses contemporains comme Budé ou ses successeurs comme Pierre de La Ramée, quand ils utilisent la même notion? A mon avis, dans l'évolution des recherches sur l'Humanisme et la Renaissance, la question ne peut plus rester sans réponse. Mais pour répondre je ne connais d'autre moyen que celui qui nous conseille de remonter à l'origine première de l'idée dont nous voulons préciser la signification qu'elle a acquise pendant les années de l'épanouissement de l'Humanisme français.

D'après les nombreux témoignages des spécialistes,[11] la culture grecque a réellement connu le rêve ou formulé l'espoir d'acquérir la science universelle. Il n'y a pas de doute que c'est, au moins, l'espoir qui a créé la notion. Toutefois, cette notion n'a pas été exprimée par le mot qui pourrait être, d'une certaine façon, à l'origine du terme français 'encyclopédie', mais par le mot πολυμαθία.[12] On se demande si les sophistes ont connu cet idéal encyclopédique et si Hippias en est le premier représentant. Evidemment, un idéal si élevé ne laissa pas indifférents Platon et Aristote, mais on peut être sûr que seulement chez leurs disciples il devint ce qui, à l'époque hellénistique, fut appelé ἐγκύκλιος παιδεία. Cette définition ne fut jamais un synonyme de πολυμαθία, puisque déjà au temps des premiers successeurs de Platon, par ce que nous dit Diogène Laërce,[13] pour Xénocrate, par exemple, et pour Héraclide le Pontique, elle signifiait seulement l'éducation normale. C'est à dire un cycle d'études propédeutiques dont le but n'était pas de fournir la totalité des connaissances humaines. Naturellement, conçue de la sorte, la notion de l'ἐγκύκλιος παιδεία réalisait le principe pédagogique de la *reductio artium ad philosophiam*. Ainsi elle était assimilée par la pensée grecque et transmise à la pensée latine par la formulation préparée par la culture hellénistique.

La première transformation importante de l'ἐγκύκλιος παιδεία a été réalisée dans la culture latine lorsque Cicéron et, à sa suite, Quintilien fondent l'éducation de l'orateur sur l'enseignement des arts libéraux classifiés dans le *trivium* et dans le *quadrivium*.[14] Ce principe nouveau—*reductio artium ad eloquentiam*—est affirmé clairement par Cicéron dans le *De oratore* 1,187.[15] Un siècle et demi plus tard, le même principe est repris par Quintilien (*Institutiones*, 1, 10, 1) lequel souhaite que l'élève soit instruit très tôt par les arts libéraux: 'ut efficiatur orbis ille doctrinae quem Graeci ἐγκυκλοπαιδείαν vocant'. J'ajouterai, pour mieux éclairer un problème complexe, que même à l'époque de Quintilien, ce principe pédagogique n'a pas encore une signification encyclopédique dans le sens moderne du mot.[16] Bien qu'il soit un catalogue des *artes liberales*, il ne représente pas encore une tentative pour rassembler, dans une organisation précise, la totalité du savoir scientifique. Le programme présente une partie encore trop limitée du grand patrimoine emprunté à la culture grecque et enrichi par la culture latine. Je répète que l'organisation latine des *artes liberales* plaidée par Cicéron et par Quintilien répond tout simplement à des exigences pédagogiques et non pas scientifiques.[17]

Ayant bien précisé ce point, restent cependant des témoignages qui ne peuvent pas être omis pour la signification qu'ils devront acquérir dans les développements successifs. Lorsque Varron dans ses *Disciplinarum libri* propose d'ajouter au système pédagogique des *artes liberales* la médecine et l'architecture[18] et lorsque Vitruve dans son *De architectura* précise le programme de l'enseignement qu'il définit '*encyclios disciplina*' en ajoutant le dessin, le droit et la philosophie aux matières du *trivium* et du *quadrivium*,[19] il me semble que, en modifiant de cette façon le schéma original, les deux auteurs révèlent leur intention de valoriser une discipline—l'architecture dans le cas de Vitruve. Ainsi, d'un côté, ils tendent à élargir en un sens encyclopédique la préparation de base et, d'un autre côté, à imposer la primauté d'une discipline différente de la philosophie, d'après ce que proposaient Platon et Aristote, ou différente de l'art oratoire, selon les règles imposées par Cicéron et Quintilien. Cette remarque est d'une très grande importance. Elle nous confirme que, déjà dans le monde classique, l'enseignement propédeutique était imposé par des préoccupations pratiques et que l'organisation des arts libéraux pouvait changer à l'intérieur—avec la prédominance de l'un ou de l'autre—et à l'extérieur avec l'apport d'autres disciplines que l'organisation primitive ne prévoyait pas. Donc, soit dans l'ἐγκύκλιος παιδεία des Grecs, soit dans l'*encyclios disciplina* des Latins deux possibilités étaient déjà présentes. La première défendait la rigidité du schéma, la deuxième en acceptait l'enrichissement. M. Etienne Gilson a justement remarqué: 'Les sept arts libéraux vont persister, à travers toute l'histoire de la culture occidentale, comme les marques propres de la civilisation latine; mais ils persisteront parce qu'on pourra indéfiniment les adapter à des fins nouvelles.'[20]

FRANCO SIMONE

2. La possibilité d'adapter à des buts nouveaux et à des niveaux divers l'organisation scolaire d'Athènes et de Rome fut utilisée de façon exemplaire lorsque le monde chrétien remplaça le monde païen. Tout comme le nouvel idéal culturel transforma lentement et péniblement le *vir bonus dicendi peritus* en *vir christianus dicendi peritus*, de même, l'organisation scolaire chrétienne dirigea vers un but nouveau l'étude des arts libéraux et elle imposa, surtout avec le *De doctrina christiana* de Saint Augustin, la *reductio artium ad Sacram Scripturam*. Celle-ci a été une transformation profonde de l'idéal classique qui pouvait être apportée seulement par un maître riche en expérience pédagogique tel que l'évêque d'Hippone. Mais cette transformation ne fut pas la seule solution pédagogique proposée par une civilisation riche en siècles différents et tous très originaux. La différence et l'originalité ont imposé à tel point des solutions différentes et même opposées que, pour bien comprendre les textes que j'ai intention de commenter, il me faut illustrer brièvement les quelques aspects d'une richesse qu'on ne peut jamais oublier.

Les penseurs chrétiens ne manifestèrent pas une réaction unanime de même qu'ils ne formulèrent pas une seule solution lorsqu'ils se trouvèrent devant le monde classique dont ils avaient parfaitement conscience d'être les héritiers légitimes.[21] Les réactions des Pères de l'Eglise vis-à-vis de l'héritage classique produisirent, selon les tempéraments de chacun et les circonstances historiques plusieurs solutions que l'on peut classer selon trois tendances précises. Il y a la solution qu'on pourrait appeler 'libérale' proposée et divulguée par les Pères grecs, lesquels étaient conscients de la grandeur de la pensée dont ils étaient les héritiers. Justin a interprété la certitude de tous les Pères grecs en soutenant que toute vérité, par définition, ne peut être que chrétienne.[22] Saint Ambroise résuma la notion avec une phrase très précise (*'omne verum a quocumque dicatur a Spiritu Sancto est'*); cette phrase sera reprise par Saint Thomas,[23] mais aussi par Pétrarque et par Erasme.[24] Cependant, il faut tout de suite ajouter que la solution, qui niait aux Chrétiens toute nécessité d'utiliser la pensée ancienne, eut autant d'importance. En se fondant sur l'enseignement de Saint Paul[25] l'idée selon laquelle *'scientia inflat'* eut de nombreux consentements. Par fidélité à cette idée, plusieurs penseurs exploitèrent toutes les occasions pour souligner l'exemple du Christ qui choisit, pour affirmer et répandre sa doctrine, des pêcheurs et non pas des savants. Cette idée eut, elle aussi, une grande renommée et fut diffusée au Moyen Age surtout par les mystiques comme Saint Bernard[26] et ses disciples. Mais elle sera encore utilisée, vers la fin de la Renaissance, par ceux qui, à la suite de Montaigne[27] et de Charron,[28] s'opposeront à l'érudition des pédants. Rousseau reprendra, encore, l'idée et même la formule biblique au moment (1751) d'écrire ses *Observations sur la réponse qui a été faite à son 'Discours sur les sciences et les arts.'*[29] Le contraste entre ces deux positions de la culture chrétienne— refus ou assimilation de la culture païenne—a été très net dès le début. Il fut si net qu'il devait engendrer une solution moyenne au cours de la formation d'une doctrine pédagogique chrétienne. Le traité *De doctrina christiana* de Saint Augustin représente, précisément, la solution qui, en tenant compte des exigences libérales et rigoristes, atteint un juste équilibre dans l'assimilation de la pensée ancienne par les penseurs chrétiens.[30] Ceux-ci, à la suite de l'évêque d'Hippone et de Saint Jérôme, acceptèrent pour la plupart la doctrine selon laquelle l'héritage ancien devait être accueilli par la pensée chrétienne, mais seulement après avoir fait un choix rigoureux dicté par le principe selon lequel 'prophani si quid bene dixerunt non aspernendum'.[31] S'appuyant sur ce principe, Saint Augustin dans le *De doctrina christiana* démontra clairement que la pensée chrétienne pouvait assimiler l'organisation pédagogique de l'ἐγκύκλιος παιδεία. Avec sa synthèse le penseur chrétien introduisit l'enseignement complet des arts libéraux, dans la pédagogie chrétienne, et il fut le premier à théoriser la *reductio artium ad Sacram Scripturam*. En transformant la *reductio artium ad eloquentiam*, qui avait été théorisée par Cicéron et Quintilien, Saint Augustin accepta, d'après une perspective chrétienne, l'organisation gréco-latine des *artes liberales*, et il utilisa ce *curriculum* scolaire non pas pour la formation de l'orateur, mais pour celle du chrétien lecteur studieux de la Bible.

Celle-ci fut la deuxième transformation capitale imposée par la direction pédagogique de l'ἐγκύκλιος παιδεία, après celle qui fut imposée par l'*encyclios disciplina* des Latins. Il n'est pas possible de reconnaître dans cette nouvelle transformation la présence active de la notion d'encyclopédie. Mais il est évident que la préoccupation des penseurs chrétiens était d'utiliser pour la formation du savant, les disciplines qui avaient été expérimentées par les classiques et qui pouvaient fournir une parfaite organisation propédeutique pour l'étude approfondie du texte sacré.

Pour répandre cette solution 'moyenne' du problème difficile des rapports entre la culture païenne et la culture chrétienne, les écrivains du Moyen Age et, après eux, toute la tradition, inventèrent quelques 'topoi' et différents symboles qui, ensuite, seront utilisés pour affirmer un principe tout à fait fondamental pour la culture occidentale. C'est ainsi que le thème de l''esclave égyptienne' sera un des premiers à se répandre pour affirmer que vis à vis du monde classique, les chrétiens se comporteront selon ce qu'enseigne un passage célèbre du *Deutéronome* (XXI, 10–13) où l'on parle de l'esclave que les Israélites ramenèrent de l'Egypte et qu'ils firent entrer dans leur maison après l'avoir lavée et parée. Ce thème (*Captiva gentilis*[32]) codifié par Saint Jérôme[33] arrive jusqu'à Boccace,[34] Coluccio Salutati[35] et Giovanni Dominici,[36] J. Gerson[37] et J. Raulin[38] en passant par Raban Maure[39] et Pierre Damien[40] et il sera répandu parmi les humanistes par les *Antibarbarorum libri* d'Erasme.[41] Un deuxième thème, celui que je définirai des 'vases d'Egypte' (*Spoliatio Aegyptiorum*)[42] aura une diffusion encore plus grande.

Même dans ce pas le point de départ est un texte biblique (*Exode*, XII, 35–36) où l'on rappelle que les Israélites, en fuyant l'Egypte, amenèrent avec eux les vases d'or qu'ils avaient pris aux païens. Les chrétiens feront la même chose avec le trésor de la culture classique. Ce conseil, avant d'être repris par Saint Augustin,[43] a été répandu par Origène, par Grégoire de Nysse[44] et, après, par la tradition la plus fidèle: Orose,[45] Cassiodore,[46] Alcuin;[47] de même que par les représentants de l'*Humanisme dévot*, jusqu'à Rollin, le recteur de l'Université de Paris qui résuma le thème, en 1694, de la façon suivante: 'Car si nous empruntons des écrivains profanes l'élégance des mots et tous les ornements du langage, ce ne sont là que comme ces vases précieux qu'il était permis de dérober aux Egyptiens sans crime, mais gardons-nous d'y verser le vin de l'erreur.'[48] Dans ce texte il est clair que la réserve finale de Rollin confirme que, même en pleine époque classique, lorsque l'encyclopédisme avait fait son chemin, l'enseignement pédagogique de Saint Augustin était présent chez les derniers représentants de l'*Humanisme dévot*. Encore au XVIIe siècle cet enseignement limitait le plus possible l'ornement des vases profanes dans le temple chrétien.

En vérité, les défenseurs de la '*vana curiositas*' furent toujours présents dans la tradition du Moyen Age. C'est à eux que l'on doit l'approfondissement du thème de Saint Jérôme 'qui se voit transporté devant le tribunal de Dieu pour son attachement aux lettres païennes'. Ce thème eut, à la différence des précédents, une très grande fortune iconographique—par exemple, Dürer[49]—et témoigne combien le problème qu'il voulait symboliser a été toujours actuel pendant tout le Moyen Age et la Renaissance.[50]

La grande fortune de la mythologie culturelle, telle qu'elle se manifesta dans les symboles et dans les thèmes du classicisme du Moyen Age et pendant l'Humanisme du XVe et du XVIe siècle, nous confirme l'actualité que le problème de l'assimilation de la culture classique eut pendant tous les siècles au cours desquels la pensée chrétienne se formait et s'exprimait. Par ailleurs, il est indispensable de bien préciser que, parmi toutes les solutions proposées et dif-

fusées par les symboles et les 'thèmes', celle de Saint Augustin acquit
la plus grande renommée puisqu'elle proposait, à l'intérieur de
l'organisation de l'enseignement, une organisation plus équilibrée,
capable de défendre l'importance et la complémentarité de chaque
discipline. Cette complémentarité et cet équilibre furent mis en
doute et, ensuite, bouleversés lorsque la *'Bataille des Sept Arts'* com-
mença, au XIII* siècle. La théologie ayant acquis sa propre autonomie, la *reductio artium ad Sacram Scripturam* se transforma en *reductio
artium ad Theologiam*. L'empire de la scolastique affirma la prédominance de la logique; cette prédominance marqua la rupture de
l'équilibre entre les arts du *trivium* et du *quadrivium*. A partir de ce
moment l'idéal classique de l'ἐγκύκλιος παιδεία changea profondément pour se préparer au développement imposé par les humanistes
auxquels nous pouvons, enfin, arriver avec l'indispensable information que j'ai fournie rapidement jusqu'à présent.

3. L'engagement civique des humanistes, l'effort de défendre
l'équilibre dans les arts du *trivium* et du *quadrivium*, le besoin de
chercher une nouvelle méthode capable de fournir une nouvelle
organisation à l'enseignement: tous ces aspects d'une crise confir-
ment que l'épanouissement de l'Humanisme était une crise avec des
valeurs positives. Cette crise marque, mieux que tout autre fait
historique—la chûte de Constantinople, la découverte de l'imprime-
rie, la découverte de l'Amérique—l'affirmation lente et difficile du
monde moderne à l'intérieur de la tradition vitale du Moyen Age.[51]

Si l'autonomie de la théologie brisa la construction rigide de Saint
Augustin, toute nouvelle discipline, qui s'affirma en dehors des arts
libéraux bien organisés, contribua au bouleversement progressif de
la construction et à sa transformation. Je suppose que la médecine
dut aussi manifester, comme la théologie, ses nécessités. Mal-
heureusement, les renseignements que j'ai pu réunir sur l'histoire de
la médecine sont encore insuffisants et je ne saurais confirmer par
les textes une situation historique très probable.[52] Au contraire, les
témoignages fournis par les juristes sont très nombreux. Avec le
grand prestige de l'école de Bologne et grâce au talent de Bartolo
da Sassoferrato, les juristes imposèrent la primauté de leur discipline. Alors, dans une perspective pédagogique bien précise, toutes
les disciplines furent soumises au droit (*reductio artium ad iurispru-
dentiam*).

Toutefois, la bataille soutenue par les humanistes avec les conseils
des auteurs grecs et latins fut plus difficile et plus longue. Elle fut
déclenchée par les humanistes non seulement pour combattre la
primauté de la logique, mais aussi pour imposer à l'intérieur des
disciplines libérales une autre primauté, celle de la rhétorique.[53]

FRANCO SIMONE

La nouvelle bataille qui avait été énergiquement amorcée par
Pétrarque sur deux fronts, l'un théologique, l'autre juridique, sut
utiliser encore une fois, l'enseignement de Saint Augustin, un
enseignement qui fut revu et repensé avec la sensibilité nouvelle
imposée par le nouveau sens de l'histoire qui, pour mieux préparer
l'avenir, identifiait les auteurs de l'antiquité avec les moyens fournis
par la philologie.

Ce n'est pas surprenant si l'Humanisme italien a engagé ses meilleurs représentants dans cette polémique contre la primauté de la
logique et, par conséquent, de la scolastique. Mais on ne doit pas
s'étonner non plus, si, en voulant remplacer l'organisation qu'impo-
sait la scolastique par une méthode nouvelle d'enseignement,
l'organisation des différentes disciplines a subi un profond changement dans l'intention de trouver un équilibre qui reflétât fidèlement
les exigences de la culture nouvelle. Cet effort fut mené à bien avec
une cohérence exemplaire pendant toutes les décennies qui vont de
Pétrarque, hostile aux Averroïstes, à Politien, défenseur du mécénat
des Médicis.[53a] Néanmoins, cet effort a été couronné par des succès
authentiques que l'on peut résumer par le retour de la primauté
classique de la rhétorique, par l'addition d'autres disciplines aux sept
traditionnelles et par la préparation d'une nouvelle méthode pour
organiser les différentes disciplines.

Enfin, on peut identifier cet effort avec la conscience historique
de l'Humanisme. Cette recherche d'une nouvelle organisation des
sciences représentait le meilleur témoignage du nouvel âge qui était
en train de préparer un nouveau schéma de l'histoire de la civilisation. Ce schéma, à partir de ce moment, reconnaîtra seulement trois
époques: l'époque ancienne, l'époque médiévale, l'époque moderne,
appelée, cette dernière, 'la Renaissance'.[54]

Avec cette nouvelle interprétation historique et historiographique,
l'organisation des disciplines fut, enfin, conçue selon une large
ouverture qui interprète l'ἐγκύκλιος παιδεία d'après une perspective différente de la tradition et qui d'une certaine façon précède
l'encyclopédisme moderne. Politien marque une étape importante
dans cette évolution de l'Humanisme. A ce propos, il est un texte
fondamental tiré de la *Miscellanea prima* et qui doit être cité ici en
entier. Dans le chapitre que l'humaniste intitule: *quam multa poetarum
interpretibus legenda*, le poète dit textuellement:

. . . qui poetarum interpretationem suscipit, eum non solum
(quod dicitur) ad Aristophanis lucernam, sed etiam ad Clean-
this oportet lucubrasse. Nec prospiciendae autem philosophorum modo familiae, sed et iureconsultorum et medicorum
item et dialecticorum, et quicumque doctrinae illum orbem

faciunt, quae vocamus encyclia, sed et philologorum quoque omnium. Nec prospiciendae tantum, verum introspiciendae magis, neque (quod dicitur) ab limine ac vestibulo salutandae, sed arcessendae potius in penetralia et in intimam familiaritatem.[55]

Un programme de travail comme celui-ci est fondamental pour notre propos et cela pour les motifs suivants. En premier lieu, parce que Politien nous donne la preuve de bien avoir présent à l'esprit la conception de l' *encyclios disciplina*, si ce n'est de l'ἐγκύκλιος παιδεία. En second lieu, parce que cette organisation des *artes liberales* ne se borne pas seulement aux disciplines du *trivium* et du *quadrivium*, mais tient compte aussi des autres disciplines. C'est le cas, parmi les premières, du droit et de la médecine—une concession importante—et ensuite des différentes spécialisations philologiques. En troisième lieu, ce programme est fondamental, parce qu'on n'exige pas une préparation si grande—vraiment encyclopédique— ni pour l'étude du texte sacré, ni pour la théologie, ni pour le droit. Il me semble essentiel que, pendant le bouleversement progressif dont la conséquence est l'enrichissement de la construction du *trivium* et du *quadrivium*, la primauté soit enfin reconnue à la critique littéraire en adoptant un principe propédeutique, qui, pour les Grecs, était au service de la philosophie, de l'éloquence pour les Latins, de l'étude de la Bible et de la théologie pendant le Moyen Age. En ayant présent à l'esprit cette succession historique que je crois bien marquée par les textes cités jusqu'ici, il est aisé de constater que l'histoire du mot et de la notion d''Encyclopédie' fera des progrès rapides parmi les humanistes italiens grâce, surtout, au Politien.[56]

Est-ce que les humanistes français connurent ce texte fondamental de la philologie florentine? L'évolution de la notion d''Encyclopédie', diffusée par les élèves et les successeurs du Politien, comment fut-elle assimilée par la culture française? La quatrième partie de cette étude se propose de donner une réponse à ces deux questions.

4. On doit encore étudier la fortune de Politien en France. Et ce n'est pas la première fois que je fais cette remarque. Cependant, à mon avis, le chercheur qui entreprendra un travail si important, devra commencer par un épisode que je crois plus que jamais significatif.[57]

Guillaume Budé fait son deuxième voyage en Italie en 1505. De retour de Rome, le grand humaniste s'arrête à Florence pour examiner le manuscrit des Pandectes dites 'pisanes' et il est reçu par Pietro Ricci, nommé le Crinito, qui fut précisément un élève fidèle de Politien. A ce moment-là l'auteur des *Stanze per la Giostra* était mort depuis neuf ans, l'année même de la mort de Pic de la Mirandole et de l'entrée à Florence de Charles VIII. Mais le souvenir du grand maître est si présent que Budé parla beaucoup avec le Crinito de l'incomparable enseignement de l'humaniste. Après de longues discussions, lorsqu'arriva l'heure du départ, voilà que les deux humanistes parlent des dernières notes, laissées inédites par Politien. Budé observe avec une immense curiosité les précieux manuscrits et tâche de les interpréter. C'est alors qu'il s'aperçoit, avec étonnement, que Politien était si jaloux de ses écrits qu'il écrivait ses observations *ut a nullo legi possent*. Tel était le talent de l'humaniste florentin (*'Sic erat ingenium hominis!'*). Voilà les jugements sévères que G. Budé formulait dans les *Annotationes in Pandectas*[58] et, encore, dans le *De asse*.[59] Mais ce sont là des jugements qui, en dehors de cet épisode, cachent à peine l'admiration pour l'humaniste florentin.[60] Celui-ci, en effet, transmettait, à l'auteur du *De philologia* et du *De studio litterarum bene et commode instituendo* (1523), la conception de l'*encyclia* qui sera reprise par Budé dans toutes ses œuvres et pour la première fois, justement, dans les *Annotationes in Pandectas* de 1508.

En vérité, les humanistes français essayèrent très tôt de savoir apprécier l'originalité de l'enseignement de Politien.[61] Ils n'ignorèrent pas que le nouvel idéal de l'ἐγκυκλοπαιδεία avait été déjà approfondi par Giorgio Valla d'après les idées de Leonardo Bruni.[62] Ils durent connaître le *Panepistemon* (1492)[63] de Politien et les textes qui en dérivèrent, c'est-à-dire: ceux de Raffaele da Volterra (1506: *Commentarii Urbani*), ceux de Paolo Cortese (1510: *De cardinalatu*),[64] ainsi que ceux de Ghiberti,[65] de Bembo[66] et de Celio Calcagnini.[67] Les œuvres du Crinito furent imprimées à Paris dans les premières décennies du XVIe siècle.[68] Cependant, la pensée même de Politien fut répandue en France, non seulement avec les sept éditions des œuvres préparées par Sébastien Gryphius entre 1528 et 1550.[69] En effet, le 15 août 1511, Josse Bade fit connaître dans une édition collective la *Centuria prima, Lamia,* et *Panepistemon*;[70] une année plus tard, le 15 mai 1512, le même éditeur publia les œuvres complètes du Florentin en deux parties avec la *Centuria prima, Lamia* et *Panepistemon*, c'est-à-dire les trois textes où les idées critiques de l'humaniste sont le mieux exprimées.[71] Enfin, en 1519, Josse Bade prépara une autre édition des œuvres complètes de Politien avec le commentaire de François du Bois.[72] Pour les éditions des œuvres particulières, qu'il me soit permis de rappeler, au moins, les six éditions des *Orationes* publiées par Bade entre 1505 et 1519.[73]

Toutefois, parmi les éditions signalées, parmi tant de lecteurs et de commentateurs, c'est à Nicolas Bérauld que revient, à juste titre, le mérite d'avoir été en France le disciple le plus fidèle de Politien.

Cet humaniste d'Orléans n'est pas un inconnu. Les recherches de Louis Delaruelle[74] nous ont donné des renseignements assez précis sur l'élève d'Aléandre,[75] sur l'ami d'Erasme qui lui dédia le *De conscribendis litteris* (1522),[76] sur le collaborateur de Louis de Berquin, sur le défenseur convaincu de l'étude de la langue grecque, sur le juriste estimé par G. Budé qui, dans l'entourage d' Etienne Porcher, participa avec conviction à la defense du droit et de son histoire.[77] C'est en 1512 que notre humaniste s'engage avec Louis de Berquin à préparer l'édition des œuvres complètes de Politien. Mais nous pouvons être sûrs que, depuis plusieurs années, il était déjà un lecteur fidèle de l'humaniste florentin. En tout cas, le résultat qui me paraît le plus éclatant d'une admirable fidélité n'est pas l'édition de 1512, mais le commentaire d'une œuvre tout à fait singulière de Politien, le *Rusticus*.[78] Bérauld avait choisi ce texte pour un cours de leçons parisiennes qu'il publia probablement dans l'année 1514.[79] C'est précisément dans la *praelectio* de ce cours parisien que l'humaniste orléanais nous assure avoir parfaitement assimilé l'enseignement du maître florentin et, surtout, avoir compris dans quel sens il entendait utiliser et diffuser la notion d'*encyclopédie*. Une page de cette *praelectio* me semble très importante. Nicolas Bérauld nous confirme qu'il reste fidèle à l'esprit et à la lettre de l'enseignement de Cicéron et de Quintilien. Son discours est la preuve qu'il a compris comment Politien entendait utiliser l'enseignement classique et l'appliquer de son mieux pour donner la base indispensable à une nouvelle théorie de la critique littéraire. L'humaniste orléanais développe la pensée de Politien dans sa plus profonde originalité quand il démontre la nécessité de connaître toutes les disciplines pour bien commenter un texte classique; quand il reproche aux maîtres d'oublier 'philosophorum familias [et] iurisconsultorum et medicorum item et dialecticorum et quicumque doctrinae orbem illum faciunt quae vocamus encyclia, sed et philologorum quoque omnium';[80] quand il souligne les défauts de tous les maîtres qui s'arrêtent à l'enseignement de la grammaire sans comprendre que n'importe quel texte poétique exige, pour être interprété, la connaissance de toutes les disciplines.[81] Nicolas Bérauld résume ainsi sa pensée qui est exactement celle de Politien: 'Alia item permulta quae quamvis exilia plerisque videantur, adeo tamen sunt necessaria ut sine illis nulla omnino ars suum possit officium explere, nedum poetica quae non una qualibet arte constat sed totam *encyclopediam* absolvit ac complectitur.'[82]

Ce texte nous confirme que la notion d'encyclopédie a été parfaitement comprise et assimilée par Nicolas Bérauld. Une telle assimilation se produit dans les années même pendant lesquelles la

FRANCO SIMONE

classification des sciences était un problème d'une grande actualité
que les humanistes français continuaient à discuter.[83] Comment
s'étonner, donc, qu'une des caractéristiques les plus originales de
la pensée de Politien ait eu en France une grande diffusion? Toutefois, il n'y a pas de doute que, plus que tout autre, Budé et Rabelais,
par leur ouverture d'esprit et par leur connaissance directe des
auteurs italiens, étaient à même de comprendre et d'utiliser, encore
mieux que leurs propres contemporains, une conception qui est, à
juste titre, une gloire de l'humaniste florentin.

Guillaume Budé, dans les *Annotationes in Pandectas* démontre dans
plusieurs endroits connaître et méditer sur la conception traditionnelle de l'ἐγκυκλοπαιδεία.[84] Cependant, seulement dans le *De asse*,
notre humaniste réussira à exprimer avec originalité la notion
désormais traditionnelle. En vérité, le juriste, dans sa première
œuvre, considère l'héritage classique comme un *corpus* encyclopédique capable de fournir aux doctes une préparation globale. Au
contraire, par la digression dédiée à notre conception dans le *De
asse*, il démontre clairement vouloir défendre la *reductio artium ad
philosophiam*, c'est à dire être un commentateur fidèle de cette pensée
classique qu'il admire dans les synthèses fournies par Cicéron et par
Quintilien et qu'il adapte, par nécessité, aux exigences de la culture
de son temps. Voici le texte fondamental du *De asse*:

Dico, igitur, eos qui ad philosophiam hodie studium suum
collaturi sunt, sapientius esse facturos, si non a rudimentis
literarum statim ad eam transierint, sed velut gnari ac strenui
indagatores, per omnia omnisque disciplinae monumenta sapientiam vestigaverint, non ut ii solent hodie qui sapientiam
quaestui habere instituentes, temporis compendia sequuntur
doctrinae dispendio, quae numerosissima pars est studentium in
omni genere disciplinae. Ut enim aves in locum arduum sub-
volaturae, non solo protinus eum locum rectis lineis petunt, sed
volatu verticoso eo commodius evadunt et facilius: sic animus
humanus ad contemplationem sapientiae melius per cochleam
iustae disciplinae scandere et intelligentius potest, quam si
protinus ab intimo genere doctrinae ad summum genus dicendi
compendio evaderet, scansilem disciplinarum seriem transiliens.
Hoc modo Solomon encyclopaedia gyro lustrasse se omnia
ingeniorum significat, ut ego quidem interpretor nosque hortari
videtur ut per omnia philosophiae secularis et priscae dogmata,
vestigia sapientia si qua sunt, ut certe multa sunt, colligere non
gravemur ac lucum saltumque opacum et abstrusum, in quo
ipsa stabulatur magistra, iusta et perpeti indagine accurataque
cingamus.[85]

246

D'après ce texte il est clair que G. Budé en 1515 était convaincu de la valeur propédeutique des arts libéraux, et aussi qu'il prônait leur enrichissement par tous les moyens et d'après une connaissance encyclopédique. Cette idée est suggérée à notre humaniste par l'exemple de Salomon qu'aucun auteur et aucune œuvre ne pouvait ignorer pour sa formation intellectuelle. De toute façon, Budé nous explique encore plus clairement ce qu'il entendait par 'encyclopédie' dans un autre texte de l'*Institution du prince* où l'humaniste, pour mieux illustrer la nécessité d'unir le savoir à la science, fait appel aux disciplines

> desquelles les bonnes lettres font profession, faisans d'icelles une perfection des arts liberaux et sciences politiques qu'on appelle en grec, *Encyclopedia* qui veult autant dire (pour le declairer briesvement) erudition circulaire, ayans les dictes sciences et disciplines connexité mutuelle et coherence de doctrine et affinité d'estude qui ne se doibt ny peult bonnement separer ny destruire par distinction de faculté ou profession ... Pource que toutes les sciences s'entretiennent comme font les parties d'un cercle qui n'a ny commencement ny fin.[86]

Pour ma part, il n'y a pas de doutes que Budé était certain de la nécessité de défendre une organisation rigoureuse des disciplines propédeutiques. En outre, il pensait que cette organisation dépendait de la complémentarité de toutes les disciplines réunies dans un cercle au centre duquel se trouve l'homme, et que la formation morale de l'homme est conçue selon le principe de l'union de la science avec le savoir. C'est ce que pense Budé aux alentours de 1532, l'année de la publication du *Pantagruel*. Cependant je suis sûr que notre humaniste n'a pas les mêmes idées, quelques années plus tard, lorsqu'il écrira le *De transitu hellenismi ad Christianismum*[87] (1535). Les événements politiques, les premiers symptômes des futures guerres de religion, l'évolution de la pensée de l'humaniste, laquelle était déjà évidente dans plusieurs pages du *De studio*, poussent l'ami d'Erasme à revenir, de façon toujours plus fidèle, aux principes pédagogiques que le Hollandais avait déjà expliqués dans les *Antibarbarorum libri* et ensuite, pour ce qui concerne notre problème, dans l'*Enchiridion militis christiani*, dans la *Methodus* et dans la *Ratio verae theologiae*.[88]

Erasme s'orienta définitivement vers l'étude de la Bible, après les douloureuses expériences parisiennes et grâce aux conseils de John Colet et Thomas More. Dans les œuvres qu'il avait écrites, reprises et transformées entre 1519 et 1523, l'humaniste hollandais avait clairement affirmé une méthode pédagogique qui, tout en ayant présents à l'esprit les progrès de la philologie, renouvelait la conception de Saint Augustin de la *reductio artium ad Sacram Scripturam*. Ce renouvellement était essentiel et non seulement parce qu'il était conçu selon la nouvelle interprétation humaniste de l'histoire. Le retour au principe de Saint Augustin était motivé par une position polémique contre deux siècles de primauté théologique. Ce retour démontrait, en outre, ne pas tenir compte, si ce n'est partiellement, du principe exprimé par l'humanisme italien qui enrichissait l'enseignement propédeutique par des disciplines qui n'étaient pas comprises dans le *trivium* et le *quadrivium* et qui semblait les orienter vers un idéal *laïc* de la culture.

Budé, dans les dernières années de son activité, entre Politien et Erasme, choisit ce dernier, et même de façon décisive. Ce choix est capital parce qu'il nous permet de comprendre, à travers les nombreuses difficultés et plusieurs doutes de cette période, l'évolution de la notion d'*encyclopédie*, l'organisation pédagogique des différentes disciplines et la recherche d'une nouvelle méthode.

Peut-on, maintenant, dire que, lorsque Rabelais composa la célèbre lettre de Gargantua à Pantagruel, celui qui le 30 novembre 1532 écrivit une lettre aussi célèbre à Erasme[89] fit le même choix que Budé? En d'autres termes, peut-on croire que 'le vray puys et abisme de encyclopedie' découvert par Thaumaste chez Pantagruel exprime la même conception culturelle assimilée, approfondie et répandue par Budé?

Avec cette question je n'entends pas discuter les sources du huitième chapître de *Pantagruel*. On connaît tous les noms auxquels on a fait appel, toutes les dépendances, ainsi que les nombreuses interprétations souvent contradictoires.[90] On a même formulé l'hypothèse selon laquelle le ton du chapître ne s'éloigne point de l'atmosphère grotesque de toute l'œuvre, et l'un des témoignages les plus éloquents de la conscience historique de la Renaissance française doit être interprété comme une satire dirigée contre l'érudition définie *a priori* comme pédantisme. A mon avis, la discussion a atteint un point ferme et sûr lorsque Charles Béné a admirablement démontré tout ce que la deuxième partie du chapître—où sont énumérées les disciplines conseillées à Pantagruel—doit au *curriculum* propédeutique que Erasme a emprunté au *De doctrina christiana*.[91] Naturellement, je n'entre pas dans les détails parce que je suis pressé d'arriver droit à mon but. En effet, je veux faire remarquer la différence importante qui existe entre la source érasmienne et le passage célèbre de Rabelais. Personne mieux que Charles Béné n'a observé avec précision cette différence. Le critique bien renseigné souligne que: 1°) la conception érasmienne, exposée dans la *Methodus* en 1516 et dans la *Ratio verae theologiae* en 1518, dépend du *De doctrina christiana* de Saint Augustin; 2°) que la lettre de Rabelais correspond à la découverte, de la part du romancier, de la doctrine pédagogique de l'humaniste hollandais; 3°) que la lettre coïncide avec la lettre du 30 novembre, envoyée à Erasme et qu'elle exprime le même enthousiasme; 4°) qu'on peut dire, comme conséquence logique de ce rapport étroit, que Rabelais répète, mot à mot, le programme érasmien. A la fin de cette série de données sûres, M. Béné, auquel nous devons un éclaircissement si important, conclut: 'Rabelais oublie, dans son enthousiasme qu'Erasme visait à former un exégète et un orateur chrétien et non un futur chevalier'.[92]

Mais sommes-nous sûrs qu'il s'agit d'un oubli ? Pouvons-nous croire que Rabelais se soit trompé sur un problème si capital qui représentait toute la conception de la culture humaniste et le nouvel idéal vers lequel cette culture devait être dirigée ? Pouvons-nous imaginer qu'il a voulu éviter de s'engager à fond ?

En citant plusieurs textes, et en me posant plusieurs questions je crois être arrivé à un autre moment important de l'histoire de la notion d'*encyclopédie*. Aux alentours de 1532 Budé fait sa plus grande concession en direction d'une sécularisation de notre notion, c'est à dire, une libéralisation de la pédagogie des humanistes. Quelques années plus tard il rebroussera chemin en suivant fidèlement l'enseignement érasmien. Pendant la même période, Rabelais, de son côté, et de façon autoritaire, poussé peut-être par les tentatives italiennes, accepte le programme de l'éducation encyclopédique proposée par Erasme; mais il ne destine pas ce programme à la formation du savant chrétien, mais à celle du chevalier parfait: 'Somme que je voye ung abysme de science, car doresenavant que tu deviens homme et te fais grand, il te fauldra issir de ceste tranquillité et repos d'estude et apprendre la chevalerie et les armes pour défendre ma maison et noz amys secourir en tous leurs affaires contre les assaulx des malfaisans . . . .'[93] Ce sont là des intentions généreuses, mais ces desseins et un idéal pareil n'avaient rien en commun avec l'idéal du *miles Christi*, ainsi que le proposait Erasme dans l'*Enchiridion militis christiani*. Ils étaient peut-être plus proches de l'*Institution du prince* de Budé.[94] Mais, dans l'état actuel des recherches on ne saurait dire avec précision l'importance de cette œuvre en tant que témoignage d'un moment précis de l'évolution de la pensée de l'humaniste.

D'après les textes qu'on a comparés, je ne crois pas me tromper quand j'affirme que, si le pas qu'a franchi Rabelais en direction de la sécularisation de l'idée d'*encyclopédie* n'était pas autorisé par ses maîtres en pédagogie humaniste, il est certain que ce pas était imposé par l'évolution d'une civilisation qui s'apprêtait à entreprendre des guerres fratricides à cause de la libéralisation des esprits et des consciences; je donnerai un exemple, peu connu mais non moins significatif pour autant, du climat culturel de cette période précise. Au mois de septembre 1530, un italien du Frioule, Giulio Camillo Delminio arrive à la cour de François 1er.[95] L'arrivée de cet Italien chez le père des lettres intrigue et éveille la curiosité, car il se propose de répondre aux exigences culturelles du roi et de ses courtisans de façon complètement nouvelle; on a comme preuve de ce propos une lettre bien précise d'Andrea Alciato.[96] Giulio Camillo Delminio, qui était conscient du besoin que les Français avaient d'apprendre les langues anciennes et modernes pour pouvoir accéder plus facilement à une culture encyclopédique, déclare qu'il possède une méthode d'enseignement si nouvelle qu'elle permet à tout le monde de parler latin et grec en quelques mois.[97] Comme il était sûr de sa méthode, Giulio Camillo Delminio s'adresse directement à François 1er et s'engage à le faire parler comme Démosthène et Cicéron en six mois s'il accepte de se soumettre une heure par jour à cette nouvelle méthode d'enseignement. On peut facilement imaginer que l'Italien demande une grosse somme d'argent comme récompense pour un miracle pareil. La stupeur, l'incertitude et la méfiance, à la cour, sont à l'ordre du jour. Ils se demandent tous si Delminio est un charlatan, un imposteur, un érudit infortuné.[98] Dolet, qui avait connu Delminio à Padoue, leur répond que le vrai but de cet Italien c'est de *'reges emungere nummis'*.[99] Bonaventure Des Périers tirera le conte 88 de cet épisode où il parle 'du fanfaron qui promet au roi de faire parler son âne au terme des ans'.[100] Mais il me semble clair que cet épisode dépasse la simple dénonciation d'un fait historique lié à un texte littéraire. D'ailleurs, ce n'est pas seulement un autre épisode de la fortune de l'italianisme ou de l'anti-italianisme en France au xvie siècle.

Dans la réalité, l'aventure de Giulio Camillo Delminio nous propose un témoignage inattendu d'un plus grand désir de connaître et d'apprendre. Ce désir suggérait à toute une génération, du roi à ses courtisans, des humanistes engagés dans la recherche d'une nouvelle méthode aux défenseurs de l'autonomie de chaque discipline, d'élargir l'horizon du savoir.[101] Mais, surtout, il permettait de chercher des voies nouvelles pour acquérir des connaissances plus grandes et plus sûres.[102] Ainsi l'idéal encyclopédique enrichissait la méthode pédagogique. Ce n'est pas un hasard, si, vers la moitié du siècle, Louise Labé conseillait aux dames lyonnaises l'étude des 'sciences vertueuses . . . pour acquerir cet honneur que les lettres et sciences ont acoutumé porter aux personnes qui les suivent'.[103] A peu près dans les même années, Du Bellay[104] et Pontus de Tyard[105] utilisent la notion d'encyclopédie, préoccupés l'un et l'autre d'imposer la nouvelle méthode pédagogique seule capable de bien comprendre et commenter les auteurs pour avancer dans la connaissance de la vérité philosophique. Donc, on peut être sûr que, à ce moment de l'évolution historique de notre notion, la sécularisation de l'idéal encyclopédique est acceptée par la majorité des humanistes français.

Toutefois, le grand mérite d'avoir formulé de la façon la plus claire possible la 'sécularisation' de la notion d'encyclopédie revient à Pierre de La Ramée. A juste titre, le discours célèbre prononcé par notre humaniste à l'Université de Paris dans l'année 1550[106] doit être mis en évidence non seulement pour sa défense d'une méthode d'enseignement, mais surtout pour sa préoccupation fondamentale de souligner l'importance que la notion encyclopédique doit avoir dans une conception générale d'une nouvelle pédagogie. Sensible aux exigences de la vie pratique, Pierre de La Ramée est hostile aux vaines disputes scolastiques et désireux de contribuer, de toutes ses forces, à la formation d'une classe nouvelle d'intellectuels, capables de soutenir la monarchie française.

Il n'a pas de doutes à suivre la tendance que le cercle rigoureux des disciplines voulait destiner à la préparation d'un savoir nouveau 'utile et profitable aux citoyens et aux républiques'. Sa lutte fut difficile, dure et généreusement payée par la mort; mais elle n'a pas été inutile.

Pierre de La Ramée proposait aux jeunes une conception 'civile' de la culture, en partant du principe que les études devaient être basées sur l'idéal de l'union entre la philosophie et l'éloquence. Cet idéal n'était pas contraire à la tradition, puisque ce grand maître voulait justement faire appel à cette tradition gallicane, en plein essor à ce moment, grâce à la conception vitale du *reditus regni Francorum ad stirpem Karoli*.[107] Cependant Pierre de La Ramée voulait enrichir avec l'aide de la tradition sa méthode d'enseignement. Cette méthode jugeait complémentaires l'enseignement scientifique et celui de la rhétorique et de la dialectique, et avec le même processus elle mettait à côté de Virgile, d'Ovide et de Lucrèce, les *Naturales quaestiones* de Sénèque et l'*Historia naturalis* de Pline. De cette façon l'humaniste unissait la doctrine à l'éloquence et faisait parcourir à l'élève tout le système des arts pour lui donner une formation complète qui fait de l'élève un homme complet, le vrai citoyen d'un monde conquis et dominé par le cœur et la raison. C'est à ce moment d'une longue évolution historique que l'idéal encyclopédique résume, encore une fois, une méthode d'enseignement. Fine fleur de la culture, cet idéal devient la vie consciente de l'esprit. Voici comment dans un texte fondamental Pierre de La Ramée formule sa pensée la plus originale:

> Grammaticam, rhetoricam, philosophiamque totam in schola relinquimus et regularum jam nihil egemus, puritatem orationis et ornatum, rationis acumen, numerandi, metiendi peritiam, coeli et mundi universi notitiam, ad animum formandum, erudiendum, componendum, ornandum, perspiciendum conjungimus et copulamus. Hanc animi perfectionem rhetores eloquentiam perfectam, philosophi melius et verius philosophiam perfectam ex perfecta artium explicatione, ex perfecta artium exercitatione, nonnulli completum quendam velut orbem doctrinae ἐγκυκλοπαιδίαν vocant. Haec, judices, disciplina mea est; quae si vestro judicio magnis poenis suppliciisque digna est, omnes in me cruciatus convertite, discipulos meos delicti vel erroris animadversione liberate.[108]

L'analyse de ce texte démontre de la manière la plus convaincante avec quelle rapidité les idées pédagogiques ont évolué en France dans les années centrales du xvie siècle. Après quelques décennies seulement, on peut constater combien on s'est éloigné des idées d'Erasme, de Budé, même de Rabelais. Probablement c'est la rapidité de cette évolution qui a échappé à M. Marcel Françon dans l'analyse qu'il nous a donnée de quelques uns des textes cités par moi-même.[109]

Il n'y a pas de doute que la pensée pédagogique française procède rapidement parce que l'évolution de la culture s'impose avec la même rapidité. Cette culture, pendant les années des guerres de religion, opposa les factions l'une contre l'autre de façon très nette. C'est alors que la voix de Montaigne et celle de Charron s'opposèrent à celle de Ramus et à celle de Bodin. Encore une fois, comme au temps de Platon et d'Aristote, la vieille dispute entre l'Humanisme et l'Encyclopédisme fut de nouveau actuelle. L'idéal d'une science complète s'opposa à l'idéal de l'Humanisme qui tendait à une perfection harmonieuse faite d'abstention et de choix. La *vana curiositas* des mystiques du Moyen Age fut défendue, avant Rousseau, par le scepticisme de ceux qui ne croyèrent pas à l'assimilation rapide des livres, mais à un choix bien précis des maîtres et des œuvres. La querelle continua au xviie siècle, marquée par l'ironie des Baroques qui isolèrent le pédant et le poète crotté. La même querelle parvint jusqu'à Descartes et dans le *Discours* bien connu trouva un point de repère pour une autre classification des sciences à laquelle contribua, avec beaucoup de succès, Francis Bacon qui est une source du *Discours* de D'Alembert.

. . .

Le champ que j'ai à peine exploré est vaste et très riche en perspectives nouvelles. En regardant le chemin parcouru, j'ai moi-même l'impression d'avoir laissé de côté des aspects importants d'une histoire sur laquelle il faudra revenir après avoir récolté d'autres témoignages et fixé des rapports pour le moment encore insoupçonnés. Au moins, à la fin de cet exposé, je voudrais avoir suffisamment éclairé ce que j'entends quand j'affirme que la notion d'encyclopédie caractérise la culture française de la Renaissance. Si jamais mon lecteur a été convaincu, voici la dernière conclusion que je voudrais lui soumettre: pour comprendre les modernes dans leur originalité, il faut comprendre les anciens dans leur nouveauté. C'est une vérité que j'ai apprise moi-même pendant cette analyse rapide de l'évolution de la notion d'encyclopédie dans la culture française de la Renaissance.

NOTES

1 Je crois avoir prouvé comment une telle perspective peut être utile pour mettre en valeur l'actualité de la mythographie du xvie siècle dans un article sur *Historiographie et Mythographie dans la culture française du XVIe siècle* publié dans le volume collectif dédié à l'*Humanisme lyonnais au XVIe siècle* (Grenoble 1974) 125–48.
2 E. Garin, *Dal Rinascimento all'Illuminismo; studi e ricerche*, Pisa, coll. 'Saggi di varia umanità', n. 11, 1970.
3 Ibid., Avvertenza, 19.
4 R. Collison, *Encyclopaedias: their history throughout the Ages* (London 1964).
5 L. M. De Rijk, 'ἐγκύκλιος παιδεία a study of its original meaning', *Vivarium* iii (1965) 24–93.
6 H. I. Marrou, *Saint Augustin et la fin de la culture antique* (Paris 1938) idem, *Histoire de l'éducation dans l'antiquité* (Paris 1948); idem, *Retractatio* (Paris 1949); idem, 'Les arts libéraux dans l'antiquité classique' dans *Arts libéraux et Philosophie au Moyen Age. Actes du quatrième Congrès international de Philosophie médiévale* (Montréal-Paris 1969) 5–27.
7 J. Fontaine, *Isidore de Séville et la culture classique dans l'Espagne visigothique* (Paris 1959).
8 M. de Gandillac, J. Fontaine, J. Châtillon, M. Lemoine, J. Gründel, P. Michaud-Quantin, *La Pensée encyclopédique au Moyen Age* (Neuchâtel 1966). Voir, aussi, R. Giacone, 'Sul concetto di "Enciclopedia" nel pensiero classico e medioevale: nota introduttiva' *Rivista di Studi classici* xxi, 1 (genn. 1973) 1–7; idem, 'Arti liberali e classificazione delle scienze: l'esempio di Boezio e Cassiodoro' *Aevum*, xlviii, 1 (1974) 58–72; G. Federici-Vescovini, 'La "perspectiva" nell'enciclopedia del sapere medioevale' *Vivarium*, vi, 1 (maggio 1968) 35–45.

9 Cf. F. Simone, 'La "reductio artium ad Sacram Scripturam" quale espressione dell'Umanesimo medioevale fino al sec. xII' *Convivium* (1949) 887–927; T. Gregory, 'La "reductio artium ad theologiam" come fondamento della pedagogia medioevale' dans B. Nardi, *Il pensiero pedagogico nel Medio Evo* (Florence 1956) 279–301.

10 Rabelais, *Pantagruel*. Introduction et présentation de V.-L. Saulnier; texte établi et annoté par P. Michel, Paris, Le Club du meilleur livre (1962) 134.

11 Qu'il me soit permis de renvoyer pour ce paragraphe aux pages exhaustives de Marrou, *Saint Augustin*, 211–35: *Les sept arts libéraux*, l' ἐγκύκλιος παιδεία *et l'encyclopédisme*. On trouvera une synthèse de ces pages dans *Histoire de l'éducation dans l'antiquité* (Paris 1948) 244–5. Tous les textes ont été repris par notre auteur dans son essai cit. sur 'Les arts libéraux dans l'antiquité classique'.

12 Marrou, *Saint Augustin*, 230.

13 Diogene Laërce, 2, 79 cit. par Marrou, op. cit., 221.

14 Cf. A. Gwynn, R*oman Education from Cicero to Quintilian* (Oxford 1926), 79–122.

15 *De oratore*, 1, 187: 'Omnia fere quae sunt conclusa nunc artibus dispersa et dissipata quondam fuerunt: ut in *musicis* numeri et voces et modi; in *geometria* liniamenta, formae, intervalla, magnitudines; in *astrologia* caeli conversio, ortus, obitus motusque siderum; in *grammaticis* poetarum pertractatio, historiarum cognitio, verborum interpretatio, pronuntiandi quidam sonus; in hac denique ipsa *ratione dicendi* excogitare, ornare, disponere, meminisse . . .'.

16 Marrou, *Histoire de l'éducation dans l'antiquité*. 244: 'On trouve, en effet, chez les écrivains d'époque hellénistique et romaine, de nombreuses allusion à ce terme, qu'il ne faudrait pas transcrire littéralement par "encyclopédie", notion toute moderne . . . qui ne correspond nullement à l'expression antique. 'Encyclopédie' évoque pour nous un savoir universel; si élastiques qu'aient pu être ses limites, l'ἐγκύκλιος παιδεία n'a jamais prétendu embrasser la totalité du savoir humain.'

17 Marrou, 'Les arts libéraux dans l'antiquité classique', op. cit., 23: 'Comme à l'époque hellénistique, le programme des arts libéraux apparaît à l'époque impériale comme la formation préliminaire que doit recevoir quiconque veut atteindre aux divers niveaux de culture supérieure.'

18 Marrou, *Saint Augustin*, 226–7.

19 Ibid., 222 rappelle le texte du *De architectura*, 1, 1(3–10).

20 E. Gilson, *La Philosophie au Moyen Age* (Paris 1962²) 175.

21 Cf. F. Simone, 'La "reductio artium ad Sacram Scripturam"', op. cit., 887–93.

22 Justin, *IIᵃ Apologia*, 13, 2–4; P.G., t. 5, col. 465B (éd. Picard (Paris 1904) 177)).

23 Cf. E. Gilson (*L'Esprit de la philosophie médiévale* (Paris 1944²) 24) qui rappelle ces textes avec le commentaire suivant: 'Il y a là un trait constant de l'esprit chrétien qui échappe à beaucoup de ses interprètes.'

24 Cf. C. Béné, *Erasme et Cicéron* dans *Colloquia Erasmiana Turonensia* (Paris 1972) vol. II, 574.

25 1 *Cor.*, VIII, 1: 'Scientia inflat, caritas vero aedificat'.

26 S. Bernard, *In Cant. Cant., Sermo XXXVI*, art. 2–3; P.L., t. 183, col.

967 (trad. M.-M. Davy (Paris 1945) 46): 'Car il y en a qui ne veulent savoir que pour cette fin, connaître pour connaître: c'est là une curiosité honteuse'). Mais il ne faut pas oublier Pierre Damien, *Epist.* lib. VIII, ep. 8 (P.L. CXLIV, 476: 'Aucupatur nimirum scientiam quae inflat; charitatem autem quae aedificat non miratur'. Cf. J. Gonsette, *Pierre Damien et la culture profane* (Louvain 1956) 8–15.

27 Montaigne, *Essais*, III, 12 (*De la Phisionomie*); éd. Thibaudet, 1000: 'J'ay pris plaisir de voir en quelque lieu des hommes, par devotion, faire vœu d'ignorance, comme de chasteté, de pauvreté, de pénitence.' Cf. F. Simone, *Il pensiero francese del Rinascimento* (Milan 1964) 9.

28 P. Charron, *De la sagesse*, éd. Paris 1783; chap. LVII du livre I: *De la science*, 282–4.

29 J. J. Rousseau, *Observations sur la réponse qui a été faite à son "Discours"* dans *Œuvres complètes*, éd. Gagnebin-Raymond, vol. III, 45. Le texte continue de la façon suivante: 'Et dans les instructions qu'il donnait à ses disciples, on ne voit pas un mot d'étude ni de science, si ce n'est pour marquer le mépris qu'il faisait de tout cela. Après la mort de Jésus-Christ, douze pauvres pêcheurs et artisans entreprirent d'instruire et de convertir le monde.' Une filière bien précise développe le 'topos' '*non oratores sed piscatores*' jusqu'à Rousseau. Voici, parmi beaucoup d'autres témoignages, le texte offert par Grégoire de Tours: 'Sed quid timeo rusticitatem meam, cum dominus Redemptor et deus noster ad distruendam mundanae sapientae vanitatem non oratores sed piscatores, nec philosophos sed rusticos praelegit?' Ce texte dans E. Auerbach, *Mimesis*, traduction italienne (Turin 1956) 98.

30 Cf. Marrou, *Saint Augustin*, troisième partie: *Doctrina christiana*, 329–540.

31 Saint Augustin, *De doctrina christiana*, II, 18; P.L., t. 34, col. 49; Cf. F. Simone, 'La "reductio artium ad Sacram Scripturam"', op. cit., 890–1.

32 Cf. E. A. Quain, 'The Medieval *Accessus ad Auctores*' *Traditio*, III (1945) 224.

33 Saint Jérôme, 'Epistola ad Magnum oratorem urbis Romae' dans *Lettres*, éd. Labourt (Paris 1949) t. III; 210–1.

34 Boccaccio, *Commento alla 'Divina Commedia'*, éd. Guerri (Bari 1918) vol. I, 250.

35 C. Salutati, Ep. du 25 janvier 1405 (*Vidi nuper*) à Giovanni di Samminiato dans *Epistolario*, éd. Novati, lib. XIV, n° XXIII, vol. IV¹, 189–90.

36 G. Dominici, *Lucula noctis*, éd. R. Coulon (Paris 1908) 65.

37 J. Gerson, 'Secunda lectio contra vanam curiositatem' dans *Opera omnia*, éd. Du Pin, t. I, 99.

38 J. Rollin, *Sermo LX* dans *Sermonum quadragesimalium pars prima, Opera omnia* (Anvers 1612) t. II, 372.

39 Rabanus Maurus, *De clericorum institutione,* III, 18; P.L. 107, col. 396.

40 P. Damiani, *De perfectione monachorum*, cap. XI, P.L. 145, coll. 306–7.

41 Erasme, *Antibarbarorum libri*, éd. Hyma, 313.

42 Cf. Quain, art. cit., 223.

43 Saint Augustin, *De doctrina christiana*, 2, 11; P.L., t. 34, col. 42 et suiv. Cf. Quain, *art. cit.*, 224: 'The universal acceptance of the *De doctrina christiana* in the Middle Ages would have made this passage the *locus classicus*.'

FRANCO SIMONE

44 Les textes de l'époque des Pères ont été signalés par Marrou (*Saint Augustin*, 393).
45 Orose, *Historiarum adversus paganos libri VII*, 7, cap. 39.
46 Cassiodore, *De institutione divinarum litterarum,* cap. 28; P.L.,t. 70, col. 1142.
47 Alcuin, *Epistola CCCVII,* M.G.H., *Epistolae,* t, IV, 470.
48 L'importance de ce texte et de la tradition qu'il résume n'a pas échappé à Sainte-Beuve (*Causeries du Lundi*, éd. Garnier, t. VI, 265).
49 Cf. E. Panofsky, *The Life and Art of Albrecht Dürer*, 1955² (traduction italienne Milano, 1967, 201–3).
50 Cf. Erasme, *Lettre* à G. Budé du 22 déc. 1518 dans *Opus Epistolarum*, éd. Allen, t. I, n⁰ 906 (*La Correspondance d'Erasme et de G. Budé* par M.M. de la Garanderie (Paris 1967) 176).
51 Cf. E. Garin, 'Cultura filosofica toscana e veneta nel quattrocento' dans *L'età nuova. Ricerche di storia della cultura dal XII al XVI secolo* (Naples 1969) 330: 'Non si tratta, come a volte il tono di certi documenti potrebbe far credere, di eleganti virtuosismi oratori, un po' sofistici, volti a tradurre pettegolezzi universitari, e gelosie ed ambizioni di facoltà. E' la messa a fuoco di uno squilibrio, e la ricerca di un equilibrio nuovo fra le varie scienze; è un tentativo di riorganizzare in quadri diversi l'enciclopedia del sapere, stabilendo un rapporto più adeguato fra le varie zone dell'attività e della ricerca. Qualcosa di simile era accaduto già fra il XII e il XIII secolo, quando era scoppiata una prima violenta battaglia fra le "arti"; ma ora la crisi del sapere e della sua sistemazione è più acuta, e si traduce nella elasticità delle articolazioni delle discipline e dei loro nessi, tanto maggiore quanto minore è la forza di una tradizione.'
52 W. P. D. Wightman, *The Emergence of Scientific Medicine* (Edinburgh 1971) 39–71: 'The Nature of the medical Renaissance'.
53 Cf. C. Vasoli, *La dialettica e la retorica dell'Umanesimo. 'Invenzione' e 'Metodo' nella cultura del XV e XVI secolo* (Milan 1968). Fondamental pour notre argument le chap. I: '"Antichi" contro "Moderni"', 9–27.
53a Cf. E. Garin, *L'educazione in Europa* (Bari 1957) 127–37: 'Scuole e maestri italiani'; idem, *L'Umanesimo civile* (Bari 1952) chap. II: 'La vita civile', 51–102.
54 Cf. F. Simone, *Storia della Storiografia Letteraria Francese* (Turin 1969) 22–3.
55 A. Politien, *Opera*, Lugduni, I (1539) 517 et suiv. (éd. Bâle, 229). Le texte a été signalé et commenté, pour la première fois à ma connaissance, par E. Garin ('L'ambiente del Poliziano' dans *La cultura filosofica del Rinascimento italiano* (Florence 1961) 335).
56 L'histoire de l'assimilation, lente mais sûre, de cette idée de Politien dans la culture italienne de la Renaissance a été esquissée par V. Cian ('Contributo alla storia dell'enciclopedismo nell'età della Rinascita: la "Methodus Studiorum" del card. Pietro Bembo' dans *Miscellanea di Studi storici in onore di Giovanni Sforza* (Turin 1923) 289–330), qui, à la suite de plusieurs textes de l'humaniste florentin (300–7) cite les témoignages de Vespasiano da Bisticci, de Sadolet et de Bembo sans oublier Longueil et Budé. Cf., aussi, A. Scaglione, 'The Humanist as Scholar and Politian's Conception of the "Grammaticus"' dans *Studies in the Renaissance*, VIII (1962) 61. Ici l'A. nous rappelle un texte oublié de B. Platina, *Victorini Feltrensis vita* dans Vairani, *Cremonensium monumenta Romae extantia* (Rome 1778) où la notion

256

d'ἐγκύκλιος παιδεία est déjà appliquée à Vittorino da Feltre; A. Scaglione signale un des plus anciens exemples de l'assimilation de la notion gréco-latine d'encyclopédie dans un texte de Boccace (*Genealogiae*, XIV, 7).

57 Cf. F. Simone, 'La componente fiorentina nella formazione dell'Umanesimo francese' dans *Umanesimo, Rinascimento, Barocco in Francia* (Milan 1968) 30–1; V. Branca, 'L'autografo dell'ultima opera del Poliziano' dans *Atti del quinto congresso internazionale di Bibliofili* (Venise 1967) 55–6.

58 G. Budé, *Annotationes in Pandectas*, éd. Gryphe (Lyon 1546) 178: 'Cum aliquando apud Petrum Crinitum, cuius nunc liber de honesta disciplina aliique suavissimi in manibus habentur, inter contrectandos nonnullos eius libros in quaternionem incidimus manu Politiani scriptum: in quo annotationes pauculae erant, consulta, ut videbatur, obscuritate congestae, ut si forte interciderent, a nullo legi possent. Sic enim erat ingenium hominis, pleraeque tamen frigidae scrupulositatis et contemnendae. Has cum celeri lectione per Criniti facilitatem saltuatim percurrere nobis licuisset (strati enim fraenatique equi ad vestibulum nos expectabant et ille me amicitiae causa ad mansionem primam deducturus erat) unum tantum et alterum locum quae ad hoc nostrum institutum pertinerent, memoriae mandavimus.' Le premier à signaler l'importance historique de ce texte a été L. Delaruelle: *Guillaume Budé: les origines, les débuts, les idées maîtresses* (Paris 1907) 82.

59 Budé, *De asse*, éd. Gryphe (Lyon 1550) à propos de la notion d' ἐντελέχεια 33: 'A Graecis, igitur, neotericis "*entelechiae*" interpretatio Ciceroni criminose obiecta est, idque meritissimo: cuius defensionem Politianus ad sui magis ostentationem suscepisse mihi videtur, quam diluendi criminis fiduciam habuisse'. Il passo non è sfuggito a E. Garin ("*Ενδελέχεια* e *ἐντελέχεια* nelle discussioni umanistiche' dans *Atene e Roma*, V, 3 (1937) 5–15); 511: 'In his autem carminibus intelligendis quoties quamque luculentis erroribus Politianus lapsus sit ex sequentibus apparebit, ut nisi Politiani stylum agnoscerem Politiani epistolam esse omnino negaturus fuerim.'

60 Ibid., 46: 'Angelus Politianus vir egregie doctus'; 510: 'Angelus Politianus vir memoria nostra utraque lingua apprime doctus.'

61 F. Joukovsky, *La gloire dans la poésie française et néolatine du XVIe siècle* (Geneva 1969) 64: 'Les artistes du quattrocento avaient lutté pour que leurs professions fussent admises parmi les arts libéraux. De même que Cellini déclare qu'un sculpteur doit parfaitement connaître différentes sciences, de même les artistes français de la Renaissance s'efforcent de mettre en valeur les éléments de leur art: Jean Pélerin dans le *De artificiali perspectiva* (1505), Delorme dans *Le Premier tome de l'Architecture* ... insistent sur les connaissances mathématiques nécessaires à leur profession.'

62 L. Bruni, 'De studiis et litteris (1423–1424)' dans *Humanistisch—philosophische Schriften*, éd. H. Baron (Leipzig 1928) 169 et suiv.; le texte en traduction italienne chez E. Garin, *Il pensiero pedagogico dell' Umanesimo* (Florence 1958) 167–9. Cf. H. Baron, *The Crisis of the early Italian Renaissance* (Princeton 1955) vol. I, 356; vol. II, 613–4; D. Hay, *The Italian Renaissance in its Historical Background* (Cambridge 1962) 137 (traduction italienne Florence, 1966, 154).

FRANCO SIMONE

63 *Praelectio cui titulus Panepistemon*, leçon d'ouverture de l'année
scolaire 1490–91 du cours sur *l'Ethique à Nicomaque* d'Aristote imprimée à Florence par Antonio Miscomini le 21 février 1492. Cf.
R. Sabbadini, *Il metodo degli Umanisti* (Florence 1920) 37: 'Egli [le
Politien] traccia ivi una laboriosissima e minutissima enciclopedia dello
scibile umano.' Pour ce texte cf. I. Maïer, 'Un inédit de Politien: la
classification des "Arts"' dans *BHR* t. XXII (1960) 338–55.
Il ne faut pas oublier son succès immédiat. Avant 1500 il fut publié
encore en 1496 à Brescia, en 1497 à Venise et, naturellement, dans
les deux éditions des *Opera* de 1498 (Venise) et 1499 (Florence). Sur
l'importance de ce texte dans l'évolution de la pensée de Politien cf.
V. Juren, 'Politien et la théorie des arts figuratifs', *BHR* XXXVII, 1
(1975) 131–8.
64 Cf. C. Dionisotti, *Gli Umanisti e il Volgare fra Quattro e Cinquecento*
(Florence 1968) chap. IV. Cf. le commentaire d'A. Scaglione dans
Romance Philology, XXII, 1 (août 1969) 121: 'Due uomini di simile
formazione e carriera [R. Maffei et P. Cortese] ... produssero simil-
mente due fra i maggiori tentativi di esprimere l'ideale umanistico
(sancito dall'alta autorità del Poliziano) di una 'encyclopaideia'. Il
più illustre precedente immediato ne era stato quello di Giorgio
Valla, più che il piuttosto schematico *Panepistemon* del
Poliziano.'
65 Cf. A. Chastel, *Art et Humanisme à Florence au temps de Laurent le
Magnifique* (Paris 1961) 97: 'Au début de son troisième livre, Ghiberti
soutient que l'artiste doit connaître tous les "arts libéraux"; il énumère
ainsi une foule impressionnante de disciplines ... On a là une
formule toute faite, une règle d'or empruntée à Vitruve; au début de
son traité d'architecture, celui-ci avait posé la nécessité d'un savoir
encyclopédique pour son héros, l'*Architecte*, de la même manière que
Cicéron l'avait fait pour le sien, l'*Orateur*'.
66 P. Bembo, *Methodus studiorum*; texte publié par V. Cian à la suite de
son art. cit., 323–30.
67 C. Calcagnini, *Opera aliquot* (Bâle 1544) 23: 'Nemo ergo physica sine
logicis, nemo logica sine mathematicis, nemo omnia sine orationis
praesidio assequatur. Quare belle hanc armoniam nonnulli
ἐγκυκλοπαιδείαν dixere'. Ce texte a été mis en valeur par E. Garin,
L'educazione in Europa (Bari 1957) 180; idem, 'Motivi della cultura
filosofica ferrarese nel Rinascimento' dans *La cultura filosofica del
Rinascimento italiano* (Florence 1961) 430–1.
68 Cf. *Imprimeurs et libraires parisiens du XVIe siècle*. Ouvrage publié
d'après les manuscrits de Philippe Renouard (Paris 1969) tome II: *De
honesta disciplina*, éd. Josse Bade, 1508 (n° 90 = n° 55 dans *Inventaire
chronologique des éditions parisiennes du XVIe siècle*, vol. I, Paris, 1972);
1511 (n° 158 = n° 73 dans *Inventaire cit.*, mais avec la date: 1510);
1513 (n° 221); *De poetis latinis*, éd. Josse Bade, 1508 (n° 90); 1511
(n° 158); 1513 (n° 221); *Poematum libri II*, éd. Josse Bade, 1508
(n° 90); 1511 (n° 158); 1513 (n° 221).
69 Baudrier, *Bibliographie lyonnaise*, VIIIe série (Paris 1964) 46, éd. 1528,
t. primus: *Epistolarum lib. XII*; *Miscellaneorum centuriam unam complectens*. Aucun exemplaire des tomes 2 et 3 n'a pu être retrouvé; 68,
éd. 1533; t. premier avec les mêmes œuvres de l'éd. 1528; t. secundus:
Complectens ea quae ex graeco in latinum convertit; t. tertius: *Praelectiones,*

258

orationes, epigrammata complectens; 89, éd. 1536; 100, éd. 1537, 122, éd. 1539; 199, éd. 1546; 236, éd. 1550.

70 Cf. *Annotationes doctorum virorum in grammaticos, oratores, poetas, philosophos, theologos et leges* avec une épître de Josse Bade à Michael Hummelberg. V. *Imprimeurs et libraires parisiens du XVIe siècle* (Paris 1969) vol. 11, 76, n° 145. N'oublions pas que, dès 1505, Josse Bade avait publié un texte de Politien dans son édition des *Satyrae* de Perse. Cf. *Imprimeurs et libraires parisiens*, vol. 11, 37, n° 40 et 50, n° 76.

71 Ibid., vol. 11, 97, n° 195. La première partie publie comme préface une lettre de Josse Bade à Nicolas Bérauld; la seconde une lettre de Josse Bade à Louis de Berquin.

72 Ibid., vol. 11, 182, n° 428. Cette nouvelle édition contient en plus de l'édition de 1512 la traduction latine des *Epigrammata graeca* par Jacques Toussain. La présente édition, spécialement dédiée à Louis Ruzé, regroupe les différentes épîtres de Josse Bade relative à la publication de textes de Politien.

73 Ibid., t. 11, 34, n° 31: Beroaldo, Poliziano, Barbaro, Maino, *Orationes, praelectiones, praefationes et quaedam mythicae historiae*. Les *Orationes* de Politien (ff. LXI à LXIIII) sont adressées au pape Alexandre VI et à Alphonse 11, roi de Naples et de Sicile; éd. 1508, 54, n° 85; ed. 1511, 77, n° 149; éd. 1513, 105, n° 213; éd. 1515, 133, n° 278; éd. 1516, 144, édition douteuse; éd. 1519, 172, n° 399.

74 L. Delaruelle, 'Notes sur les deux Bérauld et quelques uns de leurs contemporains' dans *Bulletin Soc. Orléanais*, VII (1878) 242–47; 'Notes biographiques sur Nicolas Bérauld' suivie d'une bibliographie de ses œuvres et de ses publications' *Revue des Bibliothèques*, XII (1902) 420–45; 'Etudes sur l'Humanisme français: Nicolas Bérauld' *Musée Belge*, XIII (1909), 253–312; 'Notes complémentaires sur deux humanistes', *Revue du seizième siècle* (1928) 311–23.

75 J. Paquier, *L'Humanisme et la Réforme: Jérôme Aléandre de sa naissance à la fin de son séjour à Brindes (1480–1529)* (Paris 1900) 47.

76 Erasme, *Opus epistolarum*, éd. Allen, vol. III, 503.

77 D. R. Kelley, 'The Historical School of Roman Law' dans *Foundations of modern Historical Scholarship: Language, Law and History in the French Renaissance* (New York 1970) chap IV, 87–115.

78 Ce commentaire a été bien connu et utilisé par Isidoro Del Lungo. Cf. A. Poliziano, *Prose volgari inedite e poesie latine e greche edite e inedite* (Florence 1867) vol. 11, XXXII et 305–32.

79 Angeli Politiani, *Sylva cui titulus est 'Rusticus' cum docta elegantissimaque Nicolai Beraldi interpretatione*, Parisiis, éd. Regnault Chaudière, s.d. (1514?). Exemplaire de la BN de Paris, *Rés*, m Yc 709. Dans la lettre préface à Germain de Ganay, Bérauld fait l'éloge le plus convaincu de son auteur: 'Hoc unum adfirmare posse videtur Politianum cum antiquis non contendisse modo, sed etiam multos veterum praecessisse. Sive maximam exactissimamque utriusque linguae diligentiam ac peritiam, sive egregia eius monumenta prosa ac versa oratione scripta intueri et ad Critolai (quod aiunt) staterem appendere libeat.'

80 *Nicolai Beraldi Praelectio in Angeli Politiani 'Rusticum' habita Lutetiae in Tricorenzi Gymnazio* dans op. cit.

81 Ibid., 'Quod utinam nostri magistri (non de theologis loquor), utinam, inquam, intelligerent triviales nugivenduli et imperiti isti credule iuventutis impostores qui cum vix ultra primas grammatices

radices processerint (ut Fabius ait) eam tamen sibi scientie persua-
sionem induerunt, ut illotis pedibus ad poetarum sacra protinus
irrumpere non vereantur et optimorum probatissimorumque
poetarum interpretationem suscipere, nihil ad rem tantam adferentes
praeter inverecundam frontem et scholastica quaedam nugalia
indigna quae vel in triviis recipiantur.'

82 Ibid., 4v.

83 Voir, entre autres, l'œuvre suivante de Charles Bovelles: *Libellus de
constitutione et utilitate artium humanarum in quo et applicatio sermo-
cinalium ad rerum disciplinas atque imprimis dialecticae edocetur* (1506). A.
Renaudet (*Préréforme et Humanisme*, op. cit., 495) rappelle que dans ce
livre Bovelles 's'efforcait d'y classifier les sciences et d'en définir
l'objet et les principes'. Sur le problème de la classification des
sciences et son actualité cf. P. O. Kristeller, 'The modern System of
the Arts' *JHI*, xii (1951) 496–528; xiii (1952) 17–45.

84 G. Budé, *Annotationes in Pandectas* dans *Opera omnia*, éd. 1557,
réimpression Gregg International Publishers Limited (1969²) 5:
'Haec est illa encyclopaedia de qua Fabius' (*De oratore*, 1, 10, 1); 177:
'Architecturam omnium disciplinarum cognitione constare et (quod
maxime quis miretur) legum etiam et iuris nonnulla peritia, Vitruvius
libro primo (*De architectura*, 1, 1) persuadere contendit. Ne autem
mirum videatur nonnullis, posse naturam humanam tantum
numerum doctrinarum addiscere et memoria complecti, animadver-
tendum omnes disciplinarum inter se coniunctionem rerum et
communicationem habere, unde encyclopaedia dicta, quasi orbiculata
disciplinarum serie, veluti ductus quidam scientiae ex multis disciplinis consertus et aptus, de qua nos alibi diximus'; 211: 'Latina enim
patet philosophia, cum pedissequis suis comitata orbem illum
doctrinarum complectitur, qui encyclopaedia dicitur, ut alibi
vidimus.' Cf. D. R. Kelley, op. cit., 64: 'This ideal had ancient roots,
of course, especially in Cicero's view of the liberal arts and in the
'encyclopedia' of Quintilian and Vitruvius; but more directly, it was
a combination of the art of grammar according to the famous
tradition of Poliziano and the art of rhetoric according to the notori-
ous views of Valla'. Je signale avec plaisir cette confirmation de
D. R. Kelley qui dans la première rédaction de son travail était
beaucoup moins sûr de l'influence de Politien sur Budé. Cf.
'Guillaume Budé and the First Historical School of Law', *The American
Historical Review*, lxxii, 3 (avril 1967), 814.

85 G. Budé, *De asse*, éd. Gryphius (Lyon 1550) 739–40.

86 Budé, *De l'institution du prince*, (éd. Paris 1547) réimpression Gregg
Press Limited (1966) 88.

87 Dans cette œuvre qui témoigne de la dernière évolution de la pensée
de notre humaniste, il y a au moins deux textes qui nous assurent de sa
nouvelle façon de concevoir la notion d'encyclopédie. Cf. *De transitu
hellenismi ad Christianismum*. Texte traduit, accompagné d'index et
présenté pour la première fois en français par M. Lebel, Sherbrooke,
Canada, 1973, 238 v.: 'quodnam autem alioqui dignum erit operae
pretium disciplinae orbicularis, quam encyclopaediam Graeci
vocant, per tot annos aetatis decursae florentissimae, si senectuti
fortasse amoenum praebitura est, animi tantum causa, non etiam
animae diversorium? Nec veteres eadem opera (ut inquit ille

[= Perse]) 'avias mihi de pulmone revellet'? Atqui nulli erit usui memorabili, nisi gradum nobis factura est ad studia altiora, sanctiora atque salubriora.' Par ce texte, il est clair que, à un moment important de son activité érudite, Budé reprend et valorise la conception médiévale de la *vana curiositas* pour défendre la *reductio ad Sacram Scripturam*, Voir, aussi, à la p. 240v un texte qui répète la même idée: 'Ex illa encyclopaedia sylva nihil praeter grandem legitur. Ad cereale studium transeundum quo ager domini confitus est.'

88 Pour cette originalité de la pensée d'Erasme, je ne fais que résumer rapidement ce qui a été très bien expliqué par Charles Béné, *Erasme et Saint Augustin ou Influence de Saint Augustin sur l'Humanisme d'Erasme* (Geneva 1969). Cf. surtout, dans le livre second, la deuxième section, 127–88: *Etude de l'* '*Enchiridion militis christiani*'.

89 Rabelais, Lettre (*Georgius ab Armeniaco*) à Erasme écrite de Lyon. Cf. *Œuvres complètes*, éd. P. Jourda (Paris 1962) vol. II, 497–500.

90 G. J. Brault, '"Ung abysme de science": on the Interpretation of Gargantua's Letter to Pantagruel' *BHR*, t. XXVIII (1966) 615–32.

91 Charles Béné, 'Erasme et le chapitre VIII du premier "Pantagruel" ' *Paedagogica Historica*, I (1961) 39–66; texte repris dans *Rabelais*, herausgegeben von A. Buck (Darmstadt 1973) 315–43. Dans la réédition du texte on fait état des observations de M. A. Screech dans *BHR*, XXV, 2 (1963) 477–85; de G. Mombello dans *Studi Francesi* (1962) 332–3; de M. Françon, 'Autour de la lettre de Gargantua', éd. cit., 178–9; de G. J. Brault, art. cit., 616–7.

92 Ibid., 65 (nouv. éd. 342).

93 Rabelais, *Lettre de Gargantua à Pantagruel*, ed. cit., 75, 169–75.

94 Le rapport entre Rabelais et Budé a été déjà souligné par L. Sainéan, *La langue de Rabelais* (Paris 1922) vol. I, 9 et vol. II, 58.

95 Pour cet épisode bien significatif cf. L. Sozzi, *Les contes de Bonaventure Des Périers. Contribution à l'étude de la nouvelle française de la Renaissance* (Turin 1964) 197–200; idem, 'La polémique anti-italienne en France au XVIᵉ siècle' *Atti della Accademia delle Scienze di Torino*, vol. 106 (1971–2), 136–40.

96 Cf. G. L. Barni, *Le lettere di Andrea Alciato giureconsulto* (Florence 1953), 112–3.

97 Cf. A. Alciato, *Lettera (Subverebar)* del 3 sett. 1530 à Francesco Calvo dans éd. cit., 112: 'Accepi et in aulam venisse Julium quendam Camillum a Foro Julii doctum hominem, qui Regi obtulerit brevissimo tempore, puta mense, facturum se ut Rex tam eleganter graece et latine, prosa et verso sermone dicere possit, quam Demosthenes et Cicero et Virgilius aut Homerus, dum horam diurnam illi Rex solus praestare operam velit. Nolle enim ea arcana cuiquam inferiori a Rege patefieri; et nec id quidem gratis, sed reditum annuum duorum millium aureorum in sacerdotiis pro mercede petere. Persuasit constantia vultus ipsi Regi: bis interfuit docenti, emunxitque ille sexcentos aureos et dimissus est. Vereor ne in fabulam res transeat.'

98 Cf. E. V. Telle, *L'Erasmianus sive Ciceronianus d'Etienne Dolet* (Geneva 1974) 21–2.

99 E. Dolet, *In Italum quendam* dans *Carminum libri quatuor* (Lyon 1538) I, 37–8; Cf. Sozzi, 'La polémique anti-italienne', op. cit., 139; Telle, op. cit., 21: 'Le jugement de l'Orléanais sur Giulio Camillo devait être teinté de jalousie'.

100 Cf. Sozzi, *Les Contes de B. Des Périers*, 197–201.
101 Cf. F. Secret, 'Les cheminements de la kabbale à la Renaissance: le Théâtre du Monde de Giulio Camillo Delminio et son influence', *Rivista critica di storia della filosofia* xiv (1959) 418–36; F. A. Yates, *The Art of Memory* (London 1966) 129–59; F. Secret, 'Un témoignage oublié de Giulio Camillo Delminio sur la Renaissance en France' *BHR*, t. xxxiv, 2 (1972) 276–8.
102 Cf. N. W. Gilbert, *Renaissance Concepts of Method* (New York 1960).
103 L. Labé, *Lettre à Mademoiselle Clémence de Bourges* du 24 juillet 1555 dans *Opere poetiche*, éd. E. De Michelis (Florence 1955) 16.
104 Du Bellay, *La Deffence et illustration de la langue françoyse*, i, x; éd. Chamard (1948) 58–9: 'Quand aux autres parties de literature et ce rond de sciences que les Grecz ont nommé *Encyclopedie*, j'en ay touché au commencement une partie de ce que m'en semble.' Dans le chap. v Du Bellay avait déjà témoigné d'avoir parfaitement assimilé la notion d'encyclopédie selon la plus fidèle tradition classique; cf. éd. cit., p. 33: 'Or ceste faculté de parler ainsi de toutes choses ne se peut acquerir que par l'intelligence parfaite des Sciences, les queles ont été premierement traitées par les Grecz et puis par les Romains imitateurs d'iceux. Il fault donques necessairement que ces deux langues soient entendues de celuy qui veut acquerir cete copie et richesse d'invention, premiere et principale piece du harnoys de l'orateur.'
105 Pontus de Tyard, *Œuvres: Le Solitaire premier*, éd. S. Baridon (Geneva 1950) 4, 84–92: 'Toutesfois ny la peur de telles empesches, ny encor la cognoissance que j'ay de mon insuffisance . . . ont jamais peu me commander avec assez d'imperiosité, pour faire que les lettres, tant en respect des sciences particulieres que de la spherique Enciclopedie et plus haute imagination, ne m'ayent appellé à leur service . . .'. Sur l'utilisation de la notion d'encyclopédie par Pontus de Tyard cf. K. M. Hall, *Pontus De Tyard and his 'Discours Philosophiques'* (Oxford 1963) 56–7 et 172–6.
106 *Petri Rami pro philosophica Parisiensis Academiae disciplina oratio* dans *Collectaneae Praefationes, Epistolae, Orationes* (Parisiis, apud Dionysium Vallensem, 1577) 309–401. Ce texte a déjà été valorisé dans toute son importance par E. Garin, *Il metodo e il programma di Ramo* dans *L'Educazione in Europa* (Bari 1957) 183–7.
107 Cf. F. Simone, Introduction à *Culture et Politique en France à l'époque de l'Humanisme et de la Renaissance* (Turin 1974).
108 P. de la Ramée, *Oratio pro philosophica disciplina*, éd. cit., 342.
109 M. Françon, 'Encyclopédie et culture générale' dans '*Aquila: Chestnut Hill Studies in Modern Languages and Literatures*', vol. ii (The Hague 1973) 230–43.

INDEX

Mercator, Gérard, *see* Kremer
Mercury, 8, 173
Mersenne, 180, 181, 182, 184n
Mesmes, Henri de, 195
Mesmes, Jean-Pierre de, 92n, 93n
Mesnard, P., 231n, 232n
Mettayer, 148n
Meurer, Wolfgang, 89, 92n
Michaud-Quantin, P., 253n
Michel, Alain, 47n, 48n, 49n, 50, 51n
Michel, P., 254n
Migrodius, 197
Milone, Pro, 49n
Minerva, 26, 68n
Minotaur, 101
Miscomini, Antonio, 258n
Mizault, Antoine, 148n, 150n, 195, 197, 202, 210n
Molière, 166
Molinet, 230n
Mombello, G., 261n
Monantheuil, Henri de, 117, 121, 147n
Monluc, Jean de, 217
Montaigne, Michel de, 5, 17, 20n, 43, 47n, 51n, 69n, 100, 156–69, 172, 179, 182n, 189, 191, 193n, 238, 252, 255n
Montdoré, Pierre de (Montaureus), 137, 138, 195, 196, 206n
Montpellier, 72
More, Sir Thomas, 159, 219, 247
Morel, Féderic, 204–5, 211n
Morel, Thierry, 52, 55, 56, 58
Morphos, Panos Paul, 49n
Morvilliers, J. de, 217
Moses, 97, 99, 223
Mouchy, Antoine de (Antonius de Mocharis), 50n
Munster, 216, 231n
Muret, M.-A. de, 4, 9, 16–17, 18, 19, 19n, 20n, 232n
Mylius, Crato, 68n

Naiden, J.R., 194, 201, 202, 204, 205, 206n, 207n, 208n, 209n, 210n, 211n, 212n
Nancel, Nicolas de, 18, 20n, 220, 231n
Naples, 259n
Narcisse, Le nouveau, 22
Nardi, B., 254n
Navarre, Collège de, 5, 116–17
Neobarius, 201, 209n
Neptune, 93n

Nicholas of Cusa (Cusanus), 71, 91n, 111, 178
Nicocles, 223
Nicomaches, 126, 258n
Nicot, 48n
Nizolio, Mario, 176–7, 183n
Noah, 129
Nosopon, 219
Novati, 255n
Noyon, 113, 114, 115, 143n, 145n
Nozeroy, 229
Nuñez, Pedro (Nonius), 123, 149n, 194, 209n
Nuremberg, 73, 112, 194
Nürnberger, Richard, 183n

Ockham, 39
Odyssey, 59
Œcolompadius, 145n
Olaus Magnus, 216, 231n
Ong, W. J., 5, 7, 19n, 36, 37, 38, 39, 47n, 48n, 49n, 51n, 52, 65, 67n, 69n, 152n, 183n, 231n
O'Prey, Philip, 69n
Origen, 49n, 241
Orléans, 12, 137, 216, 245
Orosius, 240, 256n
Orpheus, 27, 28, 99, 127
Osiander, Andreas, 73–4
Ossat, Cardinal d', 153n
Ourscamp, 113, 114, 145n
Ovid, 8, 58, 59, 68n, 202, 251
Owen, D.D.R., 211n

Pachtler, 152n
Pacioli, Luca, 140
Padua, 69n, 82, 250
Palephatus, 58
Palingenius, 202, 210n
Panofsky, E., 256n
Pantagruel, 8, 19n, 45, 162, 166
Pantagruel, 157, 160, 162, 174, 236, 247, 248, 254n, 261n
Panurge, 164, 166
Papon, Jean, 227
Pappus, 127
Paquier, J., 259n
Paracelsus, 71, 78, 163
Paré, A., 164
Paris, 19n, 20n, 34n, 39, 48n, 50n, 51n, 52, 67n, 68n, 69n, 72, 73, 74, 82, 91n, 92n, 95, 97, 98, 99, 105, 106, 107, 108,